THE GAWAIN POET
COMPLETE WORKS

Patience
Cleanness
Pearl
Saint Erkenwald
Sir Gawain and the Green Knight

THE GAWAIN POET
COMPLETE WORKS

PATIENCE

CLEANNESS

PEARL

SAINT ERKENWALD

SIR GAWAIN AND THE GREEN KNIGHT

VERSE TRANSLATIONS BY

Marie Borroff

YALE UNIVERSITY

W • W • Norton & Company • New York • London

W. W. Norton & Company has been independent since its founding in 1923, when William Warder Norton and Mary D. Herter Norton first published lectures delivered at the People's Institute, the adult-education division of New York City's Cooper Union. The firm soon expanded its program beyond the Institute, publishing books by celebrated academics from America and abroad. By mid-century, the two major pillars of Norton's publishing program—trade books and college texts—were firmly established. In the 1950s, the Norton family transferred control of the company to its employees, and today—with a staff of four hundred and a comparable number of trade, college, and professional titles published each year—W. W. Norton & Company stands as the largest and oldest publishing house owned wholly by its employees.

Editor: Peter Simon
Assistant Editor: Conor Sullivan
Project Editor: Melissa Atkin
Production Manager: Sean Mintus
Manufacturing by Maple-Vail

Library of Congress Cataloging-in-Publication Data

The Gawain Poet : Complete Works : Patience, Cleanness, Pearl, Saint Erkenwald, Sir Gawain and the Green Knight / verse translations by Marie Borroff. — 1st ed.
    p. cm.
  Includes bibliographical references.
  ISBN: 978-0-393-91235-7 (pbk.)
  1. Enligh poetry—Middle English, 1100–1500—Modernized versions. 2. Gawin (Legendary character)—Romances. 3. Knights and knighthood—Poetry. 4. Erkenwald, Saint, ca. 630–ca. 693—Poetry. 5. Arthurian romances. 6. Romances, English. I. Borroff, Marie.
II. Patience (Middle English poem) III. Purity (Middle English poem) IV. Pearl (Middle English poem) V. Saint Erkenwald (Middle English poem) VI. Gawin and the Green Knight.
  PR1972.G35 2011
  821'.1—dc22

                                                                2011013964

W. W. Norton & Company, Inc., 500 Fifth Avenue, New York, N.Y. 10110
www.wwnorton.com
W. W. Norton & Company Ltd., Castle House, 75/76 Wells Street, London W1T 3QT

1 2 3 4 5 6 7 8 9 0

For whoever he was

Contents

Note

Throughout this book, the Bible is quoted in the Douay-Rheims version, based on the Latin Vulgate version in which it was known to the poet. References to the Authorized, or King James, Version are marked "A.V."

Acknowledgments

The series of events that has culminated in this volume began in the mid-1950s, when I was enrolled in a graduate program in English literature and English philology at Yale University. Professor John C. Pope, with whom I had studied the Old English language and Old English metrics, suggested that I write my dissertation on *Sir Gawain and the Green Knight*. The dissertation became a book entitled *Sir Gawain and the Green Knight: A Stylistic and Metrical Study* (Yale University Press, 1962). In it, I put to use the knowledge of English philology I had acquired in courses taught by Professor Helge Kökeritz. During the 1960s, I combined my expertise as a practicing poet with my understanding, as a philologist, of the original metrical patterns of *Sir Gawain and the Green Knight* and translated the poem into verse. With the encouragement and advice of Professor E. T. Donaldson, with whom I had studied Chaucer, I published my translation of *Sir Gawain* and later translated and published *Pearl*, both with W. W. Norton. *Patience* came next, and all three were published together by Norton in 2001. I went on to translate *Cleanness* and last, *Saint Erkenwald*, whose author, I had become convinced, was the *Gawain* poet. In an essay at the end of this volume entitled "The Authorship of *Saint Erkenwald*," I present in less technical form the arguments supporting my belief in the *Gawain* poet's authorship that were published in an essay in *Studies in the Age of Chaucer* in 2006.

My earliest indebtedness is thus to Professors Pope, Donaldson, and Kökeritz, to whom I continue to be grateful. In translating *Pearl*, I received helpful suggestions and criticism from Professors Robert B. Burlin, John Freccero, and A. Bartlett Giamatti. I was fortunate in having the assistance in research of Professor M. Teresa Tavormina. I owe a special debt to Professor Sherry Reames for the thoroughgoing criticism, laced with encouragement, that gave a needed impetus to my work on *Pearl* in the eleventh hour. My translation of *Patience* is dedicated to Professor Dorothee Metlitzki in acknowledgment of our friendship and in gratitude to her for sharing with me her knowledge in depth of both the original poem and its biblical source. My translation of *Cleanness* is dedicated to Professor E. G. Stanley, who sustained me as I persevered in that long task and shared with me his knowledge of Middle English in general and of the *Gawain* group in particular. I am grateful also to Professor Elizabeth Keiser, author of an important book on *Cleanness*. From both Professor Stanley and Professor Keiser I received detailed critiques of my translation that were most

xi

helpful to me in arriving at a definitive version. I am indebted to Professor Fred C. Robinson for giving me the benefit of his great learning in reading and commenting on the General Introduction.

Marie Borroff
New Haven, Connecticut
April 2011

General Introduction

During the last two or three decades of the fourteenth century, in a period of the history of the language called Late Middle English, a man whose name we do not know but whose dialect places him in or near Cheshire, about two hundred miles northwest of London, wrote five poems. Two of them, *Sir Gawain and the Green Knight* and *Pearl*, are recognized as superb examples of their genres; they continue to be widely read, both in the original language and in translation. *Sir Gawain* is an Arthurian romance. *Pearl* is a dream vision governed by Christian doctrine and symbolism. Their author is called the *Gawain* poet or, less frequently, the *Pearl* poet. We know nothing about his life except what we can infer from the poems themselves.

Why should we read the works of this poet today? Aside from their shared value as literature worthy of a permanent place in the inherited treasury we call the humanities, each deserves to be remembered in its own right. As a group they demonstrate the poet's remarkable versatility. In *Sir Gawain and the Green Knight*, a story melding elements of supernatural menace with high comedy holds the reader's interest through its startling denouement, while at the same time raising profound questions about the relationship between human fallibility and transcendent standards of spiritual perfection. *Pearl* lavishes on its moving drama of the spiritual education of a benighted human soul a richness of Christian imagery and symbolism unexcelled elsewhere in medieval—even, some would say, in later—religious poetry. In the suspenseful unfolding and culmination of its narrative and its powerful evocation of the divine realm in juxtaposition with the secular, the saint's legend *Saint Erkenwald* is by no means unworthy of comparison with *Pearl*. *Patience* adds humor and realistic vividness to its moralized version of the tale of Jonah and the whale. And *Cleanness*, though episodic in narrative structure, offers brilliant reworkings, from the point of view of an independent-minded medieval Christian, of Old Testament stories such as the destruction of Sodom and Gomorrah and Belshazzar's feast. Taken together, these five works are the artistic achievement of one of the three most important medieval English poets (the two others being Geoffrey Chaucer and William Langland). At the same time, they show us that the human predicament, despite the social changes that have inevitably taken place in the course of six centuries, has remained essentially the same.

The author of these poems possessed, to a superlative degree, the power of placing us within scenes where we witness events that matter as much to us as they do to the fictional characters involved. In *Sir Gawain and the Green Knight*, we lie with the hero inside the curtains of a luxurious bed and cautiously peek out to see who has entered the room.

> Lo! it was the lady, loveliest to behold,
> Who drew the door behind her deftly and still
> And was bound for his bed—abashed was the knight,
> And laid his head low again in likeness of sleep.   (1187–90)

In *Patience*, we join the terrified passengers of the sailing vessel carrying Jonah (as he thinks) away from God, as they try to save it from sinking in a great storm.

> they hauled and they hoisted and they heaved over the side
> Their bags and their featherbeds and their bright-hued clothes,
> All to lighten their load, if relief could be had.
> But the winds, unwearying, blew wilder than ever,
> And the maelstrom ever madder and more to be feared.   (157–62)

In *Cleanness*, we listen to the heavenly musicians hovering over Mary as she gives birth to Jesus.

> For angels with their instruments, organs and pipes,
> And majestic strains of well-matched strings,
> And all harmonies that honorably enhance a heart's joy,
> Made music for my lady at her lying-in.   (1081–84)

Later, at Belshazzar's profane banquet, we become the auditors of a quite different kind of music:

> ever the din undiminished of drumming and piping;
> Tambourines and tabors beat time together,
> Cymbals and shrill bells resounded in answer,
> And the booming of the big drums battered all ears.   (1413–16)

In *Pearl*, we find ourselves, with the central figure, transported in a dream to a landscape of unearthly splendor:

> Embellished were those hills in view
> With crystal cliffs as clear as day
> And groves of trees with boles as blue
> As indigo silks of rich assay;
> The leaves, like silver burnished new,
> Slide rustling rife on every spray;
> As shifts of cloud let sunshine through,
> They shot forth light in shimmering play.   (73–80)

Finally, in *Saint Erkenwald*, we share the amazement of the spectators as the richly clothed and perfectly preserved body of a pagan judge, after joyously reporting that its soul is now seated at the eternal banquet of the blessed in heaven, undergoes a wholly unforeseen change:

> Then his voice ceased to sound; he said no more,
> And suddenly and swiftly his sweet looks failed,
> And his bright hue grew black, as if mold had besmirched it,
> As ruinous as the dry rot that rises in powder.   (341–44)

All these passages except the one from *Pearl* are composed in alliterative verse, a prosodic form that has long been obsolete and is thus unfamiliar to the modern reader. The basic form of this kind of verse requires the stressed syllables of two or more important words in each line to begin with—that is, alliterate on—the same sound. In lines 341–44 of *Saint Erkenwald*, quoted above, the alliterating sounds are *s*, *s*, *b*, and *r*, respectively. The lines also have a continuous four-beat rhythm, though they exhibit varying patterns of strongly stressed, moderately stressed, and unstressed syllables. As the quoted excerpts demonstrate, the *Gawain* poet made masterly use of the metrical and phonic resources offered by the tradition in which he wrote.

The Manuscripts

Our literary inheritance from medieval times has included, luckily, the survival of unique texts of all five poems. *Pearl*, *Patience*, *Cleanness*, and *Sir Gawain* appear side by side, in that order, in MS. [manuscript] Cotton Nero A. x. They are thought to have been copied about 1400. *Saint Erkenwald* survives in MS. Harley 2250 and was copied about seventy-five years later. It is clear that none of the texts in their extant versions was written down by the author himself, though we do not know how many stages of copying may have intervened between them and their presumed originals. Both manuscripts are named for collectors of medieval texts; both are kept in the British Museum. The *Gawain* group, originally bound with two works in Latin from which it has since been separated, came to the museum from the library of the sixteenth-century antiquarian Sir Robert Cotton. *Saint Erkenwald* is found in a large compilation of texts, chiefly religious in content, that the museum acquired in the eighteenth century from a library built up by Robert and Edward Harley, the first and second earls of Oxford. Names written in the margins of the poem in Harley suggest earlier ownership by families in Cheshire, the area in which dialectical evidence places all five poems.

All five poems were first edited and published by nineteenth-century scholars. The poems of the *Gawain* group were recognized immediately as constituting collectively an outstanding literary achievement, establishing their author as one of the major poets of his time. *Saint Erkenwald*, too, has had admirers from the time of its earliest publication (in Germany in 1881), and there have always been scholars who thought it was the work of the *Gawain* poet. Needless to say, the author of the five translations published here concurs with their opinion. (See the essay entitled "The Authorship of *Saint Erkenwald*" at the end of this volume.)

Subject Matter and Form

As was pointed out above, each of the four poems of the *Gawain* group differs from the others. *Pearl* is a monologue spoken by a man who mourns inconsolably the loss of a precious "pearl without a spot" that he valued above all else. A maiden appears to him in a dream, and he recognizes her as his pearl, the mortal being he thought he had lost. Speaking to him from the spiritual plane to which she has been translated after her death, she leads him to see that what was truly of value in her exists forever, and that he, as a faithful Christian, can hope to be reunited with her in the eternal bliss of heaven. *Cleanness* and *Patience* are homilies in verse—that is, they resemble sermons intended to give instruction on the popular level. The subject of *Cleanness* is not so much the virtue named in the title as its opposite: the sin of uncleanness or filth, which, as the poet defines it, infuriates God above all other sins, and which is exemplified at its worst by sexual relationships between males. In the course of expounding his theme, the poet retells several Old Testament stories showing how an angry God punished the unclean, notably the inhabitants of Sodom and Gomorrah. In *Patience*, the narrator again dwells on the fault that is the opposite of the titular virtue, his major illustration being the impatience of the prophet Jonah, who refused to comply with God's command to go to Nineveh. At the end of the poem, God's supernatural patience prevails, and human beings are called on to emulate it. *Sir Gawain*, the one secular poem of the five, belongs to a large body of Middle English and Old French Arthurian romances, stories combining adventure with love. In it, one of Arthur's most famous knights undergoes a protracted, mystifying, and thoroughly discomfiting ordeal that seems to put him in mortal danger. He survives, but not without committing a dishonest deed that humiliates and infuriates him in retrospect. But when he tells his friends at Arthur's court about it, they find it merely laughable.

Saint Erkenwald, too, is unlike any of the other four poems. It belongs to the vast body of medieval hagiographic literature, that is, literature about saints, in which a given saint who is the central figure of a story typically is martyred or performs one or more miracles, or both. Here, the title character is a bona fide historical figure, a seventh-century bishop of London, later canonized, whose see was based at St. Paul's Cathedral. The poem tells how, during a structural renovation, a magnificent tomb was unearthed in the cathedral's foundations. It contained a dead but uncorrupted body wearing both a lawyer's coif and a crown and holding a scepter in its hand. The discovery presents what seems an insoluble mystery, for no record that such a person ever lived can be found in the cathedral archives. Bishop Erkenwald's prayer that the body may be allowed to reveal its story is answered through the intercession of the Holy Spirit. After the body has spoken, it is inadvertently baptized by the bishop's compassionate tears. Its soul, which had been confined in darkness, is released and ascends to heaven. The poem ends in triumph as a procession led by Erkenwald passes from the cathedral through the streets of the city.

Saint Erkenwald, Patience, and Cleanness are composed entirely in unrhymed alliterative verse. In Sir Gawain, most of the narrative is contained in paragraphs of alliterating lines that vary in length. Each is followed by a two-syllable line, called the bob, and a stanza of four six-syllable lines, called the wheel. The five lines rhyme ababa. Pearl is composed throughout in twelve-line stanzas rhyming abababaabbcbc. The rhyming lines of Gawain and Pearl exemplify what I call "mixed meter." (I describe alliterative verse and mixed meter in "The Metrical Forms" below, pp. 275–301.)

In the remainder of this essay I will trace the history of the alliterative tradition represented by all the poems except Pearl, from its prehistoric beginnings, through its continuance in England in Anglo-Saxon and late medieval times, to its extinction in the fifteenth century.

The History of Alliterative Poetry

To judge from the languages in which works exemplifying it have been composed, alliterative verse is of Germanic origin. It must have been invented centuries before the beginning of the Common Era, in a community of northwest Europe whose speakers shared a prehistoric, unrecorded language. Later, population growth resulted in territorial expansion of this community, chiefly to the north and west, and the common language gradually evolved into separate national languages. The original language is called "primitive Germanic"; its hypothetical characteristics have been deduced by philologists from their studies of features shared by the descendant languages. The Germanic people themselves are thought to have separated and moved away centuries earlier from a parent community, probably located in Anatolia or southeast Russia, whose common language philologists call Indo-European. Among the earliest surviving records of the ancient Germanic languages are a number of commemorative inscriptions in primitive Old Norse, carved on stone in the runic alphabet in the fourth century C.E., and parts of the translation of the Bible into Gothic, an obsolete Eastern Germanic language, made in the same century by the Christian bishop Ulfilas. Contemporary languages of Germanic descent include German, the Scandinavian languages, Dutch, and English. (The non-Germanic European languages—including classical and modern Greek; classical Latin; the "Romance" languages of Latin ancestry, such as Italian, French, and Spanish; and the Celtic languages of Scotland, Ireland, and Cornwall—evolved in other areas where originally Indo-European populations had moved west and south from the ancient heartland.)

Alliterative verse, as the name implies, is so called because of the require-ment that two or more stressed syllables in each line must begin with the same sound. The fact that present-day English contains a store of dozens of alliter-ating phrases, such as "good as gold," "bold as brass," "tried and true," "better safe than sorry," and "gone but not forgotten," is a sign of the Germanic origins of our language. Alliteration is sometimes called "initial rhyme" because it links the sounds with which syllables begin, whereas the "end rhyme" we are accustomed to in poetry links the vowels of the final stressed syllables of words and the consonants that follow them. End rhyme was not originally a formal feature of alliterative verse. In fact, one of the key structural features of allit-erative verse proper is the *absence* from the last stressed syllable not only of end rhyme but also (with permissible minor exceptions) of the alliterating letter that links the earlier syllables. The Old English poets occasionally added rhyme to alliteration, probably influenced by the rhymed Latin verse of early Chris-tian Europe. End-rhymed couplets are a standard feature of Old French verse, from which formal alliterative patterns are entirely absent. In the two centu-ries that followed the Norman conquest, end rhyme came to prevail in English poetry as an aspect of the gradual gallicizing of culture, especially London, the royal seat, and the surrounding South Midland and southern areas.

Why did alliterative poetry originate in Germanic, rather than Italic, Hel-lenic, or Celtic culture? The answer must have something to do with a linguistic change that took place exclusively in the primitive Germanic language and that was inherited by its descendant languages, including English. In Germanic, syl-lables in continuous speech came to be differentiated by a system of degrees of stress. The meaningful stem syllables or lexical bases of nouns, adjectives, verbs, and adverbs carried the heaviest degree of stress, called "primary." Other sylla-bles of these words were stressed less heavily. This meant that in any group of words sharing a stem, primary stress fell uniformly on that stem. The same pat-tern appears in groups of modern words of Old English, that is, Germanic, descent, such as *speak, speaking, spoken, speaker, unspeakable* (Old English *sp[r]ecan*). Stress patterns in these groups contrast with those exhibited by groups of English words whose stems are of non-Germanic, particularly of Latin, descent, such as those containing the stem -*dict*- (from *dictus*, the past participle of the Latin verb *dicere*, "to say"). In *dictate* and *dictator*, the stress falls on the stem, but in *dictation, dictatorship*, and *dictatorial* it falls on sylla-bles in the suffix, and in *edict* it falls on a prefix. Weak stress in the Germanic languages is also carried by most of the "little words" in sentences, such as the definite and indefinite articles *the* and *a*, and words that express linguistic rela-tionships rather than having intrinsic meaning, such as *and, but, if*, and *though*. The presence in continuous language of recurrent strong stresses seems to have generated a verse form in which lines were measured by counting stresses. Since the syllables receiving primary stress in the line were normally the inde-pendently meaningful stems of nouns, adjectives, verbs, and adverbs, patterns developed linking these words not only by shared stress but also by shared sounds at the beginning of stressed syllables. Line endings then came to be marked by the absence of the alliterating letter from the last stressed word.

The history of alliterative verse in English begins with the occupation of England by settlers from several of the Germanic tribes in the westernmost regions of Europe, including Angles (from whose name the word "English" is derived) and Saxons. At the beginning of the Common Era, the British Isles had been peopled by speakers of Celtic languages, descendants of the original group of speakers of Indo-European that had migrated farthest west. Present-day languages of Celtic descent include Welsh and Gaelic (Irish and Scottish); Cornish, once spoken in Cornwall, is now extinct. From the first century C.E. on, England was subject to military incursions from Rome, became a Roman province, and was partly occupied by Roman colonists. A branch of the Christian church was established there during the Romano-Celtic period. In the middle of the fifth century, the country was invaded and then settled by Germanic warriors. They and their descendants pushed the original Celtic inhabitants north, west, southwest, and east into Scotland, Ireland, Wales, Cornwall, and Brittany in northwestern France. (Breton, a dialect spoken in Brittany, is a Celtic language.) The pagan religion they brought with them displaced the Christianity of the Romano-Celtic period. During the next two centuries, their West Germanic dialects evolved into a distinctive insular language that today is called Old English or Anglo-Saxon. Around the beginning of the seventh century, missionaries sent from Rome by Pope Gregory the Great, including Saint Augustine of Canterbury, began a new process of conversion which, during the next hundred years, led to the reestablishment of Christianity as the official religion of England. (In the opening passage of *Saint Erkenwald*, the *Gawain* poet tells the story of the two phases of early Christianity in England and the intervening lapse into paganism caused by the coming of the Germanic peoples he lumps together as "Saxons.")

Life in the Germanic communities of prehistoric Europe, as in all communities, would have allowed, at both high and low cultural levels, for periods of recreation. It is safe to assume that the activities carried on in hours taken off from work included acrobatics and jugglery, dancing, performances on musical instruments, singing, and storytelling by talented members of the community and by traveling entertainers. These entertainments would have varied in degree of sophistication and refinement, depending on social context and occasion. Some of the songs and stories would surely have been composed in verse; all the human cultures we know of have had poetic languages imposing rhythmic and phonic patterns of some sort on spontaneous utterance. Such patterns were both verbal ornamentation and aids to memory. Before writing was invented, "literary works" must have been transmitted orally from generation to generation: established performers who knew by heart the compositions of their predecessors would have recited them in public and composed or improvised new ones on the model of the old. These would have been learned in turn by the apprentices who became their successors.

As time went on, preliterate cultures, one by one, became literate. As a result, some of the poetic narratives originally composed and recited without the aid of writing came to be copied out, and some of the resultant manuscripts survived to modern times. From these extant works we can conclude that poetry of cultural importance began as history and as myth-based religion. From comparative studies of the Homeric poems, whose composition is thought to date back to the preliterate Hellenic era, and the earliest surviving English and Continental poems of Germanic heritage such as *Beowulf*, we learn that both cultures celebrated the "heroic" ethos of an elite warrior class, recording and praising the great deeds of ancestral warriors linked to their chieftains by a reciprocal bond of loyalty and magnanimity. The Germanic poetic language, like that of the Homeric poems, would have been formulaic— that is, largely made up of metrically shaped combinations of words inherited from the past and distinguished from the spontaneous language of every day. Its vocabulary included sets of synonyms designating persons and objects often referred to in the heroic tradition, such as *warrior, company of warriors, chieftain, warhorse, sword* and *shield*. It also included sets of adjectives designating the virtues celebrated in the poems, such as *courageous, strong,* and *loyal.*

Poets themselves have important roles in the narratives of both *Beowulf* and Homer's *Odyssey*. In *Beowulf*, the hero travels by sea from his native Scandinavian kingdom to Denmark in order to put an end to the ravages inflicted on the Danes by the marauding monster Grendel. After Beowulf has killed the monster, a poet attached to the court of Hrothgar, the Danish king, tells of a similar exploit performed by a Germanic hero of the past, adding "other words" to the traditional ones to pay tribute to the new hero as well as the old. At the celebratory banquet that evening, the poet performs again, taking now as his subject a famous battle in which ancestors of the Danes took part. The poet is referred to as a "thane" of the king, that is, a member of the royal retinue, comparable to a knight in later times. In the *Odyssey*, after Odysseus has been washed up on the shores of the kingdom of the Phaeacians, he is entertained by their king as a guest, not recognized by name but clearly a man of prowess and noble birth. Here too, a court poet performs at a banquet; the actors in his stories are Hellenic counterparts, including Odysseus himself, of the Germanic warriors told of in Denmark. In both poems, the poet is said to sing or chant his story, accompanying himself on a musical instrument, the Germanic harp or the Hellenic lyre. We can assume that the artistry involved in performances on such occasions for such audiences was sophisticated—as is the artistry of the two great poems themselves, *Beowulf* and the *Odyssey*. The fictional identities of the performing Germanic and Hellenic bards merge with the identities of the bards who composed and presumably recited the poems. The description in *Beowulf* of the minstrel at Hrothgar's court as "a carrier of tales, a traditional singer deeply schooled in the lore of the past" applies equally to the *Beowulf* poet himself and to Homer.

But to think of ancient poetry in terms only of poems such as *Beowulf* and the *Odyssey* is to disregard productions of a more popular, less dignified nature of which no written records remain. The audiences for these would have included not only people of royal and noble birth, but those of lower status: servants, artisans and peasants. We can assume that the former as well as the latter would on occasion have preferred crudeness and vulgarity to subtlety and refinement. The works performed for these audiences would have included comic stories, many of them indecent, told in verse or prose. These tales were ancestral to the stories told by characters of low social status (but apparently enjoyed by the gentlefolk as well) in Chaucer's Late Middle English *Canterbury Tales* and to the dirty jokes, bawdy limericks, and the like that circulate orally today. Much of the literature produced at this cultural level has been lost. In thinking of the transmission of English poetry from Anglo-Saxon to medieval times, it is important to remember that literacy came first to religious communities. It was the administrators of the monasteries and the great churches who decided which literary works should be copied out and their subordinates who were assigned the copying.

The body of words and phrases used in traditional heroic poetry, considered as a whole, signified an imagined world marked as much by exclusion as by inclusion. It was an almost wholly masculine world, populated by male warriors and their male chieftains. The comparatively few women who figure in it are typically of royal birth. They are "peace-weavers," given in marriage by their fathers and brothers to chieftains of other nations in order to form or confirm political alliances. Servitors, peasants, and artisans are absent: meals are eaten and beer is drunk in hall, but those who cook the food, grow grain for the bread, and brew the beer are of no interest to the poets or their audiences. The important characters are painted in black and white. "Our" heroes are ideally brave, strong, and loyal; if treacherous deeds are recounted, their perpetrators are "our" enemies. This world, its inhabitants, and its values are taken for granted: perpetuated in memory, exempt from challenge or change.

Of the Old English poems that survive in manuscript (a pitifully small remnant of the body of poetry that must actually have been composed and recited), *Beowulf*, extant in a single manuscript, is one of the high-water marks of artistic merit. It may well have been composed as early as the ninth century, though it was copied centuries later. The Old English period of language and literature is usually defined as beginning in the eighth century and continuing through the first half of the eleventh; 1066, the date of the Norman Conquest, makes a convenient end point. By the second half of the fourteenth century, during the productive lifetimes of both Chaucer and the *Gawain* poet, French-style metrical patterns and French-style end rhyme prevailed in poetry in the south of England. Bards proficient in alliterative verse no longer performed at court or at the residences of the noble lords corresponding to the chieftains of Anglo-Saxon times. Nor was alliterative poetry widely read, with the important exception of Langland's *Piers Plowman*, a popular allegorical poem treating issues of social injustice and corruption from the point of view of the lower classes.

In this same half century, in areas far to the north and west of London, a large body of alliterative poetry devoted to traditional topics was composed and copied. This development is sometimes called the Alliterative Revival, though it more likely was the emergence, into the daylight of written record, of a vital popular tradition whose transitional products have for the most part been lost. The Late Middle English alliterative style of these poems is similar enough to that of Old English poetry to suggest an uninterrupted line of descent. For example, their vocabulary includes a number of descendants of the Old English poetic words whose meanings were relevant to traditional heroic narrative, such as *warrior, warhorse,* and *courageous.*

Late Middle English Alliterative Poetry

Though the Late Middle English alliterative poetry of the fourteenth century resembles Old English poetry in that alliteration is the basic structural link in the lines of both, the two contrast markedly in the details of metrical patterning and in style. To some extent, this contrast is due to differences between the English language of the eighth and ninth centuries and that of the late fourteenth century. For example, the expression of grammatical relationships had undergone a thoroughgoing change. In Old English, as in Latin, grammatical relationships were commonly expressed by inflectional endings, such as our *s* for plurality and apostrophe plus *s* for the possessive singular. By the second half of the fourteenth century, Old English grammar had become much less elaborate, and phrases containing prepositions and other function words were often used in place of inflections. In *Beowulf,* for example, the monster Grendel is described as maliciously slaughtering the Danes "in the dark nights." The corresponding Old English phrase, *deorcum nihtum,* consists solely of adjective and noun, each marked by the dative plural inflectional ending -*um.* Later, in an elegiac passage, the poet refers to a rusted coat of mail that had once endured the bite of iron swords amid the clashing of shields. The Old English original omits "of" and uses the possessive plural form of "shield" with the inflectional ending -*a.* In addition, the definite and indefinite articles *the* and *a* are often omitted in Old English, at least in poetry, where they would appear in Late Middle (and modern) English. Beowulf's instruction to his retainer Wiglaf to go quickly and look at the treasure guarded by the slain dragon under the gray stone of his cave, reads, literally, "Go look at treasure under gray stone." As a result of these changes, the later alliterative line contains more lightly stressed syllables than the earlier, and thus lends itself to a more rapid reading tempo.

The subject matter of alliterative poetry had already widened in Old English times; after England was converted to Christianity, stories from the Old and New Testaments were retold in verse in the native language. This expansion continued in Middle English. New alliterative poems were composed about the legendary Celtic king Arthur, the siege of Troy, and the life of Alexander the Great. The alliterative works of the *Gawain* poet include adaptations of biblical materials, such as the story of Jonah and the whale in *Patience* and the destruction of Sodom and Gomorrah and Belshazzar's feast in *Cleanness*. The drama of the rhyming poem *Pearl* is shaped by Christian doctrines about salvation and the eternal bliss of heaven; in *Saint Erkenwald* the Christian church acts as intermediary between secular and divine realms; and the narrative of *Sir Gawain* takes place in two communities, the courts of King Arthur and of Lord Bertilak, where the birth of Jesus is celebrated at Christmas, and masses are frequently sung. Another important enlargement of poetic subject matter between Old and Middle English involved the treatment of women as important characters in fictional narratives. Knights and ladies were shown involved in relationships governed by what was then called *amour courtois*. (The phrase literally means "courteous love," but the word *courtesy* is itself derived from the word *court*, and the code of behavior involved is usually called "courtly love" in English.) Our poet draws on the courtly love tradition in the language of *Pearl* and the action of *Sir Gawain and the Green Knight*.

Some of the differences in style between Old English and Middle English alliterative poetry may be due to the fact that for two centuries or more, the alliterative tradition had been carried on at popular, subliterary levels. The language of Old English poetry, as exemplified by *Beowulf*, is elevated, slow-paced, spare, and artificial, comparable in some ways to that of the poetry of Milton. Its sentences tend to be intricate in syntactic structure, beginning in midline and running on for two or three lines more. The syntax of Late Middle English alliterative poetry is much simpler; structural units, such as sentences and clauses, characteristically coincide with the metrical unit of the line. And despite the partial survival of the groups of distinctively poetic words that had been used in Old English, the language of Late Middle English alliterative poetry has the vehemence, exaggeration, and directness of the spoken language of every day, the hyperbolic intensity of "I've told you a hundred times not to do that," or "When is dinner? I'm starving," or "I thought I'd die laughing." In the alliterative *Morte Arthure*, King Arthur pulls out his sword and with it cuts through the knees of an enemy he confronts in battle, calling to him, "Come down and talk with your comrades, you are too tall by half" (2123–26). In *Cleanness*, telling of the failure of the sages summoned by Balthasar (Belshazzar) to translate the writing on the wall, the poet says that when they had looked at the letters, they were as wise as if they had looked into the leather of his left boot.

The style of Late Middle English alliterative poetry has another, and important, affinity with the spoken language, namely, the recurrent use for descriptive purposes of "sound effects" deriving from the phonetic values of vowel and consonant sounds. We often manipulate expressively the sounds of words in everyday speech, as when we say "It's a co-o-o-o-ld day," making the vowel vibrate like the *r* in "b-r-r-r-r-r," or prolonging it, as in "It'll be a lo-o-o-o-ng time before I forget that." Moreover, the vocabulary of the spoken language includes a large component of words labeled "imitative" in dictionary entries: words such as *hiss, boom, blabber,* and *giggle*. When the occasion called for it, the Late Middle English alliterative poets drew freely on the sound-symbolic vocabulary of the English of their time. Descriptions of storms in the alliterative poems *Destruction of Troy* and *The Wars of Alexander,* for instance, use Middle English ancestral forms of the modern words *burble, flash, shatter, shudder,* and *totter,* as well as the phrase "at a wap [with a single stroke]," which also occurs in *Sir Gawain*. Finally, the rhythmic patterns of Late Middle English alliterative verse have important affinities with those of nursery rhymes, such as "Pease Porridge Hot" and "Sing a Song of Sixpence," which have been transmitted orally at the popular level. I discuss these affinities in the essay on "The Metrical Forms" below.

The Late Middle English alliterative tradition virtually ceased to be productive after the fourteenth century. When printing came to England at the end of the fifteenth century, the poetry of Chaucer, which had existed in many manuscripts, entered the classical canon of published poetry in English, where it has remained ever since. *Patience, Purity, Pearl,* and *Sir Gawain and the Green Knight* were consigned to the oblivion of a single manuscript owned by an antiquarian and later acquired by the British Museum. It was not until the nineteenth century that philologists, specialists in the history of the language, recovered the Old and Middle English alliterative poems, edited them for publication, and made them available to scholars. The first editions of *Beowulf* and *Sir Gawain and the Green Knight* appeared in 1835; that of *Saint Erkenwald* in 1881. In the twentieth century, a few American and English poets tried their hands at alliterative verse, notably Ezra Pound in his translation of the Old English *Seafarer,* and W. H. Auden in *The Age of Anxiety. Sir Gawain* has been translated into verse a number of times. But none of these translations has fully reproduced the poem's original alliterative and metrical patterns.

The effect of the *Gawain* poet's Middle English can be only partially recaptured in modern English. We have no equivalent for the groups of synonyms of distinctively poetic quality that were a staple of the traditional alliterative style. These might well have added to the language of the *Gawain* poet and his contemporaries a literary dimension that counterbalanced its vigorous, down-to-earth quality. This latter, however, can be carried over in translation, along with the all-important sound-symbolic effects of the original language. So too can the cumulative momentum of the verse, whose skillfully varied patterns are subsumed under a uniform, easily sensed, rhythmic beat. The translation project culminating in this volume was inspired by my conviction, founded on a historical investigation into the pronunciation of late fourteenth-century English in the poet's native region, that the metrical patterns of Late Middle English alliterative poetry could be not merely approximated but actually replicated today (see "The Metrical Forms" below).

This project was surely worth undertaking. The *Gawain* poet's verse, with its barrages of alliterating consonants and density of descriptive detail, will in all likelihood fall strangely at first on the ears of modern readers. But once they have made themselves at home in his imagined world, his superb artistry will surely delight the ear and captivate the imagination as it did long ago. His works, read as a whole, provide a window on a culture far distant in time from our own. They enable us to participate vicariously in human experiences and fortunes dramatized with a power still manifest in modern translations that do justice to the originals.

Patience

For Dorothee Metlitzki

Introduction to *Patience*

Story and Style

For most readers, insofar as they know it at all, the story told in the biblical book of Jonah is remote from reality. It unfolds not only in a far-off time and place but on a plane higher than that on which we live our everyday lives. Its major character is a prophet who converses regularly with the one God of the Old Testament; and its major event, the swallowing of the prophet by a whale followed by his three-day sojourn in its belly, is not only miraculous but impossible to imagine as happening to us or anyone like us. Reading the story in the Old Testament, we find it told in spare, terse language, ungarnished by descriptive detail or commentary. The first chapter begins:

1. Now the word of the Lord came to Jonas the son of Amathi, saying:
2. Arise, and go to Ninive the great city, and preach in it: for the wickedness thereof is come up before me.
3. And Jonas rose up to flee into Tharsis from the face of the Lord. . . .

(The book of Jonah in its entirety is printed in "Biblical Sources," pp. 28–31. I have used the modern forms of biblical names in my translation. The manuscript of *Patience* has *Jonas, Nynyve,* and *Tarce.*) Not until the fourth and final chapter of the book do we hear, from Jonah himself, an explanation for—or at least a rationalization of—his refusal to obey God's command. In biblical translations such as the one I have quoted, the story is further distanced from us by its language. Words such as *arise* and *thereof* and idioms such as *is come* have for a long time been largely restricted to religious and ceremonial contexts; they have taken on a corresponding elevation and solemnity of tone.

An important part of what the poet does in retelling the book of Jonah is to turn its story into a human comedy, though the poem also includes a number of serious passages that enlarge its meaning, as I shall explain later. Its central figure, we soon see, is someone who, though he is a divinely ordained prophet, is very much like our fallible selves, someone who responds with reluctance, much as we would, to the peremptory and disagreeable commands of his lord. (In this, he is typical of the Old Testament prophets generally.) His sea journey, the storm that nearly wrecks his ship, his descent into the belly of the whale,

3

his three days' sojourn there, and his adventures in and around Nineveh—all are dramatized with brilliant realism. As when we look at a stereoscopic image or watch a 3-D movie, we are drawn into simulated three-dimensional space. Observing Jonah's actions and reactions, even if we are aware that we are in a sense reading the Bible, we are more likely to shake our heads and smile than to nod solemnly.

The Moral Message

But the author of *Patience* is not entertaining us with comedy for comedy's sake; he is intent on driving home an overt moral message. For him, the biblical story of Jonah illustrated the importance in human life of what he thought of as "patience": *patience* is the first word in the poem, and its first line singles patience out as a "point," or topic, or aspect of behavior, worth talking about. (In my translation, I take advantage of the proverb "Patience is a virtue.") But the concept of patience, in the poet's time, was larger and more important than it is in ours. We think of a patient person as one who, in an unpleasant or tedious situation—say, standing in a long line—waits uncomplainingly for it to come to an end. Conceived of in this way, it is a relatively trivial and, as it were, occasional, virtue. But in the medieval period, especially in religious thought, the meaning of the word reflected fully its Latin origin in the present participle, *patiens*, of the verb *patior*, "to bear or endure" (from the past participle of the same verb comes the word *passive*). To be patient was to be submissive in the very general sense of accepting one's situation in life, especially when it was unfortunate, as decreed by God. *Patience* and *suffering* thus were akin in meaning, and indeed "to suffer," in Middle English, meant not only "to endure pain" but "to wait patiently." (Our adjective *long-suffering* reflects this earlier sense.)

Inevitably, patience in medieval thought was associated in particular with low social status and thus with poverty, and the poor were regularly exhorted to aspire to it. One of the proverbs in the *Dicta* or sayings of Dionysius Cato, a collection popular in medieval times and often cited by Chaucer, advocates patient endurance of the burden of poverty. The connection between the two goes back to the life of Jesus: he himself had been "patient" in submitting himself to mortality, and finally to suffering and death on the cross to redeem humankind. He had remained poor by choice and had imposed poverty on his disciples as part of their way of life. And he had advocated patience as a response to aggression, saying that whoever was struck on one cheek should turn his head and offer the other. Patience continued to be of central importance among Christian virtues in early times, when the church was suffering persecution at the hands of those in power. In the Gospel of Luke, Jesus predicted that his followers would be imprisoned and some of them put to death for his sake. He told them, "In your patience (*patientia*) you shall possess your souls" (21:19). Saint Paul in his letters spoke of his own patience in enduring the punishments imposed on him during his travels as a missionary and exhorted his followers to follow his example.

Use of Biblical Sources

The poet who wrote *Patience* knew his Bible thoroughly. Like other scholars of his time, he thought of it as one great whole whose every part literally or symbolically signified some aspect of Christian history or doctrine. A ready way of interpreting a given passage was to bring other passages to bear on it; anything in the Old Testament, in particular, could be seen as prefiguring something in the New. Identifying his theme in the book of Jonah, the *Patience* poet found it also in the famous series of eight virtues, each bringing its possessor a blessing or reward, known as the Beatitudes. These appear in a sermon by Jesus recorded in chapter 5 of the Gospel of Matthew; there is a much shorter version in Luke 6. (The passages from Matthew and Luke are printed in "Biblical Sources," p. 28.) The first and the eighth Beatitudes in Matthew read, "Blessed are the poor in spirit" and "Blessed are they that suffer persecution for justice' sake," respectively. Exactly the same reward is predicted in both, namely, "For theirs is the kingdom of heaven." In the Vulgate Bible that was known to the *Patience* poet, the eighth Beatitude reads "Beati qui persecutionem patiuntur" (Blessed who suffer persecution), *patiuntur* being a form of the same Latin verb that I identified earlier as the source of the word *patience*. In interpreting the first Beatitude, the poet disregards the qualification of "poor" by "in spirit" and interprets *poor* as having its primary, material meaning (he has a precedent in the Gospel of Luke, where the corresponding verse reads simply "Blessed are ye poor"). He thus can see the two as linked not only by the fact that they promise the same reward but also by the traditional connection between poverty and patience.

In the opening section of the poem (1–60), the speaker, after praising patience, paraphrases the series of eight Beatitudes and goes on to personify them playfully as eight "dames," calling the first one "Dame Poverty" and the last one "Dame Patience." He himself, he says, is fated to live in poverty, so it behooves him to acquire patience also, for where poverty is present, men and women must summon up patience to endure it. He goes on to speak of the futility of resisting the hardships a poor man must endure, particularly as a servitor who, whether he likes it or not, must do the bidding of his lord. Even if he were told to ride as far as Rome, there would be no use grumbling. Complaints are futile; in the end, he will have to carry out the original order, and he will have made his lord angry at him. This reminds him of how God commanded Jonah to undertake a long journey, how Jonah tried to evade the command, and what happened to him as a result. For the first time, the speaker explicitly addresses an audience that presumably has been listening to him all along; if they will pay attention to him for a little while, he will tell them the story as it is told in the Bible.

The putting together of the Old and New Testaments had begun in the New Testament itself. Jesus alluded to the book of Jonah when he prophesied, "For as Jona[h] was in the whale's belly three days and three nights: so shall the Son of man be in the heart of the earth three days and three nights" (Matthew 12:40). The swallowing of Jonah by the whale and his emergence from its belly unharmed were thus considered to be "types" of the death and resurrection of Jesus—that is, they were interpreted as real events that anticipated later ones. Such correspondences were part of the design of "salvation history": the fall of humankind as recounted in Genesis, the history of Israel, the compensatory incarnation of God's son as the man Jesus, his suffering and death, his resurrection, and the resultant redemption of those who believed in him as the Messiah. The whale in the book of Jonah was further identified by medieval scholars with the sea monster referred to as "leviathan" in the book of Job, in the rhetorical question asked of Job by God: "Canst thou draw out the leviathan with a hook?" Because the whale's action in swallowing Jonah prefigured the death of Jesus, the whale was thought of as a type of Satan, the bringer of death into the world, who seized figuratively on Jesus's mortal flesh when he died on the cross but had to release it when death was defeated by the Resurrection. On the medieval stage, the monster whose enormous gaping mouth represented the entrance to hell was sometimes portrayed as a whale.

We could have assumed that the *Patience* poet was aware of these interpretive connections. But in fact we know he was, because he makes use of them in telling his story. The obstinately rebellious behavior of Jonah in refusing to go to Nineveh to preach is the exact opposite of the behavior of Jesus—Jonah is not so much a type of Jesus as an antitype—and the poet sharpens this antithesis by reminding us of Jesus as he recounts Jonah's actions. When he says, for example, that Jonah set out for Tarshish (biblical Tharsis) because he was unwilling to suffer any of the torments that were likely to befall him at the hands of the Ninevites, he uses, to signify "torments," the word *pines*. *Pine* as a noun has died out by now; as a verb, it is restricted to a few expressions such as "to pine away." In Middle English, however, the noun was in common use. It primarily meant "suffering"; it had strong religious associations; and it specifically designated the sufferings of Jesus on the cross. (Chaucer has one of his pilgrims in *The Canterbury Tales* swear "by God's sweet pine.") And the torments themselves, as Jonah anxiously imagines them, conspicuously include crucifixion: God will care little, he thinks, if he is stripped naked and torn apart on a cross.

As for the whale, his satanic character is indicated at several points in the narrative. The poet calls him a *warlowe* or demon in line 258 (I translate "hell monster") and says that the inside of his belly "stank like the devil" and "reeked of hell" (274–75). When Jonah prays to God from the whale's interior, he says that God has heard him out of "Hell's dark womb" (306). He also complains that his body is imprisoned in the "abyss" (318). The Middle English form of this word meant both the "depths of the sea" and the "bottomless pit," i.e., "hell."

Variation of Tone

These references to Satan and to damnation, like the references to the "kingdom of heaven" in the paraphrased Beatitudes, remind the members of the poem's audience that they live in a world in which sin is punished and goodness rewarded in the afterlife, according to the judgment of the Christian God. But the outlook of the poem as it begins is pragmatic, and its morality is firmly grounded in this world. The rewards of patience described in the opening section (and in part in the poem's conclusion) are to be expected in this life rather than in the next. We should avoid impatience primarily because it aggravates our earthly troubles rather than relieving them; if we tear our clothes in exasperation, we will just have to sew them up later (527–28).

Even God, who in the final episode emerges as the most important character in the story, is portrayed as understandable in human terms. It is true that he is the Sovereign sitting on his celestial throne (93–94) who created the world out of nothing and has absolute power over it; Jonah identifies him to his shipmates as "the one God whose will all obey," who "wrought with his word" the heavens, the earth, and all living things (206–8). God himself points out in his speech at the end of the poem that he created not only the inhabitants of Nineveh (including among these, presumably, the "dumb beasts" that eat the grasses and the broom plants) but the primordial "matter" out of which, in turn, they were shaped (503). But if he is the Lord all powerful, he is equally the Father all merciful—"oure mercyable God" (238), as the poet calls him. The king of Nineveh, who knows him by reputation, is aware that graciousness is an aspect of his nobility; God may well decide to spare him and his people when they have repented. And Jonah's angry justification of his original refusal to go to Nineveh stems partly from his knowledge of this aspect of God's nature:

> I knew well your courteous ways, your wise forbearance
>
> . . . .
>
> Your leniency, your longsuffering, your delayed vengeance;
> And ever mercy in full measure, though the misdeed be huge.   (417–20)

Even God's omnipotence, however, seems to differ from human power in degree rather than in kind. The passage the poet quotes from Psalm 93 (numbered 94 in the A.V.), to the effect that the creator of human sight and hearing must have those faculties himself, implies that God is the same sort of being that we are. He is also made "human" in being, or at least seeming, fallible. When he first speaks to Jonah of his vexation with the Ninevites, his manner strongly suggests the impatience we have just heard criticized. He addresses Jonah "roughly and rudely," without any provocation that we know of. Nor is he long-suffering. On the contrary, he says he is so angry that he can't wait to be avenged; Jonah must drop whatever he is doing and go to Nineveh immediately (69–72). What is more, both the Bible and the medieval poet state flatly that in sparing the city, God is going back on his word. And his inconsistency makes a liar out of his prophet. Jonah's words to God in the biblical story leave this charge implicit, but the Middle English Jonah comes right out with it (428). Jonah, then, has some cause to be aggrieved. But the poet makes him seem so petulant, so childishly self-centered in his complaints about both the sparing of Nineveh and the destruction of his sheltering woodbine, that amusement qualifies our sympathy. It is God's point of view that prevails: after he has explained why he acted as he did, we hear nothing more from Jonah. And this is as it should be: What, after all, is one prophet's reputation for accuracy as against the destruction of a great city filled not only with repentant sinners but with many, including dumb beasts, who never sinned at all (508–18)?

The moral the poem began with, that patience is the best remedy for the pains life inflicts on us, is thus finally supplemented by another: that God, because he loves the human beings he created, is patient with them, ready to pardon them if, having done evil, they repent. As we look back from Jonah's angry outbursts toward the end of the story to his earlier words, we find God's infinite mercy, along with his infinite power, praised in passages that are not part of the comedy, passages that add to it a strain of poignant eloquence. Such a passage is Jonah's profession of faith on shipboard:

> I worship the one God whose will all obey:
> The wide world with the welkin, the wind and the stars,
> And all that range in that realm, he wrought with his word.   (206–8)

Such, too, is his prayer from the whale's belly, which in the Bible, as in the poet's Middle English, is reminiscent of the mixture of complaint, prayer, and reverent praise characteristic of the Psalms. (I have cited some specific echoes in the notes.) These passages must be taken seriously. The mixture of the ludicrous and the sacred, of familiarity and reverence, presented by the poem is typical of an age in which religious imagery was part of the fabric of everyday life. It may remind us of the realistic drawings and caricatures in a medieval psalter, on a page where we also see a picture of the Virgin holding her child.

The Ending

Some scholars, reading the poem in the original, have been perplexed by a problem of wording posed by its first line. As is also true in *Pearl* and *Sir Gawain and the Green Knight*, the end of the poem echoes its beginning. But in *Patience* there is a conspicuous difference between the two. The first line, as I said earlier, calls patience "a point," but the last line calls it "a noble point." Did the poet mean to include the adjective at the beginning as well, and did the copyist then omit it by mistake? I am among those who think not: the heightened praise of patience at the conclusion reflects an enlargement of thought that has taken place over the course of the narrative. Patience is now associated not just with "pain" but with "penance" (531). This additional concept, of course, comes out of the story of the Ninevites, who wore hair shirts and fasted, lamenting their sins. And it bears directly on the lives of the medieval Christians who made up the audience of the poem, guided as they were by the authority of the church. God's patience with the repentant Ninevites shows that the sorrow of sinners over having sinned and their willing endurance of the assigned pains of penance will assuredly bring not only God's forgiveness, but the ultimate happiness promised in the Beatitudes to those who are patient: theirs will be the kingdom of heaven. Conceived of thus, patience is more than just a virtue helping us to bear our troubles from day to day. It is a great virtue indeed, operating on a scale transcending the human life span as part of the perfection of God himself.

A Note on the Embarkation (Lines 101–8)

The poet's description of the departure from Joppa of the ship Jonah had boarded there is of interest because it illustrates not only his habitual expansion and elaboration of his biblical source but his interest in and knowledge of

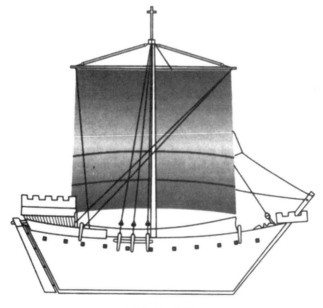

A Medieval Cog

technical skills and the terms pertaining to them, as is also shown in the hunting scenes in *Sir Gawain and the Green Knight* and the account of the opening of the tomb in *Saint Erkenwald*. Both the description and the account of the voyage strongly suggest that he had at some time before he wrote the poem experienced an actual voyage at sea.

He refers to the ship specifically as a *cog*. The cog, a large sailing ship, came into use in the thirteenth and fourteenth centuries. It had a single mast amidships and a single square sail, called in the language of the original poem

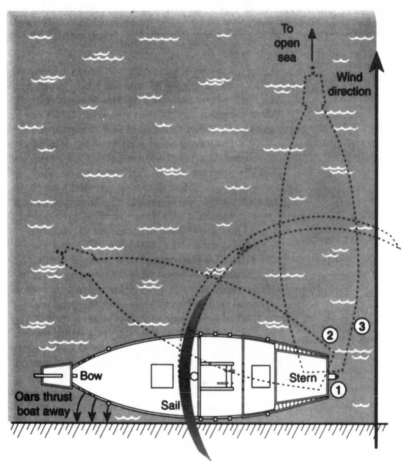

Port, or larboard, side
How Jonah's Ship Was Propelled Out of the Harbor

a *crossayl* (102) (see illustration, page 9). This was hoisted aloft while still furled on its spar, and let down by guy ropes or guide ropes when the ship was about to get under way (105). Such a ship could sail only directly, or somewhat obliquely, before the wind; in the latter case, a sheet called the *bowline* was led forward from the windward side of the sail to the bowsprit (104) so that the sail would not swing around and spill the wind. The poet's account indicates that the ship was anchored at the dock with the wind blowing across it. After letting down the sail, the sailors pushed off with oars on the port, or larboard, side of the bow (106); this is evidently what is meant by the wording of the original, "they laid in to larboard." Oars are resorted to later, during the storm (217). (The poet's word, *ladde-borde*, in line 106 is an earlier form of *larboard*, which originally meant "loading side." *Larboard* was later changed to *port*, i.e., "port" or "dock" side, apparently to avoid confusion with the similar word *starboard*.) The sail "luffed," or flapped (106), until the wind was astern of it, at which point its "bosom," or belly (107), filled and the ship began to move forward (108) (see illustration, page 10).

Patience*

Prologue[1]

Patience is a virtue, though vexing it prove.
When heavy hearts are hurt by hateful deeds
Longsuffering may assuage them and soothe the smart,
For she mends all things marred, and mitigates malice.
5 Who possessed his soul in patience would prosper in time;
Who balks at his burdens is beset the more;
Then better for me to bear the brunt as it befalls
Than harp on my hardships, though my heart mislike.
I heard on a holy day, at a high mass,
10 How the Master taught the multitude, as Matthew tells,
Eight blessings in order,[2] each with a reward,
Set singularly, in sequence, as suited each one.[†]
They are happy, he said, who in heart are poor,
For theirs is heaven's kingdom to hold for ever;
15 They are happy who have the habit of meekness,
For they shall reign as they will in every realm of this world;
They are happy likewise who weep for their harms,
For comfort in many countries shall come to their souls;
They are happy also who hunger after right,
20 For they shall freely be refreshed and filled with all good;
They are happy also who in heart have pity,
For mercy shall be meted them in measure unstinting;
They are happy also who in heart are pure,
For they shall see the best of sights: the Savior enthroned;
25 They are happy also who hold their peace,[3]
For the sons of God's self they shall solemnly be called;
They are happy who guide well and govern their hearts,[4]
For theirs is heaven's kingdom, as you heard before.
These blessings were preached us in promise of bliss
30 If we would love these ladies and liken us to them:
Dame Poverty, Dame Pity, Dame Penance the third,

---

* Notes for *Patience* appear on pages 25–28.
† Matthew 5:3–10.

Dame Meekness, Dame Mercy, Dame Purity most pleasant,
And then Dame Peace and Dame Patience put in thereafter;
He were happy who had one; to have all were better.
35 But since a plight called Poverty is appointed me here,
I shall pair her with Patience and play along with both;
For these two are a team, in the text as they stand;
They are fashioned in one form, the first and the last,
And the wages of their wise ways are one and the same;
40 And also, as I see it, they are the same in kind:
Where Poverty is in place, no power can dislodge her,
For she lingers on at her leisure, like it or not,
And where Poverty oppresses and pinches a man,
Let him prate never so loud, perforce he must bear it.
45 Thus Poverty and Patience are playfellows, I find;
Since I am beset by them both, it behooves me to suffer.
Then let me rather like them and laud their ways
Than frown and be froward and fare all the worse.
If a destiny is dealt me and duly comes round,
50 What avail my vexation and venting of spleen?
Or if the lord of my land, whose liege man I am,
Bids me ride or else run to Rome on his errand,
What gain I by grumbling but greater grief still?
He would make good his mastery, or I much mistake,
55 And threaten me, and think me an unthankful knave,
When the terms of my tenure should have taught me to bow.
Did not Jonah in Judea a bold jaunt begin?
In search of his own safety, he serves himself ill.
If you will tarry a little time, and attend to my story,
60 You shall have the whole truth, as Holy Writ tells.

Part I

It is entered of old in the annals of Judea:
Prophet there to the Gentiles was Jonah professed.
He got words from God that gave him no joy:
A rough summons and rude resounds in his ears:
65 "Rise, rest no longer, make ready to travel;
Fare forth to Nineveh without further speech;
Sow my words in the ways of that wide city,
As at that place, at that point, I put in your heart.
For all are so evil that harbor therein,
70 And their malice is so monstrous, I can no more withhold
My vengeance from their vile deeds, with venom ingrained.
Speed now to Nineveh and speak as I bid."

When the stern voice fell still, that astounded him sore,
His mind was moved to anger—he muttered to himself,
75 "If I obey His bidding and bring them this tale,
And am taken and detained there, my troubles begin.
He says those sinners are consummate knaves;
I come with those tidings, they accost me straightway,
Pen me in a prison, put me in stocks,
80 Gall my feet with fetters, gouge out my eyes.
A marvelous message for a man to preach
Among cruel foes countless, and cursèd fiends!
—Unless my dear Lord on my downfall is bent
For the sake of some misdeed deserving of death.
85 At all costs, I shall take care to keep my distance:
I shall go off some other way, out of His ken;°   *sight*
I shall take a trip to Tarshish and tarry there a while,
And if I lie low and am lost, He will leave me in peace."
He rises, rests no longer, makes ready to travel,
90 Jonah to Port Joppa; joyless, he growls
That by no means will he meekly submit so to suffer,
Though his Father value little the life that He formed.
"He sits there," says he, "on His seat so high
In His glory and grandeur—small gloom He feels
95 If I am seized now in Nineveh and naked displayed,
Racked on a rough cross by ruffians ungodly."
So he passes to the port, his passage to seek,
Finds there a fair ship fitted out to sail,
Parleys with the mariners, pays his money
100 To be taken with no tarrying to Tarshish that day.
He goes across by the gangplank; they get their gear ready,
Bend on° the big sail, belay° their cables,   *attach / make fast*
Set the windlass working, weigh° anchors forthwith;   *raise*
The bowline to the bowsprit briskly they fasten,
105 Grip well the guy ropes: the great canvas falls.
They lay oars to larboard, she luffs in the breeze
Till the blithe breath at her back finds the bosom of the sail
And sweeps their sweet ship for them swift from the harbor.⁵
Was never so joyous a Jew as Jonah was then,
110 Who had schemed to escape unscathed from his Lord.
He thought the Almighty, who made all the world,
Could do him no damage on the deep sea—
Why, the witless wretch! He who would not obey
Soon finds himself in a fix and faces more danger.
115 That was a senseless presumption that seized his mind,
When he set out from Samaria, that God saw no farther:

Yes, His gaze went wide enough, as he well might have known.
The wise words of the king had warned him often,
Royal David on dais, who indited this speech
120   In a psalm that he sang and set in the Psalter:
"O fools that walk the world, find wisdom for once,
And strive to understand, for all your stark folly:
Think you He has no hearing, whose hand formed the ear?
It cannot be that He is blind who built each bright eye."*
125   But this dull-witted dotard° dreads not God's hand;   *fool*
He is out on the high seas, heading for Tarshish.
But he was traced in a trice as he traveled, I find,
And the shaft he had shot fell shamefully short,
For the Master whose mind commands all knowledge,
130   Who wakes ever and watches, His will is well served.
He called on his craftworks, creatures of His hand;
The angrier was their answer, for angrily He called:
"Eurus and Aquilon, east-dwelling winds,[6]
Blow with both your breaths over bleak waters."
135   There was little time lost once the Lord had spoken:
Straightway they bestir them to strike as He bids.
And now out of the northeast the noise begins
As they blow with both their breaths over bleak waters;
The cloud rack runs ragged, reddening beneath;
140   The ocean howls hellishly, awful to hear;
The winds on the wan water so wildly contend
That the surges ascending are swept up so high
And then drawn back to the depths, that fear-dazed fish
Dare not rest, for that rage, at the roiled sea bottom.
145   When wind and waves as one had worked their will
All joyless was the jolly boat Jonah had boarded;
For she reeled all around upon the rough waves;
The shock of the after wind shattered all her gear,
Hurled helter skelter the helm and the stern,
150   Tore loose her tackle, toppled her mast;
The sail swam on the sea; the deck swaying down
Must drink ever deeper, and now the din rises.
They cut cords from the cargo and cast it away;
Many a lad leapt forth to unloose and to cast;
155   They bailed the baneful water, bent on escape,
For though we like our lot but little, life is ever sweet.
So they hauled and they hoisted and heaved over the side
Their bags and their featherbeds and their bright-hued clothes,

---

* Psalm 93:8–9 (A.V. 94).

Their coffers of costly goods, their casks and their chests,
160 All to lighten their load, if relief could be had.
But the winds, unwearying, blew wilder than ever,
And the maelstrom° ever madder and more to be feared,   *violent surges*
Till, wearied out and woeful, they worked no more,
But each turned to the god in whose grace he trusted.
165 Some to Vernagu devoutly vouchsafed their prayers;
Some addressed them to Diana and doom-dealing Neptune;
To Mohammed and Magog,[7] the Moon and the Sun,
As each followed his faith and had fixed his heart.
Then up spoke the wisest, well nigh despairing:
170 "I believe there is some outlaw, some disloyal wretch,
Who has grieved his god and goes here among us;
For his sins we are sinking and soon will perish.
Let us now lay a lottery alike upon all,
And whoso is singled out, send him into the water,
175 And when the evil one is ousted, what else can we trust
But that the ruler of the rain cloud will let the rest be?"
They assented to this speech, and summoned were all
From every corner of that craft, to come and stand trial.
A steersman stepped lively to search under hatches
180 For any who were absent, to add to the roll.
But of those he thought to find, he was thwarted by one,
And that was Jonah the Jew, abject in hiding.
He has fled for fear of the fury of the storm
Into the bottom of the boat, a board for his bed,
185 Huddled aft in the hold, hard by the rudder,
And there he snoozes and snores and slobbers unsightly.
The man gives him a good kick to make him get up—
May Ragnel in shackles[8] shake him out of his dreams!—
By the clasp of his cloak he clutches him fast,
190 Drags him up on deck, and down he sits him,
And rudely requires of him what reason he has
In such onslaughts of the sea to sleep so sound.
Now they tally their tokens; each takes one in turn,
And from first round to last, the lot falls on Jonah.
195 Then they glare at him grimly, and gruffly demand,
"What the devil have you done, dotard wretch?
What seek you out at sea, sinful knave,
With your damnable deeds that will drown us all?
Have you no governor nor god to give ear to your prayers,
200 That in danger of death you drop off to sleep?
From what country do you come? What crave you abroad?
Whither lies your way, and what is your errand?

See, your doom now descends for your deeds ill done:
Do homage to your deity ere we dip you under."
205 "I am a Hebrew," said he, "and Israel-born;
I worship the one God whose will all obey:
The wide world with the welkin,° the wind and the stars,   sky
And all that range in that realm, He wrought with His word.
All this mischief on my account is made at this time,
210 For I have grieved my God, and guilty He finds me,
So send me over the rail into the rough sea,
Or you get of Him no grace, I give you my word."
He made them understand, by the story that he told,
That he had fled from the face of his far-seeing lord;
215 Then such a fear befell them, they fainted in heart,
And heeded him no longer, but made haste to row.
They laid hands on long oars and lugged them in place,
And set them along the sides, for their sail was lost,
And strained with every stroke, and strove to escape,
220 But their power was as nothing; it would not prevail.
In the black boiling surge their oarblades broke;
Then they had no help in hand in that hapless plight,
Nor was there comfort to cling to, nor course to follow
But deal Jonah the judgment that justice decreed.
225 First they prayed to the Prince that prophets serve
That he let them off lightly, nor unleash his wrath
Though in innocent blood they bathed their hands,
And it was his man and messenger they meant to destroy.
Then by top and by toe they tossed him out,
230 Handed him over in haste to the hateful water;
No sooner had he touched it than the tempest ceased;
The waves made peace with the wind in the wink of an eye.
Though they teetered and tilted, with tackle torn loose,
Strong streaming currents constrained them awhile,
235 And briskly bore them on, by behest of the deep,
Till a sweeter one swept them swift to the shore.
When they reached that place of rest, they reverently prayed
To our merciful God, as Moses taught,
With sacrifice unstinted, and solemn vows,
240 And said he was the sole God, and forsook all others.
Though they are jocund° and joyous, Jonah yet fears;   merry
Yes, he finds his fortune fickle, who fled from all harm.
What befell that foolish man from the time he hit water,
It were hard to believe, had Holy Writ not been.

Part II

245 Now is Jonah the Jew in jeopardy dire;
From that storm-shaken ship they shoved him straightway.
A wild wallowing whale, by some whim of fate,
That had been driven from the depths, drew near that place
And saw a man seized and sent into the sea,
250 And swerved and swiftly swooped, on swallowing bent.
The men still holding his toes, the huge mouth takes him;
Untouched by any tooth, he tumbles down his throat.
Then he° sounds° and descends to the sea bottom,   *the whale /*
Amid ridges of rough rock and racing currents,   *submerges*
255 And the man in his maw° half demented with dread,   *mouth*
As little wonder it was if woe possessed him,
For had the hand of heaven's King, that holds all the world,
Not helped this hapless wretch in hell monster's guts,
What lore or what law could lead us to think
260 That any life might be allowed him so long there within?
But he was succored° by the Sovereign that sits on high,   *helped*
Though he had no hope of help in the innards of that fish,
And was driven through the deep and dashed about in darkness:
Lord, cold was his comfort and his care huge!
265 For he remembered each mishap that he had met with that day,
How 'twixt the boat and the briny he was borne off by a whale,
And thrown into his throat without threat or warning;
As a mote° at a minster° door, so mighty were his jaws.   *speck of dust /*
He glides in by the gills through glistening slime,   *church*
270 Goes down a gut that guides him like a road,
Ever head over heels hurtling along,
To a broad block of space as big as a hall,
And there he fixed his feet firmly and stretched forth his arms,
And stood up in his stomach, that stank like the devil;
275 Thus in rot and corruption that reeked of hell
Was his dwelling ordained, who deigned not to suffer!
Then he casts about busily, where best he can find
Some haven in that hulk, but beholds evermore
No place of rest or rescue, but rampant filth,
280 Whichever gut his eyes gaze on, but God is still sweet,
And so he held him steady a space, and spoke to his Lord:
"Now, Prince, have pity on your prophet here;
Though I am foolish and fickle, and false of heart,
Let the power of compassion put vengeance aside.
285 I am guilty of guile, I am gall and wormwood,
But you are God, and all good in your governance lies.

Have mercy now on your man and his misdeeds,
And show yourself true sovereign over sea and land."
With that he crept to a corner and couched him therein,
290   Where he was free of the filth that defiled the place,
And there he sat as safe and sound, save for darkness only,
As in the bottom of the boat where before he had slept.
So in a bowel of that beast he bides his time,
Three days and three nights, ever thinking of God,
295   His might and his mercy, his measured judgments;
Now he knows him in dire need, who knew him not in plenty.
And this whale wallows on over watery wastes,
Through many regions wild and rough, so restive he was,
For that mote in his maw, though by measure of bulk
300   It were nothing next to him, made a niggling in his belly.
And as he sailed on and on, incessantly he heard
The big sea on his back and beating on his sides.
Then the prophet composed a prayer to his God;
These were his thoughts, and thus did he speak them:[9]

Part III

305   "I have looked to you, Lord, lamenting my cares;
You heard me when I was hid in Hell's dark womb;
My feeble voice failed, yet you found me out;
You dipped me into the dim heart of the deep waters;
The great surge of your seas besets me about:
310   Your freshets° overflowing, your unfathomed pools,   *streams*
And your currents in their courses contending together,
All raging in a race, roll over my head.
And yet I said, when I was set at the sea bottom,
Doleful am I, denied the dear light of your eyes,
315   And dissevered from your sight, yet some day I know
I shall tread your temple floor and return to your service.
I am walled around with water through my woe's term;
The abyss binds my body, I bide there in thrall;
The seething of the sea swirl sounds over my head;
320   I am borne to the last bourne,° the base of the mountains.   *boundary*
Each bank is a barrier beating me back
From the landfall I long for; my fate lies with you.
You shall yet save your servant, set justice aside
Through the mildness of your mercy that is most to trust.
325   For when the onset of anguish ached in my soul
Then I hoped, as behooved, in heaven's great Lord,
That he would pity his prophet, pay heed to my prayer,

That my orisons° might enter his most holy house.   *prayers*
I have listened to your learned folk many a long day,
330 But now I see for certain that those unsound minds
That devote them to vanities and vain pursuits,
Forego the grace they are given for gewgaws and trifles.
But I vow most devoutly, and in veriest truth,
That I shall solemnly sacrifice when I am safe at last,
335 And honor you with an offering whole and entire,
And hold to your each behest,° have here my word."   *commandment*
Then our Father bids the fish with forceful voice
To heave him out hastily on land high and dry.
The whale at this word finds his way to a shore,
340 And there he pukes up the prophet as compelled by our Lord.
Then he was swept onto the sand in beslobbered clothes—
It would have been as well to have washed his mantle!
The beach and lands beyond that he beheld there
Were of the very region he had run from before.
345 Then a wind of God's word whipped past his ears:
"So, you'll not go to Nineveh? You know no way thither?"
"Yes, Lord of my life—do but lend me the grace
To go with your good will; else gain I nothing."
"Rise, approach then to preach—lo, the place lies beyond!
350 My lore is locked within you; unloose it there!"
Then he rested no longer, but rose and set forth;
By night he had drawn near to Nineveh's walls.
Now this city was wondrous in width and in length:
To traverse it entirely took a man three days.
355 A full day's journey had Jonah performed
Ere he said a single word to a soul that he met,
And then he cried with such a clamor as caught every ear;
The tenor° of his true text he told in this way: *central meaning*
"When forty days fully are finished and past,
360 Nineveh shall be made nought, as it had never been.
I tell you, this town shall be toppled to the ground;
You shall be dumped upside down, deep into the abyss,
Buried within the bowels of the black earth,
And all alike shall lose the life they hold dear."
365 This speech sprang abroad, and was spread on all sides
To burghers in their big halls and bachelors in service;
Such terror overtook them, such torments of dread
That their faces went white, and woe clutched their hearts.
Yet he ceased not his sermoning, but said ever alike:
370 "God's vengeance verily shall devastate this place."
Then the citizens fell silent and sank into grief,

And for dread of God's doom despaired in heart.
Harsh hair shirts they hauled out, hateful to feel,
And these they bound to their backs and to their bare sides,
375 Dropped dust on their heads, and dully besought
That their pains might please Him who would punish their crimes.
And ever he cries in that country till the king heard
And he rose then and there and ran from his throne
Ripped his royal raiment right off his back,
380 And huddled with bowed head in a heap of ashes.
He asks for a hair shirt and hastily dons it,
Sewed sackcloth thereon, sighing for grief;
Lay dejected in the dust, let the tears drop down,
Bewailing wondrous bitterly all his bad deeds.
385 Then he said to his sergeants, "Set out in haste
To declare this decree, devised by myself:
All beings that draw breath within the bounds of this place,
Males and their animals, females and children,
Each prince, each priest, each prelate as well,
390 Shall fast henceforth for their foul deeds.
Let no babe suck the breast, be it healthy or sick,
Nor beast bite the broom plant° or the bentgrass° either,   *edible shrub /*
Or be put out to pasture, or pull the rich herbs,   *field grass*
Nor shall the ox have his hay, nor the horse have water.
395 We shall crowd all our starved strength into one cry
Whose power shall pierce His heart whose pity shall save us.
Who can predict or presume what will please that Lord
Who governs so graciously in His glory on high?
Though we gravely have grieved Him, his godhead is great:
400 His mood may melt to mildness, and mercy ensue.
And if we veer from our vile ways and divest us of sin,
And pursue the very path He points out Himself,
He will tame His distemper, and turn from His wrath,
And forgive us our guilt, if we grant that he is God."
405 Then all believed in God's law, and left their sins;
Performed fully the penance that the prince advised,
And God in His goodness forgave as foretold:
Though He had otherwise vowed, withheld His vengeance.

Part IV

Much sorrow then settles on the soul of Jonah;
410 Anger against his God engulfs him like a storm;
Such fury has filled him, he fervently calls
A prayer of complaint to the Prince above:

"I beseech You now, Sire, Yourself be the judge:
Were they not my words that forewarned of this change,
415 That I said when You summoned me to sail from Judea
To travel to this town and teach them Your will?
I knew well Your courteous ways, Your wise forbearance,
Your abounding beneficence,° the bounty of Your grace,   *kindness*
Your leniency, Your longsuffering, Your delayed vengeance;
420 And ever mercy in full measure, though the misdeed be huge.
I knew well, when I had wielded such words as I could
To menace all these mighty men, the masters of this place,
That for a prayer and a penance You would pardon them all,
And therefore I would have fled far off into Tarshish.
425 Now, Lord, take my life, it lasts too long;
Deal me my death blow, be done with me at last,
For it seems to me sweeter to cease here and now
Than teach men Your message that makes me a liar."
Then a sound from our Sovereign assailed his ears,
430 As he takes the man to task with trenchant words:
"Hark, friend, is it fair so fiercely to rage
For any deed or decree I have dealt you as yet?"
Jonah all joyless, dejected and grumbling,
Goes out to the east of the high-walled city;
435 He looks around the land for some likely place
To wait in and watch what would happen after.
There he built him a bower, the best that he could,
Fashioned of hay and fern, and a few herbs,
For no groves grew on that ground whose green-clad boughs
440 Could give shelter or shade in the shimmering heat.
So he sat in his little booth, his back to the sun,
And soon fell asleep there, and slumbered all night
While God of His grace made grow from that soil
A green vine, the goodliest a gardener could boast.
445 When God turned dark to dawn and daylight returned,
He wakened under woodbine[10] and was well pleased:
He looked up at the leaves, that lightly moved:
In a lovelier leaf hall no lodger e'er dwelt,
For the walls were wide apart, arched well above;
450 Sealed on either side, as snug as a house;
An entry nook on the north, and nowhere else,
All closed around like a copse that casts a cool shade.
He gazed up at the green leaves that graced his bower,
Where breezes ever blew, so blithe and so cool.
455 Though the sun glared grimly, no glint of its rays
Could pierce the sheltering shade to shine there within.

So glad is this guest of his gay lodging
That he lounges there at ease, looking toward town;
Lazing and lolling in the lee of his vine—
460 As for his diet that day, let the devil take it!
And he laughed with delight as he looked all about,
And wished with all his heart that he had such a place
High on Mount Ephraim or Hermon's hill:[11]
"I never hoped to own a more honorable dwelling!"
465 And when darkness drew on, and desire to sleep,
He slipped into slumber, slow under leaves,
While a worm, as God willed, laid waste the root,
And when next he awakened, his woodbine was no more.
Then the Watcher of the winds bade the west blow soft,
470 And warm the world well with the sweet sighs of Zephyr,°   *Greek god of*
That no cloud shape might shadow the clear-shining sun,   *west wind*
Whose broad face broke forth and blazed like a candle.
When the man roused at morning from the maze of his dreams
He saw well that his woodbine was woefully marred—
475 All blighted and blasted, those beauteous leaves:
The hot sun had harmed them ere ever he knew.
Now the heat rose relentless and raged like a fire:
The warm wind from the west withered every plant
Till he perished, or nearly, for hiding place was none;
480 His woodbine was bereft him; he wept for sorrow
And, overcome with anger, indignantly he calls:
"Ah, You maker of man, what mastery is this,
To afflict so with ill fortune Your faithful servant?
Mischiefs of Your making mock me evermore.
485 The sole solace vouchsafed me was soon snatched away:
My thrice-blessèd woodbine that blocked out the sun.
But I see that all my sorrows are sent at Your command.
So lay the last stroke on me—I live too long."
And God, hearing his grievance, again gave answer:
490 "Is this right, rash man, all your unruly speech,
Vainly for a mere vine to vent so your spleen?
Why suffer such sorrow for something so little?"
"It is not little," said Jonah, "but more like justice.
Would I were out of this world, away under ground!"
495 "Then consider this, sir, since so sore you are vexed:
If I would help my own handiwork, how is that strange?
You lament loud and long over your lost vine,
And never took an hour's time to tend or maintain it,
It was here and went away in the wink of an eye,
500 Yet so ill pleased you are, you loathe your own life.

Then chide me not if I choose to cherish my work
And pity those poor penitents, their pains and their cries.
First, I molded them of matter I myself had made,
Then watched over them a while, and steered well their course;
505 And if now at long last I should lose my labor
And plunge them into the pit when they are purged of sin,
Sorrow for so sweet a place would sink in my heart:
So many cruel men there are mourning their crimes;
And some are dull dunces who cannot discern
510 The step from the steep pole of a standing ladder,
Or say what secret rule sustains the right hand
In its link with the left, though their lives were at stake.
[And there are some beside these who deserve not to die,]¹²
Such as infants in arms that are innocent still,
515 And light-headed ladies who lack wit to tell
The one hand from the other, for all this wide world;
And there are many dumb beasts in barn and in field
Who never sinned in any season, nor were sorry after.
Why rush to revenge me, since some will repent
520 And come and call me king and acknowledge my words?
Were I as hasty as you here, much harm had been done;
Could I forbear no better than you, few souls would be safe.
I may not deal such a doom and be deemed a mild Lord,
For the power to punish must be paired with mercy."

Epilogue

525 Then be not so ungracious, man—go on your way;
Be patient and prudent in pain and in joy,
For he who in ill temper takes to tearing his clothes
Is the sorrier beset as he sews them together.
So, when poverty oppresses me, and pains are strong,
530 I must ally me with longsuffering, and live without strife,
For penance and pain make it plain to see
That patience is a great virtue, though vexing it prove.
Amen.

Notes: *Patience*

1. **Prologue.** I have divided the narrative proper of the poem into four parts, corresponding to divisions indicated in the manuscript by ornamental capital letters at the beginning of lines 61, 245, 305, and 409. The opening section, lines 1–61, I call the Prologue. I call lines 525 to 532 the Epilogue, though line 525 is not marked by an ornamental capital. Parts I through IV correspond for the most part to the

four chapters of the book of Jonah in the Vulgate Bible as we have it today. But Part II ends as Jonah, in the belly of the whale, is about to utter his long prayer to God, whereas the biblical chapter 2 ends later in the narrative, after Jonah's prayer, with the whale's vomiting of Jonah "upon the dry land." Part III begins with Jonah's prayer, followed by the whale's vomiting of Jonah "onto the sand in beslobbered clothes." Chapter 3 begins with God's second command to Jonah to preach in Nineveh. Part III and chapter 3 end with God's decision to spare the penitent Ninevites. Part IV and chapter 4 begin with Jonah's anger at God's decision, followed by God's destruction of Jonah's woodbine (ivy in the Vulgate); Part IV and chapter 4 end with Jonah's complaint about God's action and God's self-justification.

There has been some disagreement among editors as to the division between God's final speech and the narrator's commentary, if indeed it is the narrator who speaks at the end of the poem. I interpret the address to "man" in line 526 (*godman*, "goodman" in the original) as indicating a shift from words spoken by God to Jonah to words spoken, like those at the beginning of the poem, by the narrator to an auditor or reader. The instruction to "go on your way" (525) seems more appropriately addressed to members of an audience who are about to return to their daily lives than to Jonah, who is still in Nineveh when God speaks and whose further travels are irrelevant to the story.

2. line 11: **Eight blessings in order.** The Beatitudes; see "Introduction" (p. 5) and "Biblical Sources" (p. 28).

3. line 25: **They . . . who hold their peace.** In the most familiar version of the Bible, the Authorized or "King James," the seventh Beatitude reads "the peacemakers." The meaning of *pacifici*, or "the peaceful ones," in the Latin Bible was sometimes taken to include "the keepers of peace within themselves"; this sort of peacekeeping would of course include remaining silent. I have kept the wording of the original, which meant in the poet's time, and still means, "who keep quiet."

4. line 27: **Who guide well and govern their hearts.** The Latin version of the eighth Beatitude reads "who suffer persecution" (see Biblical Sources, p. 28 and "Introduction," p. 4). The poet adapts this as "who can steer, [i.e., control] their hearts," referring to self-possession, that is, patience, in suffering.

5. lines 101–8. See "A Note on the Embarcation (Lines 101–8)," p. 9.

6. line 133: **Eurus and Aquilon, east-dwelling winds.** The poet imagines a convergence of two winds on the ship, one from the southeast (Eurus) and the other from the northeast (Aquilon). Two probable sources of these names in the poet's reading were the descriptions of destructive storms in Acts 27 and in Virgil's *Aeneid*, book I. The violent wind that first cripples Paul's ship in Acts is called "Euroaquilo"; in the *Aeneid*, Eurus and Aquilo are among the winds loosed by Aeolus on Aeneas' fleet. Each of these passages contains descriptive details similar to those in *Patience*.

7. lines 165–67: **Vernagu . . . Diana . . . Neptune . . . Mohammed and Magog.** Characteristically, the poet fleshes out the spare Old Testament account with an abundance of detail, supplying a list of miscellaneous non-Christian divinities. In the Book of Jonah, the narrator simply says that Jonah's shipmates "prayed to their god" (the poet's copy of the Bible may have had the plural form *gods*). Vernagu comes from the medieval Charlemagne epics; Diana and Neptune, from Roman mythology. I have substituted *Magog* for the poet's *Mergot*, which is thought to be a corrupt form of *Magog* in the medieval romances; Magog appears, with satanic

associations, in the biblical books of Ezekiel and Revelation. The invocation of *Mohammed* is an amusing anachronism, which the poet apparently overlooked; the story of Jonah is part of Old Testament, pre-Christian, history, whereas Muhammad came after Jesus, founding a faith that was viewed in medieval times as a heretical departure from Christianity.

8. line 188: **Ragnel in shackles.** In Middle English, the word *ragnel* was used both to mean "devil" and as the name of a devil; devils were laden with chains as a sign of their subordination to God's power.

9. line 304: **These were his thoughts, and thus did he speak them.** Jonah's prayer, in both the Bible and the poet's version, seems to echo the Psalms at several points. Relevant verses include:

> Out of the depths I have cried to thee, O Lord (129:1; A.V. 130:1)
> . . . All thy heights and thy billows have passed over me (41:8; A.V. 42:7)
> . . . I have come into the depth of the sea, and a tempest hath overwhelmed me (68:3; A.V. 69:3)
> [D]eliver me . . . out of the deep waters. Let not the tempest of water drown me, nor the deep swallow me up. . . . Hear me, O Lord, for thy mercy is kind: look upon me according to the multitude of thy tender mercies (68:15–17; A.V. 69:15–16)
> But I said in the excess of my mind: I am cast away from before thy eyes. Therefore thou has heard the voice of my prayer, when I cried to thee (30:23; A.V. 31:22)
> In my affliction I called upon the Lord, and I cried to my God: And he heard my voice from his holy temple: and my cry before him came into his ears (17:7; A.V. 18:6)

10. line 446: **He wakened under woodbine.** The name of the plant that shelters Jonah in the Latin Vulgate Bible the poet would have known is *hedera*, "ivy," and is so translated in Douay-Rheims. In Middle English, "woodbine" or "woodbinde" was a name for ivy and other plants; it is used by the poet, and I have retained it, anachronistically, in my translation. (In the Authorized Version, the plant is called "a gourd.")

11. line 463: **High on Mount Ephraim or Hermon's hill.** Both Mount Ephraim and Mount Hermon are mentioned several times in the Old Testament, but neither is associated in any way with Jonah. Presumably the prophet is thinking of them simply as places where there would be views as fine as the one from his booth.

12. line 513: **[And there are some beside these who deserve not to die.]** I have devised and inserted this line to solve a problem presented by the text of the poem as it stands. Throughout, the lines fall naturally into groups of four; they are in fact printed as four-line stanzas by one modern editor, though this in my view distracts the reader's eye from the continuity of the narrative. But in the single extant manuscript of the poem, there is an anomalous group of three lines corresponding to my lines 510–12. There is also a problem of logical sequence: in God's list of those living in Nineveh with whom he had no reason to be angry, the "dull dunces" referred to in line 507 are more clearly exemplified by people who can't tell the rung of a ladder from the upright, and don't know their left hand from their right (511–13 in the manuscript) than by infants and "light-headed ladies" (508–10). I therefore follow Malcolm Andrew and Ronald Waldron's edition of *The Poems of the Pearl*

Manuscript (University of Exeter Press, 1996) in reversing the order of the two passages. But this leaves the relative clause "who cannot tell the rung of a ladder from the upright" without a governing noun or pronoun. I conclude that a line is missing from the manuscript; my conjectural restoration both supplies the grammatically necessary antecedent and makes the pattern of four-line stanzas consistent throughout the poem, which then proves to be 532 rather than 531 lines long.

Biblical Sources

The Beatitudes

MATTHEW 5:3–10

3. Blessed are the poor in spirit: for theirs is the kingdom of heaven.

4. Blessed are the meek: for they shall possess the land.

5. Blessed are they that mourn: for they shall be comforted.

6. Blessed are they that hunger and thirst after justice: for they shall have their fill.

7. Blessed are the merciful: for they shall obtain mercy.

8. Blessed are the clean of heart: for they shall see God.

9. Blessed are the peacemakers: for they shall be called the children of God.

10. Blessed are they that suffer persecution for justice' sake: for theirs is the kingdom of heaven.

Luke 6:20–23

20. . . . Blessed are ye poor, for yours is the kingdom of God.

21. Blessed are ye that hunger now: for you shall be filled. Blessed are ye that weep now: for you shall laugh.

22. Blessed shall you be when men shall hate you, and when they shall separate you, and shall reproach you. . . .

23. Be glad in that day and rejoice; for behold, your reward is great in heaven. . . .

The Book of Jonah

CHAPTER 1

1. Now the word of the Lord came to Jonas the son of Amathi, saying:

2. Arise, and go to Ninive the great city, and preach in it: for the wickedness thereof is come up before me.

3. And Jonas rose up to flee into Tharsis from the face of the Lord, and he went down to Joppe, and found a ship going to Tharsis: and he paid the fare

thereof, and went down into it, to go with them to Tharsis from the face of the Lord.

4. But the Lord sent a great wind into the sea: and a great tempest was raised in the sea, and the ship was in danger to be broken.

5. And the mariners were afraid, and the men cried to their god: and they cast forth the wares that were in the ship, into the sea, to lighten it of them: and Jonas went down into the inner part of the ship, and fell into a deep sleep.

6. And the shipmaster came to him, and said to him: Why art thou fast asleep? rise up, and call upon thy God, if so be that God will think of us, that we may not perish.

7. And they said every one to his fellow: Come, and let us cast lots, that we may know why this evil is upon us. And they cast lots, and the lot fell upon Jonas.

8. And they said to him: Tell us for what cause this evil is upon us, what is thy business? of what country art thou? and whither goest thou? or of what people art thou?

9. And he said to them: I am a Hebrew, and I fear the Lord the God of heaven, who made both the sea and the dry land.

10. And the men were greatly afraid, and they said to him: Why hast thou done this? (for the men knew that he fled from the face of the Lord: because he had told them.)

11. And they said to him: What shall we do to thee, that the sea may be calm to us? for the sea flowed and swelled.

12. And he said to them: Take me up, and cast me into the sea, and the sea shall be calm to you: for I know that for my sake this great tempest is upon you.

13. And the men rowed hard to return to land, but they were not able: because the sea tossed and swelled upon them.

14. And they cried to the Lord and said: We beseech thee, O Lord, let us not perish for this man's life, and lay not upon us innocent blood: for thou, O Lord, hast done as it pleased thee.

15. And they took Jonas, and cast him into the sea, and the sea ceased from raging.

16. And the men feared the Lord exceedingly, and sacrificed victims to the Lord, and made vows.

CHAPTER 2

1. Now the Lord prepared a great fish to swallow up Jonas: and Jonas was in the belly of the fish three days and three nights.

2. And Jonas prayed to the Lord his God out of the belly of the fish.

3. And he said: I cried out of my affliction to the Lord, and he heard me: I cried out of the belly of hell, and thou hast heard my voice.

4. And thou hast cast me forth into the deep in the heart of the sea, and a flood hath compassed me: all thy billows and thy waves have passed over me.

5. And I said: I am cast away out of the sight of thy eyes: but yet I shall see thy holy temple again.

6. The waters compassed me about even to the soul: the deep hath closed me round about, the sea hath covered my head.

7. I went down to the lowest parts of the mountains: the bars of the earth have shut me up for ever: and thou wilt bring up my life from corruption, O Lord my God.

8. When my soul was in distress within me, I remembered the Lord: that my prayer may come to thee, unto thy holy temple.

9. They that are vain observe vanities, forsake their own mercy.

10. But I with the voice of praise will sacrifice to thee; I will pay whatsoever I have vowed for my salvation to the Lord.

11. And the Lord spoke to the fish: and it vomited out Jonas upon the dry land.

CHAPTER 3

1. And the word of the Lord came to Jonas the second time, saying:

2. Arise, and go to Ninive the great city: and preach in it the preaching that I bid thee.

3. And Jonas arose, and went to Ninive, according to the word of the Lord: now Ninive was a great city of three days' journey.

4. And Jonas began to enter into the city one day's journey: and he cried, and said: Yet forty days, and Ninive shall be destroyed.

5. And the men of Ninive believed in God; and they proclaimed a fast, and put on sackcloth from the greatest to the least.

6. And the word came to the king of Ninive; and he rose up out of his throne, and cast away his robe from him, and was clothed with sackcloth, and sat in ashes.

7. And he caused it to be proclaimed and published in Ninive from the mouth of the king and of his princes, saying: Let neither men nor beasts, oxen nor sheep, taste any thing: let them not feed, nor drink water.

8. And let men and beasts be covered with sackcloth, and cry to the Lord with all their strength, and let them turn every one from his evil way, and from the iniquity that is in their hands.

9. Who can tell if God will turn, and forgive: and will turn away from his fierce anger, and we shall not perish?

10. And God saw their works, that they were turned from their evil way: and God had mercy with regard to the evil which he had said that he would do to them, and he did it not.

CHAPTER 4

1. And Jonas was exceedingly troubled, and was angry:

2. And he prayed to the Lord, and said: I beseech thee, O Lord, is not this what I said, when I was yet in my own country? therefore I went before to flee

into Tharsis: for I know that thou art a gracious and merciful God, patient, and of much compassion, and easy to forgive evil.

3. And now, O Lord, I beseech thee take my life from me: for it is better for me to die than to live.

4. And the Lord said: Dost thou think thou hast reason to be angry?

5. Then Jonas went out of the city, and sat toward the east side of the city: and he made himself a booth there, and he sat under it in the shadow, till he might see what would befall the city.

6. And the Lord God prepared an ivy, and it came up over the head of Jonas, to be a shadow over his head, and to cover him (for he was fatigued): and Jonas was exceeding glad of the ivy.

7. But God prepared a worm, when the morning arose on the following day: and it struck the ivy and it withered.

8. And when the sun was risen, the Lord commanded a hot and burning wind: and the sun beat upon the head of Jonas, and he broiled with the heat: and he desired for his soul that he might die, and said: It is better for me to die than to live.

9. And the Lord said to Jonas: Dost thou think thou hast reason to be angry, for the ivy? And he said: I am angry with reason even unto death.

10. And the Lord said: Thou art grieved for the ivy, for which thou hast not laboured, nor made it to grow, which in one night came up, and in one night perished.

11. And shall I not spare Ninive, that great city, in which there are more than a hundred and twenty thousand persons that know not how to distinguish between their right hand and their left, and many beasts?

Cleanness

For E. G. Stanley

Introduction to *Cleanness*

Of the five poems by the "*Gawain* poet," the one called *Cleanness* (or, in some editions, *Purity*) is the least accessible to the modern reader. Compared with the other four, it lacks an intelligible shape. Each of the others tells one story; *Cleanness* tells three stories at length and two more briefly. And it is difficult to see how all three of the stories told at length in the poem are concerned with the virtue the poet calls *clannesse*, though the concluding summary insists that they are. Moreover, the poet's attitude toward the behavior he condemns as *fylthe* offends present-day sensibilities. To understand "cleanness" and "filth" as the poet conceives of them is the main problem the poem presents to its would-be modern interpreters.

Despite these difficulties, *Cleanness* is well worth reading today. Its author was a devout and deeply thoughtful man whose views offer us a window on one version of medieval Christianity. He was also a poet whose superb narrative art places us imaginatively in the midst of such horrific scenes as the Flood and the destruction of Sodom, making us feel the panic of the condemned members of the human race as the waters swirl around their feet, and see and hear, as if we were among the guests at Belshazzar's feast, the apparition of a disembodied hand scraping its message on the wall.

Moral Discourse and Exemplary Narratives

Clannesse, the Middle English ancestor of the modern word *cleanness*, is the first word in the original poem. The poet begins expounding on his theme by saying that anyone who wanted to praise this virtue could easily find language to serve his purpose. He then shifts to disparagement of its opposite, speaking of God's anger with priests "who affront Him with filth" (6) with a vehemence that suggests an involvement in the church on his part, perhaps as a minor official. God and his heavenly kingdom are wholly clean; it would thus be surprising if he did not detest filth in all its forms. The importance of cleanness in the Christian ethic is shown by its appearance in one of the eight Beatitudes listed by Jesus in the Gospel of Matthew. In the Douay-Rheims translation of the Vulgate Bible that the poet would have known, the relevant verse reads, "Blessed are the clean of heart: for they shall see God" (5:8); for *clean*, the Authorized Version has *pure*. (The poet's biblical sources are footnoted in the text, and printed in order in "Biblical Sources," pp. 93–107.) It follows that anyone who is in the least tainted by uncleanness is barred from the divine realm.

The analogy the poet now develops, in which sinful actions are symbolized by soiled and unkempt clothing, was hinted at earlier in his visionary description of the pure and radiant attire worn by the angels in heaven. It is based on an unspoken but important assumption: God, though greater than human beings, is also like us, and we can assume that his moral judgments are the same as ours, though on an infinitely larger scale. Since visible filth and inward viciousness are alike offensive to us, it follows that he finds them offensive as well. A lord seated at a great feast in our world would be angered if a guest came in wearing dirty and torn clothes; he would be justified in expelling such a person violently and threatening him with imprisonment. The divine Lord would judge such a person even more harshly, as is shown in a parable Jesus tells in the Gospel of Matthew. A man holds a feast to celebrate the marriage of his son. While the feast is in progress, he sees a guest who is not properly clad for the occasion, and orders his men to bind him and cast him out into darkness. The host stands for God, and the son whose marriage he celebrates stands for Christ, God's Son. The feast itself symbolizes the bliss of the saved souls in heaven; the expulsion from the feast of the inappropriately clothed guest stands for the damnation of the sinful. Although Matthew says only that the guest is not wearing a wedding garment (22:11), the poet tells the story as it had been elaborated in Christian tradition, describing his clothing as ragged and dirty. He then interprets its meaning in terms of the analogy between material and spiritual filth that is basic to the conceptual structure of the poem: the soiled clothes worn by the guest stand for the sins that will cause the men who commit them to be denied the joys of heaven, including the reward promised to the "clean of heart" in the Beatitude: the sight of God on his throne (176).

At this point, the poet comes closer to naming explicitly a form of moral viciousness that he finds particularly detestable and that figures in the first two of the major stories he tells in the course of the poem. After giving a long list of the sins that estrange men from God, he asserts that though God is displeased by all of them, what displeases him most is "filth of the flesh" (202); this sin, unlike the others, makes him uncontrollably angry. In support of his opinion, the poet recounts three episodes of the "salvation history" that is part of Christian doctrine: the revolt in heaven of the angels whose leader became the archdevil Satan; the Fall of man, engineered by Satan; and the great Flood in which all humanity, except for Noah and his family, was drowned. The punishments imposed by God for the first two were moderate. The eternal exile from heaven of Satan and his followers was fitting because they never repented, and humanity was redeemed after the Fall through the Virgin Mary, who bore God's Son. But the third punishment, in which God gave full vent to his fury, was brought about by the degeneration of the descendants of Adam. In a free interpretation of Genesis 6, the poet refers to this as "the discovery of filth in fleshly deeds." Disregarding nature, human beings engaged in willful and perverse sexual relations, to the point where fiends found mortal women sexually attractive and coupled with them. The evil giants engendered by this miscegenation became rulers whose reigns were marked by universal corruption. When God saw this, he was overcome by grief and fury as he had not been by the rebellious pride of the angels or the disobedience of Adam and Eve. The punishment he imposed was accordingly unrestrained; it brought about nothing less than the destruction of all living beings except the virtuous Noah, his family, and the pairs of animals that, in accordance with God's instructions, he stowed away safely in the Ark.

Commenting on God's action, the poet calls it a justified response to the "disgusting deeds" of mankind, and warns all men who wish to come to his heavenly court that they must keep themselves free of defilement. He goes on to speak of the covenant God established with mankind after the Flood, in which he promised that he would not again destroy all life on earth (Genesis 8:21). Though he never broke his promise, he did destroy an entire country later on for "that same sin," the sin the poet now describes as resulting from a man's contempt for his own body. The country God punished was Sodom. In the poet's retelling of the story of the destruction of Sodom, it becomes clear that by the "filth of the flesh" that most infuriates God he means perverse sexual relations, especially sexual relations between males. As he narrates the episode in which the citizens of Sodom peremptorily order Lot to hand over his angelic guests, so that they may be taught the local form of love, he momentarily gives vent to his own indignation:

> Agh! they spat out and spewed such despicable speech,
> Agh! they raged and they ranted of such rampant filth,
> That the wind and the weather and the world still stink
> Of the breach whence broke forth those abominable words! (845–48)

This expression of moral repugnance in physical terms is reminiscent of an earlier passage in which God, talking to Noah, expresses His disgust at the sinfulness of mankind in language suggestive of physical nausea:

> The sight of their unseemliness sickens me within;
> The great glut of their grossness grieves me sore.   (305–6)

Here, as throughout the poem, the divine state of consciousness is projected from the human state, in which mind and body are inseparably joined.

The story of the destruction of Sodom culminates in a lengthy description of the Dead Sea, which now fills the void that opened and engulfed the city. It is a noxious pool of "destroyed sin" (1018); the soil that surrounds it consumes men's skin and flesh and rots their bones. Beside it stand trees bearing beautiful fruit that, when broken open, prove to be filled with ashes.

Turning from this sustained contemplation of evil and decay, the poet now engages in a pleasanter meditation. The fact that God punished the people of Sodom for their filth shows that he loves noble behavior. Those who wish to see him in heaven must model themselves on Christ, his Son, who throughout his life manifested the purity of a flawless pearl. All men are evil, soiled by the "foul mire" of mortality (1114), but once defiled, they can make themselves clean again by confessing their sins to a priest and performing whatever penance he assigns them. After they have been divested of sin, however, men must take care not to resume their evil ways, because God becomes especially angry when something that has belonged to him and partaken of his purity becomes soiled again. This warning looks forward to the poem's final episode, in which the vessels of the Jewish temple, which had been consecrated to God, are used by the drunken revelers at Belshazzar's feast.

The rest of the poem—about a third of it—consists of a series of narratives derived from the Old Testament books of Paralipomenon (Chronicles), Jeremiah, and Daniel. These stories tell of the defeat of Zedechias (Zedekiah), heir of Solomon and last of the kings of Judah, by the Babylonians under Nabugodonosor (Nebuchadnezzar); the destruction of Jerusalem and the transfer of the sacred vessels of the temple to the Babylonian treasury; the death of Nabugodonosor; the reign of his heir, the sinful and arrogant Balthasar (Belshazzar); the profane feast staged by Balthasar; the appearance of the prophetic writing on the wall; its interpretation by Daniel; and its fulfillment in the slaying of Balthasar by the invading soldiers of Darius, king of the Persians, and Porros, king of India. These stories are linked with the earlier ones by a familiar analogy in Christian doctrine whose source is the Bible, particularly the writings of Saint Paul: the conception of the human body as a "vessel" destined to be the recipient of God's grace or the object of His wrath. (For example, in the second Epistle to Timothy, Paul speaks of the vessels made of various substances that are found in a great house, and says that any man who departs from iniquity "shall be a vessel unto honour, sanctified and profitable to the Lord" (2 Timothy 20:21).) The Sodomites and others whose actions the poet thinks of as "filthy" are thus figuratively committing the sin that Balthasar commits literally when he uses the treasures taken from the temple in a drunken feast: they are defiling vessels created by God that should be kept pure in his honor.

These last stories also introduce an important new theme: that of idol worship. While Zedechias sat on the throne in Jerusalem, he "used abomination, bowing to idols" (1173), turning away from the God whom the Jews had worshiped faithfully and who had helped them many times in the past. To punish the king's disloyalty, God brought an enemy down on him in the person of Nabugodonosor, whose army besieged Jerusalem for so long that those within became famished. When Zedechias attempted to steal away from the city one night with a company of his best men, they were captured by the Babylonians and taken prisoner; his sons were killed before his eyes, and he himself was blinded and imprisoned for life. Nabugodonosor then dispatched to Jerusalem a tyrannical general named Nabuzardan, who killed or took captive all those who remained in the city and despoiled the temple, sending all the consecrated vessels within it to Babylon. Seeing them, Nabugodonosor recognized them as surpassing in costliness and beauty any artifacts he had ever seen and stowed them away carefully in his treasury.

After Nabugodonosor's death, his eldest son Balthasar succeeded to the throne. Preoccupied with his own glory as the greatest king in the world, he failed to honor the king of heaven, instead worshiping idols adorned with gold and silver to whom he prayed for help in time of need. To celebrate himself and his reign, Balthasar decided to give a great and lavish banquet, to which he would invite the kings of every land and where they, in turn, would acknowledge themselves his vassals. As he sat drinking at the high table surrounded by his mistresses, the wine went to his head and made him foolish. In a fit of bravado, he ordered that the sacred vessels of the Jews should be brought from the treasury where his father had placed them and used to serve wine to him, his concubines, and his guests. Once the wine had been served to all, he and his guests drank together to their false gods. Suddenly a disembodied hand appeared and wrote on the wall an inscription visible to everyone in the room. Terrified, Balthasar consulted the scholars in his household about its meaning, but neither they nor the wise men he summoned to his court from every part of the country could explain it. Finally, at a suggestion by the queen mother, he consulted Daniel, a Jewish prophet who had been brought to Babylon as a captive in his father's days and had become highly esteemed there. Daniel told Balthasar how his father, Nabugodonosor, had once blasphemed by setting himself on a par with God. God had punished him by banishing him to the wilderness, where he lived with wild beasts, believing himself one of them. Finally, he came to his senses and acknowledged God's transcendent power; he was then restored to the throne. Daniel warned Balthasar that he, like his father, had turned against God, and that he too had acted blasphemously in using the sacred vessels of the Jews at a profane feast and drinking from them to gods made of wood and stone. As a result, his kingdom was doomed to imminent destruction, and he himself would soon die at the hands of the victorious Medes and Persians. That night, Balthasar was beaten to death in his bed by the invaders. In lines reminiscent of the Beatitude he cited at the beginning of the poem, the poet ironically predicts that Balthasar will experience little pleasure in the afterlife, and that it will be a long time before he enjoys the sight of "our Lord" (1804) promised in the Beatitudes to those clean of heart.

The Concept of Cleanness

In his concluding summary, the poet states that he has shown us "in three ways" how deeply uncleanness wounds the heart of God. To understand how it is that he can consider the sexual perversity punished in the stories of the Flood and the destruction of Sodom and the idolatry punished in the stories of Zedekiah and Balthasar as forms of the same vice, we must examine his complicated and somewhat idiosyncratic concept of the virtue that is its counterpart. It is distanced from us today partly by the fact that we think of "cleanness" chiefly in negative terms as the absence of dirt or pollution. The adjective *clean* usually denotes a physical state (as in "clean hands" and "clean water"), though its significance is sometimes moral (as in "clean living"). In this latter sense, it has largely been displaced by *pure*. But in Middle English the ancestral word had a number of now obsolete positive meanings. In the comprehensive *Middle English Dictionary*, the definitions of *clene*, in addition to "unsoiled" and "morally pure," include "bright, shining" and "splendid, elegant; shapely, comely." In its earliest appearance in the poem, the word describes God in His court (17), and here it cannot simply mean "unsoiled." We take it for granted that God's abode is free of impurity of every kind, but the poet goes on to describe it in positive terms as an honorable household where heaven's King is fittingly served by a company of angels who are radiant both intrinsically and in their bright attire. The conception of cleanness implied in this passage includes ceremony and visible or envisioned splendor. It is further developed when the poet tells for the second time the story of a feast at which a guest appears in unclean clothes, presenting it now explicitly as a parable and adding to it many details lacking in the New Testament sources. The host who represents God—a "king" in Matthew 22 and a "man" in Luke 14—becomes in the poet's version "a man of great wealth." The resources of what must be a vast estate—the bulls and boars; the fattened poultry; the partridges, swans, and cranes—amply provide for a lavish variety of dishes. The household includes not only the servants who presumably prepare the food and wait on those who are feasting but also a steward who greets the guests as they arrive and a marshal, or master of ceremonies. Judging their social status by their clothing, the marshal seats each one at the high table or at a suitable distance from it. At the banquet, all alike are lavishly served. Music played by minstrels provides entertainment, and good drink makes everyone glad.

As a symbol of the bliss of the saved souls in the afterlife, this feast, in its combination of magnificence and decorum, exemplifies the "cleanness" celebrated throughout the poem. Reimagining the parable, the poet projects into the divine realm the luxury and ceremonious formality of a great household on earth, clearly valuing these qualities for what they symbolize and in themselves as well, as they existed in the late-fourteenth-century world in which he lived. Cleanness so understood is not only spiritual but also esthetic and social, and is manifested on a continuum that includes both earthly and divine realms. The difference between the two, though vast, is one of degree rather than of kind. As an esthetic value, cleanness is manifested in the visible beauty of living beings and costly artifacts: the youthful angels who visit Lot, the "burnished" (1085) baby in the manger, the flawless beryls and pearls possessed by the wealthy, and the intricately wrought vessels of gold, adorned with gems. These last having been respectfully admired and kept safe by Nabugodonosor, are profaned by his son Balthasar at the feast.

The poet's views on sexual behavior are influenced by an aspect of God that has not yet been brought into this discussion, though it is hinted at in the poem's opening line. Cleanness is named there as a subject of discourse that will pro-

vide whoever wants to talk about it many "fair forms of language"—provided
that he knows how to commend it *kindely*. The noun *kinde*, from which the
adverb is derived, was a common word for "nature" in Middle English. To com-
mend cleanness *kindely*, or naturally, would be to understand and praise it as an
attribute of the world of nature, which is God's creation and reflects his purity.
When Christ lay in the manger, the oxen and asses recognized the baby by his
brightness as the "kyng of nature" (1087). The first descendants of Adam, who
had not yet fallen into evil ways, were endowed by God with "all the bliss with-
out blame that bodies might have" (260); the only law imposed on them was that
they were to look to *kinde* and fulfill its course cleanly. They broke this law by
engaging in unnatural sexual relations. The Dead Sea, which is the legacy on
earth of the destroyed city of Sodom, is unnatural and therefore unclean: poi-
sonous and foul. Furthermore, its properties contradict every rule of nature.
A lump of lead will float on it, but a feather will sink.

When God denounces to Abraham the sinfulness of the people of Sodom
and Gomorrah, he defines it explicitly as male homosexuality:

> Each man takes as his mate a man like himself,
> And counterfeits the woman in witless coupling.   (695–96)

A remarkable passage follows: the poet imagines God as saying that he him-
self devised and secretly taught men and women the "craft" of sexual inter-
course, considering it, indeed, the most precious of his ordinances. When loving
and committed partners come together in private, their amorous play yields
delight so intense that it all but equals the joys of paradise. Those who disre-
gard this divinely sponsored mode of coupling have "consorted uncleanly in
contempt of nature" (710) and in so doing have shown contempt for God, thus
making themselves unclean. This praise of the joys of lovemaking for their
own sake is extraordinary and unexpected in a medieval poem, particularly
since it omits all reference to the one circumstance that, according to Chris-
tian doctrine strictly interpreted, justified the otherwise sinful enjoyment of
sexual pleasure in marriage: the intention on the part of both man and woman
to conceive a child.

When Daniel explains the handwriting on the wall to Balthasar, he ridi-
cules the king for worshiping things made of wood and stone, since they are
lifeless by nature, incapable of moving or speaking as animate beings do. They
are "senseless stocks and stones, unstirring forever" (1720). The ominous mes-
sage inscribed by the hand on the wall was sent by God as a punishment for
this sin, which Daniel refers to as *frothande fylthe*, "frothing filth." The repug-
nant idea of a yeasty mess bubbling up and threatening to overflow is charac-
teristic of the poet's style in that he imagines an object of moral disapproval as
also being physically repugnant. Idolatry and sexual perversity are coupled in
the poem as forms of uncleanness because the practitioners of both sins act in
disregard of what is natural and therefore pure.

Sources

Though *Cleanness* begins as if it were a treatise on an assigned topic, the poem as a whole is more like a homily, a sermon intended for popular consumption. The poet addresses the members of his audience from time to time as if they were a Christian congregation, something he does not do in any of the other four poems, warning them that they must achieve and maintain the purity spoken of in the Beatitudes if they wish to see God after death. As in a sermon, he illustrates his opinions and precepts with stories he has read in the Bible called *exempla*, "examples." But he also speaks in the poem as a man defending his personal views:

> I have listened hard and long to many learned clerks,
> And in writings well-reasoned read it myself,
> That that peerless Prince who in Paradise rules
> Is displeased at every point appertaining to sin.
> But never have I seen it set down in a book
> That he punished so impatiently the people he had made,
> . . . .
> As for filth of the flesh that fools have practiced. (193–98, 202)

The exemplary narratives that make up most of the poem—the stories of the Fall of man, Noah's flood, the destruction of Sodom and Gomorrah, the conquest of Jerusalem, and Balthasar's feast—are taken primarily from the Old Testament; the poet would also have consulted some of the biblical paraphrases and commentaries available in his time. The story of the rebellion against God of the angels led by Lucifer, their expulsion from heaven, and the transformation of Lucifer to Satan was developed by early Christian writers from hints in the Bible such as in Isaiah chapter 14: "How art thou fallen from heaven, O Lucifer, who didst rise in the morning? . . . And thou saidst in thy heart: I will ascend into heaven, I will exalt my throne above the stars of God." (Isaiah 14:12–13; see also the note to lines 207 ff.) At one point, the poet identifies a specific source: a famous medieval French poem called *Le roman de la rose* (*The Romance of the Rose*). The *Roman* has two parts; the first, whose author was a poet named Guillaume de Lorris, is a dream allegory. Its narrator, a young man, enters the Garden of Mirth or Delight, where he sees and ardently desires a beautiful rosebud. De Lorris's narrative breaks off about a fifth of the way through the poem and is continued by a poet known as Jean de Meun or Jean Chopinel (also Clopinel). The author of *Cleanness* refers to him simply as "Clopyngnel," and it is from him that he takes and uses for his own purposes a piece of advice given to the lover (see note 23, on li. 1057ff.).

The poet also makes use, though without acknowledgement, of John Mandeville's *Travels*, a book well known in his time that he would have read in French. Its author gave what he claimed were firsthand accounts of wondrous sights and legendary personages, dwelling in remote lands, who had magical powers or great wealth, such as Prester John and the Great Chan or Khan. Details from Mandeville embellish our poet's descriptions of the Dead Sea (1015–48), of Belshazzar's palace (1389–96, 1316) and of the sacred vessels displayed at the feast (1456–88). His description of the vessels is also reminiscent of several passages in the Old Testament. In Exodus 25, God gives instructions to Moses for the making of the tabernacle and the ark: the furnishings to be prepared included "dishes, and bowls, censers, and cups . . . of the purest gold" (29) as well as a candlestick with ornate branches "of beaten work of the purest gold" holding seven lamps (31–40). Solomon's construction of the temple is described in 3 Kings (1 Kings), chapters 5–7 (printed below in biblical sources), and in 2 Paralipomenon (2 Chronicles), chapters 2–4.

Finally, there is evidence in the poem of the author's acquaintance, unusual for an Englishman of his time, with certain rabbinical commentaries on the Old Testament; these would presumably have been available to him in Latin translation (see note to li. 820).

Cleanness

Introduction[1]

He who commended Cleanness, considering her aright,
And treated every point that pertains to her praise,
Would find fair forms of language to further his speech
And in the contrary course, encumbrances huge.
5 For the Maker of all things is irked beyond measure
When the folk of His following affront Him with filth,
As reverend religious men who read and who chant
And approach the Lord's presence as priests of the church.
They betake them to His temple and attend on Him there;
10 Rightfully, with reverence, they arrange His altar;
They handle His own body, and use it as well;
If cleanness clasps them round they command rich rewards,
But if they deal in discourtesy, dishonoring their craft,
And are outwardly fair, but within all filth,
15 Then they are sinful themselves, and besmirched altogether—
Sully God's sacred gear[2] and incite Him to wrath.
So clean in His court is the King who rules all,
And His household on high so honorably served
By angels ranged round, with radiance suffused
20 Both within and without, in raiment well-wrought—
Were He not strict, and a stickler, and could stomach no evil,
It were too great a wonder; it would never happen.
Christ himself discoursed of it, commending in order
Eight states of happiness, each with its reward.[3]
25 I remember one among others, as Matthew records them,°
That discourses of cleanness in clear words and wise:
"He who is clean in heart has a happy fate,
For he shall look with delight on our Lord's fair face,"
As if to say, none succeeds who seeks that sight,
30 On whom aught of uncleanness has ever appeared.

Biblical sources indicated at the bottom of the pages are printed in order in the appendix that follows the endnotes, pp. 93–107.
° Matthew 5:3–12, esp. 8; Luke 6:20–23.

For He from whose heart all ordure is banished
Cannot bear the brunt that it should bide next His body.
So do not head for heaven with clothes all in rags
Or with unwashed hands, or the hood of a fool,
35   For who high in rank and honor on earth
Would like it if a lad came in loutish attire
When he was solemnly seated in ceremonial state
Above dukes on the dais, with dainties before him—
And then this boy bursts in and boldly sits down,
40   His trousers torn at the knees, his shoes tied with string,
And his tabard° all tattered, and two elbows out,   *tunic*
Or any one of all these, he will be ousted straight
With blame and berating and a buffet, perhaps,
Hauled off by rough hands and heaved out the door,
45   And forbidden to be found in that bright hall after
On pain of imprisonment and putting in stocks.
And thus he shall be shamed for his shabby dress
Though he never erred again in act or in speech.

The Parable of the Wedding Feast

And if he were unwelcome to a worldly prince,
50   The high King of heaven is harsher still,
As Matthew tells in the Mass of the man of great wealth[4]
Who held a feast in hall when his heir was wed,°
And sent all and some a summons to assemble
In clothes clean and comely, and come to his table,
55   "For my bulls and my boars have been battened° and   *fattened*
      slaughtered,
And my fine fat fowls fresh killed for our pleasure,
My poultry that is pen fed, my partridges too,
With collops° of wild swine, with swans and cranes.   *slices*
All is catered and concocted to a king's taste;
60   Quick, come to my court, ere the cooked food cools."
When all had heard the message for whom it was meant,
Each was ready with a reason to refuse outright.
One had purchased a property, he promptly explained,
"I must travel there today, to take things in hand."
65   Another said no, and announced this cause:
"I have troubled me to obtain teams of oxen
To help with my husbandry; I must hasten there
To see them pull the plough—your pardon, I pray."
"And I have wedded a wife," was the third one's plea;

° Matthew 22:1–14; Luke 14:16–24.

70 "Excuse me at the court; I cannot attend."
So they balked and held back and begged off, each one,
And none offered to enter, though all had been asked.
Then the lord of that land found little to praise
In their unfriendly answers—angrily he speaks:
75 "Now dire be their doom who withdraw from me thus;
More merit they my ire than any misguided heathen.
Go out, good friends, into the great streets;
Search through the city's each precinct in turn;
The wayfarers you find there, afoot and on horse,
80 Both the men and the women, the better and the worse,
Call them all cordially to come to my feast;
Blithely bring them in, as if they were barons born,
That every part of my palace may be packed full of folk;
Those others that are absent were unworthy wretches."
85 So they went and came again, who kept watch over the land,
Brought with them many young men they met with abroad,
Squires that on steeds swept swiftly along,
And not a few on foot, both freemen and bound.
When they came to the court, they were courteously welcomed;
90 A steward at his station was standing to greet them,
And a sage marshal solemnly saw them to the table,
Assigning each a seat as suited his rank.
Then the servants to their sovereign said these words:
"Lo, lord, by your leave, as your liegemen all,
95 At your behest we have brought, as you bade us do,
Many strange men to your meal, and more room remains."
On learning this, the lord said, "Look farther still:
Go forth into the fields and fetch more guests;
Hunt up those that harbor in hedgerows and thickets—
100 Whatever folk you find there, fetch them here;
Be they notables or nobodies, neglect them not;
Be their limbs sound or lame, be they lacking an eye,
And though they be wholly blind or blundering cripples,
That no least nook of my lodge may be left unfilled.
105 For I tell you, those traitors that turned their backs
And set the summons at nought that I sent but now,
Shall never gather with my guests at my great feast
Or sip one sup of my sauce, though I saw them starve."
When he had spoken, the sergeants set forth at once,
110 Carried out his orders to hunt up more people
And collected a crowd, all conditions of men—
They were not suckled by one mother, or sired by one father!
Were they prosperous or poor, they were properly placed:
The best ever before, that were brightest attired;

115 The greatest grouped on the dais, whose garments were richest,
And the lesser along the sides, at the lower tables.
As dress and adornment distinguished each one,
A marshal seated them severally, with ceremonious mien;°   *manner*
Few of the finest folk lacked full honors,
120 And yet the humblest in that hall were amply served
With meat and with merriment, and minstrelsy too,
And all the gaiety a great lord's guests should enjoy.
And they began to be glad, that were given good drink,
And each man with his table-mate made himself at ease.
125 Now in the midst of the meal the master was minded
To descend to the assembly he had summoned there,
To welcome all present, both wealthy and poor,
And greet them with gracious words to gladden their hearts.
He enters the high hall, and on he walks
130 To the best on the benches, and bids them be merry;
Plies them with pleasantries, then passes along
To each table in turn, talking and laughing,
And as he came across the floor, a sight caught his eye—
It was not fit attire for a festive time—
135 A coarse fellow in the crowd, unkempt and unclean,
In no Sunday suit, but one soiled with labor;
He was not dressed for dealing with decent folk.
And the great lord was aggrieved, and gave vent to his wrath.
He demanded of the man, with a menacing look,
140 "How got you here, friend, in guise so foul?
That outfit you have on—it honors no feast;
You have not come into this company clothed for a wedding.
The boldness boded ill that brought you here
In a robe all ragged and rent at the sides.
145 You are a downright disgrace in that dingy gown;
Small homage have you offered my hall or me
That presume to appear in my presence thus clad.
Am I a low-born lout, to laud your surcoat?"°   *loose outer garment*
The fellow was frightened by the lord's fierce words;
150 He ducked his head dumbly, looked down at the earth.
So dazed he was with dread, lest harm be done him,
That not a single syllable could he say for himself.
Then the lord lifts his voice and loudly cries
And talks to his torturers: "Detain him," he says,
155 "Take his two hands and tie them at his back,
Fix both his feet in fetters locked fast,
Seat him in the stocks, and set him thereafter
Deep in my dungeon where dolor dwells ever,

Where there are groans most grievous, and agonized sounds
160 Of teeth grinding together, to teach him discretion."
Thus Christ has compared the kingdom on high
To this magnificent feast whereto many are called,
For all are warmly welcomed, the worse and the better
Who were baptized in font, to be fed at that banquet.
165 But take care, if you would come there, to wear clean clothes
And fit for a feast day, lest a dire fate befall you,
For approach His presence, of princes most noble—
He hates hell no more hotly than him who is foul.
What, then, are the garments to gird yourself with,
170 That shall array you in radiance, raiment of the best?
They are the deeds, beyond doubt, that you have done in your life,
And enlivened and illumined, as your liking led you.
Care for them constantly, and keep them fresh
And fashioned in fair forms to fit foot and hand,
175 And cleanly cut and trimmed to conform to your body.
Then you may see your Savior on His celestial throne.

Uncleanness Is the One Sin That Rouses God to Merciless Anger

Other faults may force us to forfeit our bliss[5]
And lose sight of the Sovereign—sloth, for one;
Bragging and boasting and overbearing pride
180 Thrust men in throngs down the throat of the devil;[6]
For coveting, and crooked and crafty deeds,
For marred oaths, and manslaughter, and too much drink
For banditry and brawling, men are loved but little;
For robbery and ribaldry and outright lies,
185 For depriving of their dowries desolate widows,
For making mock of marriage, for maintenance of ruffians,
For treason and for treachery, and tyranny to boot,
And for defaming fair names, and enforcing false laws:
Men may lose the delight that is lauded most
190 For offences such as these, and suffer affliction,
And never enter the court of the King of Heaven,
Nor ever behold Him in bliss, for such bad tricks.
But I have listened long and hard to many learned clerks,
And in writings well reasoned read it myself,
195 That that peerless Prince who in paradise rules
Is displeased at every point appertaining to sin.
But never have I seen it set down in a book
That He punished so impatiently the people He had made,

Nor avenged Him so violently on vice or on sin,
200 Nor so hastily did harm in the heat of His anger,
Nor so severely and swiftly sought to destroy
As for filth of the flesh that fools have practiced,
For then, I find, He forgot all His courteous forbearance
And, maddened past relenting, moved to take revenge.

The Fall of the Angels

205 Now the first of all felonies was the false fiend's work
While he held a place of honor, raised high in heaven,
Of the many noble angels most admirably fair.[7]
But he repaid those rich gifts with a rude reward—
He saw only himself, his surpassing splendor,
210 And forsook his sovereign, and said these words:
"I shall lift my throne aloft in the lands of the north
And be honoured like Him whose hands made the sky."
With this proud pronouncement, his punishment came:
God drove him to damnation, deep in the abyss—[8]
215 Measured the chastisement, His mood held in check,
But there the tenth part of His retinue was taken and lost.
Though the traitor took pleasure in his princely attire
And the radiance that arrayed him in rays so bright,
As soon as God's sentence descended in force,
220 Thousands thrown from heaven went thronging the air;
Down from the firmament, devils turned black
Swirled at the first swipe like snow in the wind,
Hurtled into hell hole as the hive swarms home.
The fiend and all his folk fell forty days
225 Ere that stinging storm had stinted its force,
But as flour drifts in dust motes under a fine sieve,
So from heaven to hell ran that hateful torrent
On each side of the world, everywhere alike.
This was a dire disruption, and a downfall huge,
230 Yet the Lord did not rage, nor the wretch relent,
Nor would serve again his sovereign, so set was his will,
Nor implore and play the suppliant, pleading for mercy;
So though the shock was sharp, the shame was small;
Though he is cast into care, he is constant in sin.

The Fall of Man

235 But the second disaster was suffered by mankind
Through the failure in faith of one faulty man,°

° Genesis 2:15–17; 3:1–6.

Adam disobedient, destined for bliss,
Put into paradise, a place all his own,
In liberty and liking to live for a term
240 And then inherit the land that angels had lost.
But Eve egged him on to eat of an apple[9]
That poisoned their progeny, all peoples of this world,
A ban there behooved them, bidden by the Lord,
And a penalty was appended and openly suffered;
245 The ban was on the fruit that the first man tasted,
And the doom was the death that is due us each one.
Measured was the punishment, meet for the misdeed,
And amended by a maid unmatched among women.[10]

The Corruption of Adam's Progeny°

But in the third all were injured that ought to have thrived;
250 Then was ill will unstinted, ire unrestrained,
Because the folk had fallen into filthy ways
That lived in the land without lords to rule them.
They were the fairest of form, and of face likewise,
The greatest and goodliest ever given life,
255 The strongest and most stalwart that stood ever on feet,
And had the longest life spans allotted to men;
For they were the primal progeny that peopled the world;
Sons of the great ancestor, sired by Adam
To whom God had given all good that behooved:°   *was proper*
260 All the bliss without blame that bodies might have;
And they favored most their father, as his foremost heirs,
So that no others afterward were handsome as they.
No law was laid down for them save "Look to nature,
And conform to its course, and cleanly fulfill it."
265 And then they forsook their form of life for fleshly filth
And devised unnatural deeds in deviance° perverse.   *unrighteousness*
They mingled promiscuous, mating together,
And with others, willfully, in wanton misusing.
Such defilement did they wreak that the demons saw
270 How much to be desired were the daughters of men,
And came to consort with them in carnal lust,
And engendered giants in their joinings unseemly.
These were men without mercy, mighty on earth,
That were hailed with high praise for their hateful deeds.
275 He was lauded as lordly who loved fighting most,
And the author of most evil was ever deemed best.

° Genesis 6:1–2, 4–7.

So iniquity on earth increased, and grew grave,
And multiplied among men, many times over;
The prideful and powerful so preyed on the rest
280 That the Author of all things grew angry at last.
When each country's corruption was clear in His sight,
And they that lived in each land no longer loved virtue
Then anger grew hot in the heart of our Lord;
Like a man mourning within, He mused to Himself,
285 "Much do I repent me that ever I made man,
But I shall wreak my revenge on all wrong-headed folk;
Of all creatures clad in flesh will I cleanse the world—
Both men and every beast, both birds and fish
All shall be doomed and dead and driven from the earth
290 That ever I set soul in, and sorry I am
That I myself made them; but if I may hereafter
I shall watch them well, and be wary of their tricks."

Noah and the Ark°

Now one man there was in the world at that time
Ever ready to do right, and ruled himself well,
295 In dread of the dear Lord he disposed his days,
And as he walks with his God, he wins the more grace.
Noah was his name, as is known to many;
Three boys had been born to him, bound to three wives;
Shem he fathered first, and Ham followed next,
300 And Japhet joined them after, engendered third.
Now God speaks to Noah, denouncing men's deeds
With harsh hateful words and hostile intent:
"The demise of all things mortal that move upon earth
Has risen before my face, and fulfill it I must.
305 The sight of their unseemliness sickens me within;
The great glut of their grossness grieves me sore.
I shall stretch wide my strength, and destroy altogether
All these folk and their fair lands and their fellow creatures.
But make yourself a mansion—and that is my will—
310 A cabin crafted of tree trunks, cleanly planed;
With stables built stoutly for wild stock and tame.
Cover well with clay the enclosed walls within,
And where board joins with board, bedaub it without.
And make it by these measurements—mark them well:
315 Three hundred cubits be its compass in length,

° Genesis 6:8–22; 7; 8.

With fifty of the same assigned to the breadth;
Let the height of your ark be an even thirty,
With a window opening wide, well above water,
One cubit in width, likewise in height,
320 And, set in the side, a snug-fitting door.
Have halls there, and hutches, and deep-hollowed dens,
Both bowers built of brush and well-bound coops,
For I shall waken up a water to wash all the world
And drown all that dwell there with down-rushing floods.
325 All that writhe or walk erect in the realm of the living
Throughout the wide world, I shall lay waste in anger.
But a pact I proclaim and impart to you here,
For righteousness and reason have ruled you ever;
You shall enter this ark with the heirs of your body,
330 And your own wedded wife; with you shall come
Your sons and their spouses: solely these eight
I shall leave among the living, and let the rest drown.
Of each kind of animal search out couples;
Of those accounted clean you may keep seven pairs,
335 Of the unclean, your ark may harbor one only,
To spare for me the seeds of all species on earth.
And match with every male a female beast,
That, pair by pair, they may please one another.
With all food that may be found, fill well the hold
340 As sustenance for yourself and also those others."
Then briskly he sets about to obey God's behests
In great dread and danger, who dared not refuse.
When it was fashioned and fitted out and furnished within,
Then God to that good man gravely speaks.
345 "Now, Noah," says our Lord, "are you all ready?
Is each seam made seaworthy, sealed well with clay?"
"Yes, Lord, by your leave," said the loyal man then,
"I have worked by your word and the wit you lent me."
"Go in, then," He said, "Let your wife enter with you,
350 And then your three sons and their three wives together.
Let beasts come aboard, as I bade you before.
Once all is loaded and lodged, let the hatches be closed.
When seven days are done, I shall swiftly dispatch
A tempest so terrible, such teeming rains
355 As shall flood away the filth that infects the world.
No flesh near or far shall be found alive
Save only you eight in the ark abiding
And the seed I send with you, assigned to be saved."
Now Noah never rests—that night he begins—

360　Until all were brought aboard, by God's high behest.°　　　*order*
　　　Soon came the seventh day; assembled were all
　　　Within that wooden craft, the wild beasts and tame.
　　　Then from the bowels of the abyss boiled up the big waters;
　　　Each wellhead spewed wide its wild-racing torrent;
365　No bank but burst apart, by river or pool;
　　　The seas in great surges swelled toward the sky;
　　　The clouds cleft in pieces, that carried the rain:
　　　From rifts high in the heavens it rushed down to earth;
　　　Forty days undiminished the deep flood rises.
370　The woods were awash, and the wide fields,
　　　For when the weather of the welkin° had wet the whole world,　　*sky*
　　　All beings that drew breath were bound to perish.
　　　They who marked the mischief lamented their fate,
　　　That they were doomed to drown in the deep streams.
375　Torrents towered higher, toppled down houses,
　　　Rushed raging into rooms where wretches harbored.
　　　All fled at the first shock whose feet would serve them;
　　　Women with children wended their way
　　　To banks and bluffs that abode above water,
380　And all made for the uplands, where hills were highest,
　　　But their efforts were futile—the force of the storm
　　　And the rage of the risen flood would never relent
　　　Until each broad bottomland brimmed like a lake
　　　And rain filled to the rim each rift and valley.
385　By then the tallest of the mountain tops were taking on water;
　　　Folk fled there in flocks, who feared the great doom.
　　　The wild things went to water, when woods were drowned;
　　　Some set out to swim, in search of safe harbor;
　　　Some, stranded on the steeps, stared up to heaven
390　With heart-rending roars that reechoed afar;
　　　Hares and harts hastened to the high ground;
　　　Bucks, badgers, and bulls beset the steep banks;
　　　All called, confounded, on the King of heaven,
　　　Cried out for clemency to the Creator of all,
395　But the maelstrom° grew madder; His mercy was no more,　　*violent surges*
　　　And His pity passed away from people that He hated.
　　　When the swift-swelling flood swirled around their feet,
　　　Not a soul but saw he must sink and be lost;
　　　Comrades crowded round and clung to each other
400　To endure the dire doom that destiny decreed;
　　　Lover looked to lover in last fond farewell,
　　　To end once for all, and ever be parted.
　　　After forty full days, no flesh stirred on earth

That was not seized and consumed by the rough seas' rage,
405 For it climbed fifteen cubits, past cliffs and crags,
Above the mightiest mountains measured on earth.
Then all creatures were condemned to decay in the mud
That breathed the breath of life—they lashed about vainly—
Save the captain of that strange crew, closed under hatches,
410 Noah, ever crying his Creator's name,
One of eight in the ark, as pleased heaven's King,
Where all creatures in cabins were kept safe and dry.
The ark was hurled about by heaving waves,
Carried close to the clouds in countries unknown.
415 It wallowed on the wild sea, went where it would,
Drove over the deep, in danger, it seemed,
Without boom crutch, or mast, or bowline made taut,
Cable or capstan to secure their anchors,
Helm to keep a course, or hand-held tiller,
420 Or any swelling sail to speed them to harbor,[11]
But floated forth, flogged on by furious winds.
From each buffet of the brine it rebounded in turn;
Often it rolled round and reared up on end;
Had the Lord not been their helmsman, their lot had been dire.
425 To expound in true speech the life span of Noah:
The sum of his age was six hundred years;
When the seventh month had passed, and seven days more,
All wellheads burst at once, and the waters flowed,
And the flood followed after, thrice fifty days.
430 Each hill was awash in wan-hued waves;
All were lost and left to drown that lived in the world,
That ever floated, or flew, or fared forth on foot,
Save the wretched remnant that rode over the sea
Where creatures of all kinds were confined together.
435 But when God thought it good, who governs the sky,
To make known to His man His mercy unfailing,
He wakened a wind over the wide waters,
And then the lake grew less, that was large before.
He checked the churning pools, choked up the wells,
440 Bade the rain cease—it desisted straightway.
Then the deep sea diminished, drawing together.
After hard days had passed one hundred and fifty
As that buoyant box was borne all about
Wherever wind and weather willed it to go,
445 On the morning of a mild day it made land at last:
On the ridge of a rock resting unmoved,
On Ararat Mount, amid Armenia's hills

(Though otherwise, in Hebrew, they have the name Thanez[12]).
But though the craft was caught secure in the crags,
450   The deep water remained, nor drained to the bottoms,
But the loftiest ledges were a little uncovered
So that the boatman on board beheld the bare earth.
Then he unseals a window, consigns to the wind
An envoy from that household to look out for land.
455   That was the raven unruly, rebellious at heart;
Coal black in color, careless of his word.
And he speeds into space on outspread wings,
Hovers high in heaven, intent to learn tidings.
When he came upon carrion, he croaked for joy,
460   That had drowned and drifted up on a dry ledge.
The stench smells sweet to him; he swoops down at once,
Falls on the foul flesh, and fills his belly.[13]
He has dismissed from his mind the command that came
From the mouth of the man who was master of the ship;
465   He keeps his own course, concerned no whit
Whether all creatures starve, so his craw be stuffed.
But the man aboard the boat, who was brought no tidings,
Beshrewed° him most bitterly, and all beasts with him!   *cursed*
He decides on a second try, and sends the dove;
470   Brings her above board, blesses her, and says,
"Fare forth, fair one, find homes for us all;
Depart over the dark water; if dry land appear,
Bring word of that blessèd sight, bliss to us all.
Though that bird disobeyed me, be you ever honored!"
475   She takes her turn in the weather on taut-webbed wings,
Flies along a full day, afraid to alight,
And when she finds no foothold on land firm and dry,
She retraces her route to return to the ark.
At sundown she sees it; descends forthwith;
480   Noah has her in hand and houses her snugly.
Another day Noah renews his quest
Bids the dove soar forth to seek dry banks;
She skims over the seascape and scouts all about,
And when night draws near, to Noah she flies.
485   One evening on the ark, behold! the dove sits;
On the bow of the boat, benign, she awaits him.
Ah! she brought in her beak a branch of olive,
Graced all with green leaves that grew from the stem.
That was the sign of salvation sent by our Lord,
490   How He had reconciled Himself with those simple beasts.
Then bliss was in the box where before all was gloom,

Much comfort in that cabin that was clay daubed.
Merrily one fair morning—the first month it was,
That falls foremost in the year, and the first day,
495 They laughed in that little boat, and looked all about,
How the waters had waned and the world had dried.
Each lauded our Lord, but was loath to debark
Till they had word from the One whose will had confined them.
Then God sent good tidings that gladdened them all,
500 Bade them draw near the door; deliverance was at hand.
They went to it at once; straightway it opened.
The captain with his comely sons came out first;
With them walked their wives; the wild things last
Poured forth pell mell in a pack together.
505 But Noah from each clean kind culled out a single,
And raised up an altar and hallowed it fair,
And offered up solemnly one of every sort
That is pure of pollution; God prizes no other.
When the beasts burned briskly and smoke billowed forth,
510 The savor of the sacrifice ascended to Him
Who deals out all destinies; He addresses His man
In companionable kindness, with courteous words:
"Now, Noah," He said, "nevermore shall I curse
All the mighty mass of earth for any men's sins,
515 For I plainly perceive that the people of this world
Are ever drawn to evildoing by their dark designs,
And so have been and will be, from their birth on;
The mind of each man is malicious wholly.
And so I shall not send down so suddenly again
520 Such a doom for man's deeds, all the days of this world.
But go forth, grow great, beget many heirs:°
Be fruitful and fill the earth—fair fame befall you!
Seasons shall not cease of seedtime or harvest,
Nor day's heat, nor deep frost, dark clouds or drought,
525 Nor the sweetness of summer, nor the stark winter,
Nor the nights, nor the days, nor the renewing years,
But run without rest—rule there unrivaled."
Then he blessed each beast, bade them overspread the earth.
Wittily° through the wide world the wild things scattered: *knowledgeably*
530 Each fowl took to flight on well-feathered wings;
Each fish sought out seas, where fins served best,
The livestock found level lands where lush grass grew;
The long snakes glided into lairs under ground;

° Genesis 9:1–2.

The fox went to the forest, the fitchew° as well;   *polecat*
535 Harts to the highlands, hares to the thickets,
And lions and leopards to the rain-lashed canyons;
Eagles and hawks to the highest rocks,
The web-footed fowl to the fresh-flowing streams,
And each beast abides where best he may prosper;
540 The four men commence their mastery of the world.

A Warning against Uncleanness

See! how dread a disaster for disgusting deeds
The high Father inflicted on folk He had made!
Whom He had chosen to cherish, He chastised harshly,
For their vileness and villainy had vanquished His patience.
545 Wherefore beware, you who wish for a worthy place
In the company of the court of the King of bliss,
Lest filth of the flesh infect you so deep
That no water in the world can wash it away.
For though a man's demeanor be much to admire,
550 If he be steeped in sin that has stained his soul—
One speck or one spot of aspect foul
Can hinder us from beholding the King high enthroned.
For whatever shall be shown in those shining mansions
As the polished beryl must be pure and clean,
555 That is sound on every side, a seamless sphere
Without flaw or fleck, like the finest pearls.
After the Sovereign on His high seat had sore repented
That He had made human beings to inhabit the earth,
Their fall into filth He fearsomely avenged
560 When all the flesh He had formed perforce must perish.
He was sorry He had set and sustained them on earth,
And that He harshly had harmed them seemed hard to Him after.
For when sorrow assailed Him and softened His heart,
He crafted a covenant to keep with mankind,
565 In His mild magnanimity and merciful will,
That He would nevermore be moved to mar the whole world
And destroy all who dwelt there, for deeds ill done
As long as time should last in the land of mortals.°
In evil days after He held to that pledge,
570 Though He pitilessly punished a people who sinned—
Enraged by that same wrong, He ruined a rich land
In the fierceness of His fury that frightened many.

° Genesis 9:8–11.

And all for that one evil, the unwholesome glut
Of the venom and the vileness and the vicious filth
575 That sullies the soul of the sick-hearted man
And bars him from looking on our Lord in His bliss.
For He hates all evil as hell that stinks
Yet none He finds so noxious, by night or by day,
As unabashed obscenity: abusing of self.
580 Who brazens out his base deeds, may bad luck betide him!
But consider yourself, man, though you are set upon folly,
Though you babble like an imbecile, bethink you now;
He that put the power of sight in each pair of eyes,[14]
If He were born blind, it were a boundless wonder,
585 And He that framed each face with well-fashioned ears,
If He lacked a way to listen, it were no less strange;
Have no faith in that fancy—you will find it false.
No deed is hid so deep that His eyes do not see it;
No man so conceals the course he intends
590 That He has not found it out before he has thought it.
For He is the soul-searching God, the source of all action,
Probing at every moment the purposes of men,
And always when He finds a man inwardly fair,
His heart honest and whole, He pays him high honor
595 And suffers° him sweetly to see His own face,   *allows*
And the others He abhors and harries from His kingdom.
But when the folk fall into foul deeds of defiling lust,
He loathes so that lewdness, He lashes out at once,
Cannot bear to hold back, but abruptly strikes,
600 And that was openly proven by a punishment once.

Abraham Is Visited by God in the Form of Three Angels

At ease in his own land, old Abraham sits[15]
By the entry to his house, under oak leaves green.°
The sun blazes bright from the broad heaven;
At the height of the day's heat, Abraham rests.
605 As he sheltered in the shade, under shining leaves,
He beheld heading toward him three handsome youths.
That they were gracious and glad of cheer and goodly to behold
We may take to be true, from the tale's ending.
For he who looked out at leisure under leafy boughs
610 As soon as he had seen them, he sat there no longer
But goes as if toward God to give them fit greeting,

° Genesis 18:1–16.

And hailed them as One only, and said, "Honored Lord,
If ever aught of mine has earned your favor,
Linger a little while, I lowly beseech,
615 Do not part with your poor man, I pray most humbly,
Till you have supped with your servant, seated in shade;
And I shall go with a glad heart to get some water,
And busy me forthwith that your feet may be washed.
Rest here on this root until I return
620 And you shall have a bit of bread, to bring your heart comfort."
"Go forth, friend," said they, "and fetch as you promised;
By this wide-branching tree we shall watch and await you."
He hastened to his house and had words with Sarah,
Commanded her to be quick and compliant this once;
625 "Take three measures of meal and make three cakes;
Hide them well with ashes hot for the baking.
While I fetch a fatted beast, add fuel to the fire,
To prepare a platter promptly to please my guests."
He goes to the cowshed and gets him a calf
630 That was tender and not tough; had the hide taken off
And instructed his servant to season and stew it,
And he quickly and capably accomplished the task.
With head humbly bared, he plays the host's part,
Casts wide a clean cloth to cover the grass.
635 Arranges in order three unleavened cakes,
Brings butter as well, and sets it by the bread,
With milk in ample measure, the more to refresh them
And steaming soup and stew in sturdy platters.
As a retainer well trained he tended to their needs;
640 Gravely and agreeably gave them of his best,
And God, as a good guest, spoke gracious words,
Who was fond of His friend, and praised the feast highly.
Abraham, hoodless, with upfolded sleeves,
Ministered to those men whose might rules the world.
645 Then they said, as they sociably sat there all three,
When the cloth was cleared, and they conversed at ease,
"I shall come here again, Abraham," they said,
"Before your spark of life is spent upon earth,
And then Sarah shall conceive, and a son be born
650 That shall be Abraham's heir, and after him beget
With wealth and with worship the worthy folk
That shall hold in high honor the heritage I promised."
Then the dame behind the door laughed in derision,
And Sarah spoke to herself these scornful words:
655 "Can you believe that in wantonness your womb will swell,

And I grown so old, and my husband also?"
For they were both bowed with age, as the book relates;
The old lord and his lady—they had left off such work.
She was barren, as it befell, and had been so ever;
660 No sons had Sarah borne, nor seemly daughters.
Then our Sire as He sat said, "See, Sarah laughs,
Not trusting the tale that I told you at table.
Does she think any task overtaxes my hands?
Yet the same words I said I solemnly repeat:
665 I shall return in good time, my intent to fulfill,
And Sarah shall conceive, and a son be born."
Then Sarah rushed to their side and swore by her honor
That no laugh had passed her lips while she listened to their talk.
"Now, enough," said our noble Lord; "Say not so, Sarah;
670 For you did laugh a little—but now let it pass."
With that they rose up refreshed and ready to travel.
They set their eyes on Sodom and sallied forth at once,
For this city that they sought had its site in a valley
Not more than two miles from Mambre plain[16]
675 Where he lived who went along with the Lord as He traveled
To attend on Him, and talk with Him, and teach Him the way.
Now God goes on apace; the good man follows,
Abraham obedient, bound, as their guide,
Toward the city of Sodom, that was sinfully steeped
680 In the fault of this filth.°

God Confides to Abraham His Intent to Destroy Sodom; Abraham Convinces Him to Spare the Righteous Few

The Father in anger
Speaks thus to the one who walks by His side:[†]
"How can I hide my heart from Abraham the true,
Nor refrain from revealing my righteous intent,
Since he is assigned to be sire to seed without number
685 Whose progeny shall prosper and people the world,
And all born of his blood shall be blessed in his name.
I must tell that true servant what has tried my temper
And openly to Abraham unveil my purpose.
The infamy of Sodom sinks into my ears,
690 And the guilt of Gomorrah has goaded me to wrath.
I shall visit those environs and view for myself
If they behave as we have heard in heaven on high.

° Genesis 18:16.
† Genesis 18:17–33.

They have learned a lust that I like not at all,
And found in their flesh the foulest of faults;
695 Each male takes as his mate a man like himself,
And counterfeits the woman in witless coupling.
I framed a fair craft for them, confiding it in secret,
And of all my many ordinances, held it most dear;
I planted pleasure therein, love's passionate joy,
700 And the sweet play of paramours I plotted myself
And made a manner of mingling, most blissful of any:
When two were tied together with true minds and hearts,
Between a man and his mate would mount such delight
That the pure joys of paradise could scarce prove better.
705 But they must use each other honorably, with equal desire,
At a set secret hour, unseen and unseeing,
The blaze of love between them so bright and so fierce
That all the mishaps on earth could not hold back its heat.
Now they have despised my providence, perverting my plan
710 And consorted uncleanly in contempt of nature.
I shall visit them with violence for their vile ways
That all who live in later days may learn from their doom."
Then Abraham grew uneasy, and all his mood changed
When he heard these hot words of hostile intent,
715 And he said to Him sighing, "Sir, by your leave,
Shall sinful and innocent suffer together?
Was it ever like my Lord to allot such dooms
As that the worthy and the wicked received one sentence,
And those count as criminal who caused you no grief?
720 That was never your wont,° whose handiwork we are.   custom
Now if fifty fair friends were found in that town,
In the city of Sodom, and also Gomorrah,
Who never belittled your law, but ever loved truth,
And were righteous and reasonable and ready to serve you,
725 Shall they be accused of the crimes of others,
And joined with them in jeopardy and judged the same?
That was never your nature—let no one think it—
Who are so merciful a Master and mild in your ways."
"No, for fifty," said the Father, "and your fair speech,
730 If they be free of the fault that defiled so many
I shall forgive the guilty as well, and grant them pardon;
They shall escape scot free, unscathed by my hand."
"Ah, blessings on You, Lord, so abounding in virtue,
And hold in Your hands both the heavens and the earth!
735 But since I have talked this much, take it not amiss
If I who am earth and ashes should add somewhat more.

If five less than fifty are found to be righteous
And the remainder unrepentant, how runs Your decree?"
"If there are five less than fifty, I shall forgive all alike,
740 And withhold my hand, and do harm to none."
"And what if forty be faultless, and faithless the rest—
Shall you deal out destruction and doom them out of hand?"
"No, lest forty such be lost, I shall let time pass
And set my wrath aside, though to do so displease me."
745 Then Abraham made obeisance and bowed low in homage:
"Now blessed be a Savior so blameless in His wrath!
I am earth and sooty ash, and utterly unfit
To presume to hold parley with the Prince who rules all.
But I have begun with my God, and He gives me leave;
750 If He finds me foolish, His forbearance may spare me.
What think You, if that town hold thirty good men?
Shall I believe of my Lord that He will let them perish?"
Then God in His goodness gave him His answer:
"If thirty such there be, I shall think myself bound
755 To rein in My rage, and be ruled by patience,
And restrain My rancor for your well-reasoned words."
"And if twenty be trusty, will you take their lives?"
"No, if you ask it, all shall be pardoned;
If twenty be true, I shall trouble them no more,
760 And wreak no revenge for their rampant sins."
"Noble Lord," said the loyal man, "allow me one speech,
And I shall cease to intercede and be silent henceforth.
If there are ten in that town whom Your truth has guided,
Shall You withhold Your anger in hope of amendment?"
765 "I grant it," said the great God; the other gave thanks
And put aside his pleading and pressed Him no further,
And God goes His way under those green branches,
And as He fares forth, he follows with his eyes.
And as he looked along the road where the Lord traveled,
770 He called out a complaint with disconsolate voice:
"Meek Master, if your man might speak for a moment:
Lot lives in that place, my belovèd nephew;
In the city of Sodom your servant he dwells
Among those malicious men that have made you grieve.
775 If You overturn that town, temper Your wrath—
As mercy may move You, let meek men live."
Then he turns and wends homeward, weeping for sorrow;
Makes his way to Mambre, mournful in heart,
And all night he lies and waits, wakeful in longing,
780 While the Lord sends His spies to inspect the city.

Lot Entertains Two Angels in Sodom

His embassy to Sodom was sent at that time:°
Early in the evening, two angels together,
Moving along modestly, as young men well-mannered,
As Lot at his lodging stood alone by the door,
785 In a porch of his palace, where the portal was set,
That was fine and well-furnished, befitting its master.[17]
As he stared into the street where sportive folk loitered,
Two comely men in concert came walking his way.
They were brave fellows both, with beardless chins
790 And loose waving locks like lengths of raw silk,
Fair as the briar flower where the flesh was bare;
Open of countenance, with clear eyes alight,
Clothed all in white, of colors most fitting;
Their features finely formed, without fault or blemish;
795 Nothing ugly about them: they were angels both,
The one who stood watching knew well who they were;
He tarried not an instant, but toward them he ran
And bowed down before them, in abasement unfeigned,
And soberly said to them, "Sirs, I beseech you,
800 Stop here at my homestead and stay for a time;
Visit your varlet, if I may venture to ask.
I shall bring you a basin to bathe your feet.
Stay near me one night—no more do I seek—
And when the bright day dawns, depart on your errand."
805 But no, they insisted, they needed no houses;
They would stay in the street where they stood by his gate,
And lodge the long night there, and lie out of doors;
The heavens overhead they thought house enough.
But Lot prayed and pleaded, and persisted so long
810 That they agreed to go in, and argued no more.
The man to his manor admits them at once,
No luxuries were lacking, for he had long been rich.
They had as warm a welcome as the wife could give,
And the two dear daughters deferred to them duly,
815 That were maidens demure, unmarried as yet,
And they were amiable and earnest, and handsomely attired.
Then Lot, like a good host, looks to his guests;
Commanded his men that a meal be prepared,
"But mind, whatever you make, to mix in no leaven,
820 For nothing sour or salt may be served to my guests."[18]

° Genesis 19:1–26.

But the wayward wife was otherwise minded,
And said softly in scorn, "These numbskulls here
Like no salt in their sauce, but I see no sense
In depriving other people, though this pair lack wit."
825 Then she salts well her soups and her sauces each one,
All heedless of the order the host had given,
And went against their wishes who knew well her thoughts;
Wretch! why was she so reckless? She enraged our Lord.
Then they sat down to supper, with servants attending;
830 The guests gay and glad, and gracious of speech,
Lordly and lighthearted, till at last they washed
And the trestles and tabletop were tilted to the wall.
Soon after they had supped, and sat a while together,
Before 'twas time to retire, the town was all up,
835 All that could wield weapons, the weaker and the stronger,
Had hurried to Lot's house to lay hands on his guests.
The folk in great flocks forgathered at his gates;
As when sentries rouse a regiment, the rude clamor rises;
With great clubs and cudgels they clatter on the walls,
840 And in sharp shrill voices they shout these words:
"If you value your life, Lot, in this place,
Yield us up those young men who came to you lately,
That they may learn about love as our lust dictates,
As is decreed and required of all who come to Sodom."
845 Agh! they spat out and spewed such despicable speech,
Agh! they raged and they ranted of such rampant filth,
That the wind and the weather and the world still stink
Of the breach whence broke forth those abominable words!
Lot looked toward the noise, and listened in fear;
850 For shame of that lewd show, his heart shrank within,
He was well aware of the ways of those wastrels ungodly.
So deep a dismay had never daunted his heart.
"Alas!" said Lot then, and leapt up alarmed
And rushed from the room and ran to the gate.
855 The menacing of evil men dismayed him no whit,
No, nor stayed him from stepping forth to face strong foes.
He went out by a wicket gate; at once it swung shut;
With the light click of a latch it closed behind him.
Then he called to that crowd with courteous words,
860 For he hoped his good manners might make them ashamed:
"Oh, my free-spirited friends, you are far too wild.
Have done with this din; withdraw these demands.
Your wishes are unwelcome; your ways are unclean;
And you are fine gentlefolk—fie on your pranks!

865 But I commend to you a craft more becoming by far;
My abode here is blessed by two beauteous daughters;
They live with me alone—no lover has had them;
None seemlier dwell in Sodom, though I say so myself.
They are ripe and ruddy fleshed; they are ready for men;
870 To embrace such bonny maids will bring you more pleasure.
I bestow them with my blessing, that are buxom and blithe,
And lie with them as you like, and let my guests be."
Then those riotous ruffians raised such a row
That their ribaldry rang and reechoed in his ears:
875 "You are nothing but a newcomer, no native here,
A stranger, an upstart—we'll strike off your head!
By what pretext do you presume to pose as our judge,
Who was brought a boy to our city, though now you be rich?"
Thus their threats flew thick and fast as they thronged all about
880 And constrained him with their strength, and distressed him sore,
Till the royal youths ran out, on rescue bent,
Went through the wicket gate, and won to his side,
And soon had their hands on him and hurried him within
And barred the broad gate like a bastion° of stone.   *strong fortification*
885 They blew a blast that blinkered that blasphemous band
So that they blundered about like blind Bayard the horse[19]
And were cheated of the chance to achieve an entry
As in futile befuddlement they fumbled about.
Then each fellow fled the scene, who had found no sport,
890 And repaired to his room for such rest as remained;
But they were roused all awry, who returned to their homes,
By the most horrible mishap that ever befell.

The Destruction of Sodom and Lot's Escape

A red ray rose over the east rim of earth
When the murk of midnight might no more prevail;
895 By early light the angels were at Lot's side,
And startled him with stern words, instructing him to rise.
And he was filled with fear, and flung out of bed.
Brusquely they bade him to bring what he had:
"Take with you wife and daughters, womenfolk and men,
900 For we send you forth, Sir Lot, to save your life.
Depart without delay, lest doom overtake you,
Hasten with all your household till you reach a high hill.
Go fast, fix your eyes before you unswerving;
To look back is forbidden—disobey at your peril!
905 See you stay not one step, nor stop for one moment;

Till you reach a place of refuge, no rest may you take;
For we shall lay this town low, level it to ground,
And the wicked folk who dwell there, once and for all.
The people of this place shall perish together.
910 Sodom shall suddenly sink into the earth
And Gomorrah go down into the gulf of hell,
And every district, defenseless, be dashed in pieces."
Then Lot, at a loss, said, "Lord, what is best?
If I find I am forced to flee hence on foot,
915 How shall I hide me from Him whose hate is made known
In the blaze of His breath that blasts all things?
I know of no cranny to creep from my Creator,
Nor whether I face Him as my foe before or behind."
"No foe of yours is the Father," the fair angel said,
920 "But He has lifted your life above the lost who must perish.
Now seek out a site where you can safely dwell
And He will spare it for your sake who sent us here.
For you are singularly saved, unsullied by this filth—
And also Abraham, your uncle, on your behalf asked it."
925 "Now may the Lord," said Lot, "be lauded on earth!
There is a city not far off, and Segor is its name;[20]
On the summit of a round rise it sits by itself;
I would like, if He allows it, to live in that place."
"Then get you gone," he said, "and go without stopping;
930 "Take with you whom wish to walk with you thither;
Lead them briskly along without a backward look,
For all this land shall be lost long before daybreak."
Then he wakened his wife and his two winsome daughters,
And two trusty men who were betrothed to those maids;
935 But they imagined he mocked them, not meaning his words—
Though Lot pleaded long, they lay still abed.
The angels bade them hasten, uttering dire portents,
And followed after the four to enforce their departure—
Those were Lot, and his lawful wife, and their lovesome daughters:
940 Not another soul was saved of fair cities five.
They were ushered by the angels to the outer gates,
And informed of dire perils and urged to depart:
"Lest you be damned and condemned with evildoers here,
Go out, as we order you, and be off quickly."
945 And they turned without tarrying, and straight took to flight.
They arrived at a hill ere the advent of dawn.
Then God in His grim wrath begins in heaven
To waken wild weather—the winds heard his call,
And, rising up in a rage, came wrestling together

950 From the earth's every quarter, in argument loud.
Clouds, clustered in heaps, climbed into mountains
Which threatening thunderclaps cleft through and through;
The rain rushed earthward in rattling torrents
With flaring of fires and flaming of sulphur,
955 All smoking and smouldering in foul-smelling murk.
Beset on every side was the city of Sodom.
And the ground of Gomorrah gaped and gave way—
With Admah and Zeboim, four cities in all—
They were riddled by the rain, roasted and burnt,
960 And their denizens demented with dread of that doom,
For Hell, when he had once heard the hounds of heaven,
In ungodly glee ungirt his grim power.
The great bars of the abyss were broken into pieces,
And the region was rent by rifts all about;
965 The cliffs, cleft by chasms, clattered asunder
As leaves, when the binding breaks, leap from a book.
By the time the stench of brimstone had stifled all breath,
Those sin-ridden cities had sunk down to hell.
Then bereft of recourse was the rabble within
970 When they saw the same disaster descend on all sides.
The yowls that arose there, the yelling and roaring
So reechoed from the clouds that Christ might have mercy.
He heard well the sound, who was heading for Segor
And the three women with him who walked at his heels;
975 Their flesh crawled for fear as they fled with one accord,
Faring fast afoot, who feared to look back,
Lot and those lovely maids, his lily-white daughters
Hastening straight onward, their eyes fixed before them,
But the baleful beldame, disobedient ever,
980 Looked behind her back to behold the great fire:
It was lusty Lot's wife, who over her left shoulder
Saw the sight she sought, but with that same glance
She stood a stiff stone, a statue unstirring,
As salt as any sea, and so she still stands.
985 They rushed blindly by, who had been her companions,
Till they had settled in Segor; our Sovereign they blessed;
With hands raised heavenward they humbly praised Him
Who had succored so His servants, and saved them from danger.
By then all was done for, damned and drowned deep;
990 The people of that place had plunged to their deaths
In that godforsaken sea that swallowed them whole,
And nought survived but Segor, that sat on a hill.
They settled in that city, the sire and his daughters,

For his mate was missing, who remained on the hill,
995 A stone-still statue that savored of salt
For two faults that the fool had been found in before:
First, she served our Sovereign with salt at her table,
And second, though forbidden, she looked back at Sodom.
For the first she was transfixed, for the second turned salt,
1000 And all beasts like to lick her that live in the wild.
Early was old Abraham up and about;°
No pleasant repose to his pillow had come,
For in longing for Lot he had long lain wakeful.
He sped to the spot where he had spoken with our Lord.
1005 And his eyes sought out Sodom in sorrow and fear,
That had long been a land deemed loveliest of any,
Being planted near paradise, most pleasant of gardens.
Now it is plunged into a pit of pitch of the foulest.
Such a reek of red smoke arose all around,
1010 With ash filling the air and embers flying,
As scum seethes and swirls in a scalded vat
When fresh brush and branches are brought to the fire.
That was a violent vengeance that vanquished these places,
When a fair folk foundered and fell into darkness.
1015 Where cities five were set,[21] a sea now stands
That is darksome and drear, and deathly in nature,[22]
A bog black and burbling, baleful of aspect,
Like a stale stinking pond, where destroyed sin dwells,
That makes the senses smart with its smell unwholesome.
1020 Wherefore the Dead Sea it deserves to be called,
For its death-dealing deeds endure to this day,
For broad it is, and bottomless, and bitter as gall,
And nought may last in that lake that has life on earth,
And the known laws of nature it denies and perverts,
1025 For throw a lump of lead in, and lo! it will float,
But set a light feather there, and forthwith it sinks,
And if its waters should well forth and wet its banks,
Nothing green will ever grow there—grass, bush or tree.
If a captive were condemned to be cast in that water,
1030 Though he were mired in that morass for a month or more,
In loss everlasting he should languish still,
Doomed yet never dying, days without end.
And its attributes accord with its accursèd state:
The clays that cling to its banks are corrosive in kind,[23]
1035 Such as alum and black pitch, eager to bite,

° Genesis 19:27–28.

Sour sulphur and sandiver and other such stuff.
And great waxy geysers in gobbets gush forth
Of the spumy asphalt that spice dealers sell,
And such is all the soil at the side of that sea
1040 That it infects men's flesh and festers their bones;
And there are trees by that tarn° of traitorous kind   *pool*
That burgeon and bear most beautiful blooms,
And the fairest fruits that men foster on earth:
Great oranges and other fruits and pomegranates huge,
1045 All as ripe and as red and as rich in hue
As befits a princely feast where fare is of the finest.
But be they bruised or broken or bitten in twain,
No worldly good is within, but wind-winnowed ashes.

The Purity of Christ: How Mortals May Emulate It

These are tokens to trust in, from that time to this,
1050 That bear witness to the wickedness and the woeful vengeance
That the Father performed for the filth of that folk.
From this lesson we learn that He loves what is noble,
Then if gracious deeds gladden Him who governs on high,
And you would come to His court and be recognized there,
1055 And see His bright throne and His blissful face,
I can no clearer counsel than "Keep ever clean."
For Clopinel, in the compass of his clean-wrought *Rose*,[24]
Speaks words of wisdom to one who aspires
To win a woman's love. "Watch her," he says,
1060 "Her deportment, her pastimes, what pleases her best,
And such as you see her, so you too must be,
Ever following in the footsteps of her you find fair,
And if you heed my counsel, though her heart be hard,
She will like most the ways that are most like her own."
1065 If, then, in love's delight you would dally with the Lord,
And give Him all your heart, and have His in turn,
Pattern your soul on Christ in pure words and deeds,
Who is polished in every part like priceless pearls.
For look, when first He alighted in the elected maiden,
1070 By how comely a contrivance He was cloistered there,
When no virginity was vanquished, nor violence used,
But far cleaner was her body: there God became flesh!
And after, when He was born in Bethlehem the noble,
How purely in her poverty she parted with her child.
1075 Was never bedchamber as bright as a barn was then,
Nor sacristy as sumptuous as a simple stable.

Nor any as glad as the girl who should have groaned in pain,
For there was sickness made sound, that is said to be sorest,
And there was fragrance of roses where flesh has been rankest,
1080 And solace and song where sorrow has ever cried,
For angels with their instruments, organs[25] and pipes,
And majestic strains of well-matched strings,
And all harmonies that honorably enhance a heart's joy,
Made music for my lady at her lying-in.
1085 Then, so burnished bright was her blithe babe
That both the ox and the ass bowed humbly before Him;
In his cleanness they acknowledged Him king of nature,
For none so clean from such confines came ever till then.
And if He came forth clean, He was courteous after:
1090 Each taint or trace of evil He detested wholly;
So noble was His nurture, He never would touch
Aught that was unwholesome or inwardly foul.
Yet many came to Him unclean: scab-encrusted beggars,
Some leprous, some lame, some who lacked sight,
1095 Poisoned, and paralyzed, and painfully burned,
Dried up, and dropsical, and dead at the last.
All called on that courteous one, laid claim to His grace;
He helped them with healing words, as each one asked;
For whatever His hands touched was instantly healed,
1100 Far cleaner than any medicine could ever have made it:
From His pure hands' power all pollution fled.
And so gracious was the grasp of God and man both,
And His fingers' craft so fine, He found no need
To cut or to carve with a keen-ground edge,
1105 Wherefore He broke bread without brandishing of blades,
For it parted more perfectly in His princely hands,
And was more verily revealed when He divided it thus
Than if a sword of French steel had split it in two.
So He insists upon cleanness, whose court you seek;
1110 How should you come unclean to His kingdom, then?
Now we are stained and sullied and sinful, each one;
How should we see, so we ask, that Sire on His throne?
No, that Master is merciful—though you, man, be muddy,
All immersed in foul mire in your mortal life,
1115 You may shine through confession, though shame you deserve,
And be polished by penance like a pearl of price.
Pearl is highly praised among precious stones,
Though not costliest accounted in commerce of pennies;
What can be the cause but her clean hue
1120 For which she is worshipped over all white stones?

For her shape in its roundness so radiant shines
Without fault or flaw, if she is finest appraised,
And let her be worn in the world for long weary years,
She is never impaired while she is prized by men;
1125 And if by unlucky chance she is cherished no longer,
And loses her luster while laid up in chest,
Only wash her worshipfully in wine, as behooves,
And she will become by her nature more bright than before.
So if ill-fated folk into foul ways have fallen,
1130 And sadly soiled their souls, let them seek out a priest
And confess, and be polished by pains freely borne
Till they are brighter than beryls or beads of pearl.
But beware, when once you are washed in that water
And polished like a parchment planed free of flaws,
1135 That you keep your soul unsullied by sin ever after,
For you displease the dear Lord with your distasteful deeds
And he rises up relentless, more wrathful than ever,
And hotter in his hate than if you had not washed.
For when a soul is absolved, and consecrate to God,
1140 He holds it wholly His, and would have it thenceforth,
And when it turns away to evil, He takes the loss hard
As if robbers' hands rudely had wrenched it away.
Then beware the rebuke that His rage brings down
If what once was His ever wishes to be foul.
1145 Though it be but a basin, a bowl or a platter,
A dish or a drinking cup dedicate to God,
He flatly forbids that any filth should touch it,
So abhors He uncleanness whose law is ever true.
And that was brought about in Babylon in Balthasar's days,
1150 How a hard fate befell him, and fearfully soon,
For he took the vessels in vain that men revered in the temple
In the service of the Sovereign some time before.
If you would let me take the time, I would tell you the tale,
How he found a worse fate, who refused them honor
1155 Than his godforsaken father, who filched them by force
And robbed of its relics the religion of old.

Jerusalem, in the Reign of the Idolatrous King
Sedecias (Zedekiah), Is Conquered by the Chaldeans
under King Nabugodonosor

Daniel in his discourses discloses the story,[26]
As proved by his prophecies expressly stated,
How the gentry of Judea and Jerusalem the great

1160   Were destroyed with great distress, and dashed down to earth.°
     For the foolish folk were found faithless at last
     Who had promised the high Prince to pray to Him ever,
     And He had held them His own and helped them at need
     In many a great mischance, most marvelous to hear.
1165   And they forsook their faith, and followed other gods,
     And His rage was aroused, and rose to such heat
     That He befriended the faithful to the false law
     To destroy the traitors that had turned from the true.
     In the time of Sedecias these tribulations came
1170   In Judea, where Jewish kings had justly reigned.
     He was solemnly seated on Solomon's throne,
     But in faith to our fair Lord he fell far short;
     He used abomination, bowing to idols,
     And prized little the laws he should loyally have kept,
1175   Wherefore the Lord found a foe to afflict him on earth:
     Through Nabugodonosor ignobly he perished.
     He pressed into Palestine with many proud knights,
     And laid waste the little towns and the lodgings within
     He harried all Israel, hauled off their treasures,
1180   And confined in Jerusalem the finest of Judea.
     He ringed the city round with redoubtable men,
     Placed a prince at each gate, and penned them within,
     For the battlements of the bastion° loomed baleful above,   *fortification*
     And there were fierce folk within to forestall all entry.
1185   Then the sides of the citadel were besieged and beset
     With clamor and clash of arms and cleaving of flesh;
     Installed on every bridge, an engine on wheels
     Assailed the city gates seven times in a day;
     The defenders fought back from fortified towers
1190   And platforms of wood placed high on the walls;
     They fight and they fend off in conflict unceasing
     Until two years were told, yet the town was not taken.
     After many long months, misfortune befell them:
     Famine confronted them as food stores failed;
1195   The fierce pangs they felt afflicted them more
     Than any hurt they had had at the enemy's hands.
     Then the dwellers in those domiciles despaired of all counsel;
     When they found no food before them, their fair flesh wasted—
     And so strait were they constrained, no step could they stray
1200   From the confines of that fort to seek for provisions.
     Then the king of that country conceived of a plan

° 2 Paralipomenon (II Chronicles) 36:11–12, 17–20; Jeremias (Jeremiah) 52:1–11.

With a band of his best men to try a bold trick:
They stole out from the stronghold on a still night,
And hurled themselves headlong through the enemy lines.
1205 But before they won their way past the watchful guards,
An outcry rose in the camp, that echoed through the air,
With loud noise of alarums, relayed near and far.
Roused from their rest, men run for their armor,
Clap helmets on their heads, on horses they leap;
1210 The clear call of clarions° clamoring about them.   *trumpets*
Then they all headed out, riding hot on the heels
Of the foe that fled in fear; they found them forthwith,
Fell upon them fiercely, flung them to earth,
Till each man's peer lay prostrate before him.
1215 Then the king was taken captive by Chaldean nobles,
With the princes of Judea, on Jericho's plains
And presented to please the all-powerful king,
Nabugodonosor, noble on his throne,
And he the happiest on earth, who had humbled his foe.
1220 He spoke to them spitefully, dispatched them soon after;
Had the king's sons slain as their sire looked on,
And angrily gave orders to gouge out his eyes,
And bade that he be brought to Babylon the mighty,
And deep in a dungeon doomed ever to dwell.
1225 Now see, how the Sovereign has sent down His vengeance.
Yet it was not Nabugodonosor nor his noble warriors
That caused this king's discomfiture, and cost him such pain
But the base deeds that betrayed his benevolent Lord,
For had the Father been his friend, as in former days,
1230 And he had never turned traitor or trespassed against Him,
All the armies of Chaldea and India combined—
And throw in Turkey too—would have troubled him little.
Yet Nabugodonosor would never desist
Till he had torn the town to pieces and trampled it down;
1235 He appointed as his deputy a prince high born,
Nabuzardan by name, to bring them new hardships.°
He was a master of men, and mighty himself,
A chieftain unchallenged among champions in war;
He broke through the barriers, the bulwarks he leveled,
1240 And entered in unsmiling, with ire in his heart.
Ah, petty was that triumph: the troops had departed;
The best long before had been killed with their king
And the remnant so weary and weakened with hunger

° Jeremias (Jeremiah) 52:12–14.

That one woman of Babylon was worth the best four.
1245 But no help could they hope for at Nabuzardan's hands:
The folk that had not fled were felled by bare blades;
The fairest maids and meekest were martyred untimely,
Babes bathed in blood, their brains split open,
Prelates pressed to death, and priests in the temples;
1250 They slew wenches and wives, slit open their wombs,
With bowels burst from their bellies they lay by the ditches.
All those that they could catch, they killed then and there,
And those that slipped away from the slaughtering swords
Were seized and stripped bare and set astride horses,
1255 Foot fastened to foot by fetters beneath,
And to Babylon brought to endure bitter days,
Consigned there to servitude, whose sires had been noble.
Now they are changed to churls and charged with tasks,
To haul carts by hand, and help milk the cows
1260 Who as honored lords and ladies sat lately in hall.
And the wrath of Nabuzardan still knows no bounds:
He musters his men and makes for the temple.
They beat at the barriers, break the gates open,
Slay all who serve there in one swift assault;
1265 Haul priests by the hair and hack off their heads,
Put deacons to death, dash down clerks;
All the maids in the minster they mercilessly slew
With stern strokes of the sword that swept them away.
Then they ran to the relics like a rude band of robbers
1270 And pillaged all the priceless things so proudly displayed:[27]
The great brass pillars embellished with gold,
And the chief chandelier, that was charged with the task
Of lifting up the lamp whose light ever shone
Before the *sanctum sanctorum*,[28] where oft were seen wonders.
1275 They carried off the candlestick, and the crown as well
That sat in state on the altar, of solid gold,
The gridiron, and the goblets garnished with silver,
The bases of the pillars, the polished basins,
The plates of pure gold, and the great platters;
1280 The vials and the vessels of valuable gems.
Now of those noble things is Nabuzardan master;
He pillaged that precious place, and packed up his booty,
From the treasury he took its great troves of gold
With all the ornaments of the house, in hampers together.
1285 He despoiled all the splendors, with spiteful intent,
That Solomon sought to make so many a long year[29]
With all the wisdom and workmanship his wit could muster.

He devised the costly vessels, designed the vestments;
With his sciences and skills, in his Sovereign's praise
1290 He adorned that noble edifice and bedecked it within.
Now Nabuzardan has possessed it wholly,
And battered down the building and burned it to ashes.

Nabuzardan Returns to Chaldea with Daniel and Other Prisoners; Nabugodonosor's Reign and Death

Then, commander of his company, he made for Chaldea,
Ransacking and ravaging wherever he rode.
1295 With wagons well laden, he went to his chief,
Bestowed on him the stores he had stolen in the war;
Consigned to him the captives conveyed from their homes:
Peers of high repute, while their prosperity lasted;
Heirs of haughty sires, and high-born maidens,
1300 The proudest of the province—and prophets' children:
Ananias, Azarias, and also young Michael,
And dear Daniel as well, a diviner most noble,[30]
With mettlesome mothers' sons, more than enough.
And Nabugodonosor knew never such joy.
1305 Now he has conquered the kingdom and captured the king,
And murdered all the men who were mightiest in arms;
And the foremost in their faith have been felled to the ground,
And their highest-praised prophets imprisoned forever.
But he rejoiced most in the jewels: the gems beyond price
1310 When they were first brought before him, filled him with wonder;
Of vessels of such value, devised at such cost,
Had Nabugodonosor never yet heard.
He received them solemnly; the Sovereign he praised,
The high King of heaven, Israel's God;
1315 Such goods, such garments, such gorgeous vessels
Came never from any country into Chaldean realms.
He secured them in his coffers, carefully stowed,
With reverent regard, as their rightful keeper,
And there he proved prudent, as will appear after,
1320 For had he failed to prize them fully, he might have fared worse.
In royalty unrivaled he reigned throughout his life;
As conquerer of all countries he was called caesar,
Sole sovereign of the world, and sultan as well,
And his great name was engraved as god of earthly ground.
1325 And this was due to Daniel, who disclosed to him truly
That all the goods a man gains are given him by God,
And he freely confessed himself faithful at last,

And was the meeker in heart, and milder in deeds.
But life draws ever toward death and a doleful end;
1330 Lofty though a lord sits, at last he must bow;
And so Nabugodonosor, as necessity bade,
For all his empire so haughty, in earth he is buried.

Balthasar, Nabugodonosor's Idolatrous Son, Succeeds Him; He Decides to Hold a Great Feast

But then Balthasar the bold, his first-born son,
Was installed in his stead and established his reign;
1335 He boasted himself the best that in Babylon dwelled,
Unequaled by anyone on earth or in heaven.
For he began in all the glory the great man had won,
Nabugodonosor, who was his noble sire;
No king so bold in Chaldea had come into power.
1340 But he honored not Him who dwells high in heaven,
But had faith in false phantoms formed by men's hands,
Hewed out of hard wood and hoisted upright,
And standing stocks and stones he calls strong gods
When they are gaudily gilded or garnished with silver.
1345 Then on bended knee he bows and begs them for help;
If their words guide him wisely, he rewards them well,
And if they grudge the grace he seeks, to grieve his heart,
He clutches a great club and clobbers them to pieces.
Thus puffed up with pride, his empire he holds
1350 In lust and in lechery and in loathly deeds,
And he had a wedded wife, a worthy queen,
And paramours aplenty, passed off as ladies.
With his complaisant° concubines and curious adornments,   *obliging*
With dress overbedizened° and dishes ever new,   *excessively adorned*
1355 All the mind of that man was on misshapen things,
Till the Lord who reigns aloft allowed it no longer.
Then this bold Balthasar bethinks him one day
To invite the world to view his vainglorious pomp;°
It does not suffice a fool to perform foul deeds
1360 Unless his shame be shown and shouted abroad.
His bidding in Babylon was borne to all ears,
And from the kingdom of Chaldea his call went forth,
That the mightiest men on earth must make their way thither
To assemble on a set day at the sultan's table.
1365 So magnificent a meeting he was minded to hold

° Daniel 5:1.

That each king who ruled a country should come from afar;
Each prince, with his paladins and other proud peers,
Should come to his court to proclaim him their lord,
And offer him homage and hark to his revels,
1370 And salute all his harlots as high-born ladies.
To gape at his grandeur great men came
With many a baron bold, to Babylon the noble.
Such flocks of fine folk forgathered that day—
Crowned kings and emperors, come to the court,
1375 Lords from many lands, and their ladies with them—
That to tell their number truly would overtax my wits.
For Babylon was so big, and its borders so wide,
No city on a fairer site sat beneath the stars;
Pitched on a plain, whence proudly it towered,
1380 And encircled on every side by seven great rivers,
With a wall all around it, that rose wondrous high,
And battlements above, with embrasures° well furnished;   *gaps for archers*
Towers at intervals of twenty spears' length,
And palings placed crosswise to protect from assault.
1385 The ground girt round by these goodly ramparts
Was long and large in scope, laid out in a square;
Each side of the precinct was seven miles long,
And the sultan's seat sat in the center.
It was a palace of pride, surpassing all others
1390 In the wonder of its workmanship, walled all about;
High houses within, the hall in proportion,
With wings so wide that one could let horses run.
When the hour was at hand when all should eat,
Mighty throngs of noblemen met at the dais,
1395 And proud prince Balthasar was prompt to sit—
Great gems gleamed on his gorgeous throne.
Then the floor of that festive hall was filled with knights,
And barons, as behooved, at the side boards sat,
For the sovereign himself presided on the dais,
1400 With his bevy of beauties in their bright array.
When the assembly was settled, the service begins;
With fanfares of trumpets and flourishes quaint
Clear notes carried, echoing from the walls
Where broad banners fluttered, embellished with gold.
1405 Men bore in the meats on immense platters
That were of solid silver, with sauces to sup;
Palaces with pinnacles, of paper cut fine,
Were contrived to grace the table—the tips were of gold;
Brutish apes above, wild beasts below,

1410 With forms of birds aflutter in foliage between,
In azure and indigo artfully enameled,
Were borne by men on horseback into the bright hall.
And ever the din undiminished of drumming and piping;
Tambourines and tabors beat time together,
1415 Cymbals and shrill bells resounded in answer,
And the booming of the big drums battered all ears.
So the banquet was brought to the tables by turns,
With savor in each serving, where the lord sat in state
With his ladyloves about him, lolling at ease.

Balthasar Gets Drunk and Decides to Use the Treasures of the Jewish Temple at the Feast°

1420 So well they plied him with wine, it warmed his heart,
And the breath rose to his brain, and befuddled his mind;
His wits grew weak, and he waxed half mad,
For his eyes sweep the assembly; he sees his sweet wenches
And his band of bold barons about by the walls;
1425 Then this drunkard descends into deepest folly,
And an ill-conceived counsel comes to his mind,
In pursuit of his design, he summons the marshal
And commands that coffers be quickly set open
And the vessels fetched forth that his father had kept,
1430 Nabugodonosor, noble in his strength,
Who had ravaged unrestrained and ransacked the temple
In Jerusalem, in Judah—and judged their worth truly.
"Bring them here, brimming with brew of the best;
Let these ladies lap their fill—I love them dearly!
1435 My kingly courtesy shall make clear to all
That none abounds in bounty like Balthasar the great."
Then the treasurer in turn was told of this plan,
And he with clustered keys unclosed the locked chests.
Many a bright burden was borne into hall,
1440 And many a side board spread with spotless white cloths;
The jewel-encrusted treasures from Jerusalem's temple
Round the sides of the room were arrayed in splendor;
And the bright brass altar borne into place.
The great crown of gold, gleaming aloft,
1445 That had been blessed in better days by bishops' hands,
And signed° with the blood of consecrated beasts   *ritually marked*
In the solemn sacrifice that savored sweet

° Daniel 5:2–3.

Before the Lord who reigns aloft, with love and with praise
Is assigned to the service of Satan the black
1450 Before bold King Balthasar, with boasting and pride.
Placed upon the altar were priceless vessels
That had been cunningly contrived with consummate skill.
Seven years and somewhat more had Solomon striven,
Assisted by the sapience° his Sovereign had bestowed,   *wisdom*
1455 To fashion them flawless, fit for His service;
For there were beauteous basins of brightest gold[31]
Enameled in azure, and ewers° to match,   *pitchers*
And cups made like castles, with covers that fitted,
Battlements° embellished them, with corbels° beneath,   *notched parapets /*
1460 Fashioned into figures fancifully shaped.   *projecting layers*
The elaborate lids overlying the cups
Were intricately tooled, with turrets set round
And high-pointed pinnacles projecting between;
And embossed on the cups were branches and leaves,
1465 Magpies and parakeets were perched among them
As if pecking on pomegranates, proud in their plumage,
For all the blossoms on the boughs were beauteous pearls,
And all the fruits were fashioned of flashing gems,[32]
Sapphire and sardius and saffron-hued topaz,
1470 Almandines and emeralds and amethysts rare,
Chalcedony, and chrysolite,[33] and clear red rubies,
And peridots and pinkardines,° with pearls set between.   *carnelians*
Trefoils° and traceries of trailing branches   *threefold leaf patterns*
Bravely embellished each beaker and bowl.
1475 Each goblet was of gold, engraved around the top,
And flowers adorned each phial, and butterflies of gold.
All these were gathered together on the great altar.
The candelabrum was carried in by a costly contrivance
On a platform set on pillars—they praised it who saw—
1480 Bases of polished brass bore up its weight.
Boughs stretched wide above, all of bright gold,
With branches where birds beguiled men's gaze,
Of many kinds and colors, curious and rare,
Whose wings seemed wondrously to wave in the wind.
1485 Lamps shone lustrous upon leaves and twigs,
And other lights lavishly illumined the scene,
Such as bowls filled with wax, embellished without
By effigies of fierce beasts wrought of fine gold.
It was not wont in that wicked place to waste its tapers,
1490 But in the temple of the true faith to take its stand
Before the *sanctum sanctorum*, where heaven's sole Lord
Expounded His speeches to the spiritual elect.

You may well believe, the Lord of the lofty sky
Was angered by those antics in that unseemly place,
1495 That His prized things were profaned by impious fools
That He had once prized as precious in priestly hands;
Solemnly in sacrifice some had been anointed
By instructions He himself had sent down from heaven;
Now a boaster on bench imbibes from them freely
1500 Till, drunk as the devil, in dotage he sits.
So abhorrent He finds it, whose hands made the world,
That as their revels rage on He arrives at a purpose;
Yet He had no wish to harm them in haste in His wrath,
But awed them with an omen that all thought a wonder.
1505 God's service now graces a gathering of gluttons;
Installed on a rich stage, it stands in splendor.
Balthasar the bold bids the banquet begin:
"Serve wine to one and all! Wassail!" he cries.[34]
Swiftly the servants swing into action,
1510 Clap hands on cups to carry them to kings;
Others in bowls set the bright wine abrim,
And each man minds his own master's affairs.
There was clinking and clanking of costly metals
When retainers in that room crowd round for the wine,
1515 Covers cast aloft come down with a clamor,
Like struck strings of a psaltery° strident and gay. *small instrument played by hand*
Then the dotard on the dais drank all he could,
And proud peers and princes were properly served,
And lesser lords and lady friends, all along the tables;
1520 As each found his cup full, he finished it off.
Long did those lords lap up these sweet liquors,°
And proudly praised their gods, and prayed for their grace,
That are made of sticks and stones, stock still forever:
They said never a syllable, so sealed are their tongues.
1525 Yet all these golden gods the great fools invoke:
Belphegor, and Belial, and Beelzebub as well,[35]
With as reverent regard as if they ruled in heaven;
But He that gives all good, that God they forgot.

*A Hand Appears and Writes on the Wall; Balthasar Offers
a Reward to Anyone Who Can Interpret the Inscription*

Wherefore a wonder befell that was witnessed by many;
1530 The king caught sight of it first, and all the court after;
In the principal palace, upon the plain wall,

° Daniel 5:4–12.

Across from the candle, where it cast most light,
Appeared the palm of a hand, with a pen in its grip,
That was ghostly and great, and grimly it writes;
1535 A fist with fingers folded, and no flesh beside,
Scraped and scored the plaster, inscribing signs.
When Balthasar the bold king beheld that hand
Such a horror came on him and overwhelmed his heart
That his face blanched bloodless, that was blithe before;
1540 The sudden stress startled him and strained his joints;
His knees knocked together; he kneaded his thighs
And clutched his head with his hands and clawed his cheeks
And bawled like a big ox that bellows for fear,
Watching ever the hand while it worked away
1545 And made marks on the wall, mysterious signs.
When it had scratched the inscription with its scraping pen,
As a coulter° cuts the clay and cleaves it in furrows,   *blade on a plow*
It vanished from view and was visible no more,
But left the letters behind, writ large on the plaster.
1550 When the king had recovered command of his speech,
He sent for his sages most sapient esteemed
To interpret the text and tell him its meaning,
"For my heart faints for fear of that fateful hand."
Scholars scanned the script to discover its intent,
1555 But not one was so wise as to read one word,
Nor learn to what language those letters belonged,
Or what tiding or tale was betokened thereby.
When they confessed this to the king, he became half crazed,
And ransacked the city to search out men
1560 That were well versed in witchcraft, warlocks° and others   *male witches*
Who dealt in dark spells and divining of letters;
"Call them all to my court, these Chaldean clerks,
Bring word of the wonder we have witnessed here
And clearly proclaim, 'He who counsels the king
1565 And can expound the speech that is spelled by these marks
And make the matter meet for my mind to encompass
So that I see for certain the sense of the words,
He shall go about grand in gowns of purple,
And a kingly collar of gold shall clasp his throat;
1570 He shall be primate and prince in all precincts of learning;
Among my proudest peers third place he shall hold,
Most renowned and respected, to ride at my side;
Two higher in the realm, and he ranked third.'"
Many came to the court to compete for the prize:
1575 Clerks accounted wisest in Chaldean lands,

Sage satraps° as well, and soothsayers wily;   *provincial governors*
Witches and valkyries[36] vied with each other
And diviners of dreams who vaunted their lore
And exorcists who said they could summon forth demons,
1580   And the letters they looked at enlightened them as much
As if they had looked into the leather of my left boot.
Then the king tore his clothes and cried in distress;
He cursed all his clerks and called them knaves;
Often he had a mind to hang them forthwith;°   *immediately*
1585   So wild his wits wandered, he nearly went mad.
The queen heard him chide in her chamber above;
When attendants had told her how the trouble began—
So uncanny a happening in the hall below—
The lady, to lighten the load on his mind,
1590   Steps lightly down the stair, and stands by his side;
She kneels down on her knees and makes known her thought,
In respectful speech expounds a wise plan.
"Bold sovereign," she said, "sole emperor of earth,
May your life be everlasting in length of days!
1595   Why do you rend your robe, all wretched and helpless,
Though those men cannot make out the meaning of letters,
When there is one in your household, as often I have heard,
Who is guided by the God that governs all truth?
The sense of dark sentences his sage soul discerns,
1600   He construes the hidden signs in strange events;
He it was who often exhorted your father
And wooed away his rage with words wise and holy;
When the king from time to time was troubled in heart,
By true signs and tokens he interpreted his dreams.
1605   He escaped through his counsel many a cruel mischance;
All questions he was asked he answered aright,
Inspired by the spirit, that spoke from within him,
Of the goodliest of the gods to whom men give homage.
For his learning in religion and his well-loved words
1610   'Baltassar' your bold sire bade that he be named,[37]
Who is Daniel now, adept in lore deep and dark;
He was caught in the conquest of the kingdom of Judah,
Lord Nabuzardan's prisoner, and now resides here,
A prophet from a far place, praised among his peers.
1615   Send into the city, seek him out in haste;
Persuade him by your princely power to proffer you his help,
And though the meaning be murky, of the marks on the wall,
He shall declare it as clearly as on clay they stand."

Daniel Interprets the Words on the Wall
as Prophesying Balthasar's Destruction

The queen's courteous counsel was quickly followed;
1620 The blessèd youth to Balthasar was brought before long.°
When he comes before the king, and courteously greets him,
The sovereign salutes him and says, "Fair sir,
I am told by folk I trust that you were truly called
A prophet of the people oppressed by my father,
1625 And that your heart is a storehouse of holy knowledge,
And you are sage of soul, to see and say the truth.
God's spirit is given you, who guides all the world,
And you open each hidden thing that heaven's King intends,
And a wonder has been witnessed here, and now I would learn
1630 The sense of the strange writ that stands on the wall,
For all the clerks of Chaldea have cravenly failed.
Fathom it, and faithfully I shall fulfill my promise;
If you can render it aright into reasonable sense,
Then tell it to me truly; take the letters together;
1635 The matter that they mean make clear to my mind,
And I shall keep every clause of the contract I made:
I shall accoutre° you like a king in cloth of purple,   *outfit, clothe*
And a gorget° of gold shall gird your throat,   *ornamental collar*
And in my royal retinue your rank shall be third.
1640 You shall be a baron on bench, so binds me my promise."
Then Daniel with due deference delivers this speech:†
"Great leader of this land, may our Lord guide you!
It is said and held certain that the Sovereign of heaven
Ever aided on earth your honorable father,
1645 Promoted him, preeminent, to princely rank,
And bowed the world to his will, to wield as he liked.
Those he wished to foster fared well in their lives,
And those he would destroy were struck down at once;
Those he wished to help were raised to high station,
1650 And those he would hinder lay helplessly low.
Such was the renown of Nabugodonosor,
In royal state established by the strength of God;
For a faith unfaltering was fixed in his heart
That all power proceeds from the Prince on high,
1655 And while he kept that conviction closed in his heart,
No other mortal monarch was mighty as he.

° Daniel 5:13–16.
† Daniel 5:17–21; cf. 4:15, 21–22, 26–34.

But as time passed, pride overpowered him at last;
So wide stretched his lordship, such wealth he had won,
So egregiously he gloried in his own great deeds
1660 That he paid no heed to the power of the Prince above.
Nor did he blench from blasphemy, but belittled his Lord,
Matched his might with God's in immodest words:
'I am the god of earthly ground, to govern as I like,
As He oversees his angels in heaven on high;
1665 If He ordained the earth and all those upon it,
I have built Babylon, biggest of cities;
Set stone upon stone with the strength of my arms;
No man is so mighty as to make such another.'
No sooner had this same speech sped from his mouth
1670 Then the sound of the Sovereign's voice assailed his ears:
'Let Nabugodonosor boast no longer;
Your preeminence has passed; your pride is put down;
Remote from men's sons, in the moors you must dwell,
And abide among beasts in the barren waste,
1675 And browse like a beast on bracken and herbs,
And wander under the welkin with wolves and wild asses.'
At the highest point of his pride he departed alone
From his ceremonial seat, forsaking all joy,
A care-cumbered outcast in uncouth lands,
1680 In a forest far away, unfrequented by men.
His heart and soul were sick; he soberly believed
He had become a brute beast, a bull or an ox;
He forages on all fours, feeding on grass,
And eats hay like a horse when the green herbs wither.
1685 Thus he who was a king accounts himself a cow
Till seven seasons have passed, summers and winters.
Thickly thatched about by then was his body,
That had been doused and bedabbled with the dew of heaven;
Hanks of matted hair, as heavy as felt,
1690 Fell from his shoulders to the fork of his groin,
And, twining twentyfold, it trailed to his toes
As if the paste of a poultice° had plastered it down.   *medicinal application*
His great beard had grown until it grazed the bare ground;
His brows bristled like briars above his broad cheeks:
1695 Set beneath those shaggy hairs, his eyes showed hollow.
He was grey as a kite,° with great claws and grim,   *bird of prey*
That were crooked and curved like keen-pointed talons;
In aspect like an eagle, utterly transformed,
Till he remembered who measures out all mortal power
1700 And can ruin realms at will and restore them again.

Then He sent him back his sanity, who had suffered long,
And he was ignorant no more, and knew who he was;
And then he lauded that Lord, and believed for certain
That it was He and He alone whose hand governed all.
1705   Soon he had resumed his high seat of power;
His barons bowed before him, blithe at his coming;
The headdress he had doffed he donned once again
And so his state was restored, reestablished in glory.
But you, Balthasar, begotten and born his heir,
1710   Saw those signs with your eyes, and set them at nought;°
You rose up in rancor, rebelled against God
Boasted boldly before Him, with blasphemous words.
You made vile with your vanity the venerated treasures
That had honored Him ever in His holy house;
1715   Placed them before your peers, poured them full of wine
To refresh your lady friends in an ill-fated hour;
You put beside your dinner plates the priceless vessels
That had been blessed long before by bishops' hands,
While you adored false deities that never drew breath,
1720   Senseless stocks and stones, unstirring forever,
And for that flagrant filth, the Father in heaven
Sent you those signs as you sat there in hall:
The fist with its fingers that so frightened your heart,
That scratched a strange script with its scraping pen.
1725   The words on the wall, without more ado,
I shall say as I perceive them through the Sovereign's power;†
'Mane, Techal, Phares,' a threefold message
That threatens you three ways with three strange words.
I shall expound them speedily, in speech brief and plain.
1730   *Mane* means as much as: 'Almighty God
Has counted up your kingdom and cast its number,
And its fate is fulfilled, its final hour at hand.'
To teach you of *Techal*, the term means this:
'The worth of your kingdom is weighed in the balance,
1735   And but few faithful deeds have been found therein.'
What follows from these faults, *Phares* foretells;
In *Phares* I find this fearsome sentence:
'Your kingly state is canceled; outcast shall you be,
Your dominion is done for, destroyed by the Persians.
1740   The Medes shall be your masters; no more shall you reign.'"
The king then gave command to clothe the sage
In rich garb and grand, as agreed on between them;

°   Daniel 5:22–24.
†   Daniel 5:25–29.

In precious purple cloth the prophet was clad,
And a collar of costly gold clasped round his throat.
1745 Then a decree came forth from the king himself;
Bold Balthasar bade to bow low before him
All commoners that dwelt in the domain of Chaldea,
As companion to the prince, appointed one of three,
With all others his underlings, two only excepted,
1750 Ever to keep close to him in court and in field.
This news was announced, made known abroad,
And all the folk that followed him were filled with joy.
But however the prophet fared, the feast day passed;
Darkness drew on; disaster was at hand.°
1755 For ere the dark was dispelled, and dawn turned to day,
The fate Daniel foretold was fully accomplished.
The pomp and the pleasures of that princely feast
Lasted in the lofty hall till sunlight failed;
Then the bright sky above grew bleak and wan,
1760 Darkness and damp dispelled the fine weather
And on the margins of the meadows the mist lay low.
Good folk, as darkness fell, found their way home;
Sat down to supper, sang together after;
At last, when it grew late, took leave of each other.
1765 Balthasar betimes was brought blithely to bed;
Let him rest there at ease; he rose not again.

The Medes and Persians Invade Chaldea;
Balthasar Is Murdered

For there were fighting men afield, foes in their numbers,
That long had sought the life and the lands of the king,
And had suddenly assembled at that same hour—
1770 None within the walls was aware of their coming.
It was the monarch of the Medes, mighty King Darius,
The proud Persian prince, and Porros of Ind,
With legions massed and marshalled, fierce men-at-arms
Intent now to attack and topple down Chaldea.
1775 They thronged in by thousands through thickening darkness;
Beyond the bright waters, walls barred their way;
They lifted long ladders and climbed in quickly,
Stole through the streets—none stirred as they passed.
Ere night was an hour old, all had gained entrance,
1780 Unheard and unhindered; onward they go

° Daniel 5:30–31.

And proceed unopposed to the principal palace;
Then the marauders rushed in in raging throngs;
From bright brass trumpets the shrill blasts rose;
War cries were heard, unwelcome to many;
1785 They murdered men in their beds before they could move,
And despoiled the town speedily, sparing no household.
Balthasar in his bed was battered to death:
His blood and his brain on the bedclothes mingled.
The king within his curtain was caught by the heels,
1790 Fetched out by the feet and foully mishandled.
He who audaciously had drunk from the vessels
Has the worth of a hound huddled dead in a ditch.
For the monarch of the Medes in the morning arose:
Great Darius that day was duly enthroned;
1795 Having taken over the town, he set terms of peace,
With all the barons about him, who bowed to him as one.
And thus the land was lost for that lord's sin
And his filth and foolish pride who presumed to profane
The ornaments of God's house, long hallowed by men;
1800 He was cursed for his uncleanness and caught unaware,
Degraded and debased for his dastardly deeds, -
And from the worship of this world cast away forever,
And also banished, I believe, from blessedness hereafter—
It will be long and late ere he looks on our Lord.

Conclusion

1805 Thus in three ways I have thought good to show you
That uncleanness cuts deep into the courteous heart
Of the Lord whom men love, who lives ever on high—
Goads Him to wrath and to grim revenge;
And cleanness is His comfort, and comely wisdom,
1810 And they that are seemly and sweet shall see His face.
May we go in festive guise by the grace of God,
And serve in His sight where solace never ends.
Amen.

Notes: *Cleanness*

1. **Introduction.** As is true of the other poems in the manuscripts of the *Gawain* group and *Saint Erkenwald*, some of the lines of *Cleanness* begin with large ornamental capitals. But aside from this decorative feature, the other poems are clearly divided into sections of one sort or another. *Patience* begins with an introductory passage discussing the titular virtue, followed by a narrative whose parts corre-

spond roughly to the chapters of the biblical book of Jonah as we have it today. It concludes with a summarizing epilogue. In *Pearl* and *Saint Erkenwald*, divisions reflect numerical designs. The stanzas of *Sir Gawain*, each defined prosodically, fall naturally into groups making up the four "chapters" of the story (see the introductions to these poems). *Cleanness*, however, is loosely organized; it is made up of passages expounding branches of the main topic, sometimes illustrated by stories from the Bible. Only a small number of the lines beginning with ornamental capitals correspond to these divisions. As an aid to the reader, therefore, I have composed and inserted headings indicating the subjects of the passages that follow them.

2. line 16: **Sully God's sacred gear and incite Him to wrath.** By God's gear, the poet means the vessels used by the priest in celebrating mass, including the chalice for the wine and the ciborium for the bread. Since, according to Christian doctrine, the bread and wine become the body and blood of Christ, the officiating priest is literally handling the divine body. God thus feels the kind of revulsion that would be felt by a human being in intimate contact with the dirty hands of an unwelcome lover. Cf. Isaiah 52:11: "Be ye clean, you that carry the vessels of the Lord."

3. line 24: **Eight states of happiness, each with its reward.** The poet translates all eight Beatitudes in *Patience* 13–28 and goes on to personify them as eight "Dames" whom everyone should love. The Beatitude referred to in *Cleanness* is the sixth.

4. line 51: **As Matthew tells in the Mass of the man of great wealth.** The poet's version of the parable contains details from each Gospel that are not found in the other. The version in Matthew does not include the speeches made by those who decline the host's invitation (62–70); the version in Luke does not include the host's encounter with the guest who has failed to put on a wedding garment.

5. line 177: **Other faults may force us to forfeit our bliss.** The passage that follows is perhaps reminiscent of Matthew 15:19–20: "For from the heart come forth evil thoughts, murders, adulteries, fornications, thefts, false testimonies, blasphemies. These are the things that defile a man."

6. line 180: **Thrust men in throngs down the throat of the devil.** The entrance to hell was often represented in the sets of the medieval mystery plays by "Hell-Mouth," the wide open jaws of a sea monster at one side of the stage. The poet may have had this in mind when, in *Patience*, he described Jonah as descending into the whale's "throat," whereas the Bible simply says that God "prepared" a fish to swallow him (Jonah 2:1).

7. line 207: **Of the many noble angels most admirably fair.** See the Introduction, p. 42. In line 211 of the original text, the poet has the rebellious angel say that he will raise his throne in the "tramountayne," the north. In Isaiah 14:13, Lucifer says, "I will sit in the mountain of the covenant, in the sides of the north."

8. line 214: **God drove him to damnation, deep in the abyss.** Over two hundred years later, John Milton narrated this same event in quite a different style in *Paradise Lost*, Book I, lines 44–53:

> Him the Almighty Power
> Hurled headlong flaming from th' Ethereal Sky
> With hideous ruin and combustion down
> To bottomless perdition, there to dwell
> In Adamantine Chains and penal Fire,
> Who durst defy th' Omnipotent to Arms.

9. line 241: **But Eve egged him on to eat of an apple.** The idea that the Fall of Man came about because Eve urged Adam to taste the apple was widespread in medieval times. In the *Man of Law's Tale*, Chaucer says that "thurgh wommannes eggement / Mankind was lorn and damned ay to dye" (842–43). The poet alludes to the tradition in *Gawain* (2416), though he does not mention it when the Fall is referred to in *Saint Erkenwald* (214–16).

10. line 248: **And amended by a maid unmatched among women.** The poet refers here to the Virgin Mary, who gave birth to Christ and thus made the Redemption possible. In the original, he uses a pun no longer available to us, describing her as "a mayden that make had never": *make* in Middle English meant both "partner in marriage" and "equal." A famous medieval lyric praising the Virgin begins, "I sing of a maiden / That is makeles." See also *Pearl*, XIII.5–XIV.1.

11. line 420: **Or any swelling sail to speed them to harbor.** Here, as in the description of the embarkation in *Patience* 101 ff., the poet gives evidence of nautical knowledge. See "A Note on the Embarkation," pp. 9–11 above. The *boom crutch* (or *crotch*) is a notched or forked fitting that supports the *boom*, the horizontal spar at the bottom of the sail, when the sail is not set. The *bowline* was fastened to the windward side of the sail and the bowsprit or prow, to enable a boat to sail obliquely before the wind. The *capstan* is a cylinder around which a *cable* or heavy rope is wound to raise and lower the anchor. The *tiller*, attached to the *rudder*, steers the boat.

12. line 448: **Though otherwise, in Hebrew, they have the name Thanez.** Mandeville says that the name of the mountain where Noah landed was "Ararach, but the Jews call it Thanez."

13. line 462: **Falls on the foul flesh, and fills his belly.** The idea that the raven failed to return because it gorged itself on carrion is not original with the poet. It is added to the biblical account in a number of medieval commentaries on the story in Genesis.

14. line 583: **He that put the power of sight in each pair of eyes.** The poet makes use here of the same passage of Psalm 93 (A.V. 94), verses 8–9, that he paraphrases in *Patience* (123–24).

15. line 601: **At ease in his own land, old Abraham sits.** The poet's audience would have known Abraham as the great Hebrew patriarch with whom God had made a covenant, promising that he would be "a father of many nations" with descendants as numerous as the stars in the sky and the grains of sand on the shore, and whose barren wife, Sara, he had miraculously enabled to bear a son (Genesis 11:27–17:27).

16. line 674: **Not more than two miles from Mambre plain.** According to Genesis 13, Abraham and his nephew Lot departed together from Egypt, where they had lived for a while to escape a famine that had beset their country. They then established themselves in neighboring properties, where each possessed great herds of sheep and cattle. When strife arose between their herdsmen, Abraham suggested that he and Lot should settle elsewhere, departing in opposite directions. Abraham's new home was "by the vale of Mambre," Lot's in Sodom.

17. line 786: **That was fine and well-furnished, befitting its master.** The poet makes two additions to the story of Lot as told in the Old Testament, both derived from Jewish tradition. The first is his portrayal of Lot as a wealthy man; his wealth is not mentioned in the Bible (li. 785–86, 812, and 878). For the second, see the next note.

18. line 820: **"For nothing sour or salt may be served to my guests."** In Jewish legend, the transformation of Lot's wife into a pillar of salt, which is not explained

in the Old Testament, is accounted for in several different ways. According to the version of the story that most closely resembles the poet's, the angels visited Lot during Passover, and that is why Lot insisted that they be served unleavened bread, containing neither yeast nor salt. As a punishment for looking back at the city when she had been told not to, Lot's wife is transformed into an effigy and left by the wayside; the effigy is made of salt because of her earlier disobedience. It seems clear from the poet's treatment of the story that he had read one or more of the Jewish commentaries on Genesis, presumably in Latin translation.

19. line 886: **So that they blundered about like blind Bayard the horse.** Bayard was a legendary horse of extraordinary swiftness. A proverb, "Bold as blind Bayard," means that if a blind horse tries to emulate Bayard, it will probably fall into a ditch.

20. line 926: **"There is a city not far off, and Segor is its name."** Segor is called Zoar in the Authorized Version.

21. line 1015: **Where cities five were set, a sea now stands.** Four cities are named in line 940. Segor, originally slated for destruction, was spared at Lot's request (925–30), but according to tradition was destroyed later.

22. line 1016: **That is darksome and drear, and deathly in nature.** The description of the Dead Sea is taken in large part from the description in Mandeville's *Travels* (see Introduction, pp. 42–43), but the idea that the properties of the sea contradict nature is original with the poet.

23. line 1034: **The clays that cling to its banks are corrosive in kind.** The poet lists a number of corrosive or destructive substances known to medieval chemistry, including sandiver or glass gall, a scum that floats on molten glass.

24. line 1057: **For Clopinel, in the compass of his clean-wrought *Rose*.** See the Introduction, p. 42. In the *Roman de la Rose*, the allegorical character called "Friend" gives this pragmatic, if not cynical, advice to the lover, telling him to ingratiate himself with "Fair Welcoming," a male figure who in the allegory stands for the beloved's hoped-for graciousness in responding to his suit. "No matter how old [Fair Welcoming] may be, or what appearance he may have, adapt yourself to his manner. If he is old and serious, put all your attention on conducting yourself in a serious way; and if he acts stupidly, you act stupidly. Take trouble to follow his lead: if he is happy, put on a happy face; if he is angry, an angry one. If he laughs, you laugh, and weep if he does. Maintain your conduct in this way at every hour. Love what he loves, blame what he wants to blame, and give praise to whatever he does. He will then have much more confidence in you" (7719–37, trans. Charles Dahlberg).

25. Line 1081: **For angels with their instruments, organs and pipes.** The poet refers to portable organs, such as were in use in his time, small enough to be played by angels hovering in air.

26. line 1157: **Daniel in his discourses discloses the story.** A brief summary of the destruction of Jerusalem by King Nabugodonosor, and the plundering of the temple, is given in Daniel 1:1–2. Daniel could not have prophesied these events, however, for he was brought into the household of Nabugodonosor as a child only after they had taken place. The fuller accounts in Paralipomenon 2 (II Chronicles) and Jeremias, which the *Cleanness* poet paraphrases, may have been attributed to Daniel by some medieval scholars.

27. line 1270: **And pillaged all the precious things so proudly displayed.** The building of Solomon's temple, and a full account of the precious furnishings and artifacts within it, can be found in 3 Kings (1 Kings), ch. 7. A similar account is given,

in the story of Nabuzardan's pillaging of the temple, in Jeremias 52. The items listed in each version differ somewhat in detail from those said to have been stolen in *Cleanness* 1271–80 and displayed at Balthasar's feast in 1441–92. The latter passage also owes something to Mandeville's *Travels* (see note 30, below).

28. line 1274: **Before the sanctum sanctorum, where oft were seen wonders.** The *sanctum sanctorum*, or holy of holies, was the sanctuary in the temple in Jerusalem where the Ark of the Covenant was kept.

29. line 1286: **That Solomon sought to make so many a long year.** See 3 Kings (1 Kings) 7:1, "And Solomon built his own house in thirteen years, and brought it to perfection."

30. line 1302: **And dear Daniel as well, a diviner most noble.** In Daniel 1:6, Ananias, Misael, Azarias, and Daniel are said to be among the Hebrew children brought to Babylon by order of Nabugodonosor. Daniel later became famous as a diviner, that is, a prophet having occult knowledge.

31. line 1456: **For there were beauteous basins of brightest gold.** The details in the passage that follows seem to be drawn in part from Mandeville's account of the quasi-mythical wonders of the Great Chan's palace and the land of Prester John (see Introduction, p. 43).

32. line 1468: **And all the fruits were fashioned of flashing gems.** In his account of the Great Chan's palace, Mandeville describes a gold vine laden with grapes made of varicolored precious stones, including crystal, topaz, rubies, "alabaundines," garnets, emeralds, peridotes, onyx, and "geracites." Fantastic lists of this sort were frequent in alliterative poetry. The banks of the stream in the *Gawain* poet's *Pearl* are made of beryl, and the pebbles on the bottom are gems, including sapphires and emeralds (II.5). An important source of such descriptions in medieval literature is the list in Apocalypse (Revelation) of the twelve layers of the foundation of the celestial Jerusalem, each of which is a different precious stone. These include sapphire, chalcedony, emerald, chrysolite, and topaz (cf. *Pearl* XVII. 2–4). Lapidary encyclopedias listing exotic stones and detailing their supposed magical powers were also widely available for consultation.

33. line 1471: **Chalcedony, and chrysolite, and clear red rubies.** Sardius (1469), also called sard, is a translucent brownish-red stone; the almandine (1470) is a violet-red garnet. Chalcedony is a form of translucent quartz; chrysolite, or olivine, is an olive-green mineral found in certain kinds of rock.

34. line 1508: **"Serve wine to one and all! Wassail!" he cries.** It has been plausibly suggested that the poet is here describing a drinking ceremony such as he may have known of or participated in himself. The king begins it by calling out "Wassail," whereupon the cups of all those present are filled, first those of the noblest guests (1510, 1518) and then of the rest. Each one responds in proper fashion by promptly draining his cup (1520).

35. line 1526: **Belphegor, and Belial, and Beelzebub as well.** Belphegor is named in Numbers 25:3 as one of the idols worshiped by the Israelites. Beelzebub appears in both the Old and the New Testaments. Since he is called "the prince of the devils" in Matthew 12:24, Milton, in *Paradise Lost*, made him second in rank to Satan. The word *Belial* in the Old Testament meant "worthless," but later came to be used as the name of a demon. In the Vulgate Bible, Paul asks "Quae autem conventio Christi ad Belial?" "What concord [is there] between Christ and Belial?" (2 Corinthians 6:15).

36. line 1577: **Witches and valkyries vied with each other.** *Valkyries* (spelled *walkyries*) is the poet's word. Rather than denying the existence of the mythological divinities worshiped in religions other than Christianity, medieval Christians believed them to be demonic allies of Satan.

37. line 1610: **"'Baltassar' your bold sire bade that he be named."** In Daniel 1:7, Daniel and several other captive children living in Nabugodonosor's household are said to have been given new names. Daniel becomes Baltassar (Belteshazzar in the A.V.). The new names of the others in the A.V., Shadrach, Meshach, and Abednego, are remembered in modern times in the well-known story of the "fiery furnace" (the "furnace of burning fire" in Douay-Rheims) from which all three, protected by God, emerged unharmed (Daniel 3:8–24).

Biblical Sources

The names of books in the Authorized Version of the Bible, where they differ from the names in the Douay-Rheims translation, are added in parentheses.

Matthew 5:3–10

3. Blessed are the poor in spirit: for theirs is the kingdom of heaven.

4. Blessed are the meek: for they shall possess the land.

5. Blessed are they that mourn: for they shall be comforted.

6. Blessed are they that hunger and thirst after justice: for they shall have their fill.

7. Blessed are the merciful: for they shall obtain mercy.

8. Blessed are the clean of heart: for they shall see God.

9. Blessed are the peacemakers: for they shall be called children of God.

10. Blessed are they that suffer persecution for justice' sake: for theirs is the kingdom of heaven.

Luke 6:20–23

20. . . . Blessed are ye poor, for yours is the kingdom of God.

21. Blessed are ye that hunger now: for you shall be filled. Blessed are ye that weep now: for you shall laugh.

22. Blessed shall you be when men shall hate you, and when they shall separate you, and shall reproach you. . . .

23. Be glad in that day and rejoice: for behold, your reward is great in heaven. . . .

Matthew 22:1–14

1. And Jesus answering, spoke again in parables to them, saying:

2. The kingdom of heaven is likened to a king, who made a marriage for his son.

3. And he sent his servants, to call them that were invited to the marriage; and they would not come.

4. Again he sent other servants, saying: Tell them that were invited, Behold, I have prepared my dinner; my beeves and fatlings are killed, and all things are ready: come ye to the marriage.

5. But they neglected, and went their own ways, one to his farm, and another to his merchandise.

6. And the rest laid hands on his servants, and having treated them contumeliously, put them to death.

7. But when the king heard of it, he was angry, and sending his armies, he destroyed those murderers, and burnt their city.

8. Then he saith to his servants: The marriage indeed is ready; but they that were invited were not worthy.

9. Go ye therefore into the highways; and as many as you shall find, call to the marriage.

10. And his servants going forth into the ways, gathered together all that they found, both bad and good: and the marriage was filled with guests.

11. And the king went in to see the guests: and he saw there a man who had not on a wedding garment.

12. And he saith to him: Friend, how camest thou in hither not having a wedding garment? But he was silent.

13. Then the king said to the waiters: Bind his hands and feet, and cast him into the exterior darkness: there shall be weeping and gnashing of teeth.

14. For many are called, but few are chosen.

Luke 14:16–24

16. . . . A certain man made a great supper, and invited many.

17. And he sent his servant at the hour of supper to say to them that were invited, that they should come, for now all things are ready.

18. And they began all at once to make excuse. The first said to him: I have bought a farm, and I must needs go out to see it: I pray thee, hold me excused.

19. And another said: I have bought five yoke of oxen, and I go to try them: I pray thee, hold me excused.

20. And another said: I have married a wife, and therefore I cannot come.

21. And the servant returning, told these things to his lord. Then the master of the house, being angry, said to his servant: Go out quickly into the streets and lanes of the city, and bring in hither the poor, and the feeble, and the blind, and the lame.

22. And the servant said: Lord, it is done as thou hast commanded, and yet there is room.

23. And the Lord said to the servant: Go out into the highways and hedges, and compel them to come in, that my house may be filled.

24. But I say unto you, that none of those men that were invited, shall taste of my supper.

Genesis 2:15–17

15. And the Lord God took man, and put him into the paradise of pleasure, to dress it, and to keep it.

16. And he commanded him, saying: Of every tree of paradise thou shalt eat.

17. But of the tree of knowledge of good and evil, thou shalt not eat. For in what day soever thou shalt eat of it, thou shalt die the death.

Genesis 3:1–6

1. Now the serpent was more subtle than any of the beasts of the earth which the Lord God had made. And he said to the woman: Why hath God commanded you, that you should not eat of every tree of paradise?

2. And the woman answered him, saying: Of the fruit of the trees that are in paradise we do eat:

3. But of the fruit of the tree which is in the midst of paradise, God hath commanded us that we should not eat; and that we should not touch it, lest perhaps we die.

4. And the serpent said to the woman: no, you shall not die the death.

5. For God doth know that in what day soever you shall eat thereof, your eyes shall be opened: and you shall be as Gods, knowing good and evil.

6. And the woman saw that the tree was good to eat, and fair to the eyes, and delightful to behold: and she took of the fruit thereof, and did eat, and gave to her husband who did eat.

Genesis 6:1–2, 4–7

1. And after [the series of generations ending with Noah and his sons, described in chapter 5] men began to be multiplied upon the earth, and daughters were born to them.

2. The sons of God seeing the daughters of men, that they were fair, took to themselves wives of all which they chose. . . .

4. Now giants were upon the earth in those days. For after the sons of God went in to the daughters of men, and they brought forth children, these are the mighty men of old, men of renown.

5. And God seeing the wickedness of men was great on the earth, and that all the thought of their heart was bent upon evil at all times,

6. It repented him that he had made man on the earth. And being touched inwardly with sorrow of heart,

7. He said: I will destroy man, whom I have created, from the face of the earth, from man even to beasts, from the creeping things even to the fowls of the air, for it repenteth me that I have made them.

Genesis 6:8–9, 11–22

8. But Noe found grace before the Lord.

9. These are the generations of Noe: Noe was a just and perfect man in his generations, he walked with God. . . .

11. And the earth was corrupted before God, and was filled with iniquity.

12. And when God had seen that the earth was corrupted (for all flesh had corrupted its way upon the earth),

13. He said to Noe: The end of all flesh is come before me, the earth is filled with iniquity through them, and I will destroy them with the earth.

14. Make thee an ark of timber planks: thou shalt make little rooms in the ark, and thou shalt pitch it within and without.

15. And thus shalt thou make it: The length of the ark shall be three hundred cubits: the breadth of it fifty cubits, and the height of it thirty cubits.

16. Thou shalt make a window in the ark, and in a cubit shalt thou finish the top of it: and the door of the ark thou shalt set in the side: with lower, middle chambers, and third stories shalt thou make it.

17. Behold I will bring the waters of a great flood upon the earth, to destroy all flesh, wherein is the breath of life, under heaven. All things that are in the earth shall be consumed.

18. And I will establish my covenant with thee, and thou shalt enter into the ark, thou and thy sons, and thy wife, and the wives of thy sons with thee.

19. And of every living creature of all flesh, thou shalt bring two of a sort into the ark, that they may live with thee: of the male sex, and the female.

20. Of fowls according to their kind, and of beasts in their kind, and of every thing that creepeth on the earth according to its kind; two of every sort shall go in with thee, that they may live.

21. Thou shalt take unto thee of all food that may be eaten, and thou shalt lay it up with thee: and it shall be food for thee and them.

22. And Noe did all things which God commanded him.

Genesis 7:1–3, 5–24

1. And the Lord said to him: Go in thou and all thy house into the ark: for thee I have seen just before me in this generation.

2. Of all clean beasts take seven and seven, the male and the female.

3. But of the beasts that are unclean two and two, the male and the female. Of the fowls also of the air seven and seven, the male and the female: that seed may be saved upon the face of the whole earth. . . .

5. And Noe did all things which the Lord had commanded him.

6. And he was six hundred years old, when the waters of the flood overflowed the earth.

7. And Noe went in and his sons, his wife and the wives of his sons with him into the ark, because of the waters of the flood.

8. And of beasts clean and unclean, and of fowls, and of every thing that moveth upon the earth,

9. Two and two went in to Noe into the ark, male and female, as the Lord had commanded Noe.

10. And after the seven days were passed, the waters of the flood overflowed the earth.

11. In the six hundredth year of the life of Noe, in the second month, in the seventeenth day of the month, all the fountains of the great deep were broken up, and the flood gates of heaven were opened:

12. And the rain fell upon the earth forty days and forty nights.

13. In the selfsame day Noe, and Sem, and Cham, and Japheth his sons: his wife, and the three wives of his sons with them, went into the ark:

14. They and every beast according to its kind, and all the cattle in their kind, and everything that moveth upon the earth according to its kind, and every fowl according to its kind, all birds, and all that fly,

15. Went in to Noe into the ark, two and two of all flesh, wherein was the breath of life.

16. And they that went in, went in male and female of all flesh, as God had commanded him: and the Lord shut him in on the outside.

17. And the flood was forty days upon the earth, and the waters increased, and lifted up the ark on high from the earth.

18. For they overflowed exceedingly: and filled all on the face of the earth: and the ark was carried upon the waters.

19. And the waters prevailed beyond measure upon the earth: and all the high mountains under the whole heaven were covered.

20. The water was fifteen cubits higher than the mountains which it covered.

21. And all flesh was destroyed that moved upon the earth, both of fowl, and of cattle, and of beasts, and of all creeping things that creep upon the earth: and all men.

22. And all things wherein there is the breath of life on the earth, died.

23. And he destroyed all the substance that was upon the earth, from man even to beast, and the creeping things and fowls of the air: and they were destroyed from the earth: and Noe only remained, and they that were with him in the ark.

24. And the waters prevailed upon the earth a hundred and fifty days.

Genesis 8

1. And God remembered Noe, and all the living creatures, and all the cattle which were with him in the ark, and brought a wind upon the earth, and the waters were abated.

2. The fountains also of the deep, and the flood gates of heaven were shut up, and the rain from heaven was restrained.

3. And the waters returned from off the earth going and coming: and they began to be abated after a hundred and fifty days.

4. And the ark rested in the seventh month, the seven and twentieth day of the month, upon the mountains of Armenia.

5. And the waters were going and decreasing until the tenth month: for in the tenth month, the first day of the month, the tops of the mountains appeared.

6. And after that forty days were passed, Noe, opening the window of the ark which he had made, sent forth a raven:

7. Which went forth and did not return, till the waters were dried up upon the earth.

8. He sent forth also a dove after him, to see if the waters had now ceased upon the face of the earth.

9. But she, not finding where her foot might rest, returned to him into the ark: for the waters were upon the whole earth: and he put forth his hand, and caught her, and brought her into the ark.

10. And having waited yet seven other days, he again sent forth the dove out of the ark.

11. And she came to him in the evening, carrying a bough of an olive tree, with green leaves, in her mouth. Noe therefore understood that the waters were ceased upon the earth.

12. And he stayed yet seven other days: and he sent forth the dove, which returned not any more unto him.

13. Therefore in the six hundredth and first year, the first month, the first day of the month, the waters were lessened upon the earth, and Noe opening the covering of the ark, looked, and saw that the face of the earth was dried.

14. In the second month, the seven and twentieth day of the month, the earth was dried.

15. And God spoke to Noe, saying:

16. Go out of the ark, thou and thy wife, thy sons, and the wives of thy sons with thee.

17. All living things that are with thee of all flesh, as well in fowls as in beasts, and all creeping things that creep upon the earth, bring out with thee, and go ye upon the earth: increase and multiply upon it.

18. So Noe went out, he and his sons: his wife, and the wives of his sons with him.

19. And all living things, and cattle, and creeping things that creep upon the earth, according to their kinds, went out of the ark.

20. And Noe built an altar unto the Lord: and taking of all cattle and fowls that were clean, offered holocausts upon the altar.

21. And the Lord smelled a sweet savor, and said: I will no more curse the earth for the sake of man: for the imagination and thought of man's heart are prone to evil from his youth: therefore I will no more destroy every living soul as I have done.

22. All the days of the earth, seedtime and harvest, cold and heat, summer and winter, night and day, shall not cease.

Genesis 9:1–2

1. And God blessed Noe and his sons. And he said to them: Increase and multiply, and fill the earth.

2. And let the fear and dread of you be upon all the beasts of the earth, and upon all the fowls of the air, and all that move upon the earth: all the fishes of the sea are delivered into your hand.

Genesis 9:8–11

8. Thus also said God to Noe, and to his sons with him,

9. Behold I will establish my covenant with you, and with your seed after you:

10. And with every living soul that is with you, as well in all birds as in cattle and beasts of the earth, that are come forth out of the ark, and in all the beasts of the earth.

11. I will establish my covenant with you, and all flesh shall be no more destroyed with the waters of a flood, neither shall there be from henceforth a flood to waste the earth.

Genesis 18:1–16

1. And the Lord appeared to [Abraham] in the vale of Mambre as he was sitting at the door of his tent, in the very heat of the day.

2. And when he had lifted up his eyes, there appeared to him three men standing near him: and as soon as he saw them he ran to meet them from the door of his tent, and adored down to the ground.

3. And he said: Lord, if I have found favor in thy sight, pass not away from thy servant:

4. But I will fetch a little water, and wash ye your feet, and rest ye under the tree.

5. And I will set a morsel of bread, and strengthen ye your heart, afterwards you shall pass on: for therefore are you come aside to your servant. And they said: Do as thou hast spoken.

6. Abraham made haste into the tent to Sara, and said to her: Make haste, temper together three measures of flour, and make cakes upon the hearth.

7. And he himself ran to the herd, and took from thence a calf very tender and very good, and gave it to a young man: who made haste and boiled it.

8. He took also butter and milk, and the calf which he had boiled, and set before them: but he stood by them under the tree.

9. And when they had eaten, they said to him: Where is Sara thy wife? He answered: Lo, she is in the tent.

10. And he said to him: I will return and come to thee at this time, life accompanying, and Sara thy wife shall have a son. Which when Sara heard, she laughed behind the door of the tent.

11. Now they were both old, and far advanced in years, and it had ceased to be with Sara after the manner of women.

12. And she laughed secretly, saying: After I am grown old and my lord is an old man, shall I give myself to pleasure?

13. And the Lord said to Abraham: Why did Sara laugh, saying: Shall I who am an old woman bear a child indeed?

14. Is there any thing hard to God? According to appointment I will return to thee at this same time, life accompanying, and Sara shall have a son.

15. Sara denied, saying: I did not laugh: for she was afraid. But the Lord said, Nay: but thou didst laugh:

16. And when the men rose up from thence, they turned their eyes towards Sodom: and Abraham walked with them, bringing them on the way.

Genesis 18:17–33

17. And the Lord said: Can I hide from Abraham what I am about to do:

18. Seeing he shall become a great and mighty nation, and in him all the nations of the earth shall be blessed?

19. For I know that he will command his children, and his household after him to keep the way of the Lord, and do judgment and justice: that for Abraham's sake the Lord may bring to effect all the things he hath spoken unto him.

20. And the Lord said: The cry of Sodom and Gomorrha is multiplied, and their sin is become exceedingly grievous.

21. I will go down and see whether they have done according to the cry that is come to me: or whether it be not so, that I may know.

22. And they turned themselves from thence, and went their way to Sodom: but Abraham as yet stood before the Lord.

23. And drawing nigh he said: Wilt thou destroy the just with the wicked?

24. If there be fifty just men in the city, shall they perish withal? and wilt thou not spare that place for the sake of the fifty just, if they be therein?

25. Far be it from thee to do this thing, and to slay the just with the wicked, and for the just to be in like case as the wicked, this is not beseeming thee: thou who judgest all the earth, wilt not make this judgment.

26. And the Lord said to him: If I find in Sodom fifty just within the city, I will spare the whole place for their sake.

27. And Abraham answered, and said: Seeing I have once begun, I will speak to my Lord, whereas I am dust and ashes.

28. What if there be five less than fifty just persons? wilt thou for five and forty destroy the whole city? And he said: I will not destroy it, if I find five and forty.

29. And again he said to him: But if forty be found there, what wilt thou do? He said: I will not destroy it for the sake of forty.

30. Lord, saith he, be not angry, I beseech thee, if I speak: What if thirty shall be found there? He answered: I will not do it, if I find thirty there.

31. Seeing, saith he, I have once begun, I will speak to my Lord. What if twenty be found there? He said: I will not destroy it for the sake of twenty.

32. I beseech thee, saith he, be not angry, Lord, if I speak yet once more: What if ten should be found there? And he said: I will not destroy it for the sake of ten.

33. And the Lord departed, after he had left speaking to Abraham: and Abraham returned to his place.

Genesis 19:1–26

1. And the two angels came to Sodom in the evening, and Lot was sitting in the gate of the city. And seeing them, he rose up and went to meet them: and worshipped prostrate to the ground,

2. And said: I beseech you, my lords, turn in to the house of your servant, and lodge there: wash your feet, and in the morning you shall go on your way. And they said: No, but we will abide in the street.

3. He pressed them very much to turn in unto him: and when they were come in to his house, he made them a feast, and baked unleavened bread and they ate:

4. But before they went to bed, the men of the city beset the house both young and old, all the people together.

5. And they called Lot, and said to him: Where are the men that came in to thee at night? bring them out hither that we may know them:

6. Lot went out to them, and shut the door after him, and said:

7. Do not so, I beseech you, my brethren, do not commit this evil.

8. I have two daughters who as yet have not known man: I will bring them out to you, and abuse you them as it shall please you, so that you do no evil to these men, because they are come in under the shadow of my roof.

9. But they said: Get thee back thither. And again: Thou camest in, said they, as a stranger, was it to be a judge? therefore we will afflict thee more than them. And they pressed very violently upon Lot: and they were even at the point of breaking open the doors.

10. And behold the men put out their hand, and drew in Lot unto them, and shut the door:

11. And them that were without, they struck with blindness from the least to the greatest, so that they could not find the door.

12. And they said to Lot: Hast thou here any of thine? son in law, or sons, or daughters, all that are thine bring them out of this city:

13. For we will destroy this place, because their cry is grown loud before the Lord, who hath sent us to destroy them.

14. So Lot went out, and spoke to his sons in law that were to have his daughters, and said: Arise: get you out of this place, because the Lord will destroy this city. And he seemed to them to speak as it were in jest.

15. And when it was morning, the angels pressed him, saying: Arise, take thy wife, and the two daughters which thou hast, lest thou also perish in the wickedness of the city.

16. And as he lingered, they took his hand, and the hand of his wife, and of his two daughters, because the Lord spared him.

17. And they brought him forth, and set him without the city; and there they spoke to him, saying: Save thy life: look not back, neither stay thou in all the country about: but save thyself in the mountain, lest thou be also consumed.

18. And Lot said to them: I beseech thee my Lord,

19. Because thy servant hath found grace before thee, and thou hast magnified thy mercy, which thou hast shewn to me, in saving my life, and I cannot escape to the mountain, lest some evil seize me, and I die:

20. There is this city here at hand, to which I may flee, it is a little one, and I shall be saved in it: is it not a little one, and my soul shall live?

21. And he said to him: Behold also in this, I have heard thy prayers, not to destroy the city for which thou has spoken.

22. Make haste and be saved there, because I cannot do any thing till thou go in thither. Therefore the name of that city was called Segor ["a little one"].

23. The sun was risen upon the earth, and Lot entered into Segor.

24. And the Lord rained upon Sodom and Gomorrha brimstone and fire from the Lord out of heaven.

25. And he destroyed these cities, and all the country about, all the inhabitants of the cities, and all things that spring from the earth.

26. And his wife looking behind her, was turned into a statue of salt.

Genesis 19:27–28

27. And Abraham got up early in the morning, and in the place where he had stood before with the Lord,

28. He looked towards Sodom and Gomorrha, and the whole land of that country: and he saw the ashes rise up from the earth as the smoke of a furnace.

2 Paralipomenon (II Chronicles) 36:11–12, 17–20

11. Sedecias [Zedekiah] was one and twenty years when he began to reign: and he reigned eleven years in Jerusalem.

12. And he did evil in the eyes of the Lord his God, and did no reverence to the face of Jeremias the prophet speaking to him from the mouth of the Lord. . . .

17. For he [God] brought upon them the king of the Chaldeans, and he slew their young men with the sword in the house of his sanctuary, he had no compassion on young man, or maiden, old man or even him that stooped for age, but he delivered them all into his hands.

18. And all the vessels of the house of the Lord, great and small, and the treasures of the temple and of the king, and of the princes he carried away to Babylon.

19. And the enemies set fire to the house of God, and broke down the wall of Jerusalem, burnt all the towers, and whatsoever was precious they destroyed.

20. Whosoever escaped the sword, was led into Babylon, and there served the king and his sons. . . .

Jeremias (Jeremiah) 52:1–11

1. Sedecias was one and twenty years old when he began to reign: and he reigned eleven years in Jerusalem . . .

2. And he did that which was evil in the eyes of the Lord. . . .

3. For the wrath of the Lord was against Jerusalem, and against Juda, till he cast them out from his presence: and Sedecias revolted from the king of Babylon.

4. And it came to pass . . . that Nabuchodonosor the king of Babylon came, he and all his army, against Jerusalem, and they besieged it, and built forts against it round about.

5. And the city was besieged until the eleventh year of King Sedecias.

6. And in the fourth month, the ninth day of the month, a famine overpowered the city: and there was no food for the people of the land.

7. And the city was broken up, and the men of war fled, and went out of the city in the night by the way of the gate that is between the two walls, and leadeth to the king's garden (the Chaldeans besieging the city round about), and they went by the way that leadeth to the wilderness.

8. But the army of the Chaldeans pursued after the king: and they overtook Sedecias in the desert which is near Jericho: and all his companions were scattered from him.

9. And when they had taken the king, they carried him to the king of Babylon . . . and he gave judgment upon him.

10. And the king of Babylon slew the sons of Sedecias before his eyes: and he slew all the princes of Juda in Reblatha.

11. And he put out the eyes of Sedecias, and bound him with fetters, and the king of Babylon brought him into Babylon, and he put him in prison till the day of his death.

Jeremias 52:12–14

12. And in the fifth month, the tenth day of the month, the same is the nineteenth year of Nabuchodonosor, king of Babylon, came Nabuzardan the general of the army, who stood before the king of Babylon in Jerusalem.

13. And he burnt the house of the Lord, and the king's house, and all the houses of Jerusalem, and every great house he burnt with fire.

14. And all the army of the Chaldeans that were with the general broke down all the wall of Jerusalem round about.

Daniel 5:1

1. Baltasar the king made a great feast for a thousand of his nobles: and everyone drank according to his age.

Daniel 5:2–3

2. And being now drunk [Baltasar] commanded that they should bring the vessels of gold and silver which Nabuchodonosor his father had brought away out of the temple, that was in Jerusalem, that the king and his nobles, and his wives and his concubines, might drink in them.

3. Then were the golden and silver vessels brought, which he had brought away out of the temple that was in Jerusalem: and the king and his nobles, and his wives and his concubines, drank in them.

Daniel 5:4–12

4. They drank wine, and praised their gods of gold, and of silver, of brass, of iron, and of wood, and of stone.

5. In the same hour there appeared fingers, as it were of the hand of a man, writing over against the candlestick upon the surface of the wall of the king's palace: and the king beheld the joints of the hand that wrote.

6. Then was the king's countenance changed, and his thoughts troubled him: and the joints of his loins were loosed, and his knees struck one against the other.

7. And the king cried out aloud to bring in the wise men, the Chaldeans, and the soothsayers. And the king spoke, and said to the wise men of Babylon: Whosoever shall read this writing, and shall make known to me the interpretation thereof, shall be clothed with purple, and shall have a golden chain on his neck, and shall be the third man in my kingdom.

8. Then came in all the king's wise men, but they could neither read the writing, nor declare the interpretation to the king.

9. Wherewith king Baltasar was much troubled, and his countenance was changed: and his nobles also were troubled.

10. Then the queen, on occasion of what had happened to the king, and his nobles, came into the banquet house: and she spoke and said: O king, live for ever; let not thy thoughts trouble thee, neither let thy countenance be changed.

11. There is a man in thy kingdom that hath the spirit of the holy gods in him: and in the days of thy father knowledge and wisdom were found in him: for king Nabuchodonosor thy father appointed him prince of the wise men, enchanters, Chaldeans, and soothsayers, thy father, I say, O king:

12. Because a greater spirit, and knowledge, and understanding, and interpretation of dreams, and shewing of secrets, and resolving of difficult things, were found in him, that is, in Daniel. . . . Now therefore let Daniel be called for, and he will tell the interpretation.

Daniel 5:13–16

13. Then Daniel was brought in before the king. And the king spoke, and said to him: Art thou Daniel of the children of the captivity of Juda, whom my father the king brought out of Judea?

14. I have heard of thee, that thou hast the spirit of the gods, and excellent knowledge, and understanding, and wisdom are found in thee.

15. And now the wise men the magicians have come in before me, to read this writing, and shew me the interpretation thereof: and they could not declare to me the meaning of this writing.

16. But I have heard of thee, that thou canst interpret obscure things, and resolve difficult things: now if thou art able to read the writing, and to shew me the interpretation thereof, thou shalt be clothed with purple, and shalt have a chain of gold about thy neck, and shalt be the third prince in my kingdom.

Daniel 5:17–24

17. To which Daniel made answer, and said before the king: Thy rewards be to thyself, and the gifts of thy house give to another: but the writing I will read to thee, O king, and shew thee the interpretation thereof.

18. O king, the most high God gave to Nabuchodonosor thy father a kingdom, and greatness, and glory, and honor.

19. And for the greatness that he gave to him, all people, tribes, and languages trembled, and were afraid of him: whom he would, he slew: and whom he would, he destroyed: and whom he would, he set up: and whom he would, he brought down.

20. But when his heart was lifted up, and his spirit hardened unto pride, he was put down from the throne of his kingdom, and his glory was taken away.

21. And he was driven out from the sons of men, and his heart was made like the beasts, and his dwelling was with the wild asses, and he did eat grass like an ox, and his body was wet with the dew of heaven: till he knew that the most High ruled in the kingdom of men, and that he will set over it whomsoever it shall please him.

22. Thou also his son, O Baltasar, hast not humbled thy heart, whereas thou knewest all these things:

23. But hast lifted thyself up against the Lord of heaven: and the vessels of his house have been brought before thee: and thou, and thy nobles, and thy wives, and thy concubines have drunk wine in them: and thou hast praised the gods of silver, and of gold, and of brass, or iron, and of wood, and of stone, that neither see, nor hear, nor feel: but the God who hath thy breath in his hand, and all thy ways, thou hast not glorified.

24. Wherefore he hath sent the part of the hand which hath written this that is set down.

Daniel 4:15, 21–22, 26–34

15. I king Nabuchodonosor saw this dream; thou, therefore, O [Daniel], tell me quickly the interpretation: . . . thou art able, because the spirit of the holy gods is in thee. . . .

21. [Daniel said,] This is the interpretation of the sentence of the most high, which is come upon my lord the king.

22. They shall cast thee out from among men, and thy dwelling shall be with cattle and with wild beasts, and thou shalt eat grass as an ox, and shalt be wet with the dew of heaven: and seven times shall pass over thee, till thou know that the most High ruleth over the kingdom of men, and giveth it to whomsoever he will. . . .

26. At the end of twelve months [Nabuchodonosor] was walking in the palace of Babylon.

27. And the king answered and said: Is not this the great Babylon, which I have built to be the seat of the kingdom, by the strength of my power, and in the glory of my excellence?

28. And while the word was yet in the king's mouth, a voice came down from heaven: To thee, O king Nabuchodonosor, it is said: Thy kingdom shall pass from thee,

29. And they shall cast thee out from among men, and thy dwelling shall be with cattle and wild beasts: thou shalt eat grass like an ox, and seven times shall pass over thee, till thou know that the most High ruleth in the kingdom of men, and giveth it to whomsoever he will.

30. The same hour the word was fulfilled upon Nabuchodonosor, and he was driven away from among men, and did eat grass like an ox, and his body was wet with the dew of heaven: till his hairs grew like the feathers of eagles, and his nails like birds' claws.

31. Now at the end of the days, I Nabuchodonosor lifted up my eyes to heaven, and my sense was restored to me: and I blessed the most High, and I praised and glorified him that liveth forever: for his power is an everlasting power, and his kingdom is to all generations.

32. And all the inhabitants of the earth are reputed as nothing before him: for he doth according to his will, as well with the powers of heaven, as among the inhabitants of the earth: and there is none that can resist his hand, and say to him: Why hast thou done it?

33. At the same time my sense returned to me, and I came to the honor and glory of my kingdom: and my shape returned to me: and my nobles, and my magistrates sought for me, and I was restored to my kingdom: and greater majesty was added to me.

34. Therefore I Nabuchodonosor do now praise, and magnify, and glorify the King of heaven: because all his works are true, and his ways judgments, and them that walk in pride he is able to shame.

Daniel 5:25–29

25. And this is the writing that is written: MANE, THECEL, PHARES.
26. And this is the interpretation of the word. MANE: God hath numbered thy kingdom, and hath finished it.
27. THECEL: thou art weighed in the balance, and art found wanting.
28. PHARES: thy kingdom is divided, and is given to the Medes and Persians.
29. Then by the king's command Daniel was clothed with purple, and a chain of gold was put about his neck: and it was proclaimed of him that he had power as the third man in the kingdom.

Daniel 5:30–31

30. The same night Baltasar the Chaldean king was slain.
31. And Darius the Mede succeeded to the kingdom. . . .

Pearl

Introduction to *Pearl*

Pearl, like *Patience*, was written by a devout Christian at a time when the Christian church was also the Catholic Church. It is a poem of doctrinal instruction in time of bereavement, rich in allusions to the Psalms, the Gospels, and the Apocalypse, or Book of Revelation. (The most important of these passages are printed in "Biblical Sources," pp. 163–66.)

In the opening section of the poem, the narrator visits the place where his lost pearl had dropped to the ground and falls asleep on the plot of earth where she lies buried. In a dream he sees a maiden on the far side of a stream, and immediately recognizes her as his pearl. In the ensuing dialogue between them, an important theme emerges, namely, patience, or rather, impatience, linking *Pearl* with its sister poem—the narrator resembles Jonah in *Patience* in rebelling against God's will. The pearl maiden tells the dreamer that it is useless for him to lament his earthly loss, behaving like a wounded deer that flings itself wildly about:

> Better to cross yourself, and bless
> The name of the Lord, whatever he send;
> No good can come of your willfulness;
> Who bears bad luck must learn to bend.
> Though like a stricken doe, my friend,
> You plunge and bray, with loud lament,
> This way and that, yet in the end
> As He decrees, you must consent.   (VI.4)°

With this we may compare the narrator's advice to himself in *Patience*, lines 7–8: "Then better for me to bear the brunt as it befalls / Than harp on my hardships, though my heart mislike."

The Story

The story of the poem, on its most literal level, is easy to follow. As it opens, the narrator mourns a pearl of supreme value, and we soon realize that the terms in which he describes it apply not only to a precious gem but also to a girl. His

---

° Roman numerals refer to sections and arabic numerals to stanzas within sections.

111

"secret pearl" has slipped from him into the ground; sweet herbs and spice plants have sprung up where it is buried. The bereaved man visits the spice garden, where he gives way to inconsolable grief and at last falls into a deep swoon. As his body lies asleep, his soul is transported to a resplendent landscape of unearthly beauty. Here he wanders about, his grief forgotten. But soon his way is blocked by a river that he wants above all else to cross, for the country beyond it is even lovelier than that on the nearer side—paradise, he thinks, must surely be there. As he searches for a ford, he sees on the other side of the river a being who is at once a "child" and a "maiden" of stately bearing, dressed in royal robes and wearing a magnificent crown. Her dress is wholly white, adorned with many pearls; a single pearl of great price lies upon her breast. The sight of her stabs his heart, for he recognizes her as one he once knew well, who was "nearer to him than aunt or niece." The apparition comes down the shore on the other side of the river and greets him graciously. He hails her in return as his lost, lamented pearl, but then elicits from her the first of a series of rebukes by complaining that she, lost to him, dwells in bliss while he is left to mourn.

This speech and the pearl maiden's answer initiate a conversation between the two that takes up most of the rest of the poem. We know the narrator to be a Christian; even in his grief at the outset, he expresses his awareness of the nature of Christ and the "comfort" that is, at least theoretically, to be derived from it. But his knowledge of doctrine seems not to be matched by understanding, and the pearl maiden must dispel a number of misapprehensions on his part. He cannot understand why he may not cross the stream and join her in blessedness forthwith. He does not see how she can be a queen in heaven when that rank is held by the Virgin Mary; no one could take Mary's crown from her who did not surpass her in some respect, yet Mary is "singular," peerless, like the phoenix. He finds it unjust that royal rank should have been bestowed on one whose accomplishments in life were negligible, who did not live two years on earth and could not even say her prayers or recite the creed. To resolve this last difficulty, the pearl maiden tells him the New Testament parable of the vineyard (Matthew 20), according to which the owner of the vineyard pays each laborer the same wage, a single penny, for his day's work, no matter how late the hour at which it began; the owner of the vineyard stands for God, and the "penny" is eternal life in the heavenly kingdom. But this in turn baffles the dreamer. The equal wage is unreasonable, he says, and what is more, it contradicts a statement in the Bible that he can quote, that God "render[s] unto every man according to his works" (Psalm 61:13 [A.V. 62:12]).

At this point (which is also the halfway point of the poem), the pearl maiden's exposition shifts its emphasis from justice and right to grace and mercy. All human beings, as a result of Adam's disobedience to God, are born in sin and condemned to physical death and then to the second death of everlasting damnation. But Adam's guilt was redeemed by the voluntary death of Christ, which also expressed God's boundless love for humanity. The blood that ran from the pierced side of Christ on the cross symbolizes redemption, and the water that came with it signifies the sacrament of baptism, administered by the church, which brings redemption to the individual soul. A baptized child who dies in infancy has, it is true, done no works of righteousness, but neither has it sinned, whereas the best human beings sin constantly and must repeatedly be returned to a state of grace through contrition and penance, also under the aegis of the church. The dead infant is an "innocent"—literally, one who has done no harm; the claim of such spotless souls to the bliss of heaven is wholly in accord with reason and indeed is clearer than that of the righteous person.

The pearl maiden has spoken sternly, and she has matched the dreamer's quotation from the Psalms with another, more threatening one, to the effect that no one shall be justified in the sight of the Lord (Psalm 142:2 [A.V. 143]). Her tone now changes as she speaks of the tenderness of the living Jesus, who invited the little children to come to him. The figure of the child unspotted by sin knocking at the gate of the kingdom of heaven, which will open straightway to receive him, opens a new phase in the development of the poem in which materials from the Old Testament, the Gospels, and the Book of Revelation, as interpreted in early church tradition, are woven together in language of unsurpassed intensity and power. The pearl now enters for the first time in its major symbolic role as the "one pearl of great price" in the parable told by Jesus in the Gospel of Matthew, for which the merchant seeking goodly pearls sold all he had. The maiden explains that the pearl is like the heavenly kingdom; it is spotless, like the souls of the innocent; it is perfectly round and thus "endless," like eternity; it is "blithe" and thus represents the bliss of the redeemed.

Endlessness here does not mean "infinite continuance," as the modern reader might think. Rather, eternity means freedom from measurements of time, as the circumference of a circle is free from interruptions, that is, from beginnings and ends. In the parable of the vineyard, it is significant that the penny symbolizing the heavenly reward is circular in form, and that in some interpretations of the parable it was identified with the communion wafer, also circular. Communion, for the faithful Christian, prefigures oneness with the divine in eternal happiness. Because this reward, for all who receive it, is "beyond price," comparative values such as "first" and "last," "higher" and "lower," have no meaning within it. The pearl of great price is, in fact, the "one pure pearl" visible on the maiden's breast, bestowed on her by the Lamb at the time of their wedding in token of the peace of heaven and the spotlessness for which he loved her.

Just as the dreamer had supposed that there could be only one queen in heaven, so he now supposes that the pearl maiden, in becoming the bride of the Lamb, must have been preferred to all others, including many women who had lived and died for Christ in saintly fashion. But the maiden, carefully distinguishing between two similar words in Middle English, explains that although she is indeed spotless (*maskeles*, or immaculate), she is not unique (*makeles*, or matchless). She reveals herself to be one of the 144,000 virgins seen with the Lamb on Mount Sion in the New Jerusalem by Saint John the Divine and described by him in the Apocalypse, or (see Biblical Sources,

p. 164) Book of Revelation. These in turn were identified in medieval tradition with the Holy Innocents whose martyrdom is commemorated yearly by the church—the children under the age of two whom Herod killed, thinking thus to kill the infant Jesus. The pearl maiden, who did not live two years on earth, has joined this celestial company. The bridegroom to whom all of them alike are wedded, and with whom they live in joy, is the Lamb of God, invoked by Isaiah in the Old Testament as he that takes away the sins of the world, condemned to death in Jerusalem and crucified there, and seen in heaven beside the throne of God by Saint John the Divine (see Biblical Sources, p. 164).

This exposition gives rise to another misunderstanding on the dreamer's part. The pearl maiden has told him that she lives with the Lamb, but that cannot be in "Jerusalem," for she is there on the other side of the river and Jerusalem is on earth, in the kingdom of Judea. This confusion in turn is resolved by the maiden, who distinguishes between the Old Jerusalem, where the trial and Crucifixion of Christ took place, and the New Jerusalem, seen descending out of heaven by Saint John (Apocalypse 21). In accordance with the traditional interpretations of the name *Jerusalem* as "city of God" and "sight of peace," this latter is the city where the souls of the blessed, once their bodies have suffered earthly death and decay, dwell with God in eternal harmony and rest.

The request the dreamer now makes, as he speaks for the last time, poignantly reflects his love for the maiden in her former condition as a human child. He wants, he says, to see the place where she lives, the great city and the "blissful bower," the wedding chamber, within it. Here, late in the unfoldment of the narrative as also in *Sir Gawain and the Green Knight*, we learn what has set the entire sequence of events in motion, beginning with the narrator's swoon over the mound in the herb garden. The pearl maiden tells him that no mortal may enter the celestial city, but that she has obtained permission from the Lamb for him to see it from the outside (XVI.5). She has, that is, interceded for him that he may be brought out of his spiritual impasse, mediating between him and God, as the saints, when men pray to them, are thought to do. Beneath her seemingly impersonal, if not cold, attitude toward him during much of their conversation lies the loving concern implicit in this act.

The description of the celestial Jerusalem, seen by the dreamer across the river from a hill to which the pearl maiden has directed him, follows closely—much of the time almost word for word—the description in the Apocalypse, as if the poet wished thereby to insist on the authenticity of the vision (see Biblical Sources, p. 165). There are the twelve foundations, each made of a single precious stone; the cubic shape as Saint John saw it measured; the twelve pearly gates; the golden streets; and, within the city, the throne of God and the elders seated around it. Then, as, on earth, the risen full moon begins to shine in the east while it is still daylight (such is the poem's unforgettable simile), the dreamer becomes aware of a procession moving toward the throne, led by the Lamb and made up of the thousands upon thousands of his brides. All are dressed as the pearl maiden had been dressed; all wear the pearl of great price. In a

moment of all but unbearable poignancy, he sees among the others in the pro-
cession his "little queen" (XIX.5). As he recognizes her, the entrancement of
spiritual vision gives way to that delight in the sight of the beloved that for
earthly beings is inseparable from the desire to possess. He rushes toward the
river, determined to cross it, come what may, and wakens from his dream.

Symbolism and Theme

Such is the density of symbolic meaning in *Pearl* that the story of the poem,
maiden and all, has sometimes been interpreted wholly in allegorical terms.
But the force of certain details seems clearly circumstantial, pointing toward
the story of an individual man as much as to that of the Christian soul in gen-
eral. The commonsense view has prevailed in more recent criticism: that the
poem is at once autobiographical and allegorical, founded on an actual experi-
ence of bereavement and dealing with that experience in terms of Christian
symbols and doctrine.

  Another question of interpretation has to do with the so-called obtuseness
of the dreamer. It is implausible (the argument runs) that he, a professed
Christian, should not already understand the doctrinal points the maiden is
making, should keep asking virtually the same question again and again. But
his persistent wrongheadedness makes sense if we consider how deeply
founded it is in the limitations of the mortal perspective. Seeing the pearl
maiden standing on the other side of a river, he naturally concludes that she is
"there" in the same sense in which another person would be there, a certain
distance away, in life. Actually, the dreamed encounter by the river, within
speaking range, symbolizes the maiden's role as an intermediary between the
dreamer and the heavenly realm to which he does not belong. Even as the
maiden speaks to him, one is tempted to say, she is in the procession moving
through the streets of the celestial Jerusalem in the company of the Lamb, as
the dreamer sees her to be at the end of the poem. Yet the procession itself,
like the marriage relationship, is a symbol of spiritual union, the visible for the
invisible. Such questions as Where is she really? What is she really doing? have
no answer, indeed no meaning, on this plane.

  So too with the pearl. At the beginning of the poem, it stands for what has
been most precious to the narrator in this world—in Shakespeare's words,
there where he has garnered up his heart. Seeing the maiden, recognizing her
(so it seems) as the very being he so loves, the dreamer naturally thinks that
what he has found is what he had lost. He does not and at this stage cannot
realize that his earthly pearl has passed into another mode of existence. All
that was truly precious in her is now forever merged in the transcendent values
of the heavenly kingdom. She can be possessed only by possessing that king-
dom, and that can be possessed only by giving up the things of this world, as
the merchant sold all he had to obtain the one pearl of the parable.

But between earthly and divine orders there is a separation that cannot be bridged by the unaided efforts of the human mind. The characteristics of the pearl as the maiden describes them in telling the parable of the merchant are signs of this radical discontinuity. Having the form of a circle, the pearl, as previously observed, stands for eternity, the existence of God in a timeless present from the perspective of which human history is a completed, static pattern. Human beings are trapped in progressive time, looking back from the present to the past and forward to an unknown future. Eternity is not perpetual duration, "longer than" time; it is the absence of time. So too with the worth of the heavenly pearl. It is not "greater than" the worth of anything on earth; it is absolute, literally "beyond measure." Nearer and farther, earlier and later, lower and higher, less and more—all are interdependent manifestations of a dimensional mode of being in which human beings, under the governance of changing fortune, move toward certain death. "We look before and after, And pine for what is not": the inner dissatisfaction and perpetual striving inevitable in such a world have their otherworldly counterparts in the peace of heaven. To dwell there is to possess a happiness that, again, is not "greater than" human happiness, but perfect, without qualification.

From this disparity arise all the paradoxes and contradictions that baffle the dreamer so. That everyone in heaven is a king or queen; that the "penny" of eternal life, the wage of everyone who works in the vineyard, has no relation to comparative deserts; that everyone in heaven has the same reward "no matter how little or great his gains" (XI.1)—such statements cannot be understood in commonsense, "realistic" terms. They are attempts to express in language what language was not designed to express.

The dreamer, for all that he is transported to a "place" of visionary enlightenment, cannot escape the earthly habit of comparative measurement. *More*, in fact, is the link word of two sections of the poem: in section III, at the beginning of the dream, where, released from sorrow, the dreamer experiences a joy that intensifies until he is brought to a halt at the river, and in section X, where the laborers who came earliest to the vine want their wages commensurately increased. In section XV, when the maiden is telling of her life in heaven as a bride of the Lamb, the link word is *nevertheless*; the word *more*, which appears twice in stanza 1, now signifies values that exceed human imagining. The dream breaks off because the dreamer, having been granted a sight of his pearl in its heavenly setting, wants something more and rushes into the stream to attain it. Reproaching himself after he has awakened, he reflects ruefully that "always men would have and hoard / And gain the more, the more they get" (XX.4).

Yet the experience of the dream does change him, and the evolution of his attitudes and feelings in the course of the poem breathes dramatic life into what would otherwise have been unrelieved didacticism. At first, as we saw, he is querulous and self-centered, then brash and presumptuous in assuming that he and the glorious personage on the other side of the river exist on the same plane. For this latter misapprehension he receives her coldest rebuke. But then he takes an important step: forsaking his obstinacy and confessing his foolishness, he throws himself on God's mercy in a kind of self-administered baptism (VII.1):

> As water flows from a fountainhead
> I cast myself in His mercy clear.

More important, he stops thinking solely about what he has suffered and what he desires, and begins to sense his own ignorance about what it is he is seeing. His inquiry to the maiden about her way of life (VII.3) has, at the moment of asking, profounder implications than he or we realize. The answer, it turns out, is life itself—in terms of Christian doctrine, the life beyond mortality compared to which life as we know it is a continual dying. By the time the maiden has expounded the parable of the vineyard and justified the place in heaven of the innocent, the dreamer is filled with awe, overwhelmed by her angelic aspect and more than earthly magnificence even as he remains wrong-headed, still trying to understand her heavenly station in terms of what he knows. His last request is made with the utmost reverence and humility, though it too is humanly motivated, reflecting the same partiality that leads at last to his ill-fated attempt to cross the river.

What, in the end, has he learned? We have already heard his self-admonition in the concluding section. If, he thinks, he had been less impatient, more willing to be content with what had been granted him, he would not have been banished so soon from the country of his vision. But this facile moralizing hardly addresses the problem of his initial despair, and a far deeper lesson is implicit in the terms of his farewell to the pearl maiden (XX.3).

> Then sorrow broke from my burning breast;
> "O honored Pearl," I said, "how dear
> Was your every word and wise behest
> In this true vision vouchsafed me here.
> If you in a garland never sere
> Are set by that Prince all provident,
> Then happy am I in dungeon drear
> That He with you is well content."

In the symbol of the garland, a completed circle, we see an intimation of eternity on the speaker's part. The disparity between garland and dungeon further suggests his realization that the mortal and immortal realms are closed off from each other, that the "distance" between the two cannot be crossed as if it were a river. It is significant that nowhere in the final stanzas does he speak of his hope to be reunited with his pearl in heaven, or of his anticipation of that reunion, in expressing his reconcilement to his earthly lot. The deepest lesson he has been taught is an imaginative apprehension of what his lost pearl now is, part of an everlasting and changeless order. Such a garland, unlike one made of earthly flowers, cannot fade, nor can the man lose it who has learned to value it properly. Knowing this, and grateful for the grace that has accorded him the enlightening vision, the speaker commits to God his pearl and his poem, calling down on both the blessing of Christ and praying that all men may be made conformable to the divine will.

The Literary Background

We have so far seen *Pearl* exclusively in relation to the Bible and Christian tradition. But it is an imaginative, as well as a doctrinal, work, and we must therefore say something about its literary background as well. Knowing little or nothing about the author's life, we cannot attempt a full account of influences and sources as we might for a Yeats or a Stevens. But it is obvious that *Pearl* shares important elements of theme and dramatic presentation with two major literary works that were so widely read in the Middle Ages that the poet would inevitably have known them: *The Consolation of Philosophy* and *The Romance of the Rose.*

    The Consolation of Philosophy, like *Pearl,* has its point of departure in the circumstances and mental state of its narrator. Boethius, who lived in the late fifth and early sixth centuries, was thrown into prison and finally executed after having enjoyed prosperity and power under the Roman emperor Theodoric. At the beginning of the *Consolation* he speaks as a captive, complaining of the conditions in which he finds himself, unable to reconcile himself to the loss of his former good fortune. He is visited by a feminine being of supernatural majesty whom he belatedly recognizes as Philosophy, the "nurse of his youth." There follows a lengthy conversation between the two in which the prisoner's role is largely passive. Philosophy rebukes him for his despair and consoles him by gradually leading him to a full understanding of the relationship between transitory and lasting goods. The former are the gifts to human beings on earth of the changeable goddess Fortuna, who will inevitably take them away. The latter belong to the human soul, which is also the human rational intelligence; once possessed, they cannot be lost.

    The lesson of the *Consolation,* though it is presented in philosophic rather than religious terms, is much the same as what I have described as the implicit lesson of *Pearl.* But if the "meaning" of *Pearl* is to this extent Boethian, the emotional climate of the poem is far otherwise. *Pearl* is not only a dialogue affording doctrinal enlightenment, it is a dream vision suffused with the ardor of what we now call romantic love, and was then called *amour courtois* (See the General Introduction, p. xxiii). It is especially reminiscent of the first part of the *Romance of the Rose,* which describes a wonderful dream that begins on a May morning. The youthful narrator (he is, he tells us, at the age when love rules men's hearts) finds himself in a delightful landscape, which shares with the dream landscape of *Pearl* such features as leafy trees and bushes and joyfully singing birds, though these are more naturalistically described. Wandering about, delighting in the beauty of the scene, he pauses to bathe his face in a clear stream, then follows it along its bank. At last he comes to a garden or park surrounded by a high wall, to which he succeeds in gaining access. Neither the garden nor its inhabitants, chief among whom is the god of love, need be described here; more important with relation to *Pearl* is the dreamer's discovery, in the garden, of a fountain at the bottom of which are two brilliant crystal stones. He gazes into the fountain and sees reflected there a bush laden with blooming red roses to which he is immediately attracted. Seen close at hand, it enraptures him with its sweetness, and one especially beautiful rosebud becomes the object of his love. The story that follows tells of his frustrated attempts to gain possession of the rose.

The *Romance of the Rose* is an allegory of love on the human plane. But the conventional language of secular love poetry in medieval times was also used in a considerable body of religious poetry addressed to the Virgin Mary. In *Pearl*, the feelings of a father for his lost infant daughter, who appears to him as an angelic visitant, are expressed in this same language. As has often been noted, the maiden has the typical physical attributes of the idealized mistress—slender figure, gray eyes, hair like gold, flawless complexion—and the terms in which the dreamer addresses her—"my jewel," "my sweet," "my adored one"—are such as a lover would use to his lady. Yet she is also a virgin and a saint, and other terms applied to her—"special spice," "immaculate bride," "immaculate maid so meek and mild"—clearly associate her with Mary. The educational process dramatized in *Pearl* involves not the negation of human passion but its removal from the realm of mutability—a lifting up of the heart to higher things.

Design and Its Significance

One of the most striking and significant aspects of the poem is its conformity to an all-encompassing and highly elaborated design. Elements of this design are found separately elsewhere, but the intricacy of their combination in *Pearl* is unmatched in English poetry before or since. The twelve-line stanza used by the poet is found in other Middle English poems on religious subjects; the stanzas of these poems characteristically end in a repeated or varied refrain. The rhyme scheme, *ababababbcbc*, presents extraordinary difficulties for poet and would-be translator. It requires no fewer than four *a* rhymes and six *b* rhymes per stanza, and the repetition of the refrain calls for a number of *c* rhymes as well. *Pearl* is divided into twenty sections, each of which, with the exception of section XV, contains five stanzas. The last line of each of the five stanzas making up a given section ends in a link word that is sometimes part of a repeated phrase ("without a spot," "is enough for all"); the same link word also appears in the first lines of all but one of the five stanzas. The sections themselves are joined by the device of "concatenation," or overlapping repetition: the link word of a given section appears in the first line of the first stanza of the following section. For example, in the last stanza of section III, the link word *more* appears in the first and last lines; it makes its final appearance in the first line of the first stanza of section IV, which ends with the new linking phrase "pearls of price":

> The more I mused on that fair face,
> The person of that most precious one,
> Such gladness grew in my heart by grace
> As little before had been, or none.
> I longed to call across that space
> But found my powers of speech had flown;
> To meet her in so strange a place—
> Such a sight, in truth, might shock or stun!
> Then raised she up her brow, that shone
> All ivory pale on that far shore,
> That stabbed my heart to look upon
> And ever the longer, more and more.
>
> More dread diminished my delight;
> I stood stock still and dared not call.
> With eyes wide open and mouth shut tight
> I stood there tame as hawk in hall.
> Unearthly, I knew, must be that plight;
> I dreaded much what might befall,
> Lest she I viewed should vanish quite
> And leave me there to stare and stall.
> That slender one, so smooth, so small,
> Unblemished, void of every vice,
> Rose up in robes imperial,
> A precious pearl in pearls of price.

Finally, it is important to note that the link word of the final section also appears, in rhyming position, in the first line of the first stanza of the poem. The end is thus connected back to the beginning in a kind of temporal circularity. The presence of the statement "I am alpha and omega, the first and the last," in chapters 1 and 22 of the Apocalypse (Revelation) has been thought to be an instance of this same device. A modern example of both circularity and concatenation is Donne's "La Corona" ("The Crown"), in which each of seven sonnets has as its first line the last line of the preceding one, and the last line of the last is also the first line of the first. The thematic significance of such a pattern in a poem so entitled need scarcely be pointed out, and we are reminded that circularity is also a symbolic attribute of the pearl.

Circularity or roundness is a symbol not only of eternity but of perfection: In the *Consolation*, Philosophy quotes the ancient philosopher Parmenides to the effect that "the divine essence is 'in body like a sphere, perfectly rounded on all sides.'" Another visible symbol of perfection is symmetry, exemplified most notably in *Pearl* in the shape of the celestial Jerusalem. The poet repeats the description given by Saint John, who saw the city measured; it was twelve thousand furlongs in length, breadth, and height, a perfect cube. Symmetry is further exemplified by the outer walls of the city, each with its three gates. The number twelve is the total number of gates, the number of the trees growing beside the river of life, and the base of the city's measurement in furlongs. It is also the number of lines in each stanza of *Pearl*. The square of a number is a mathematical expression of symmetry, and the square of twelve, multiplied by a thousand, is the number of the virgins accompanying the Lamb. Given these facts, we cannot fail to find it significant that the one hundred one stanzas of *Pearl* have a total of 1,212 lines. But one hundred is also the square of the "perfect number," ten, in which the decimal sequence returns to one plus zero, and the 101st stanza of the poem can be thought of as overlapping, and thus coinciding with, the first stanza, to close the circle. Corroborating evidence of the *Pearl* poet's interest in number and numerical design is found in *Sir Gawain and the Green Knight* and *Saint Erkenwald* (see the introductions to those poems, pp. 189 and 169, respectively).

It is natural for the modern reader to wonder whether all this patterning in *Pearl* is mere display—artifice for artifice's sake. But the very question implies that the answer may be found in the relationship between display and purpose, form and content, or, to use a characteristically medieval analogy often applied to literary works, husk and kernel. Most obviously in the realm of tangible artifacts, painstaking elaboration signifies and confers value. In early times, the hand-copied manuscript was such an artifact; we think of the gorgeously bound and illuminated Bibles, missals, and books of hours whose material worth was a sign that they bore a priceless message. We think too of the medieval reliquary with its profusion of ornament worked in ivory or metal. And these in turn suggest an important group of images in *Pearl:* the jeweler, the jewel, and the enclosing box. In section V, the dreamer tells the maiden that since he has been separated from her he has been "a joyless jeweler"; the maiden replies that he is mistaken—his pearl cannot be lost to him when it is enclosed in so comely a "coffer" as the garden in which he sees her. There is a grim pun here, for *coffer* in Middle English could also mean "coffin." (I have substituted *casket*, which has a similar mortuary meaning in American English.) The root meaning of the word *garden* is in fact "enclosed place"; the garden of Eden where Adam and Eve first lived was a bounded precinct, a kind of park. Heaven was commonly visualized as a celestial version of the earthly paradise. Alternatively, it was visualized as a city, the celestial Jerusalem. This latter, having walls, is also a kind of enclosure or box—a coffer, fashioned sumptuously of precious substances, containing the treasure of eternal life. An analogy becomes irresistible: the verbal artifact called *Pearl* is itself a kind of painstakingly crafted container, embellished with every device of language in order that it may be worthy of its contents, the vision of the pearl maiden and the precious teachings she imparts.

Design in *Pearl* has an additional dimension of significance. Like any literary work, the poem exists temporally rather than spatially; it must be experienced part by part. But having been experienced, it can be contemplated—in terms of its numerical form, its sections, its stanzas, its rhymes, and its metrical patterns—as a patterned object. Moving through time toward a condition of timelessness, the poem fulfills the aspiration it dramatically represents.

The Translation

In translating *Pearl*, I have reproduced the schemes of rhyme, repetition, and concatenation described above; whatever difficulties these present, the poem could scarcely retain its identity without them. I have also followed the poet as best I could in the linking of stressed syllables by initial alliteration, especially in passages of heightened dramatic intensity. Language in these latter is at times loaded with alliteration, consonance, and other linkages among sounds to the point where the shapes of words threaten to become more conspicuous than their sense, and similar effects have found their way into my translation. Lines such as

> His gifts gush forth like a spring in spate
> Or a stream in a gully that runs in rains. (XI.1)

or

> As in his flock no fleck is seen,
> His hallowed halls are wholly bright. (XVI.3)

may strike the modern reader as overwrought, but they have their counterparts in the poem and would not, I think, have offended the ears to which it was first addressed.

Another kind of verbal extravagance in which *Pearl* abounds is wordplay. The necessity of repeating the link words leads to the sort of pun that exploits the range of senses of a single word, as when *spot* means both "speck" and "place," *deem* both "express an opinion" and "pronounce sentence," and *right* both "valid claim" and "rectitude." But the *Pearl* poet did not eschew the lowliest form of wit either. In the original, he substitutes *now* for the link word *enow* "enough" in XI.2, and in section XVI uses two words of identical form: *mote* "speck" and *mote* "walled city" (related to *moat*). (Elsewhere in the poem he puns on yet another word spelled *mote*, modern *moot*, meaning "debate" or "strife.") He seems to rejoice in the phonetic identity in his dialect of *lamb* and *lamp*, writing "God himself was their lamplight [the text has the spelling *lombelyght*], The Lamb their lantern" (XVIII.2). These homonymic puns cannot be reproduced in modern English, but in view of their presence in the original, I have felt justified in combining *wholly* and *holy* as a link word in section XVI—a pun that is in fact of the more respectable sort, because the two words go back to a single root.

As for the diction of the translation, I have tried to conform to the original in making it at once traditional and varied. It would not have occurred to the author of *Pearl* to avoid formulaic combinations of words, whether poetic or colloquial, or to think of such combinations as "clichés" in the modern derogatory sense. I have made use of some distinctively literary diction, as the *Pearl* poet himself did, though I have tried to avoid burned-out archaisms. The occasional echo of Milton, Shakespeare, or the King James Bible, when it suggested itself, was allowed to stay; and stock phrases such as "heart's desire," "daily round," "lost and lamented," "royal road," and others have been incorporated as in keeping with the style both of *Pearl* and of *Sir Gawain and the Green Knight*. I have also emulated a complementary effect of diction peculiar to *Pearl*, of the deployment or display of abundant resources. One has the impression that the poet never inadvertently repeats an adjective, a rhyming combination, or even a rhyme sound. Important attributes such as spotlessness, brightness, and happiness seem to be described in endlessly fresh combinations of words, and this aspect of the language offers a particular challenge to the translator, as well as conferring on the poem a richness befitting its character as an artifact.

In *Pearl*, if in any poem, we see the poet offering up his craft, creating expressive power out of the very restrictions imposed on expression. To emulate such an achievement is an act of the greatest temerity, especially because, as with dancing on pointe, the limitations accepted by an artist are justified only insofar as they are transcended. The result of my long labors may or may not be found worthy of comparison with the original; "if not," in the words of Emily Dickinson,

> I had
> The transport of the Aim.

Pearl[*]

1

Pearl, that a prince is well content
To give a circle of gold to wear,
Boldly I say, all Orient
Brought forth none precious like to her;
5 So comely in every ornament,
So slender her sides, so smooth they were,
Ever my mind was bound and bent
To set her apart without a peer.°   *equal*
In a garden of herbs I lost my dear;[1]
10 Through grass to ground away it shot;
Now, lovesick, the heavy loss I bear
Of that secret pearl without a spot.

2

Since in that spot it sped from me so,
Often I watched and wished for that grace
15 That once was wont to° banish woe   *used to*
And bless with brightness all my days;
That clutches my heart in cruel throe
And causes my blood to rage and race,
Yet sweeter songs could no man know
20 Than silence taught my ear to trace;
And many there came, to think of her face
With cover of clay so coldly fraught:°   *freighted, burdened*
O earth, you mar a gem past praise,
My secret pearl without a spot.

° Notes for *Patience* appear on pages 25–28.

3

25 That spot with spice must spring and spread
Where riches rotted in narrow room;
Blossoms white and blue and red
Lift now alight in blaze of noon;
Flower and fruit could never fade
30 Where pearl plunged deep in earthen tomb,
For the seed must die to bear the blade
That the wheat may be brought to harvest home.°
Good out of good to all and some:
Such a seed could never have come to nought
35 Nor spice in splendor spare to bloom
From that precious pearl without a spot.

4

To that especial spot I hied
And entered that same garden green
In August at a festive tide[2]
40 When corn is cut with scythe-edge keen.
On the mound where pearl went tumbling wide,
Leaf vied with leaf in shade and sheen:
Gillyflower and ginger on every side
And peonies peerless blooming between.
45 But fairer yet, and all unseen,
Was the fragrance that my senses sought;
There, I know, is the dear demesne°   *dwelling place*
Of my precious pearl without a spot.

5

Before that spot with head inclined
50 I stretched my hand in stark despair;
My heart lamented, deaf and blind,
Though reason reconciled my care.
I mourned my pearl so close confined
With thoughts in throng contending there;
55 Comfort of Christ might come to mind
But wretched will would not forbear.
I fell upon that flowerbed fair;
Such odor seized my brain distraught
I slipped into slumber unaware,
60 On that precious pearl without a spot.

° John 12:24.

II

1

My soul forsook that spot in space
And left my body on earth to bide.
My spirit sped, by God's good grace,
On a quest where marvels multiplied.
65 I knew not where in the world it was,
But I saw I was set where cliffs divide;
A forest flourished in that place
Where many rich rocks might be descried.
The glory that flashed there far and wide
70 Eye could not credit, nor mind invent;
Pure cloth of gold were pale beside
Such rich and rare embellishment.

2

Embellished were those hills in view
With crystal cliffs as clear as day
75 And groves of trees with boles° as blue   *trunks*
As indigo silks of rich assay;°   *assessed value*
The leaves, like silver burnished new,
Slide rustling rife on every spray;
As shifts of cloud let sunshine through,
80 They shot forth light in shimmering play.
The gravel stones that strewed the way
Were precious pearls of orient;
The beams of the sun but blind and gray
Beside such bright embellishment.

3

85 Amid those hills embellished bright
My sorrows fled in full retreat;
Fragrance of fruits with great delight
Filled me like food that mortals eat.
Birds of all colors fanned in flight
90 Their iridescent pinions° fleet,   *wings*
But lute or lyre, by craft or sleight,
Could not make music half so sweet,
For while in time their wings they beat
In glad accord their voices blent;
95 With more of mirth might no man meet
Than hear each brave embellishment.

4

So all embellished was the land
Where Fortune bears me on my way;
No tongue is worthy to command
100 Fit words those splendors to display.
I walked along with bliss at hand;
No slope so steep to make me stay;
The further, the fairer the pear trees stand,
The spice plants spread, the blossoms sway,
105 And hedgerows run by banks as gay
As glittering golden filament;°   *spun thread*
I came to the shore of a waterway:³
Dear God, what brave embellishment!

5

Embellishing those waters deep,
110 Banks of pure beryl greet my gaze;
Sweetly the eddies swirl and sweep
With a rest and a rush in murmurous phrase;
Stones in the stream their colors steep,
Gleaming like glass⁴ where sunbeam strays,
115 As stars, while men of the marshlands sleep,
Flash in winter from frosty space;
For every one was a gem to praise,
A sapphire or emerald opulent°   *rich*
That seemed to set the pool ablaze,
120 So brilliant their embellishment.

III

1

Embellished with such wondrous grace
Were wood and water and shining plain,
My pleasures multiplied apace,
Conquered my cares, dispelled my pain.
125 By the brink of a river that runs a race
Blissful I walked with busy brain;
The more I explored that plashy place
The greater strength did gladness gain.
As proof of Fortune's purpose plain
130 Makes a man's heart to sink or soar,
He whom she plies with bliss or bane
Of what he draws is dealt still more.

2

More of bliss was there to prize
Than ever my tongue could testify,
135 For earthly heart might not suffice
To sustain one tenth of that pure joy.
It could not be but paradise
Lay beyond those noble banks, thought I,⁵
And the stream itself seemed a device,
140 A mark to know a boundary by.
Those peerless precincts to espy
I need but gain the farther shore;
But I dared not wade, for the water ran high,
And longing mastered me more and more.

3

145 More than ever and ever the more
To cross that river was all my care,
For lovely though this landscape were,
What lay beyond was past compare.
I stared about, scanning the shore
150 For a ford to afford me thoroughfare,
But dangers direr than before
Appeared, the more I wandered there.
And still it seemed I should not forbear
For dangers, with delights in store;
155 But now was broached a new affair
My mind was moved by, more and more.

4

More marvels now amazed me quite:
Beyond that stream, strange to behold,
There rose a cliff of crystal bright
160 With resplendent rays all aureoled.°   *haloed*
At the foot was seated in plain sight
A maiden child of mortal mold,
A gracious lady gowned in white;
I knew her well, I had seen her of old.
165 As fine-spun floss of burnished gold,
So shone she, peerless, as of yore;
I gazed on her with joy untold,
The longer, I knew her more and more.

5

The more I mused on that fair face,
170 The person of that most precious one,
Such gladness grew in my heart by grace
As little before had been, or none.
I longed to call across that space
But found my power of speech had flown;
175 To meet her in so strange a place—
Such a sight, in truth, might shock or stun!
Then raised she up her brow, that shone
All ivory pale on that far shore,
That stabbed my heart to look upon
180 And ever the longer, more and more.

IV

1

More dread diminished my delight;
I stood stock still and dared not call.
With eyes wide open and mouth shut tight
I stood there tame as hawk in hall.
185 Unearthly, I knew, must be that plight;
I dreaded much what might befall,
Lest she I viewed should vanish quite
And leave me there to stare and stall.
That slender one, so smooth, so small,
190 Unblemished, void of every vice,
Rose up in robes imperial,
A precious pearl in pearls of price.

2

Pearls of price in ample store
Were there to see by grace divine
195 As she, approaching, shone on shore
Like *fleurs-de-lys* to kings condign.°   *suitable*
Her surcoat of white linen pure°
Had open sides of fair design,
And filigree on bands it bore
200 Where pearls in lavish lustre join,
And lappets° large, with double line   *hanging folds of cloth*

° Apocalypse 19:7–8 (A.V. Revelation); cf. VII.5.5–6.

Of pearls set round in that same guise;
Her gown of that same linen fine,
And all bedecked with pearls of price.

3

205 Her priceless crown with pearls alone
Was set, in fashion fit and fair;
High pinnacles° upon it shone,   *decorative peaks*
And florets° carved with craft and care.   *small flowers*
Other headdress had she none
210 To frame her ivory forehead bare;
As earl or duke by royal throne,
So sage she seemed, so grave her air.
About her shoulders fell her hair
Like gold spun fine by artifice,
215 Whose deepest hue yet had a share
Of pallor pure of pearls of price.

4

Pearls of price in rows ornate
On hem, on side, on wristband rest;
No other gem could suit her state
220 Who was in white so richly dressed.
But one pure pearl, a wonder great,
Was set secure upon her breast;
A man might ponder long and late
Ere its full worth were well assessed.
225 I think no tongue could ever attest°   *affirm*
A discourteous thought of that device,
So white it was, so wholly blessed,
And proudest placed of pearls of price.

5

In pearls of price she moved at ease
230 Toward the rim of the river that flowed so free;
No gladder man from here to Greece
Than I, that blessèd sight to see.
She was nearer my heart than aunt or niece:
So much the more my joy must be;
235 She proffered parley° in sign of peace,   *offered conference*
Bowed womanlike with bended knee,
Took off her crown of high degree

And bade me welcome with courteous voice;
That I was born O well for me
240 To greet that girl in pearls of price.

V

1

"O pearl," said I, "in pearls of price,
Are you my pearl come back again,
Lost and lamented with desolate sighs
In darkest night, alone and in vain?
245 Since you slipped to ground where grasses rise
I have wandered pensive, oppressed with pain,
And you in the bliss of paradise,
Beyond all passion and strife and strain.
What fate removed you from earth's domain
250 And left me hapless and heartsick there?
Since parting was set between us twain
I have been a joyless jeweler."

2

That jewel then with fair gems fraught
Lifted her face with eyes of gray,
255 Set on her crown and stood in thought,
And soberly then I heard her say,
"Sir, your tale is told for nought,
To say your pearl has gone away
That is closed in a coffer° so cunningly wrought   strongbox
260 As this same garden green and gay,
And here forever in joy to stay
Where lack nor loss can never come near;
Here were a casket fit to display
A prize for a proper jeweler.

3

265 "But, jeweler, if your mind is bound
To mourn for a gem in solitude,
Your care has set you a course unsound,
And a cause of a moment maddens your mood;
You lost a rose that grew in the ground:
270 A flower that fails and is not renewed,
But such is the coffer closing it round,
With the worth of a pearl it is now imbued.
And fate, you say, has robbed you of good,

That rendered you profit free and clear;
275 You blame a blessing misunderstood:
You are no proper jeweler."

4

A jewel to me then was this guest
And jewels her gentle sayings were.
"O blissful one," I said, "and best,
280 You have healed me wholly of heartache here!
To be excused I make request:
My pearl was away, I knew not where;
Now I have found it, now I shall rest,
And live with it ever, and make good cheer,
285 And love the Lord and his laws revere
That brought me the blissful sight of her.
Let me once cross and behold you near,
And I am a joyful jeweler!"

5

"Jeweler," said that gem at this,
290 "Such mockery comes of mortal pride!
Most ill advised your answer is
And errors grave your thoughts misguide.
Three statements you have made amiss;
Your words from your wit have wandered wide;
295 You think me set in this vale of bliss
For so you see me, the brook beside;
The second, you say you shall abide
With me in this far country here;
The third, to cross this deep divide,
300 Behooves° no joyful jeweler.   *befits*

VI

1

"I hold that jeweler little to praise
Who believes no more than meets the eye,
And little courtesy he displays
Who doubts the word of the Lord on high
305 That faithfully pledged your flesh to raise
Though Fortune made it fail and die:°
They twist the sense of his words and ways

° John 6:40.

Who believe what they see, and else deny;
And that is pride and obstinacy
310 And ill accords with honest intent,
To think each tale must be a lie
Except his reason give assent.

2

"Say, do you not, dissenting, strive
Against God's will that all should uphold?
315 Here in this land you mean to live—
You might ask leave to make so bold!
Nor can you with such ease contrive
To cross this water deep and cold;
Your body fair, with senses five,
320 Must first sink down in mire and mold,
For in Eden garden, in days of old,
Our fathers' father his life misspent;
Each man must suffer a death foretold
Ere God to this crossing give consent."

3

325 "Consent," said I, "to that hard fate
And you have cleft my heart in twain.
That which I lost I found but late—
And must I now forgo it again?
Why must I meet it and miss it straight?
330 My precious pearl has doubled my pain.
What use is treasure in worldly state
If a man must lose it and mourn in vain?
Now little I reck° what trials remain,   *care*
What bitter exile and banishment,
335 For Fortune is bound to be my bane
And suffer I must by her consent."

4

"Such dire presentiments of distress,"
Said she, "I cannot comprehend;
But grief for a loss that matters less
340 Makes many miss what might amend.
Better to cross yourself, and bless
The name of the Lord, whatever He send;
No good can come of your willfulness;

Who bears bad luck must learn to bend.
345 Though like a stricken doe, my friend,
You plunge and bray, with loud lament,
This way and that, yet in the end
As He decrees, you must consent.

5

"Dissent, indict Him through the years,
350 His step stirs not one inch astray.
No tittle is gained for all your tears,
Though you should grieve and never be gay.
Abate your bluster, be not so fierce,
And seek His grace as soon as you may,
355 For prayer has power to bite and pierce
And call compassion into play.
His mercy can wipe your tears away,
Redeem your loss, restore content,
But, grudge or be glad, agree or gainsay,°   *dispute*
360 All lies with Him to give consent."

VII

1

Then I assented, answering in dread,
"Let not my Lord be wrathful here
Though blindly I rave, with speech ill sped;
Mourning had made me mad, or near.
365 As water flows from a fountainhead
I cast myself in His mercy clear;
Heap no reproaches on my head
Though I should stray, my dearest dear,
But speak in charity and good cheer;
370 Be merciful, remembering this:
You gave me a heavy grief to bear,
Who once were ground of all my bliss.

2

"My bliss you have been and bitterest woe;
The grief was the greater as time ran on;
375 Since last I looked for you high and low
I could not tell where my pearl had gone.
I rejoice in it now as long ago,
And when we parted we were as one;

God forbid I should vex you so—
380 We meet so seldom at any milestone.
Your courtesy is second to none;
I am of earth, and speak amiss,
But the mercy of Christ and Mary and John,
These are the ground of all my bliss.

3

385 "I see you set in bliss profound,
And I afflicted, felled by fate;
And little you care though I am bound
To suffer harm and hardship great;
But since we are met upon this ground
390 I would beseech, without debate,
That in sober speech you would expound
The life you lead both early and late.
Indeed, I am glad that your estate
Is raised to such honor and worthiness;
395 It is my joy to contemplate
And royal road of all my bliss."

4

"Now bliss befall you!" she replied
In form and feature that had no peer,
"And welcome here to walk and bide;
400 Such words are grateful to my ear.
Headstrong hearts and arrogant pride,
I tell you, are wholly detested here;
My Lord the Lamb is loath to chide,°   scold
For all are meek who behold Him near.
405 And when in His house you shall appear,
Be wholly devout in humbleness,
For that delights my Lord so dear
That is the ground of all my bliss.

5

"A blissful life I lead, you say;
410 You ask in what station I reside;
You know when pearl first slipped away
I was tender of age, by time untried.
But my Lord the Lamb whom all obey,
He took me to Him to be His bride,

₄₁₅ Crowned me queen in bliss to stay,
Forever and ever glorified.
And seized of° His heritage far and wide   *endowed with*
Am I, His love, being wholly His;
His royal rank, His praise, His pride
₄₂₀ Are root and ground of all my bliss."

VIII

1

"Oh, blissful one, can this be right?"
Said I, "Forgive me if I should err;
Are you the queen of heaven's height
Whom we in this world must all revere?
₄₂₅ We believe in Mary, a virgin bright,
Who bore to man God's Son so dear;
Now who could assume her crown, by right,
But she in some feature fairer were?⁶
Yet as none is lovely like unto her,
₄₃₀ We call her Phoenix of Araby,
Sent flawless from the artificer°   *maker*
As was our Queen of courtesy."

2

"Courteous Queen!" that blithe one said
Kneeling to ground with upturned face,
₄₃₅ "Matchless Mother, most lovely Maid,
Blessed beginner of every grace!"
Then rose she up, and silent stayed,
And spoke to me across that space:
"Sir, gifts are gained here, and prizes paid,
₄₄₀ But none on another presumes or preys.
Empress peerless ever to praise
Of heaven and earth and hell is she,
Yet puts no man from his rightful place,
For she is Queen of courtesy.

3

₄₄₅ "The court of the kingdom whose crown I bear
Has a property by nature and name:
Each who gains admittance there
Is king of that realm, or queen of the same,
And none would lessen the others' share

450 But each one, glad of the others' fame,
     Would wish their crowns five times as fair,
     Had they the power of amending them;
     But she who bore Jesu in Bethlehem
     Over all of us here has sovereignty,
455 And none of our number carps at° that claim,   *complains about*
     For she is Queen of courtesy.

4

     "By courtesy, so says Saint Paul,°
     We are members of Christ in joy profound,
     As head, arms, legs, and navel and all
460 Are parts of one person hale and sound;
     Likewise each Christian soul I call
     A loyal limb of the Lord renowned;
     Now what dispute could ever befall
     Between two limbs in one body bound?
465 Though hand or wrist bear a golden round,
     Your head will never the sorrier be:
     Just so in love is each of us crowned
     A king or queen by courtesy."

5

     "Courtesy, no doubt, there is,
470 And charity rife° your ranks among;   *plentiful*
     Yet truly—take it not amiss—
     I cannot but think your words are wrong.
     You set yourself too high in this,
     To be crowned a queen, that was so young;
475 Why, what more honor might be his
     That had lived in hardship late and long
     And suffered pains and penance strong
     To purchase bliss in heaven on high?
     How might he more have thriven in throng
480 Than be crowned a king by courtesy?

IX

1

     "That courtesy too free appears
     If all be true as you portray;
     You lived in our country not two years—

° 1 Corinthians 12:12–21, 26–27.

You could not please the Lord, or pray,
485 Or say 'Our Father,' or Creed rehearse—
And crowned a queen the very first day!
I cannot well believe my ears,
That God could go so far astray.
The style of countess, so I would say,
490 Were fair enough to attain unto,
Or a lesser rank in heaven's array,
But a queen! It is beyond your due."

2

"Beyond all due His bounty flows,"
So answered she in words benign;
495 "For all is justice that He does,
And truth is in His each design.
As the tale in the Gospel of Matthew goes
In the mass that blesses the bread and wine,
In parable His words propose
500 A likeness to the realm divine.°
A man possessed a vineyard fine—
So runs the tale in sermon true—
The time was come to tend the vine
By tasks assigned in order due.

3

505 "The laborers duly gathered round;
The lord rose up by daybreak bright,
Sought at the marketplace, and found
Some who would serve his turn aright.
By the same bargain each was bound:
510 Let a penny a day his pains requite;°   *reward*
Then forth they go into his ground
And prune and bind and put things right.
He went back late by morning light,
Found idle fellows not a few;
515 'Why stand you idle here in sight?
Has not this day its service due?'

4

"'Duly we came ere break of day,'
So answered they in unison;

° Matthew 20:1–16.

'The sun has risen and here we stay
520 And look for labor and yet find none.'
'Go to the vine; do what you may,'
So said the lord, 'till day is done;
Promptly at nightfall I shall pay
Such hire as each by right has won.'
525 So at the vine they labored on,
And still the lord, the long day through,
Brought in new workmen one by one
Till dusk approached at season due.

5

"When time was due of evensong,
530 The sunset but one hour away,
He saw there idle men in throng
And had these sober words to say:
'Why stand you idle all day long?'
None had required their help, said they.
535 'Go to the vine, young men and strong,
And do as much there as you may.'
Soon the earth grew dim and grey;
The sun long since had sunk from view;
He summoned them to take their pay;
540 The day had passed its limit due.

X

1

"Duly the lord, at day's decline,
Said to the steward, 'Sir, proceed;
Pay what I owe this folk of mine;
And lest men chide me here, take heed:
545 Set them all in a single line,[7]
Give each a penny as agreed;
Start with the last that came to the vine,
And let the first the last succeed.'
And then the first began to plead;
550 Long had they toiled, they said and swore;
These in an hour had done their deed;
It seems to us we should have more.

2

"'More have we served, who suffered through
The heat of the day till evening came,
555 Than these who stayed but an hour or two,
Yet you allow them equal claim.'
Then said the lord to one of that crew,
'Friend, I will not change the game;
Take your wage and away with you!
560 I offered a penny, to all the same;
Why begin to bicker and blame?
Was not our covenant set of yore?
Higher than covenant none should aim;
Why should you then ask for more?

3

565 "'More, am I not at liberty
To dispose of my own as I wish to do?
Or have you lifted an evil eye,
As I am good, to none untrue?'
'Thus,' says Christ, 'shall I shift it awry:
570 The last shall be the first in the queue,
And the first the last,[8] were he never so spry,
For many are called, but friends are few.'
So poor men take their portion too,
Though late they came and puny° they were,   *weak*
575 And though they make but little ado,
The mercy of God is much the more.

4

"More of ladyship here is mine,
Of life in flower and never to fade,
Than all who dwell in this world could win
580 By right and right alone," she said.
"Although but late I began in the vine—
I came at evening, as Fortune bade—
The lord allowed me first in the line
And then and there I was fully paid.
585 There were others came early and longer stayed,
Worked on and on, and sweated sore,
And still their payment is delayed,
Shall be, perhaps, for many years more."

5

Then with more discourse I demurred:°   *dissented*
590   "There seems small reason in this narration:
God's justice carries across the board
Or Holy Writ is prevarication!°   *falsehood*
In the psalter of David there stands a word
Admits no cavil or disputation:*
595   'You render to each his just reward,
O ruler of every dispensation!'
Now he who all day kept his station,
If you to payment come in before,
Then the less, the more remuneration,
600   And ever alike, the less, the more."

XI

1

"Of more and less," she answered straight,
"In the Kingdom of God, no risk obtains,
For each is paid at the selfsame rate
No matter how little or great his gains.
605   No niggard° is our chief of state,   *cheapskate*
Be it soft or harsh his will ordains;
His gifts gush forth like a spring in spate°   *flood*
Or a stream in a gully° that runs in rains.   *roadside ditch*
His portion is large whose prayers and pains
610   Please Him who rescues when sinners call.
No bliss in heaven but he attains:
The grace of God is enough for all.

2

"Yet for all that, you stubbornly strive
To prove I have taken too great a fee;
615   You say I, the last to arrive,
Am not worthy so high degree.
When was there ever a man alive,
Though none were so pious and pure as he,
Who by some transgression did not contrive
620   To forfeit the bliss of eternity?
And the older, the oftener the case must be

* Psalm 61:12 (A.V. 62).

That he lapsed into sins both great and small.
Then mercy and grace must second his plea:
The grace of God is enough for all.

3

625 "But grace enough have the innocent:
When first they see the light of day
To the water of baptism they are sent
And brought to the vine without delay.
At once the light, its splendor spent,
630 Bows down to darkness and decay;
They had done no harm ere home they went;
From the Master's hands they take their pay.
Why should He not acknowledge them, pray?
They were there with the rest, they came at His call—
635 Yes, and give them their hire straightway:
The grace of God is enough for all.

4

"It is known well enough, the human race
Was formed to live in pure delight.
Our first forefather altered that case
640 By an apple of which he took a bite.
We all were damned by that disgrace
To die in sorrow and desperate plight
And then in hell to take our place
And dwell there lost in eternal night.°
645 But then there came a remedy right:
Rich blood ran down rood tree° tall   *cross*
And with it flowed forth water bright:
The grace of God was enough for all.†

5

"Enough for all flowed from that well,
650 Blood and water plain to behold:
By the blood our souls were saved from hell
And the second death decreed of old.‡
The water is baptism, truth to tell,
That followed the spearhead keen and cold,

° Genesis 3:17–19; Matthew 13:41–42; Romans 5:12.
† John 19:34; Ephesians 1:3–7.
‡ Apocalypse 20:14.

655 Old Adam's deadly guilt to dispel
     That swamped us in sins a thousandfold.
     Now all is withdrawn that ever could hold
     Mankind from bliss, since Adam's fall,
     And that was redeemed at a time foretold
660 And the grace of God is enough for all.

XII

1

     "Grace enough that man can have
     Who is penitent, having sinned anew,
     If with sorrow at heart he cry and crave
     And perform the penance that must ensue.
665 But by right reason, that cannot rave,
     The innocent ever receives his due:
     To punish the guiltless with the knave
     Is a plan God never was party to.
     The guilty, by contrition true,
670 Can attain to mercy requisite,°   *necessary*
     But he that never had guile in view,
     The innocent is safe and right.

2

     "I know right reason in this case
     And thereto cite authority:
675 The righteous man shall see His face
     And the innocent bear Him company.
     So in a verse the psalter says,*
     'Lord, who shall climb Your hill on high
     Or rest within Your holy place?'
680 And readily then He makes reply:
     'Hands that did no injury,
     Heart that was always pure and light:
     There shall his steps be stayed in joy';
     The innocent is safe by right.

3

685 "The righteous also in due time,
     He shall approach that noble tor,°   *tower*
     Who cozens° his neighbor with no crime   *deceives*

---

* Psalm 23:3–4 (A.V. 24).

Nor wastes his life in sin impure.
King Solomon tells in text sublime
690 Of Wisdom and her honored lore;°
By narrow ways she guided him
And lo! God's kingdom lay before.
As who should say, 'Yon distant shore—
Win it you may ere fall of night
695 If you make haste'; but evermore
The innocent is safe by right.

4

"Of the righteous man I find report
In the psalter of David, if ever you spied it:†
'Call not your servant, Lord, to court,
700 For judgment is grim if justice guide it.'
And when to that seat you must resort
Where each of us shall stand indicted,
Allege the right, you may be caught short
By this same proof I have provided.
705 But he who, scourged° and sore derided,°   *whipped / mocked*
Bled on the cross through mortal spite,
Grant that your sentence be decided
By innocence and not by right.

5

"Who reads the Book of rightful fame
710 May learn of it infallibly
How good folk with their children came
To Jesus walking in Galilee.‡
The touch of His hand they sought for them
For the goodness in Him plain to see;
715 The disciples banned that deed with blame
And bade the children let him be.
But Jesus gathered them round His knee
And of that reprimand made light;
'Of such is the kingdom of heaven,' said He;
720 The innocent is safe by right.

° Wisdom 10:9–10 (A.V. classified as Apocryphal).
† Psalm 142:2 (A.V. 143).
‡ Mark 10:13–16; Luke 18:15–17.

XIII

1

"Jesus on His faithful smiled
And said, 'God's kingdom shall be won
By him who seeks it as a child,
For other entry right is none.'
725 Harmless, steadfast, undefiled,
Unsullied bright to gaze upon,
When such stand knocking, meek and mild,
Straightway the gate shall be undone.
There is the endless bliss begun
730 That the jeweler sought in earthly estate
And sold all his goods, both woven and spun,
To purchase a pearl immaculate.°*   *spotless*

2

"This immaculate pearl I tell you of,
The jeweler gave his wealth to gain,
735 Is like the realm of heaven above;
The Father of all things said it plain.
No spot it bears, nor blemish rough,
But blithe in rondure° ever to reign,[9]   *roundness*
And of righteousness it is prize and proof:
740 Lo, here on my breast it long has lain,
Bestowed by the Lamb so cruelly slain,
His peace to betoken and designate;
I bid you turn from the world insane
And purchase your pearl immaculate."

3

745 "Immaculate pearl whom white pearls crown,
Who bear," said I, "the pearl of price,
Who fashioned your form? Who made your gown?
Oh, he that wrought it was most wise!
Such beauty in nature never was known;
750 Pygmalion never painted your eyes,
Nor Aristotle, of long renown,
Discoursed of these wondrous properties,[10]
Your gracious aspect, your angel guise,
More white than the lily, and delicate:

* Matthew 13:45–46.

755 What duties high, what dignities
Are marked by the pearl immaculate?"

4

"My immaculate Lamb, my destiny sweet,"
Said she, "who can all harm repair,
He made me his mate in marriage meet,
760 Though once such a match unfitting were.
When I left your world of rain and sleet
He called me in joy to join Him there:
'Come hither, my dove without deceit,
For you are spotless, past compare.'°
765 He gave me strength, He made me fair,
He crowned me a virgin consecrate,
And washed in His blood these robes I wear,†
And clad me in pearls immaculate."

5

"Immaculate being, bright as flame,
770 In royalties set and sanctified,
Tell me now, what is that Lamb
That sought you out to become His bride?
Over all others you pressed your claim
To live in honor with Him allied,
775 Yet many a noble and worthy dame
For Christ's dear sake has suffered and died;
And you have thrust those others aside
And reserved for yourself that nuptial° state,   *marital*
Yourself all alone, so big with pride,
780 A matchless maid and immaculate?"

XIV

1

"Immaculate," came her answer clear,
"Unblemished am I, my peers among;
So much I claim with honor here,
But matchless—there you have it wrong.
785 We all are brides of the Lamb so dear,
One hundred and forty-four thousand strong,

° Canticle of Canticles 4:7, 5:2 (A.V. Song of Solomon).
† Apocalypse 7:13–14 (A.V. Revelation).

In Apocalypse the words appear
As John beheld it and told with tongue.°
Thousands on thousands, virgins young,
790   He saw on Mount Sion in sacred dream,
Arrayed for the wedding in comely throng
In the city called New Jerusalem.

2¹¹

"Of Jerusalem I speak perforce,
To tell his nature and degree,
795   My jewel dear, my joy's sole source,
My Lamb, my lord, my love, all three.
In the prophet Isaiah we find discourse
Of him and his humility,†
Condemned and martyred without remorse
800   And on false charges of felony,
As a sheep to the slaughter led was he,
As a lamb to the shearers meek and tame;
His lips were sealed to all inquiry
When Jews were his judge in Jerusalem.

3

805   "In Jerusalem my true love died,
Rent° by rude hands with pain and woe;   *torn*
Freely he perished for our pride,
And suffered our doom in mortal throe.°‡   *painful struggle*
His blessèd face, or ever He died,
810   Was made to bleed by many a blow;§
For sin He set His power aside
Though never He sinned who suffered so.
For us He was beaten and bowed low
And racked on the rood-tree rough and grim,
815   And meek as the lamb with fleece of snow
He breathed His last in Jerusalem.

4

"In Jerusalem, Jordan, and Galilee,
When John the Baptist preached abroad,

° Apocalypse 14:1 (A.V. Revelation).
† Isaiah 53:7, 9.
‡ Isaiah 53:4–5.
§ Matthew 26:67.

The words with Isaiah well agree
820 That he said when Jesus before him stood;°
He made of him this prophecy:
'Steadfast as stone, O Lamb of God,
Who takes away the iniquity
That all this world has wrought in blood';
825 And He was guiltless and ever good,
Yet bore our sins and atoned for them;
O who can reckon His parenthood
Who perished for us in Jerusalem?

5

"In Jerusalem my lover true
830 Appeared as a lamb of purest white
In the eyes of the prophets old and new
For his meek mien° and piteous plight.   *manner*
The third fits well with the other two,
In Revelation written aright;†
835 Where the saints sat round in retinue
The Apostle saw Him throned in light,
Opening the book with pages bright
And the seven seals set round the rim,
And all hosts trembled at that sight,
840 In hell, in earth, and Jerusalem.

XV ¹²

1

"This Jerusalem Lamb in his array
Was whiter far than tongue could tell;
No spot or speck might on Him stay,
His fair rich fleece did so excel.
845 And so each sinless soul, I say,
Is a worthy wife with the Lamb to dwell,
And though He fetch a score each day
No strife is stirred in our citadel,°   *stronghold*
But would each brought four others as well—
850 The more the merrier in blessedness!
Our loves are increased as our numbers swell,
And honor more and never the less.

° John 1:29.
† Apocalypse 5:1, 6–7 (A.V. Revelation).

2

"Less of bliss none brings us here
Who bear the pearl upon our breast;
855   No mark of strife could ever appear
Where the precious pearl is worn for crest.
Our bodies lie on earthen bier,
And you go grieving, sore distressed,
But we, with knowledge full and clear,
860   See in one death all wrong redressed.
The Lamb has laid our cares to rest;
We partake of His table in joyfulness;
Each one's share of bliss is best,
Nor ever in honor any the less.

3

865   "Lest less you believe, incline your ear
To the Book of Revelation true:°
'I saw,' says John, 'the Lamb appear
On the Mount of Sion, all white of hue,
With a hundred thousand maidens dear
870   And forty-four thousand more in view;
On all their foreheads written were
The name of the Lamb, of His Father too.
But then in heaven a clamor grew,
Like waters running in rapid race;
875   As thunder crashes in storm cloud blue,
Such was that sound, and nothing less.

4

" 'Nevertheless, though it shouted shrill
And made the heavens resound again,
I heard them sing upon that hill
880   A new song, a most noble strain;
As harpers touch their harps with skill
Their voices lifted, full and plain;
And well they followed with a will
The phrases of that fair refrain.
885   Before his throne who ever shall reign
And the four beasts ranged about the dais†

° Apocalypse 14:1–5 (A.V. Revelation).
† Apocalypse 4:6–7 (A.V. Revelation).

And the solemn elders of that domain,°
Great was their song, and grew no less.

5

"'Nevertheless, there was none had might
890 Or for all his art might ever aspire
To sing that song, save those in white
Who follow the Lamb their lord and sire;
For they are redeemed from earth's dark night
As firstfruits given to God entire,
895 And joined with the Lamb on Sion's height,
As like Himself in speech and attire,°   *clothing*
For never, in deed or heart's desire,
Their tongues were touched with untruthfulness;
And none can sever that sinless choir
900 From that master immaculate, nevertheless.'"

6

"Never less welcome let me find,"
Said I, "for the queries° I propose;   *questions*
I should not tempt your noble mind
Whom Christ the Lord to His chamber chose.
905 I am of mire and mere mankind,
And you so rich and rare a rose,
And here to eternal bliss assigned
Where joy fails not, but forever grows.
Now, dame, whom simplicity's self endows,
910 I would beseech a favor express,°   *specific*
And though I am rough and rude, God knows,
Let it be granted nevertheless.

XVI

1

"Nevertheless, if you can see
In my request a reason sound,
915 Deny not my dejected plea,
But where grace is, let grace abound.
Have you no hall, no hostelry;°   *residence*
Where you dwell and meet in daily round?
You tell of Jerusalem rich and free

° Apocalypse 4:4 (A.V. Revelation).

920 Where reigned King David the renowned,
But that cannot be near this ground
But lies in Judea, by reckoning right;
As you under moon are flawless found,
Your lodgings should be wholly bright.

2

925 "These holy virgins in radiant guise,
By thousands thronged in processional—
That city must be of uncommon size
That keeps you together, one and all.
It were not fit such jewels of price
930 Should lie unsheltered by roof or wall,
Yet where these riverbanks arise
I see no building large or small.
Beside this stream celestial
You linger alone, none else in sight;
935 If you have another house or hall,
Show me that dwelling wholly bright."

3

That wholly blissful, that spice heaven-sent,
Declared, "In Judea's fair demesne
The city lies, where the Lamb once went
940 To suffer for man death's anguish keen.
The old Jerusalem by that is meant,
For there the old guilt was canceled clean,
But the new, in vision prescient,°   *prophetic*
John saw sent down from God pristine.°°   *pure*
945 The spotless Lamb of gracious mien
Has carried us all to that fair site,
And as in His flock no fleck is seen,
His hallowed halls are wholly bright.

4

"Two holy cities I figure forth;
950 One name suits well with both of these,
Which in the language of your birth
Is 'City of God,' or 'Sight of Peace.'†
In the one the Lamb brought peace on earth

° Apocalypse 21:2 (A.V. Revelation).
† Apocalypse 3:12 (A.V. Revelation); Ezekiel 13:16.

Who suffered for our iniquities;°   *evil deeds*
955   In the other is peace with heavenly mirth,
And ever to last, and never to cease.
And to that city in glad release
From fleshly decay our souls take flight;
There glory and bliss shall ever increase
960   In the household that is wholly bright."

5

"Holy maid compassionate,"
Said I to that fresh flower and gay,
"Let me approach those ramparts great
And see the chamber where you stay."
965   "The Lord forbids," she answered straight,
"That a stranger in His streets should stray,
But through the Lamb enthroned in state
I have won you a sight of it this day.
Behold it from far off you may,
970   But no man's foot may there alight;
You have no power to walk that way
Save as a spirit wholly bright.

XVII

1

"This holy city that I may show,
Walk upward toward the river's head,
975   And here against you I shall go
Until to a hill your path has led."
Then to stir I was not slow,
But under leafy boughs I sped
Until from a hill I looked below
980   And saw the city, as she had said,
Beyond the stream in splendor spread,
That brighter than shafts of sunlight shone.
In Apocalypse it may all be read°
As he set it forth, the apostle John.°

2

985   As John the apostle saw it of old
I saw the city beyond the stream,

° Apocalypse 21:10–27, 22:1–2 (A.V. Revelation).

Jerusalem the new and fair to behold,
Sent down from heaven by power supreme.
The streets were paved with precious gold,
990 As flawless pure as glass agleam,
Based on bright gems of worth untold,
Foundation stones twelvefold in team;
And set in series without a seam,
Each level was a single stone,
995 As he beheld it in sacred dream
In Apocalypse, the apostle John.

3

As John had named them in writ divine
Each stone in order by name I knew;
Jasper was the first in line;
1000 At the lowest level it came in view;
Green ingrained I saw it shine.
The second was the sapphire blue;
The clear chalcedony, rare and fine,
Was third in degree in order due.
1005 The fourth the emerald green of hue;
Sardonyx fifth was set thereon;
The sixth the ruby he saw ensue
In Apocalypse, the apostle John.

4

To these John joined the chrysolite,
1010 The seventh in that foundation's face;
The eighth the beryl clear and white,
The twin-hued topaz ninth to trace;
The chrysoprase tenth in order right;
Jacinth held the eleventh place;
1015 The twelfth, the amethyst most of might,
Blent blue and purple in royal blaze.
The jasper walls above that base
Like lustrous glass to gaze upon;
I knew them all by his every phrase
1020 In Apocalypse, the apostle John.

5

As John had written, so I was ware
How broad and steep was each great tier;°   *layer*
As long as broad as high foursquare

The city towered on twelvefold pier.
1025 The streets like glass in brilliance bare,
The walls like sheen on parchment sheer;
The dwellings all with gemstones rare
Arrayed in radiance far and near.
The sides of that perimeter°   *enclosing line*
1030 Twelve thousand furlongs° spanned, each one;[13]   *eighth of a mile*
Length, breadth, and height were measured there
Before his eyes, the apostle John.

XVIII

1

Yet more, John saw on every side
Three gateways set commensurate,°   *coequal*
1035 So twelve I counted in compass wide,
The portals rich with precious plate.
Each gate a pearl of princely pride,
Unfading, past all mortal fate,
On which a name was signified
1040 Of Israel's sons, in order of date,
That is, by birthright ranked in state,
The eldest ever the foremost one.
The streets were alight both early and late;
They needed neither sun nor moon.

2

1045 Sun and moon were far surpassed;
The Lord was their lamp eternally,
The Lamb, their lantern ever to last,
Made bright that seat of sovereignty.
Through roof and wall my looking passed,
1050 Pure substance hindered not to see;
There I beheld the throne steadfast
With the emblems that about it be,
As John in text gave testimony,
The Lord himself seated thereon;
1055 From the throne a river ran fresh and free,[14]
More bright by far than sun or moon.

3

Sun nor moon shone never so fair
As that flood of plenteous waters pure;
Full it flowed in each thoroughfare;

1060 No filth or taint its brightness bore.
Church they had none, nor chapel there,
House of worship, nor need therefor;
The Almighty was their place of prayer,
The Lamb the sacrifice all to restore.
1065 No lock was set on gate or door
But evermore open both night and noon;
None may find refuge on that floor
Who bears any spot beneath the moon.[15]

4

The moon has in that reign no right;
1070 Too spotty she is, of body austere;
And they who dwell there know no night—
Of what avail her varying sphere?
And set beside that wondrous light
That shines upon the waters clear
1075 The planets would lose their luster quite,
And the sun itself would pale appear.
Along the river are trees that bear
Twelve fruits of life their boughs upon;
Twelve times a year they burgeon there
1080 And renew themselves with every moon.

5

Beneath the moon so much amazed
No fleshly heart could bear to be
As by that city on which I gazed,
Its form so wondrous was to see.
1085 As a quail that couches,° dumb and dazed,   *crouches down*
I stared on that great symmetry;
Nor rest nor travail my soul could taste,
Pure radiance so had ravished me.
For this I say with certainty:
1090 Had a man in the body borne that boon,°   *gift*
No doctor's art, for fame or fee,
Had saved his life beneath the moon.

XIX

1

As the great moon begins to shine
While lingers still the light of day,[16]
1095 So in those ramparts crystalline

I saw a procession wend its way.
Without a summons, without a sign,
The city was full in vast array
Of maidens in such raiment fine
1100   As my blissful one had worn that day.
As she was crowned, so crowned were they;
Adorned with pearls, in garments white;
And in like fashion, gleaming gay,
Each bore the pearl of great delight.

2

1105   With great delight, serene and slow,
They moved through every golden street;
Thousands on thousands, row on row,
All in one raiment shining sweet.
Who gladdest seemed, was hard to know;
1110   The Lamb led on at station meet,
Seven horns of gold upon His brow,°
His robe like pearls with rays replete.°   *full to overflowing*
Soon they approach God's mighty seat;
Though thick in throng, unhurried quite;
1115   As maidens at communion meet
They moved along with great delight.

3

Delight that at His coming grew
Was greater than my tongue can tell;
The elders when He came in view
1120   Prostrate as one before Him fell;
Hosts of angels in retinue
Cast incense forth of sweetest smell;
Then all in concert praised anew
That jewel with whom in joy they dwell.†
1125   The sound could pierce through the earth to hell
When the powers of heaven in song unite;
To share His praises in citadel
My heart indeed had great delight.

4

Delight and wonder filled me in flood
1130   To hear all heaven the Lamb acclaim;

° Apocalypse 5:6 (A.V. Revelation).
† Apocalypse 5:8, 11–14 (A.V. Revelation).

Gladdest He was, most kind and good
Of any that ever was known to fame.
His dress so white, so mild His mood,
His looks so gracious, Himself the same;
1135 But a wound there was, and wide it stood,
Thrust near His heart with deadly aim.
Down His white side the red blood came;
"O God," thought I, "who had such spite?
A breast should consume with sorrow and shame
1140 Ere in such deeds it took delight."

5

The Lamb's delight was clearly seen,
Though a bitter wound He had to bear;
So glorious was His gaze serene,
It gladdened all who beheld Him there.
1145 I looked where that bright host had been,
How charged with life, how changed they were.
And then I saw my little queen
That I thought but now I had stood so near;
Lord! how she laughed and made good cheer
1150 Among her friends, who was so white!
To rush in the river then and there
I longed with love and great delight.

XX

1

Moved by delight of sight and sound,
My maddened mind all fate defied.
1155 I would follow her there, my newly found,
Beyond the river though she must bide.
I thought that nothing could turn me round,
Forestall me, or stop me in mid-stride,
And wade I would from the nearer ground
1160 And breast the stream, though I sank and died.
But soon those thoughts were thrust aside;
As I rushed to the river incontinent°   *uncontrolled*
I was summoned away and my wish denied:
My Prince therewith was not content.

2

1165 It contented Him not that I, distraught,
Should dare the river that rimmed the glade;

Though reckless I was, and overwrought,
In a moment's space my steps were stayed.
For just as I started from the spot
1170 I was reft of my dream and left dismayed;
I waked in that same garden plot,[17]
On that same mound my head was laid.
I stretched my hand where pearl had strayed;
Great fear befell me, and wonderment;
1175 And, sighing, to myself I said,
"Let all things be to His content."

3

I was ill content to be dispossessed
Of the sight of her that had no peer
Amid those scenes so bright and blessed;
1180 Such longing seized me, I swooned, or near;
Then sorrow broke from my burning breast;
"O honored pearl," I said, "how dear
Was your every word and wise behest°   *piece of advice*
In this true vision vouchsafed me here.
1185 If you in a garland never sere°   *withered*
Are set by that Prince all provident,
Then happy am I in dungeon drear
That He with you is well content."

4

Had I but sought to content my Lord
1190 And taken His gifts without regret,
And held my place and heeded the word
Of the noble pearl so strangely met,
Drawn heavenward by divine accord
I had seen and heard more mysteries yet;
1195 But always men would have and hoard
And gain the more, the more they get.
So banished I was, by cares beset,
From realms eternal untimely sent;
How madly, Lord, they strive and fret
1200 Whose acts accord not with Your content!

5

To content that Prince and well agree,
Good Christians can with ease incline,
For day and night He has proved to be

A Lord, a God, a friend benign.
1205 These words came over the mound to me
As I mourned my pearl so flawless fine,
And to God committed her full and free,
With Christ's dear blessing bestowing mine,
As in the form of bread and wine
1210 Is shown us daily in sacrament;
O may we serve Him well, and shine
As precious pearls to His content.

Amen.

Notes: *Pearl*

1. I.1.9: **In a garden of herbs I lost my dear.** We infer that the garden is enclosed, because the speaker says he entered it (I.4.1); later, as the dreamer, he sees the pearl maiden standing in what she calls a garden (V.2.8); it too is "enclosed," barred from him by the river he cannot cross (V.5.11–12). Space in the vision is symbolic rather than realistic: the garden beyond the river is also the heavenly Jerusalem, the walled city to which the maiden says the Lamb has transported her (XVI.3.9–10) and in which the dreamer sees her in the procession in section XIX. Garden and city are interchangeable symbols for the kingdom of heaven; each serves to make some aspect of it more accessible to the human imagination. The garden the speaker enters in section I is said to contain both herbs (1.9) and spices (3.1). The two are not wholly distinct; plants of both classes have medicinal and preservative powers. The former prefigure the healing of the dreamer's sorrow in the course of his dream; the latter, the blissful immortality of the pearl maiden, which, as a faithful Christian, the dreamer can hope to attain himself. Spices in particular have a fragrance symbolically associated with the divine realm and all things pertaining to it; they appear frequently in the imagery of the Old Testament Canticle of Canticles, or Song of Songs, which was interpreted as an allegory signifying the love of Christ for the Church. It is presumably the fragrance of the spices in the garden that lulls the speaker to sleep (I.5.10–12). The speaker refers to the maiden as a "spice" in section XVI (3.1); in the original poem, but not in my translation, he also refers to her thus in section IV (5.7). The poet is probably punning here on two words in Middle English; each was derived ultimately from Latin *species*, and each could be spelled either *spice* or *spece*. One was equivalent in meaning to modern *spice*, the other meant "a visible shape, appearance or semblance." Both meanings apply to the maiden.

2. I.4.3: **In August at a festive tide.** This line has been thought to refer to either of two church holidays or "festive tides": the Assumption of the Virgin on August 15, or Lammas Day on August 1. (By the Assumption of the Virgin is meant the removal of the Virgin's body to Heaven immediately after her death, to be reunited there with her soul.) The word *lammas* originated as a compound of the Old English forms of the words *loaf* and *mass*. On Lammas Day in the early English church, the bread consecrated in the Eucharistic or Communion service was made from the first grain harvested that year, called the "first fruits." The one

hundred forty-four thousand maidens, in whose company the dreamer sees the pearl maiden, were also considered "first fruits," since they were the first Christian martyrs: the children under the age of two killed shortly after the Nativity by Herod's command in order to kill the infant Jesus. They are so called in Apocalypse 14:4 and *Pearl* XV.5.6. In view of the poet's reference to the harvesting of the corn in I.4.4, as well as the importance of the communion service in the poem generally (cf. XV.2.10, XIX.2.11–12), Lammas Day seems more likely to be the holiday the poet has in mind.

3. II.4.11: **I came to the shore of a waterway.** As the dreamer will learn, the "shore" of the river at which he has arrived marks the closed boundary of the landscape within which, up to now, he has moved freely. Late in the poem, the dreamer is instructed by the pearl maiden to follow the stream uphill toward its "head" (XVII.1.2); when he has done so, he sees the heavenly Jerusalem and within it a river that runs from the throne of God (XVIII.2.11–12). This is the "river of water of life" referred to in Apocalypse (Revelation) 22.1; it does not flow in a single direction but radiates outward in all directions, filling "each thoroughfare" (XVIII.3.3) of the city. The stream that both brings the dreamer and his pearl together and separates them would seem to be continuous with it.

4. II.5.6: **Gleaming like glass where sunbeam strays.** For the modern reader, glass is a common, colorless material, found in the windows of the most ordinary of homes. But that was not true in medieval times. The poet is presumably alluding to the splendid stained-glass windows, decorated with religious motifs and scenes, that could be seen in great churches (so also in XVII.4.10 and XVII.5.5).

5. III.2.5–6: **It could not be but paradise / Lay beyond those noble banks, thought I.** It is not clear whether the speaker is mistakenly thinking of the "earthly paradise," believed to be the still existent, though unknown, site of the Garden of Eden, or the "celestial paradise," the heavenly realm. It is the latter that lies beyond the banks, on the river's farther side.

6. VIII.1.7–8: **Now who could assume her crown, by right, / But she in some feature fairer were?** These lines express one part of an important thematic opposition in the poem that I have touched on in the introduction (p. 116); it comes to the foreground in the parable of the vineyard in section IX. The opposed concepts might be called "comparative value" and "absolute value," or "that which is measurable" and "that which transcends measurement." See the note to X.1.5.

7. X.1.5: **Set them all in a single line.** The line (called a *rawe* or "row" in the original) is by definition "linear" or sequential, visibly so as time is invisibly so. Both lines and units of time can be measured; they have "first" and "last" points and are divisible into inches or minutes. The workers that arrived first at the vine plead that positions in the line should also correspond to a measured series of payments or values, from smallest to largest, corresponding to a range between shortest and longest periods of time.

8. X.3.6–7: **The last shall be the first in the queue, / and the first the last.** This statement in the parable was interpreted by the church fathers as having two different meanings: that the first and last positions are to be reversed, and that they are to be made equal. The two interpretations embody the complementarity between "comparative" and "absolute"—in spatial terms, between positions in a line and positions on the circumference of a circle. As the line of workers is the major symbol of linearity in the poem, the major symbol of circularity is the pearl.

9. XIII.2.5–6: **No spot it bears, nor blemish rough, / But blithe in rondure ever to reign.** As the immaculate brightness of the pearl betokens the freedom from sin that merits eternal life, so its rondure, or circularity, betokens eternity itself.

10. XIII.3.6–8: **Pygmalion never painted your eyes, / Nor Aristotle . . . . Discoursed of these wondrous properties.** The poet seems to have borrowed these allusions from *Le roman de la rose* ("The Romance of the Rose"), a poem he paraphrases in *Cleanness* 1057–64ff. In the *Roman*, the speaker contends, using as examples Aristotle and the mythical Greek sculptor Pygmalion, that philosophers cannot adequately discourse of natural beauty nor can the works of artists equal it. The *Pearl* poet transfers this dictum to the supernatural beauty of the pearl maiden.

11. XIV.2–3, 4, 5: The envisioning of Christ the Redeemer as a sacrificial lamb in this section proceeds in three stages of increasing profundity. In the first, it has the form of a simile: Jesus, in his silence at the time of his condemnation, is *like* a lamb. In the second, it is stated as a metaphor: John the Baptist addresses Jesus as "Lamb of God." In the third, the form of a lamb appears as a symbolic personification of Christ in heaven, part of the supernatural vision described by Saint John in the Apocalypse.

12. XV. This section, unlike the other nineteen, contains six stanzas rather than five. As a result, the number of stanzas in the poem as a whole totals 101 rather than 100 (see Introduction, p. 121). If we disregard the absurd suggestion that the poet meant to cancel one of the six stanzas he had written and never did so, the question of the placement of the irregular section in the poem arises: Why should it be the fifteenth? A plausible suggestion (see entry for Metlitzki, Dorothee in the bibliography) is based on the fact that the name of God appears in the description of the 144,000 virgins in the third stanza of that section (cf. Apocalypse 14.1):

> On all their foreheads written were
> The name of the Lamb, of His Father too.   (XV.3.7–8)

It is Metlitzki's view that the *Pearl* poet is thinking of the name of God at this point as the "tetragrammaton" YHVH or JHVH, realized as Yahweh or Jahweh and Jehovah in Jewish and Christian traditions, respectively. The three different letters of the four, J/Y, H, and V, were studied by early Jewish scholars using *gematria*, an ancient method of numerological analysis according to which numbers were assigned to the Hebrew letters. Metlitzki finds that in such an interpretation, the three letters J/Y, H, and V could be taken to represent the numbers 15, 6, and 3. These are, respectively, the number of the section, the number of stanzas in the section, and the number of the particular stanza in the section in which the name of God appears. The poet's acquaintance with Jewish lore, which can be inferred from his account of the story of Lot in *Cleanness* (see notes 16 and 17 to that poem), lends plausibility to this theory, as does his interest in numbers, shown in the numerical structures of *Saint Erkenwald* and *Sir Gawain and the Green Knight* as well as that of *Pearl* (see the introductions to the three poems).

13. XVII.5.10: **Twelve thousand furlongs spanned, each one.** The line in the original says that each side was "twelve furlongs" in width, but the corresponding detail in the source, Apocalypse 21:16, gives the measurement as "twelve thousand furlongs." Though I can offer no explanation for the discrepancy, I have kept the same number in my translation, on the assumption that "twelve furlongs" does not represent the poet's intention.

14. XVIII.2.11: **From the throne a river ran fresh and free.** See the note to II.4.11.
15. XVIII.3.11–12: **None may find refuge on that floor / Who bears any spot beneath the moon.** We spend our lives on earth "beneath the moon," dominated by changes of fortune and state that resemble the moon's waxing and waning. This "sublunary" realm of time is contrasted by the poet with the "translunary" realm of eternity where there is no need of moonlight or sunlight. We learn from stanza 5 that the speaker, translated out of the mortal body, has left the sublunary realm behind him. Had he remained there, the shock of the vision of the celestial Jerusalem would have taken his life.
16. XIX.1.1–2: **As the great moon begins to shine / While lingers still the light of day.** Here the image of the risen full moon is transitional between mortal and eternal realms. The dreamer, looking toward it from earth, seems to see the life of the celestial city within its circle, and the city itself, having been imagined as a cube in XVII.5, is now imagined as circular. The throne of God is at its center, and every street is a radius leading toward it in a kind of hyperspace, filled simultaneously by the river of life and the members of the procession.
17. XX.2.7: **I waked in that same garden plot.** The poet makes it clear that the speaker wakens exactly where he had fallen asleep, on the ground where his pearl lies buried. On awakening, he stretches out his hand, as he had stretched it out in the earlier scene (I.5.2). This correspondence between the beginning and end of the dream and the verbal correspondence between the first line of the poem and the last work together to give the poem a kind of circularity of form, as a necklace changes from a line to a circle when its two ends are linked.

Biblical Sources

In the Authorized Version of the Bible, the Apocalypse is known as Revelation.

Matthew 20:1–16

1. The kingdom of heaven is like to an householder, who went out early in the morning to hire labourers into his vineyard.
2. And having agreed with the labourers for a penny a day, he sent them into his vineyard.
3. And going out about the third hour, he saw others standing in the market place idle.
4. And he said to them: Go you also into my vineyard, and I will give you what shall be just.
5. And they went their way. And again he went out about the sixth and the ninth hour, and did in like manner.
6. But about the eleventh hour he went out and found others standing, and he said to them: Why stand you here all day idle?
7. They say to him: Because no man hath hired us. He saith to them: Go you also into my vineyard.

8. And when evening was come, the lord of the vineyard saith to his steward: Call the labourers and pay them their hire, beginning from the last even to the first.

9. When therefore they were come, that came about the eleventh hour, they received every man a penny.

10. But when the first also came, they thought that they should receive more: and they also received every man a penny.

11. And receiving it they murmured against the master of the house,

12. Saying: These last have worked but one hour, and thou hast made them equal to us, that have borne the burden of the day and the heats.

13. But he answering said to one of them: Friend, I do thee no wrong: didst thou not agree with me for a penny?

14. Take what is thine, and go thy way: I will also give to this last even as to thee.

15. Or, is it not lawful for me to do what I will? is thy eye evil, because I am good?

16. So shall the last be first, and the first last. For many are called, but few chosen.

Apocalypse 5:6, 8, 11–14

6. And I saw: and behold in the midst of the throne and of the four living creatures, and in the midst of the ancients, a Lamb standing as it were slain, having seven horns and seven eyes. . . .

8. And . . . the four living creatures, and the four and twenty ancients fell down before the Lamb, having every one of them harps, and golden vials full of odours. . . .

11. And I beheld, and I heard the voice of many angels round about the throne, and the living creatures, and the ancients; and the number of them was thousands of thousands,

12. Saying with a loud voice: The Lamb that was slain is worthy to receive power, and divinity, and wisdom, and strength, and honour, and glory, and benediction.

13. And every creature, which is in heaven, and on the earth, and under the earth, and such as are in the sea, and all that are in them: I heard all saying: To him that sitteth on the throne, and to the Lamb, benediction, and honour, and glory, and power, for ever and ever.

14. And the four living creatures said: Amen. And the four and twenty ancients fell down on their faces, and adored him that liveth for ever and ever.

Apocalypse 14:1–5

1. And I beheld, and lo a lamb stood upon mount Sion, and with him an hundred forty-four thousand, having his name, and the name of his Father, written on their foreheads.

2. And I heard a voice from heaven, as the noise of many waters, and as the voice of great thunder; and the voice which I heard, was as the voice of harpers, harping on their harps.

3. And they sung as it were a new canticle, before the throne, and before the four living creatures, and the ancients; and no man could say the canticle, but those hundred forty-four thousand, who were purchased from the earth.

4. These are they who were not defiled with women, for they are virgins. These follow the Lamb whithersoever he goeth. These were purchased from among men, the firstfruits to God and to the Lamb:

5. And in their mouth there was found no lie; for they are without spot before the throne of God.

Apocalypse 21:10–27

10. And he took me up in spirit to a great and high mountain: and he shewed me the holy city Jerusalem coming down out of heaven from God,

11. Having the glory of God, and the light thereof was like to a precious stone, as to the jasper stone, even as crystal.

12. And it had a wall great and high, having twelve gates, and in the gates twelve angels, and names written thereon, which are the names of the twelve tribes of the children of Israel.

13. On the east, three gates: and on the north, three gates: and on the south, three gates: and on the west, three gates.

14. And the wall of the city had twelve foundations, and in them, the twelve names of the twelve apostles of the Lamb.

15. And he that spoke with me, had a measure of a reed of gold, to measure the city and the gates thereof, and the wall.

16. And the city lieth in a foursquare, and the length thereof is as great as the breadth: and he measured the city with the golden reed for twelve thousand furlongs, and the length and the height and the breadth thereof are equal.

17. And he measured the wall thereof an hundred forty-four cubits, the measure of a man, which is of the angel.

18. And the building of the wall thereof was of jasper stone: but the city itself pure gold, like to clear glass.

19. And the foundations of the wall of the city were adorned with all manner of precious stones. The first foundation was jasper: the second, sapphire: the third, a chalcedony: the fourth, an emerald:

20. The fifth sardonyx: the sixth, sardius: the seventh, chrysolite: the eighth, beryl: the ninth, a topaz: the tenth, a chrysoprasus: the eleventh, a jacinth: the twelfth, an amethyst.

21. And the twelve gates are twelve pearls, one to each: and every several gate was of one several pearl. And the street of the city was pure gold, as it were transparent glass.

22. And I saw no temple therein. For the Lord God Almighty is the temple thereof, and the Lamb.

23. And the city hath no need of the sun, nor of the moon, to shine in it. For the glory of God hath enlightened it, and the Lamb is the lamp thereof.

24. And the nations shall walk in the light of it: and the kings of the earth shall bring their glory and honour into it.

25. And the gates thereof shall not be shut by day: for there shall be no night there.

26. And they shall bring the glory and honour of the nations into it.

27. There shall not enter into it any thing defiled, or that worketh abomination or maketh a lie, but they that are written in the book of life of the Lamb.

Apocalypse 22:1–2

1. And he shewed me a river of water of life, clear as crystal, proceeding from the throne of God and of the Lamb.

2. In the midst of the street thereof, and on both sides of the river, was the tree of life, bearing twelve fruits, yielding its fruits every month, and the leaves of the tree were for the healing of the nations.

Saint Erkenwald

Introduction to *Saint Erkenwald*

Saint Erkenwald, more than any of the other four poems, is grounded in history, specifically, the history of the city of London. It opens by placing its story

> In London, in England, not long since the time
> That Christ died on the cross, and Christendom began. (1–2)

As the second of these lines indicates, history for this medieval poet includes what is called "salvation history"—the history of this world, interpreted in Christian doctrine as encompassed and governed by the divine realm. It begins with the rebellion of a contingent of angels in God's heaven, led by the angel who became the archdevil Satan. It continues with the story of Adam and Eve, the first human beings created by God, who "fell" when they yielded to Satan's temptation to disobey their creator and eat the fruit of the tree of knowledge. All human beings inherit this "original sin," which dooms them to death on earth and bars them after death from the eternal bliss of heaven. But the sins of humankind were redeemed by the voluntary death on the cross of the Son of God, Jesus Christ. (The *Gawain* poet tells the story thus far in *Cleanness* 205–48.) Before he died, Jesus founded the Christian church, naming the apostle Peter as its head. To Peter and the heads of the church who were to succeed him, and through them to its officials generally, he gave the "keys of the kingdom" (Matthew 16:13–19), the power to mediate between God and human beings through the sacraments; dispelling original sin through the sacrament of Baptism, which admitted them into the church; and cleansing them of the sins they inevitably committed in the course of their daily lives through the sacrament of Penance. Thus purified, they could join the company of the saved in heaven after death. In *Saint Erkenwald*, the particular mediator between divine and secular realms is the saint named in the title. Erkenwald was a *bona fide* historical figure who lived in the seventh century, was a bishop of London, had his ecclesiastical seat at St. Paul's Cathedral, and was entombed there after his death. The action of the poem takes place in the cathedral. It ends in a vision of civic harmony, with Bishop Erkenwald leading a procession out into the London streets as church bells miraculously chime in unison:

> They passed out in procession, and all the people followed,
> And all the bells of the city broke silence together.

The poem's dramatized narrative is preceded by an account of the history of Christianity in England, which the poet probably based in part on the well-known *Ecclesiastical History of the English People* completed in the eighth century by Bede, called "the Venerable" (hereafter "Bede"). This prefatory account ends when Erkenwald becomes bishop of London at St. Paul's. The action of the poem then begins, as the digging up of the foundations of the cathedral in a renovation called "New Work" results in the unearthing of a splendid tomb containing a body untouched by physical decay.

A renovation called "New Work" is in fact part of the recorded history of St. Paul's Cathedral, though no such discovery as the poem describes resulted from it. It took place in the thirteenth century, seven hundred years after the death of the historical Erkenwald in the seventh century. The saint became the subject of several biographies, and the poet seems to know some of the recorded facts of his life. He speaks of Erkenwald as visiting "an abbey in Essex" at the time when the body is discovered (108), and the recorded facts include his founding of two abbeys there. But no record associates him with any such story as is found in the poem: the poet is clearly adapting historical chronology and fact to his own purposes. Though in the opening lines of the poem he says that Saint Erkenwald lived "not long" after the Crucifixion, he tells his story as if it were taking place in the St. Paul's Cathedral of his own late fourteenth century. Speaking, for example, of the congregation that assembles on the day when Erkenwald presides over a votive mass of the Holy Spirit (131–32), he adds, using the present tense, that "the finest folk of the land" often attend services there (135).

Legendary Sources

What we think of as history was not distinct in earlier times from legend. Stories of supernatural events are solemnly recorded, side by side with secular ones, in so scholarly a work as Bede's *Ecclesiastical History*. In his account of Saint Erkenwald, Bede says that the litter in which the saint was transported when he was crippled and could not walk has curative powers, and that even splinters cut from it cure the sick (bk. iv, ch. 6). And the motif of the body exempted from decay, as is the body discovered in the foundations of St. Paul's in *Saint Erkenwald*, appears frequently in stories of saints, though not in the biographies of Erkenwald himself.

A far more important source is a legend concerning two historical figures, Saint Gregory "the Great," who was pope from 590 to 604 (cf. *Erkenwald* 12 and note 2), and the Roman emperor Trajan, who reigned from 98 to 117 C.E. Their roles are enacted in the poem by Bishop Erkenwald and the pagan judge, never named, whose tomb is discovered in the foundations of St. Paul's. Trajan was famed for the justice and compassion of his reign, but he never became a Christian. The gist of the legend is its account of how on learning of the emperor's unfailing righteousness, Saint Gregory prayed successfully for his soul's release from hell. The story was handed down in medieval times in a number of forms. In the earliest versions, no encounter takes place between Saint Gregory and Trajan's remains. In later ones, such an encounter does take place, and the body is brought back to life long enough to be baptized and thus made a Christian. Dante alludes to the Trajan-Gregory legend in the *Purgatorio*, where he speaks of the Roman prince whose virtue moved "Gregory" to his "great victory." (Trajan also appears in the *Paradiso*, where he is seen as forming part of the eyebrow of the Eagle of Justice.) In a mid-fourteenth-century Italian edition of the *Divine Comedy* that the *Gawain* poet might conceivably have seen or heard about in London, the commentator tells a version of the legend according to which a skull, unearthed in the course of an excavation in Rome during the papacy of Saint Gregory, is found to contain a tongue wholly free from decay. When Gregory conjures the tongue "by the living God and the Christian faith" to reveal its identity, it replies that in life it had belonged to the emperor Trajan. Because Trajan had not become a Christian, his soul had been condemned to damnation in the afterlife. Gregory decides to find out more about the emperor. On learning of Trajan's wholly virtuous life, he is moved to pray for his salvation. His prayer is answered; the emperor is brought back to life and baptized. However, the narrator goes on to say that God imposed on Gregory a penance for questioning divine judgment, a malady of the stomach that afflicted him for the rest of his life.

These versions of the story, together with the one presented in *Saint Erkenwald*, raise important questions for the reader. One concerns the nature of God and his relation to human beings. According to Christian doctrine, God exists not in time as we know it, but in an eternal present from which he sees all human history as already completed in a pattern exempt from change. Moreover, God's perfection must include the righteousness of all his judgments. The imposition of a penance on Saint Gregory in the Italian story implies the view that it is impious to pray for the salvation of one of the damned. In *Saint Erkenwald*, then, what part did divine agency play in the transference of the dead judge's soul from eternal limbo to eternal bliss? A second question concerns the conditions a human being must fulfill in order to be received in heaven after death. Conflicting answers are found in the New Testament. In the Gospel of Mark, Jesus says "He that believeth and is baptized, shall be saved" (16:16). In Matthew, Jesus prophesies that at the end of the world, "the Son of man shall come in the glory of the Father with his angels, and then will he render to every man according to his works" (16:27). A vision of the Last Judgment in Apocalypse (Revelation) echoes this prophecy: "they [the dead] were judged every one according to their works" (20:13). Finally, in the Epistle bearing his name, Saint James says that "even as the body without the spirit is dead; so also faith without works is dead" (2:26). What was the *Erkenwald* poet's view as to the necessity or sufficiency for salvation of faith, works, and ecclesiastical ceremony?

The Holy Spirit

An important, though largely implicit, divine agency in the narrative of *Saint Erkenwald* is the Holy Spirit, or Holy Ghost, the third member of the Christian Trinity, defined as coequal and coeternal with God the Father and Christ the Son. It is identified in Christian doctrine with the spirit that moved over the face of the waters when God created the world (Genesis 1:2) and that descended in the form of a dove when Jesus was baptized by Saint John (Mark 1:10). Jesus promised his disciples that the spirit would come to them after his death and act for them as a "Paraclete" (from Latin *paracletus*, signifying "advocate, helper, comforter"). *Comforter* was a common designation for the Holy Spirit in the poet's Middle English, and the word is still so used in the Authorized, or King James, Bible. Of great importance to the action of the poem is the fact that the Holy Spirit was thought to be received by each person when baptized in the Christian faith. It was present, in particular, at the event recounted in Acts 2, when the disciples gathered together in an "upper room" (Acts 1:13; called *coenaculum* in the Latin Vulgate Bible known to the poet) to celebrate the Jewish holiday of Pentecost. Appearing to the apostles after his death, Jesus had told them that before long they would be baptized by the Holy Ghost. On the Pentecostal occasion, the Holy Spirit descended on them in the form of "tongues" of fire, and gave them the power of speaking in all the "tongues" spoken by the Jews of many nations living in Jerusalem (Acts 2:1–5). (The word *lingua*, in the Latin Bible, has the same two meanings.) This power in turn enabled them to convert strangers who spoke other languages. The power of the Holy Spirit, shown in the Pentecostal miracle, thus enabled the spread of Christianity across Europe, reaching its westernmost point in England.

The Holy Spirit is named in *Saint Erkenwald* as answering the bishop's prayer that he may solve the mystery presented by the nameless body in the tomb (127). On that day, he celebrates a "mass . . . of *Spiritus Domini*" (132)— that is, a mass containing prayers addressed to the Holy Spirit—before visiting the body and conjuring it to speak. But in a larger sense, the Holy Spirit is implicitly operative throughout the action of the poem, since it is present at all conversions, including the conversion of England to Christianity that makes the whole sequence of events possible and the particular "conversion" of the dead man whose body is baptized by the bishop's tears. It seems wholly possible that the "flame" that "flash[es] suddenly" in the abyss where the soul of the dead man resides and then transports it to heaven is meant to remind us of the descent of the Holy Spirit on the apostles in tongues of flame at Pentecost. Certainly, the word *cenacle*, which the poet uses to refer to the room where the eternal banquet of the saved takes place (336), alludes to the *coenaculum* of Acts 1. For other probable allusions to the Holy Spirit, see the note to line 165.

Number Symbolism

Like *Pearl* and *Sir Gawain and the Green Knight*, *Saint Erkenwald* has a numerically defined structure (see the introductions to the first two poems). The key number of the architecture of *Saint Erkenwald* is eight. The poem is 352 lines long, or 88 × 4; it begins and ends with sections that are 32, or 4 × 8, lines long. (Lines 1–32 are introductory, and I have so labeled them; the final section, lines 321–52, begins at the moment when one of the bishop's tears falls on the body's face). Eight is an important number in Christian history in that it signifies new beginnings, such as the beginning of world history after God rests from the work of creation on the seventh day, and the coming of the Last Judgment after the seventh age. Baptism is a new beginning for the soul, and baptismal fonts are traditionally octagonal. Since the dean of the cathedral reports that he and his colleagues had searched the archives for "seven days unceasing" (155) before the day on which the bishop speaks with the body, the miracle takes place on the eighth day.

Saint Erkenwald as an Occasional Poem

Finally, there is good reason to link the poem with certain late-fourteenth-century events in which the saint figured. In 1386, Bishop Braybrooke of Saint Paul's elevated in importance the two feasts of Saint Erkenwald that were celebrated in the cathedral. A few years later, he instituted an annual procession of the diocesan clergy in ceremonial dress in the saint's honor. It is wholly possible that even though he was native to Cheshire, the *Gawain* poet should have been living in London for a time, late in his life. If so, he might have been asked or commissioned to produce a poem in connection with these happenings. Certainly, his narrative portrays the official church as an essential mediator between divine and secular realms in a past time not differentiated from his own present and as bringing about a needed "confirmation" of their faith to the Christian citizens of London (124, 173).

Saint Erkenwald

Introduction

At London, in England, not long since the time
That Christ died on the cross, and Christendom began,
A bishop lived in that city, sanctified and blessed;
Saint Erkenwald, as I hear, was the holy man's name.
5 At that time, one part of the principal temple
Was torn down, and dug out, to dedicate anew,
For it had been heathen of old, since Hengist's days,
Who was sent here by the Saxons, desecrators of peace.[1]
They dealt the Britons a drubbing and drove them into Wales
10 And perverted to perdition all the people in the land.
Then it was lost to the Lord many long sad years
Till Saint Augustine to Sandwich was sent by the pope.[2]
Then he preached here the pure faith, and planted the truth,
And converted the communities to Christendom anew.
15 He took temples in hand that trafficked with the devil,
And cleansed them in Christ's name and called them churches;
He hurled out their idols, brought in holy saints,
And changed the names of churches, and charged° them better: *assigned*
The altar of Apollo he hallowed° to Saint Peter, *made sacred*
20 Mohammed to Saint Margaret or Mary Magdalen;
The Synagogue of the Sun to the service of Our Lady,
Jupiter and Juno to Jesus or James.
So he dedicated them all to deathless saints
That had been seats of Satan in the Saxons' days.
25 The town named London was then the New Troy—
The metropolis of most renown it evermore has been—
The master of the minster° there was a mighty devil, *church*
And its title, in those times, was taken from his name,
For they deemed him a deity, all idols excelling
30 And his sacrifices most solemn in Saxon lands.
Of triapolitan temples[3] it was told the third;
Within the bounds of Britain were but two besides.

175

Part I

Now is Erkenwald bishop, like Augustine before him;
In beloved London town he teaches the Law,
35   Solemnly at St. Paul's he assumes his seat,
That was the triapolitan temple, as I told you before.
Then they battered and beat it down and built it again:
A noble renovation, and New Work men called it.[4]
Many a crafty mason came on command
40   To hew the hard stones with keen-edged tools;
Many grubbers in grit gouged out the ground,
That a surer foundation might shore up the frame.
And in the midst of their mining, they met with a marvel,
As chronicles continue to call it to mind,
45   For as they delved and dug down deep into the earth,
They found on a floor a wondrous fair tomb.
It was a massive stone monument, masterly wrought,
Garnished with gargoyles of fine gray marble;
The lid that lay over its length and its breadth
50   Was a matching slab of marble, made suitably smooth,
And its border embellished with bright gold letters,
But mysterious was the message they were meant to convey.
The characters were clear—many conned them at length—
But none could say their sounds, or decipher their sense.
55   Many clerks in that enclosure with crowns clean shaven
Strove and strained vainly to construe them in words.
When word of the wonder spread wide in the town,
Many hundred men in haste thronged eagerly about,
Burgesses bustled in, beadles° and others,   *church officers*
60   Magistrates and merchants, men of all trades;
Lads left their work and ran like the wind,
Raced along in rivalry with ringing shouts.
So diverse a crowd convened there that verily it seemed
As if the whole world at once had found its way thither.
65   When the mayor with his men saw the marvel before them,
They sealed up the sanctuary with the sexton's° consent,   *church officer*
Bade men lift the lid and lay it by the chest,
For all longed to look on what lurked there within.
Skilled workmen at once went willing to the task,
70   Put prises° into place and pushed them under,   *levers*
Caught it by the corners with crowbars of iron,
And were the lid never so large, it was soon laid aside.
But amazement passed all measure where men stood watching,
Whose wits could not fathom what Wisdom had forethought,

75 For the room within was rich, with red gold lined,
    And a body lay blissful on the bottom there.
    He was royally arrayed in resplendent robes:
    All with glittering gold his gown was hemmed,
    With many a precious pearl in patterns upon it,
80 And a goodly girdle of gold grasped his waist;
    A mantle furred with miniver° was folded about him,   *decorative fur*
    Cut of costly cloth, with comely borders,
    And with a crown like a king's his coif° was encircled,   *lawyer's cap*
    And a ceremonial scepter was set in his hand.
85 As good as new were his garments, that gave no sign
    Of mold or of moth holes or mottling unsightly,
    And in color as brave and brilliant to behold
    As they had been assembled yesterday in St. Paul's Yard.[5]
    Fresh was his face where the flesh showed bare,
90 And his ears and his hands, that were open to view,
    With cheeks ruddy as roses, and two red lips,
    As if he suddenly had swooned or slipped into sleep.
    Then time went to waste as one asked another
    What body it might be that was buried there;
95 How long had he lain there, so lifelike in hue
    And his clothes uncorrupted—this question they pondered.
    "Such a man must have merited remembrance long lasting;
    He has been king of this country, as anyone can see;
    His sepulcher° sits deep, it would seem a great wonder   *burial vault*
100 If someone could not say he had seen him before."
    But no whit were they the wiser; look where they would,
    There was no title, or token, or tale of olden times,
    Or record in a register, or writing in a book
    That ever mentioned such a man, in many words or few.
105 The tidings without tarrying were told to the bishop,
    Of the buried body, the eye-abashing wonder.
    The primate° with his prelates° had departed from home;   *chief bishop /*
    In Essex at an abbey was Erkenwald that day.[6]   *high officials*
    He heard all that had happened, the unrest in the city:
110 Such an outcry over a corpse, with clamor unceasing.
    The bishop sent bans° to bid it abate,°   *decrees / calm down*
    Had a swift steed saddled, and set out at once.
    When he rode through the city and reached St. Paul's
    There were many who met him with much to tell;
115 He entered his palace, bade all hold their peace,
    And turned away from the tomb and sealed tight his door.
    The dark night departed and the day bell rang,
    But Erkenwald had early been up and about,

Who well nigh the whole night had watched and prayed
120   To beseech his sovereign, by His sweet grace,
To vouchsafe° a revelation, some vision or sign;   *grant*
"Though I be unworthy," weeping, he said,
"In His mildness and mercy, may my Lord be moved,
In confirming His Christian faith, to clarify in me
125   This marvel whose mystery amazes men so."
And he pleaded and prayed till presently he had
An answer from the Holy Ghost—and afterward it dawned.
Men flung wide the minster doors when matins° were sung; *early service*
The bishop stood in solemn state to sing the high mass;
130   The prelate was appareled in pontifical° robes;   *bishop's*
He commences the mass, his ministers attending,
Of *Spiritus Domini*,[7] supplication° sweet,   *pleading*
With choral voices vying° in variable accords,   *competing*
Great lords and grand sat gathered together—
135   As the finest folk of the land are found there often—
Until the service had ceased, all recitation done.
Then forth from the altar the officiants came;
The prelate passed on the paved floor—peers bowed low—
In his ceremonial attire he sought out the tomb;
140   Men unclasped the cloister° door with clustered keys,   *enclosed place*
But scarce was there space for the spectators who followed.
The bishop enters the burial place, barons beside him,
The mayor with mace bearers° and men of high office *carriers of staffs*
Duly now the dean discourses of the wonder,
145   The finding and what followed—with a finger he points—
"Honored lords," said he, "we behold here a body
That has lain below this minster, how long is unknown,
Yet his clothes and his color are clear of all blemish,
And his flesh, and the fine tomb where first he was buried.
150   No learned man among us, however long lived,
Can summon up a memory of such a man's reign,
Or let us know his name or his notable deeds.
Many poorer men in this place are put in the grave
Who are registered forever in the rolls of our martyrs,
155   And for seven days unceasing we have searched our books,
But can find in no chronicle a record of this king.
He has not lain here long enough, by his looks it seems,
To be lost from men's memory, unless through some marvel."
"You say true," he concurred who was consecrated bishop;
160   "What is marvelous to men amounts to but little
In the providence of the Prince that in Paradise reigns
When He is led to unlock the least part of His power.

But when man's might is overmastered, and his mind surpassed,
And his reasons lie in ruins, and remedy is none,
165 Then He readily resolves, and releases with a finger[8]
What all the hands under heaven could never hold fast.
When the creature is confounded° by considerations vain,   *confused*
The comfort of the Creator must come to his aid.
So let us do our duty, and discourse no further,
170 In seeking truth ourselves you have seen no success;
Let us turn our gaze on God—may He grant us His grace—
Whose counsels are countless, whose comfort never fails
In confirming your faith and conveying His truth.
I shall provide you presently such proof of His powers
175 That you may believe all your lives that He is Lord God Almighty,
And willingly grants your wishes when faith calls Him friend.

Part II

Then he turns to the tomb, and talks to the dead;[9]
With eyelids lifted wide, he delivers these words:
"Now, body lying before us, be silent no longer;
180 Since Jesus asks that we join Him in joy on this day,
Be obedient to His bidding, I beg on His behalf,
As He spilt and spent His blood, outspread on the cross
(As you see for a fact, and we faithfully suppose),
Answer me openly; unseal all the truth.
185 Since we none of us know you, speak now, and say
Who you were in this world, and why you lie thus,
How long you have lain here, and what law you followed,[10]
And whether you sit high in heaven or suffer in hell."
When he had said these solemn words, and sighed thereafter,
190 The fair body in the box bestirred itself a little,
And its mouth moved mournfully and made these words
Through some ghostly life granted by God, who rules all.[11]
"Bishop," said the body, "your behest° is my joy;   *command*
I were as loath to let it pass as lose both my eyes.
195 The name you have named and pronounced to me here
Holds sway in heaven and hell and the earth between.
First to say, since you ask, what I myself was—
The most ill-fated fellow that fared ever on earth!
I was no king or emperor, or a knight either,
200 But a leading light of the law that the land then used.
I was chosen and charged as chief among those
Who heard causes in court; I upheld London's laws
Under a prince of noble parentage, a pagan born,

Who followed the old faith, and his folk with him.
205 The date of my lying here is lost to your learning;
It is too much for any man to measure its number:
After Brutus first had built the bastion° of this city[12]   *fortress*
Just eight hundred years, take eighteen away;[13]
Before the coming of Christ, as recorded in your faith,
210 A thousand years and thirty more, plus three times eight.
At assizes in circuit° court I sat in New Troy   *traveling*
In the reign of the renowned king that ruled us then,
The bold Briton Sir Belin—Sir Berin was his brother;[14]
Immense was the malice that mounted between them
215 In the wrathful war they waged while their ill will lasted;
In those days was I enjoined° to deal out justice."   *directed*
While he spoke in that closed space, spellbound were all;
No man said a syllable or made the least noise,
But still as a stone all stood there and listened,
220 Struck mute with amazement, and many wept tears.
The bishop bids the body, "Let the cause be known,
Since we cannot call you king, why men have crowned you,
And why a scepter so solemnly is set in your hand,
Since never loyal liegemen owed you life and limb."
225 "Dear sir," said the dead body, "I desire to tell you,
Though it was never my will, for I wanted neither.
I was commissioned a magistrate under a mighty duke,
And this place and all its people were put in my charge.
In London town I laid down the laws of the heathen
230 Faithfully and fairly, forty winters and more.
The folk were false felons, and fractious to govern;
Often I suffered harm to hold them to right.[15]
But for woe or well-being, or warning of danger,
Or authority, or offerings, or awe of any man,
235 I removed never from right, as reason revealed it,
To deem or deal injustice, any day of my life,
Or cast conscience aside to acquire worldly goods,
Or pronounced a false pardon, or played the knave
To please a proud peer, though plenteous his wealth
240 Nor could ever a man's menacing, or mischief or pity
Constrain me to stray from the straight path of right,
As I held fast to the faith that was fixed in my heart.
Had a man felled my father, I had offered him no harm,
Nor falsely freed my father, were he found fit to hang.
245 And as I was reputed righteous and ready in counsel,
All the city resounded with sorrow at my death;
All bemoaned my passing, the mean and the great;

And so they embellished my burial bountifully with gold,
Clad me as the most courteous who convened ever a court,
250 In a mantle, as the mildest and manliest on bench,°   *judge's seat*
Girded me as the goodliest of the governors of Troy,
Furred me for the faith unfaltering within me.
In honor of my honesty and upright life,
They crowned and acclaimed me king of all judges
255 That had lived, they believed, or would live ever in Troy,
And my rule ever righteous they rewarded with the scepter."
The bishop asks urgently, with anguish at heart,
Though men honored him highly, how it might be
That his clothes had kept so clean—"I cannot believe
260 They are not already rotten and rent into rags.
Your body may be embalmed; it baffles me not
That no corruption has reached it, or ravaging worms,
But the color of your clothes: through no craft I know of
Could they have lasted without loss, having lain here so long."
265 "No, bishop," said the body, "embalmed I never was,
Nor are my clothes kept unmarred by any craft of men,
But the peerless Prince of Reason who praises right ever
And loves every law relating to the truth—
And more He honors men who are mindful of right
270 Than all the money gifts they make° to gain the   *i.e., to the church*
     more merit—
And if in reverence for right men arrayed me thus,
He has allowed me to last that loves right best."
"Yes, but say somewhat of your soul," said the bishop then,
"To what lot is she elect, if you lived without blame?
275 He who readily rewards the works of the righteous
Could not have failed to let you feel some effect of His grace.
For as He solemnly asserts in the psalms He wrote,
'The high minded and the harmless shall come home to Me.'[16]
So say somewhat of your soul, where she safely resides,
280 And the recompense° she reaped and received from our Lord."   *reward*
Then he hemmed a little who lay there, and let his head roll,
And gave a great groan, and grieving he spoke:
"O you Maker of man, Your might is great!
How could any part of Your mercy ever have been mine?
285 Was I not an untutored heathen, ignorant of Your ways
And the measure of your mercy and your unmatched power,
A lost unbeliever, unlearnèd in the creed°   *statement of belief*
That You, Lord, are ever lauded in—alas, the hard hours!
I was not among the number You nobly redeemed
290 With the blood of Your body upon the bleak cross.

When You descended into hell and hauled out the souls,[17]
Released the lost from limbo,[18] you left me there,
And there sits my soul, that can see no farther,
Doomed to the dark death descended from our father,
295 Our ancestor Adam who ate of that apple
That poisoned many a people who perished after.
You were touched by his teeth and trapped in hell's throat,
But a medicine mends you and makes you live,
Which is baptism in font, with faith never failing,
300 And we have missed that mercy, myself and my soul.
What gained we by good deeds, who were guided by right,
When we are damned and sent down into the deep pit,
And exiled from that supper so, that solemn feast
Where they that hungered after righteousness are richly filled?[19]
305 My soul may sit sorrowful, with sighs heavy and cold,
Dwelling in that dark place where dawn never comes,
Hungry here in hell-hole, and harken after meals
Long ere she sees that supper, or is summoned to table."
Thus dolefully that dead body disclosed its sorrow
310 Until all wept for woe at the words it spoke,
And the bishop as he listened lowered his eyes,
Who scarce had space to speak, so desperately he sobbed,
Till he collected him a little, and looked toward the tomb,
At the body in its burial place, with brimming tears.
315 "If our Lord," said the prelate, "would but lend you life
As long as would allow me to fetch a little water,
And cast it on your fair form, and say these few words:
'I baptize you now in the Father's name, and the name of His Son
And of the gracious Holy Ghost,'[20] though He granted nothing more,
320 Then though you suddenly died, my distress would be lightened."
When he had said these solemn words, his eyes welled over
And tears wet the tomb that contained the body,
And one fell on its face, and the man fetched a sigh,
And said in a sober voice, "Our Savior be praised,
325 Now be you lauded,° O Lord, and our Lady your mother,   *praised*
And blest be the blissful hour that she bore you in,
And blest be you, bishop, who bore away my sorrow
And lifted the loathly doom whose load was my bane,°   *everlasting misery*
For with the words that you spoke, and the water that you spilled,
330 The bright font of your tears, my baptism has befallen;
With the first one that fell on me, my pain fled away;
My soul right now is saved and seated at the table,
For with the words and the water that washes us clean,
A flame flashed suddenly, far in the abyss,

335 That sped my spirit in space with unspeakable joy
     Into the solemn cenacle²¹ where sup all the faithful,
     And there a marshal° met her with ceremony unstinting   *official guide*
     And ushered her with reverence into a room of her own.
     I praise here my high God and you also, bishop,
340 Who have changed our bale° to bliss—blessings upon you!"   *misfortune*
     Then his voice ceased to sound; he said no more,
     And suddenly and swiftly his sweet looks failed,
     And his bright hue grew black as if mold had besmirched it,
     As ruinous as the dry rot that rises in powder.
345 For as soon as the soul was received into heaven,
     That other craft decayed, that covered the bones,
     For in the blissful reign above, that abides forever,
     All the vainglory° vanishes, that avails so little.   *worldly pride*
     Then they lauded our Lord, with hands lifted high;
350 Much mourning and gladness were mingled together;
     They passed out in procession, and all the people followed,
     And all the bells in the city broke silence at once.²²

Notes: *Saint Erkenwald*

1. lines 7–8: **Since Hengist's days, / Who was sent here by the Saxons.** This and the other historical "facts" that preface the narrative proper of the poem and appear in it later seem to have been drawn by the poet from such sources as Bede's *Ecclesiastical History of the English People* (see Introduction, p. 170) and the popular *Historia Regum Britanniae* (*History of the Kings of Britain*; hereafter *History*) by Geoffrey of Monmouth (d. 1154), which tells of the founding of "Troynovant" or "New Troy" on the site of London. He also may have known Wace's translation of the *Historia* into Norman French verse in the twelfth century, and he was probably familiar with one or more of the medieval prose chronicles recounting early English history, such as the thirteenth century *Chronica Majora* (*Greater Chronicles*) of Matthew of Paris. But his own penchant as a poet for fleshing out the gist of a narrative with specific details must be taken into account as well. With his rhetorical expansion of Augustine's practice of renaming English churches (19–22), for example, compare his similar treatment in *Patience* 165–67 of the statement in the Book of Jonah 1:5 that "men cried to their god(s)."

2. line 12: **Till Saint Augustine to Sandwich was sent by the pope.** Bede tells how at the end of the sixth century Pope Gregory the Great, with the intention of converting England to Christianity, sent there a delegation of missionaries headed by Saint Augustine. This Saint Augustine is not to be confused with the earlier and more eminent Saint Augustine, bishop of Hippo in Africa (in modern Algeria), author of the *Confessions* and *The City of God*.

3. line 31: **Of triapolitan temples it was told the third.** The poet apparently coined the word *triapolitan* ("[one] of three cities") on the model of the Middle (as well as Modern) English word *metropolitan*. The cities he has in mind are

London, Canterbury, and York, which were the sites of the three churches of greatest importance in his own time.

4. line 38: **A noble renovation, and New Work men called it.** The renovation of the cathedral called "New Work" actually dates from the mid-thirteenth century. See Introduction, page 170.

5. line 88: **As they had been assembled yesterday in St. Paul's Yard.** See Introduction, page 170.

6. line 108: **In Essex at an abbey was Erkenwald that day.** See Introduction, page 170.

7. line 132: **Of *Spiritus Domini*, supplication sweet.** *Spiritus Domini* means "of the Holy Spirit." Of the several masses addressed to the Holy Spirit, the poet probably intended one that was used to invoke its power to help on occasions involving an immediate need. This mass is especially appropriate to *Saint Erkenwald* because it was associated with the legal profession; judges attended it at the beginning of each law term in England and France.

8. line 165: **Then He readily resolves, and releases with a finger.** This detail should be understood as an allusion to the Holy Spirit, which figured earlier in the action of the poem in answering Bishop Erkenwald's nocturnal prayers (127) and to which the mass celebrated that morning was dedicated. "Finger of God" was a well-known designation in medieval times for this member of the Trinity. The word *comfort*, which appears twice in the rest of Erkenwald's speech (168, 172), is similarly allusive; the Holy Spirit was called "comforter" in the poet's Middle English, and the title is still used today in the Authorized Version of the Bible. For the underlying presence of the Holy Spirit in the action of the poem as a whole, see Introduction, page 172.

9. line 177: **Then he turns to the tomb, and talks to the dead.** The first letter of this line, which begins the second half of the poem, is a large decorated capital. See the discussion of number symbolism in the Introduction, p. 173.

10. line 187: **How long you have lain here, and what law you followed.** *Law* is a keyword in the poem. The bishop seems to be using it here in the religious sense it had in Middle English and still has, less conspicuously, in the present. His question means, "What religion did you adhere to?" With the coming of Christianity, the "law of grace" was thought by the church to have supplanted the "old," specifically the Mosaic, or Judaic, law. But the old law could also be understood as heathen or pagan religious belief generally, such as prevailed in England when the dead judge lived. Since Christianity had not yet been founded, the law of grace was not available to him and he could not be saved. The word also had its modern, secular meaning in Middle English, and this meaning is equally important in the poem. The dead man had been a lawyer by profession, as shown by the lawyer's coif on his head. When the body refers to the dead man as having been, in life, "a leading light of the law that the land then used" (200, 202), the secular meaning of the word would seem to be primary, but its religious meaning is inevitably suggested as well. When the body says that the dead man "upheld London's laws" (202), and that he "laid down the laws of the heathen" (229), the word has its secular meaning. But when the poet refers to God as one who "loves every law relating to the truth" (268), he is clearly referring to Christian "laws." The poem as a whole raises the question, What laws must be fulfilled, in either the Christian or pre-Christian era, for a soul to be saved?

11. line 192: **Through some ghostly life granted by God, who rules all.** This means only that the body has been made animate and enabled to speak. It has not been restored to life, for life is conceived of in Christian doctrine as the union of body and soul, and the judge's soul is separated from his body in limbo.

12. line 207: **"After Brutus first had built the bastion of this city."** Wace's verse translation of Geoffrey's *History* was entitled *Le roman de Brut*. Both authors told the story of the founding of Britain by a descendant of the Trojan hero Aeneas named Brutus, after whom the country was named. The *Gawain* poet alludes to this same story at the beginning and end of *Sir Gawain and the Green Knight*. The "books of Brutus' deeds" referred to in line 2523 of *Sir Gawain* presumably include Wace's *Brut*.

13. line 208: **"Just eight hundred years, take eighteen away."** None of the theories purporting to explain this complicated numerical sequence has gained general assent. It should be noted, however, that eight, the key number of the poem, is conspicuous in it.

14. line 213: **"The bold Briton Sir Belin—Sir Berin was his brother."** The story of Belinus, who appears in chronicles as a king of Britain, and his protracted feud with his brother Brennius, is recounted in Geoffrey of Monmouth's *History* and elsewhere, and seems to have some foundation in fact. The events in question would have occurred in the fourth century B.C.E.

15. line 232: **"Often I suffered harm to hold them to right."** This speech by the dead body introduces another important word in the poem, namely, *right*, which in the poet's Middle English meant both "righteousness" and "justice" in both its legal and more general senses. The narrative as a whole implies that unfailing righteousness alone does not suffice for salvation, despite the high value attached to it in the later speeches of the body (267–72) and the bishop (275–78). For the latter, see note 16.

16. lines 277–78: **"For as He solemnly asserts in the psalms He wrote, / 'The high minded and the harmless shall come home to Me.'"** Here, as also in *Pearl* XII.2, the poet seems to have in mind Psalm 23 (24 in the A.V.), where the psalmist's question "Who shall ascend into the mountain of the Lord?" receives the answer "The innocent in hands, and clean of heart, who hath not taken his soul in vain, nor sworn deceitfully to his neighbor" (3–4). "Clean of heart" and what follows are interpreted in *Pearl* as designating the righteous man (685–88). In *Saint Erkenwald* 278, the original words are *skilfulle* and *unskathely*; the base of the latter word means "harm" (modern *scathe*). The *unskathely* are clearly the innocent (Latin *innocens*, *in-* "not," *nocens* "harming"). In Middle English, *skilfulle* primarily meant "endowed with reason, rational" and could also mean "righteous." The fact that both here and in *Pearl* 675–76, the poet reverses the order in which the two prerequisites for salvation appear in the Vulgate Bible is a small but significant sign of common authorship.

17. line 291: **When You descended into hell and hauled out the souls.** The poet is referring to the Christian belief that between the Crucifixion and the Resurrection, Christ invaded "limbo" (see note 18) and released the souls of those who had awaited his coming, including the patriarchs of the Old Testament. This event was formerly called the "harrowing" (plundering or sacking) of hell. It is referred to in the Creed in the statement that Christ "descended into hell."

18. line 292: **Released the lost from limbo.** The realm of limbo was variously defined in medieval theology, but was in general thought to be the abode of those

who, though free of personal guilt, had inherited the "original sin" of Adam prior to the redemption of it by Christ's death on the cross. Though denied the bliss of the saved, they were not subjected to the physical torments of the damned in hell proper. The soul of the dead judge in *Saint Erkenwald* is afflicted by grief because, having in the afterlife gained knowledge of the truth of Christianity (see line 283), he is aware of the eternal banquet of the saved in heaven, but thinks that he will never be allowed to join it.

19. lines 303–4: **that solemn feast / Where they that hungered after righteousness are richly filled.** This part of the judge's speech echoes the fourth Beatitude. (See *Patience* 19 and the biblical sources of that poem, pp. 13 and 28.) I translate as "righteousness" the poet's original word, *right*; the Vulgate Bible reads *justitia* (Matthew 5:6).

20. lines 318–19: **'I baptize you now in the Father's name, and the name of His Son / And of the gracious Holy Ghost.'** These words echo in full the official baptismal formula.

21. lines 335–36: **That sped my spirit . . . / Into the solemn cenacle where sup all the faithful.** For the allusion here, and perhaps also in line 334, to the "baptism of fire" at Pentecost, see the introduction, page 000.

22. line 352: **And all the bells in the city broke silence at once.** The motif of church bells ringing spontaneously to mark an especially blessed event appears in medieval saints' lives and is profanely alluded to in Chaucer's *Troilus and Cressida*. Rejoicing at Criseide's acceptance of Troilus as her lover, Pandarus says that he thinks he hears every bell in the town ringing "without hand" (3.188–89).

Sir Gawain and the Green Knight

Introduction to *Sir Gawain and the Green Knight*

Of all the poems of the so-called *Gawain* group, Sir *Gawain and the Green Knight* is the best known and most widely read. In addition to displaying the poet's characteristic powers of narration and description, its story includes elements of mystery, danger, and amorous intrigue that give it universal appeal. It is also the most distanced of the poems from Christian doctrine and story. Though it takes place in a Christian world, the confession on the hero's part in which the action culminates is made not to a priest but to a person who, though his exact identity is a matter of dispute, clearly has no connection with the established church. The confession leads to a kind of secular absolution that most if not all readers have found authoritative. But though the poem does not tell a specifically Christian story, its hero embodies a complex moral ideal defined only partly in Christian terms. Its emblem is a five-pointed star drawn in one continuous line, called by the poet the "Pentangle" and the "endless knot." This ideal symbolizes the moral and spiritual perfection of its possessor, including such specifically Christian elements as reliance on the five joys of the Virgin Mary for fortitude in battle, and trust in the five wounds suffered by Christ on the cross. In addition, the inner side of Gawain's shield bears an image of the Virgin. (This detail is traditionally associated not with Gawain but with King Arthur.)

Sir Gawain and the Green Knight is, so far as we know, the author's sole contribution to the large body of medieval literature recounting the adventures of the knights of King Arthur's court. As such, it harks back to a past earlier than the *Gawain* poet's late fourteenth century, when French was still the language of the English nobility and French literary works were more admired in high-cultural circles than English ones. Though he gives no explicit sign of the fact, the *Gawain* poet must have known the internationally famous romances of the French poet Chrétien de Troyes, composed in the twelfth century, whose subjects included the adventures of a number of King Arthur's knights, among them Sir Gauvain (Gawain). The action of our late-fourteenth-century English poem concerns almost exclusively Sir Gawain, the Green Knight, and Lord Bertilak. The latter appears in Part II as Gawain's host and plays an important part in the later events of the narrative. Bertilak and the Green Knight are original creations. But the poet's familiarity with Arthurian tradition is evident throughout. The story begins with Christmas and New Year feasts at King Arthur's court. The king refuses to sit down at table until he has heard of an adventure; he also behaves this way in earlier French romances, including one of Chrétien's. The many names of knights of the Round Table dropped casually in Part I are found also in Chrétien's other poems and in stories of Arthur told in the Old French prose "Vulgate" cycle. In particular, the name "Bertilak" may come from a Middle English translation of the Old French prose romance *Merlin*.

Yet the poem equally reflects its origin in the late fourteenth century, when the ideal of knighthood, based on the devoted loyalty of a mounted warrior to the feudal lord from whom he held land and for whom he fought, was slowly giving way to a less rooted military professionalism. The knight who appears among the pilgrims in the *Canterbury Tales*, written by the *Gawain* poet's contemporary Geoffrey Chaucer, personifies fidelity and honor, has served worthily in "his lord's war" and has "fought for our faith." But he has also fought in Turkey for "the Lord of Palatye," a Muslim. The time-honored ideal of knighthood, or *chivalry*, is explicitly emphasized in *Sir Gawain*. The virtues symbolized by Gawain's emblem are his in superlative degree. The narrator praises him as "devoid of all villainy" (634). He is "in speech most courteous knight" (639), and his virtues of "fellowship" and "courtesy" are, we may assume, exhibited in his behavior toward others, including his fellow knights. After his second encounter with the Green Knight, when he realizes that he has fallen short of perfection, he accuses himself of having behaved in a way "contrary . . . / To largesse and loyalty belonging to *knights*" (2380–81). The Green Knight affirms his merit in the same terms: Sir Gawain, compared with "other gay *knights*," is like a pearl compared with white peas (2364–65). In part, then, the meaning of the poem consists in its affirmation of an old ideal threatened by change.

The Story

The main elements of the plot of *Sir Gawain* derive ultimately from folklore, but the poet himself would probably have encountered them in stories told in Latin or Old French, and he was surely the first to combine them. The opening action of the poem retells a story known as the "Beheading Game," in which an unknown challenger proposes that one of a group of warriors volunteer to cut off his head, the stroke to be repaid in kind at some future date. The hero accepts this challenge and at the crucial moment of reprisal is spared and praised for his courage. Later action incorporates the "Temptation Story," in which an attractive woman attempts to seduce a man under circumstances in which he is obliged to resist her, and the "Exchange of Winnings," in which two men agree to exchange what each has acquired during a set period of time. In the plot of *Gawain*, these narrative components are intricately linked.

The hero, having contracted to accept a presumably mortal stroke from the ax of the Green Knight, whom he has beheaded, sets out to meet him at the Green Chapel on New Year's Day. Though the Green Knight has assured him that many people know where he lives, Gawain is unable to find him; instead, he comes on a magnificent castle, where he is lavishly entertained. Later, he is induced by his host, Lord Bertilak, to exchange winnings at the end of three successive days, during each of which Bertilak will go hunting. His beautiful wife visits the chamber where Gawain is lying in bed on the three successive mornings and does her best to seduce him.

In an Old French manuscript dating from the late thirteenth or early fourteenth century, unique copies of two poems whose hero is Sir Gauvain appear side by side.° In one of them, Gauvain is subjected to sexual temptation when his host, in the castle where he is a guest, orders him to spend the night naked in bed with his beautiful (and willing) daughter. When he makes an attempt to consummate their lovemaking, he is punished by a magic sword that flies from the wall to the bed and cuts off a little slice of his flesh. His ardor cooled, he abstains. Eventually it turns out that his host has in the past used the sword to kill many visiting knights but that it will not kill the best knight in the world, that is, Sir Gauvain. In the other poem, as Gauvain is about to go to bed in a castle where he is staying, his host, around whose head hangs a large ax (called a *gisarme*, a word used also in *Sir Gawain*) proposes a "game": Gauvain will cut off his host's head with the ax, on condition that he allows his own head to be cut off on the following day. Gauvain agrees. His host returns in the morning, alive and well, with his head back in place. Gauvain lays his head on the block. The other man lifts the ax high to frighten him, but spares him because he has been loyal and kept his promise. The opening passages of both these poems contain allusions to Chrétien de Troyes, and they are written in the rhymed eight-syllable couplets that Chrétien used in his narrative poems. Whether or not Chrétien was their author, there is every reason to think that the *Gawain* poet read them and was inspired to connect the beheading anticipated by Sir Gawain with the attempts at seduction made by his host's wife. These end in her farewell offer of a love gift or memento in the form of a girdle supposedly conferring invulnerability on its wearer. Gawain's acceptance of it, under the circumstances, is wholly understandable, even though it entails a lapse of fidelity or troth on his part: the lady tells him that he must conceal the girdle from her husband, thus breaking the men's agreement to turn over all their winnings to one another at the end of the day.

All the strands of the narrative of *Sir Gawain and the Green Knight* come together in the last part of the poem, when Sir Gawain and the Green Knight meet once more. By the time their encounter is over, the most honored knight in the world, famed alike as a courageous warrior and an unfailingly courteous

---

° English translations of both these poems are included in the Norton Critical Edition of *Sir Gawain and the Green Knight*, translated by Marie Borroff, edited by Borroff and Laura Howes (2009).

admirer of women, has been proven fallible. The pentangle symbolizing his perfection, described at length in Part II, has not been mentioned again, though Gawain is referred to in one of the bedroom scenes as "Mary's knight." His faulty act includes cowardice, because it was brought about by fear of death; and treachery, because it involved a breach of faith with the host to whom Sir Gawain had pledged feudal allegiance (1039, 1092). To these the poet adds a breach of courtesy when this most gracious of knights, confronted with his own susceptibility to feminine wiles, gives way to a burst of anger against women.

The *Gawain* poet, a master of juxtapositions, has constructed from these separable story elements a whole greater than the sum of its parts. The castle where Sir Gawain is entertained is vividly real. Its architecture reflects the latest Continental style; its court is elegant and gay; its accommodations and meals as sumptuous as those of a modern luxury hotel. Yet it is also the mysterious castle that has appeared out of nowhere, shining and shimmering like a mirage, in direct response to a prayer to the Virgin, and it is a way station (or so Gawain believes) on the road to certain death. This shadow looms over the Christmas festivities, though the knight takes part in them as gaily as courtesy (the "fellowship" of the pentangle) obliges him to do, and over the high comedy of the bedroom scenes, where he must struggle to resist the lady's advances without insulting her. There is a profound psychological truth to the fact that he passes all these tests successfully and then fails the most important one of all: the most dangerous temptation is the one that presents itself unexpectedly, as a side issue, while we are busy resisting another. Gawain accepts the girdle because it is clearly "a pearl for his plight," and perhaps also because the act may seem a way of granting the importunate lady a favor while eluding her amorous invitation. Its full meaning as a cowardly, and hence covetous, grasping at life is revealed to him only later and with stunning force.

To all this, the poet has added three brilliantly described hunting scenes as the host, on three successive mornings, pursues the deer, the boar, and the fox. These episodes obviously parallel the bedchamber scenes, where the lady acts the part of the huntress and Sir Gawain that of the fleeing quarry. The parallel between the wiles of the fox, before he is caught on the third and final day, and Gawain's ill-fated ruse in concealing the belt, is equally obvious. Such parallels are inherent in the presence of the three hunts in the narrative. But by his handling of them, the poet has enhanced their dramatic effect. Each hunt is divided in two, enclosing the bedchamber scene of that day like the two halves of a peapod. As each one opens, it presents a picture of vigorous, unhampered, and joyous activity, with the host as the central figure dominating the action. From these openings we move suddenly to the bed with its surrounding curtains, where all is hushed and space is narrowly confined. Nothing could more effectively enhance our sympathetic identification with the hero, hedged about morally and socially as well as physically. Each bedroom encounter is followed by the conclusion of the corresponding hunt in a scene of carnage and ceremonial butchery that follows with all the logic of a violent dream after dutiful constraints.

But the deepest "meaning" of the hunting scenes lies in the reader's vicarious experience of them. Perhaps the most salient quality of that experience is the sheer delight inherent in sport at its best, when demanding physical activity is skillfully performed in fine weather with good companions. This delight, though innocent, is of the body, bringing into play a part of experience that unites human beings with other living creatures. The poet's sympathetic understanding of it is a part of his love of the physical world, manifest also in his knowledge of and pleasure in "all trades, their gear and tackle and trim" and his imaginative identification with the point of view of the hunted creatures themselves and, later, of the creatures enduring the cold and stinging sleet of winter. Insofar as he induces us to share their experience, he places us on the side of mortality. We can forgive Gawain for his single act of cowardice, for we see that it was caused, as the Green Knight says, not by sensual lust or the desire to possess precious things, but by love of life—"the less, then, to blame." Given this affectionate sympathy, we can view Gawain's violent anger, when the meaning of his actions is revealed to him, as another aspect of his human fallibility, and we can join in the friendly laughter of the members of Arthur's court when he returns and tells his story. Yet the larger moral of the poem is serious; the pride implicit in Gawain's taking his own reputation for granted has been humbled. The lesson he has been taught applies a *fortiori* to the court he represents and, by further extension, to all human beings.

The Traditional Style and the Plot of *Sir Gawain*

All the works of the *Gawain* poet, except for *Pearl*, are composed in the traditional style of Late Middle English alliterative poetry. This body of poetry descended from Old English alliterative poetry represented by *Beowulf*, among other poems. Old English poetry descended in turn from the alliterative poetry originally composed in the preliterate Germanic culture of western Europe. As the General Introduction explains, the earliest surviving poetic narratives, in both Germanic tradition and the Hellenic tradition extant in the works of Homer, celebrate the deeds of ancestral heroes: noble lords and their loyal companions. Poets themselves appear in both traditions as honored members of royal households—men who serve the important purpose of remembering and reciting the traditional stories. The language of the "heroic" verse recounting these stories is formulaic, containing multitudes of metrically shaped word combinations and, in the Germanic tradition, groups of synonyms expressing important meanings such as *warrior, chieftain, sword,* and *steed.* These latter begin with different consonants and thus constitute repertoires from which needed alliterating words can be chosen. In addition to their ornamental value, these synonymous alternatives, incorporated into alliterative patterns, are mnemonic aids. Late Middle English alliterative verse perpetuates them, newly embodied in the English language of the late fourteenth century.

Of the *Gawain* poet's alliterative works, *Sir Gawain and the Green Knight* is most reminiscent of the ancient heroic poems in content and presentation. The poet-narrator begins by saying that he intends to "unfold . . . a marvel of might," "unmatched among the wonders" associated with the past history of England in the person of the legendary King Arthur. He will tell it, as he himself heard it, in language linking "letters tried and true" (I take this last phrase to be a reference to alliterative verse). At intervals, he alludes to the fact that the story he tells is not original with him but comes from a book he has "heard." From time to time his narrative implies an audience, as when in the second introductory stanza, he says "If you will listen to my lay [poem] but a little while . . . I shall hasten to tell it." Much later, as Sir Gawain lies in bed on the night preceding his fatal encounter (as he supposes) with the Green Knight, the narrator says

> Let him lie and wait;
> He has little more to do.
> Then listen, as I relate
> How they kept their rendezvous.   (1994–97)

The tone of the ancient heroic poems exemplified by *Beowulf* is serious and, on appropriate occasions, solemn. Their poet-narrators, like the poets who appear in them as characters, are cultural historians: custodians and commemorators of the important deeds of the past and the powers and virtues of the ancestral heroes who performed them. The narrator of *Sir Gawain* is by definition the "official" spokesman for King Arthur's court and the central figure of the story, Sir Gawain. This role is particularly important in a narrative in which reputation figures so prominently. In the second of the two opening stanzas, the narrator says that he has chosen his story from among the "wonders" associated with the man accounted "most courteous" of British kings. Later, describing the gaiety of the Christmas feast at Camelot, he calls Arthur the "king noblest famed." The theme is picked up again, with a difference, in the Green Knight's explanation for his visit: to see for himself the king whose praises are "puffed up so high" and the members of the knightly company that is "accounted" the best, "worthiest of their works the wide world over"—to see and, by implication, to put to the test.

But the poet's treatment of the encounter between the court and the stranger who "hurtles" into it on horseback, and in particular his conception of the person and manner of the Green Knight, disregards the time-honored parameters of Arthurian romance. When, at the New Year feast, Arthur behaves as usual by refusing to take his place at table until something has happened, his expectations are couched in comfortably traditional terms. He will not eat until he has heard "of some fair feat or fray," some "marvel of might . . . by champions of chivalry achieved in arms,"

Or some suppliant [who] came seeking some single knight
To join with him in jousting, in jeopardy each
To lay life for life . . .   (96–98)

In other words, he looks forward to another adventure of the sort familiar to those who know the Arthurian stories. What follows instead—and what the narrator is duty bound to relate—is the humiliation of the knightly company and its king by an outlandish, obstreperous, jeeringly dismissive stranger, a mysterious being at once worldly and otherworldly. Of all the characters in the episode, he alone is described, in some seventy lines of specific detail, with the result that he looms over the scene as a physical being far more real than anyone else. And though the court, in the persons of King Arthur and Sir Gawain, does rise to the challenge he presents, its actions are preceded by a long moment of paralysis during which everyone present sits "in a swooning silence in the stately hall" as if they had fallen asleep.

Through it all, the narration proceeds smoothly, couched in the traditional language that was originally designed to commemorate and to praise. But here that language describes events difficult to fit into the Arthurian paradigm. In the course of the action in Part I, we see heroes of high repute treated disrespectfully by an overbearing personage of indeterminate identity. He drives a hard bargain, imperiling the court's most honored knight, and finally gallops off headless, coolly throwing down a final challenge. The result of this tension between tradition and the overturning of tradition is that elements of the traditional language take on, at times, a hollow ring, or attract connotations insidiously belying or contradicting their time-honored force. This happens in a small detail early in the poem, when Arthur's company is described as "hardy . . . on hill." ("On hill" is equivalent to "in a castle [located on a hill].") But the linking of adjective and location is a little off key, as "hardiness" is more usually predicated, in such phrases as "hardy of heart" and "hardy of hand," not of warriors as dwellers in castles but of warriors as powerful contenders on the field of battle. (Compare the descriptive formula "heard under helme," i.e., "hardy under helmet," which appears several times in *Beowulf*.) Later, explaining the company's reluctance to answer the stranger as due to his uncanny appearance, the narrator says that "of answer was chary *many a champion bold*." Given the failure of nerve that is taking place at that moment, the appellation "bold champion" has an unmistakably ironic ring. (In the original language of the poem, the members of the court are called "athel frekes [noble warriors]," a combination in which both adjective and noun belong to the elevated, deferential language of the alliterative tradition.) Something similar happens when the narrator, in the original, refers to King Arthur, standing near the dinner table as he waits for something to happen, as "the stif kyng." The word *stiff* was used in the alliterative tradition in Late Middle English as an adjective of praise, meaning "resolute" or "stout hearted." But it also had its modern meaning, "rigid." When the narrator calls Arthur "the stiff king himself," he surely means the adjective as an honorific, but in this context the less dignified modern meaning intrudes itself and, once present, cannot be dispelled. (I have tried to approximate this effect by using the similarly ambiguous modern word *stout*, as if the young king were not only stalwart but also a little portly.) Disparities of the same sort arise later, when, for example, the narrator applies to Sir Gawain at moments when he is sorely tried an adjective signifying the cheerfulness of mien a courteous knight is expected to display at all times. On the morning of her first visit, when his host's wife claims to have taken him captive and threatens to "bind him in his bed," he manages a courteous reply, but at that moment the appellation "Gawain the blithe," applied to him by the narrator, seems jarringly unsuitable. Later in their conversation, when he must yet again devise a polite reply to yet another of her thinly veiled sexual overtures, the narrator refers to him as "the merry man."

In his treatment of the relationship between Sir Gawain and the seductive wife of Lord Bertilak, the poet draws on another source: the language of the "courtly love" tradition that enlarged the subject matter of alliterative poetry between the Old English and Late Middle English periods. (For a discussion of this tradition, and the important contribution to it of the Arthurian romances of Chrétien de Troyes, see the General Introduction, p. xxiii.) When the members of Lord Bertilak's court, delighted to learn that the guest who has arrived is Sir Gawain, anticipate that whoever talks with him "shall learn love's language true," they are referring to this tradition. Bertilak's wife invokes it at length in the second bedroom scene (see especially li. 1512–34). Earlier, in her first attempt to arouse Gawain's amorous interest, she has described herself as his "servant to command," using the word *servant* in what might be called its technical sense. Gawain uses the same word in its more general meaning when he adroitly responds by saying, "soberly your servant, my sovereign I hold you" (1278; see the note on li. 1239–40). The courtly love convention is further invoked when the wife, in their last encounter, describes herself as "of all women in this world most wounded in heart" (1781).

Fame and Fiction

The interplay between reality and reputation initiated in the opening episode of the poem thus becomes prominent again, with a difference, during Gawain's stay in Bertilak's castle. Among his praiseworthy qualities, one is made especially conspicuous. We find it attributed to Gawain in Chaucer's *Canterbury Tales*, when the Squire, telling his own tale, describes the salutation of the knight on the steed of brass to those present at the court of Cambuskyan, saying that "Gawayn, with his olde curteisye, Though he were comen ayeyn out of Fairye," could not have improved on it (V[F] 95–97). Bertilak's wife alludes to it when she addresses him during her first visit to his bedroom:

> For as certain as I sit here, Sir Gawain you are,
> Whom all the world worships, whereso you ride;
> Your honor, your courtesy are highest acclaimed
> By lord and by ladies, by all living men.   (1226–29)

More disconcertingly, she uses it to chide him: he cannot be Sir Gawain, she tells him, because Sir Gawain would have "claimed a kiss, by his courtesy" before they parted (1300). On her visit the following morning, she uses the same tactic: it is strange, if he is indeed Sir Gawain, that he "cannot act in company as courtesy bids" (1483). This disparity between his reputation and his actions, it turns out, consists in his having failed not only to kiss her but to use, in conversation with her, "the language of love," wooing her and then instructing her, during her husband's absence, in "new pastimes" such as may or may not be suitable for a married woman to engage in with a house guest. Here again, reality and fiction tend to merge. In a number of the Arthurian romances, Gawain is portrayed as amorous and fickle, ever susceptible to the charms of women though permanently committing himself to none. The lady, evidently aware of this aspect of the tradition, questions the identity of the man beside her as if he were a movie star—a sex symbol who might or might not live up to his image on the screen.

Courtesy, as the lord's wife seems to conceive of it, is the art of flattering a lady to lure her into amorous interplay; its goal is seduction. But the Gawain we see in action in the poem is not the womanizer his bedside visitor takes him to be. He is the Gawain who bears the pentangle on his shield, and the set of five virtues signified by that emblem includes *cortaysye* side by side with *clannes* or purity (653; I translate "pure mind and manners"). Moreover, each of the "five fives" symbolized by the pentangle, including the five wounds on the cross and the five joys of the Virgin, is linked inseparably with all the rest in an "endless knot," so that a breach in one would be a breach in the whole design (630, 655–61). For this Gawain, there is no conflict between courtesy and chastity—except, ironically, in the third bedroom scene. Here, the lady is more desirable, and her invitation to lovemaking more explicit, than ever. There is no question of his becoming her lover, however his mortal flesh may be stirred by her beauty (1760–62), for to allow himself to do so would be sinful (1774). In refusing her, he must take the lesser risk of appearing discourteous (1773). The poet avails himself of more than one opportunity to insist that the courtesy of the Gawain he has in mind is free from any taint of lewdness even when he speaks of love.

The Pentangle and the Green Girdle

Sir Gawain and the Green Knight is "circular" in design in that its conclusion harks back to its opening. The first line of the poem, "Since the siege and the assault was ceased at Troy," is echoed by the last alliterating line, "After the siege ceased at Troy and the city fared / amiss." Moreover, the poem has a numerical design, the key number of that design being five. The number of the above-quoted last alliterating line is 2525. The pentangle, Sir Gawain's emblem, has five points, each of which has a fivefold meaning. The first point described stands for the five senses, and perhaps there is some justification for associating these with the love of life that motivated Gawain when he accepted the green girdle offered him by Lord Bertilak's wife. In any case, the pentangle is called the "endless knot" because when it is drawn, the end of the continuous line joins its beginning without a break. The green girdle can be thought of as a symbol complementary to the pentangle. It is "knotted" about the lady's body, and in offering it, she breaks the knot so that the girdle becomes a line, just as Sir Gawain breaks the endless knot of the pentangle by breaking his promise to her husband. There is even a reference later in the narrative to the two "ends" of the girdle; when Sir Gawain ties it (twice) about his body, the narrator assures us that he wore it not "for its wealth, . . . though glittering gold gleamed at the ends" (2037–39), but to save himself from death. In its circular structure, in its numerical design, and in the complementary symbolism of pentangle and girdle, *Sir Gawain* resembles *Pearl*. (See the introduction and notes to *Pearl* for a discussion of the analogous opposition in that poem between circle and line. It is a further, and intriguing, fact that in both poems, the number of stanzas is 101.)

When, at the end of the poem, the Green Knight "absolves" Sir Gawain, forgiving him for concealing the green girdle because his motive was not the vulgar desire to possess a valuable object but love of life, he makes explicit a theme that has been conspicuous, though tacit, in several earlier episodes. Part of the vividness of the three hunting scenes derives from the poet's sympathetic identification not only with the joyful hunters but with their quarry. We are placed in the woods alongside the frantically racing deer as arrows whistle by at every turn; we share the point of view of the great boar as the stinging of arrow after arrow finally rouses him to a frenzy; we accompany the fox as he cautiously makes his way through a clearing, thinking he has thrown his pursuers off the scent, then is suddenly confronted by three greyhounds who block his path. All these mortal creatures want desperately to live and use their powers to the utmost to evade death; death, when it comes, is immediately followed by the cutting up or flaying of bodies. When Sir Gawain, having borne the third and last stroke of the Green Knight's ax, sees his own blood on the snow, he joins the hunted creatures as a fleshly being who does not want to die.

The *Gawain* poet was a devout Christian. As such, he was well aware (as he shows us in *Pearl* and *Saint Erkenwald*) of the joys of the saved soul after death. But *Sir Gawain and the Green Knight*—the poem that I think was his last—looks forward to a time when society would no longer be dominated in its every aspect by a single religious establishment. The definitive judgment of its hero is made, not by the church, but by a representative of his profession: a lord at the head of a knightly company, such as the members of Arthur's court, mourning Gawain's loss as he sets out on what they consider his fatal errand, believe he was likely to become, had he lived. The poet ends his "best book of romance" by assuring us that life on earth, for all the trials and hazards in which it ensnares body and soul, is worthy of our love.

Sir Gawain and the Green Knight

Part I

Since the siege and the assault was ceased at Troy,[1]
The walls breached and burnt down to brands and ashes,
The knight that had knotted the nets of deceit
Was impeached for his perfidy,° proven most true.[2]   *treachery*
5   It was high-born Aeneas and his haughty race
That since prevailed over provinces, and proudly reigned
Over well-nigh all the wealth of the West Isles.
Great Romulus to Rome repairs in haste;
With boast and with bravery builds he that city
10 And names it with his own name, that it now bears.
Ticius to Tuscany, and towers raises.
Langobard in Lombardy lays out homes,
And far over the French Sea, Felix Brutus[3]
On many broad hills and high Britain he sets,
15   most fair,
      Where war and wrack and wonder
      By shifts have sojourned there,
      And bliss by turns with blunder
      In that land's lot had share.

20   And since this Britain was built by this baron great,
Bold boys bred there, in broils° delighting,   *fights*
That did in their day many a deed most dire.
More marvels have happened in this merry land
Than in any other I know, since that olden time,
25   But of those that here built, of British kings,
King Arthur was counted most courteous of all,
Wherefore an adventure I aim to unfold,
That a marvel of might some men think it,
And one unmatched among Arthur's wonders.
30   If you will listen to my lay° but a little while,   *narrative poem*
As I heard it in hall, I shall hasten to tell
            anew
      As it was fashioned featly°   *skillfully*

201

In tale of derring-do,
35   And linked in measures meetly°   *suitably*
By letters tried and true.

This king lay at Camelot at Christmastide;
Many good knights and gay his guests were there,
Arrayed of the Round Table rightful brothers,
40 With feasting and fellowship and carefree mirth.
There true men contended in tournaments many,
Joined there in jousting these gentle knights,
Then came to the court for carol dancing,[4]
For the feast was in force full fifteen days,
45 With all the meat and the mirth that men could devise,
Such gaiety and glee, glorious to hear,
Brave din by day, dancing by night.
High were their hearts in halls and chambers,
These lords and these ladies, for life was sweet.
50 In peerless pleasures passed they their days,
The most noble knights known under Christ,
And the loveliest ladies that lived on earth ever,
And he the comeliest king, that that court holds,
For all this fair folk in their first age
55   were still.
Happiest of mortal kind,
King noblest famed of will;
You would now go far to find
So hardy a host on hill.

60 While the New Year was new, but yesternight come,
This fair folk at feast twofold was served,
When the king and his company were come in together,
The chanting in chapel achieved and ended.
Clergy and all the court acclaimed the glad season,
65 Cried Noel anew, good news to men;
Then gallants gather gaily, hand gifts to make,[5]
Called them out clearly, claimed them by hand,
Bickered long and busily about those gifts.
Ladies laughed aloud, though losers they were,
70 And he that won was not angered, as well you will know.
All this mirth they made until meat was served;
When they had washed them worthily, they went to their seats,
The best seated above, as best it beseemed,
Guenevere the goodly queen gay in the midst
75 On a dais° well decked and duly arrayed   *platform*
With costly silk curtains, a canopy over,

Of Toulouse and Turkestan tapestries rich,
All broidered and bordered with the best gems
Ever brought into Britain, with bright pennies
80   to pay.
    Fair queen, without a flaw,
    She glanced with eyes of gray.
    A seemlier that once he saw,
    In truth, no man could say.

85 But Arthur would not eat till all were served;
So light was his lordly heart, and a little boyish;
His life he liked lively—the less he cared
To be lying for long, or long to sit,
So busy his young blood, his brain so wild.
90 And also a point of pride pricked him in heart,
For he nobly had willed, he would never eat
On so high a holiday, till he had heard first
Of some fair feat or fray,° some far-borne tale   *battle*
Of some marvel of might, that he might trust,
95 By champions of chivalry achieved in arms,
Or some suppliant° came seeking some single knight   *seeker of help*
To join with him in jousting, in jeopardy° each   *danger*
To lay life for life, and leave it to fortune
To afford him on field fair hap or other.
100 Such is the king's custom, when his court he holds
At each far-famed feast amid his fair host
            so dear.
        The stout king stands in state
        Till a wonder shall appear;
105   He leads, with heart elate,
        High mirth in the New Year.

So he stands there in state, the stout young king,
Talking before the high table of trifles fair.
There Gawain the good knight by Guenevere sits,
110 With Agravain à la dure main° on his other side,   *of the hard hand*
Both knights of renown, and nephews of the king.
Bishop Baldwin above begins the table,
And Yvain, son of Urien, ate with him there.
These few with the fair queen were fittingly served;
115 At the side tables sat many stalwart knights.[6]
Then the first course comes, with clamor of trumpets
That were bravely bedecked with bannerets bright,
With new sounding of drums and the noble pipes.
Wild were the warbles that wakened that day

120 In strains that stirred many strong men's hearts.
    There dainties were dealt out, dishes rare,
    Choice fare to choose, on chargers° so many   *platters*
    That scarce was there space to set before the people
    The service of silver, with sundry meats,
125   on cloth.
        Each fair guest freely there
        Partakes, and nothing loath;°   *not at all unwilling*
        Twelve dishes before each pair;
        Good beer and bright wine both.

130 Of the service itself I need say no more,
    For well you will know no tittle was wanting.
    Another noise and a new was well-nigh at hand,
    That the lord might have leave his life to nourish;
    For scarce were the sweet strains still in the hall,
135 And the first course come to that company fair,
    There hurtles in at the hall door an unknown rider,
    One the greatest on ground in growth of his frame:
    From broad neck to buttocks so bulky and thick,
    And his loins and his legs so long and so great,
140 Half a giant on earth I hold him to be,
    But believe him no less than the largest of men,
    And that the seemliest in his stature to see, as he rides,
    For in back and in breast though his body was grim,
    His waist in its width was worthily small,
145 And formed with every feature in fair accord
           was he.
        Great wonder grew in hall
        At his hue most strange to see,
        For man and gear and all
150   Were green as green could be.

    And in guise all of green, the gear and the man:
    A coat cut close, that clung to his sides,
    And a mantle to match, made with a lining
    Of furs cut and fitted—the fabric was noble,
155 Embellished all with ermine, and his hood beside,
    That was loosed from his locks, and laid on his shoulders.
    With trim hose and tight, the same tint of green,
    His great calves were girt,° and gold spurs under   *encircled*
    He bore on silk bands that embellished his heels,
160 And footgear well fashioned, for riding most fit.
    And all his vesture° verily was verdant green;   *clothing*
    Both the bosses° on his belt and other bright gems   *circular ornaments*

That were richly ranged on his raiment noble
About himself and his saddle, set upon silk,
165   That to tell half the trifles would tax my wits,
The butterflies and birds embroidered thereon
In green of the gayest, with many a gold thread.
The pendants of the breast band, the princely
      crupper,°   *strap around horse's rump*
And the bars of the bit were brightly enameled;
170   The stout stirrups were green, that steadied his feet,
And the bows of the saddle and the side panels both,
That gleamed all and glinted with green gems about.
The steed he bestrides of that same green
               so bright.
175   A green horse great and thick;
          A headstrong steed of might;
          In broidered bridle quick,
          Mount matched man aright.

Gay was this goodly man in guise all of green,
180   And the hair of his head to his horse suited;
Fair flowing tresses enfold his shoulders;
A beard big as a bush on his breast hangs,[7]
That with his heavy hair, that from his head falls,
Was evened all about above both his elbows,
185   That half his arms thereunder were hid in the fashion
Of a king's cap-à-dos,[8] that covers his throat.
The mane of that mighty horse much to it like,
Well curled and becombed, and cunningly knotted
With filaments° of fine gold amid the fair green,   *threads*
190   Here a strand of the hair, here one of gold;
His tail and his foretop° twin in their hue,   *lock of hair on brow*
And bound both with a band of a bright green
That was decked adown the dock° with dazzling stones   *clipped tail*
And tied tight at the top with a triple knot
195   Where many bells well burnished rang bright and clear.
Such a mount in his might, nor man on him riding,
None had seen, I dare swear, with sight in that hall
             so grand.
          As lightning quick and light
200   He looked to all at hand;
          It seemed that no man might
          His deadly blows withstand.

Yet had he no helm, nor hauberk° neither,   *tunic of chain mail*
Nor plate, nor appurtenance° appending to arms,   *item of equipment*

205 Nor shaft pointed sharp, nor shield for defense,
But in his one hand he had a holly bob
That is goodliest in green when groves are bare,
And an ax in his other, a huge and immense,
A wicked piece of work in words to expound:
210 The head on its haft was an ell° long;   *forty-five inches*
The spike of green steel, resplendent with gold;
The blade burnished bright, with a broad edge,
As well shaped to shear as a sharp razor;
Stout was the stave in the strong man's gripe,
215 That was wound all with iron to the weapon's end,
With engravings in green of goodliest work.
A lace lightly about, that led to a knot,
Was looped in by lengths along the fair haft,
And tassels thereto attached in a row,
220 With buttons of bright green, brave to behold.
This horseman hurtles in, and the hall enters;
Riding to the high dais, recked he no danger;
Not a greeting he gave as the guests he o'erlooked,
Nor wasted his words, but "Where is," he said,
225 "The captain of this crowd?⁹ Keenly I wish
To see that sire with sight, and to himself say
          my say."
      He swaggered all about
      To scan the host so gay;
230   He halted, as if in doubt
      Who in that hall held sway.

There were stares on all sides as the stranger spoke,
For much did they marvel what it might mean
That a horseman and a horse should have such a hue,¹⁰
235 Grow green as the grass, and greener, it seemed,
Than green fused on gold more glorious by far.
All the onlookers eyed him, and edged nearer,
And awaited in wonder what he would do,
For many sights had they seen, but such a one never,
240 So that phantom and faerie the folk there deemed it.
Therefore chary° of answer was many a champion bold,   *cautious*
And stunned at his strong words stone still they sat
In a swooning silence in the stately hall.
As all were slipped into sleep, so slackened their speech
245   apace.
      Not all, I think, for dread,
      But some of courteous grace

Let him who was their head
Be spokesman in that place.

250 Then Arthur before the high dais that entrance beholds,
And hailed him, as behooved, for he had no fear,
And said, "Fellow, in faith you have found fair welcome;
The head of this hostelry° Arthur am I;   *inn*
Leap lightly down, and linger, I pray,
255 And the tale of your intent you shall tell us after."
"Nay, so help me," said the other. "He that on high sits,
To tarry here any time, 'twas not mine errand;
But as the praise of you, prince, is puffed up so high,
And your court and your company are counted the best,
260 Stoutest under steel gear on steeds to ride,
Worthiest of their works the wide world over,
And peerless to prove in passages of arms,
And courtesy here is carried to its height,
And so at this season I have sought you out.
265 You may be certain by the branch that I bear in hand
That I pass here in peace, and would part friends,
For had I come to this court on combat bent,
I have a hauberk at home, and a helm beside,
A shield and a sharp spear, shining bright,
270 And other weapons as well, war gear of the best;
But as I willed no war, I wore no metal.
But if you be so bold as all men believe,
You will graciously grant the game that I ask
                              by right."
275   Arthur answer gave
             And said, "Sir courteous knight,
             If contest here you crave,
             You shall not fail to fight."

"Nay, to fight, in good faith, is far from my thought;
280 There are about on these benches but beardless children.
Were I here in full arms on a haughty steed,
For measured against mine, their might is puny.°   *weak*
And so I call in this court for a Christmas game,
For 'tis Yule and New Year, and many young bloods about;
285 If any in this house such hardihood claims,
Be so bold in his blood, his brain so wild,
As stoutly to strike one stroke for another,
I shall give him as my gift this gisarme noble,
This ax, that is heavy enough, to handle as he likes,
290 And I shall bide the first blow, as bare as I sit.

If there be one so wilful my words to assay,°   *put to the test*
Let him leap hither lightly, lay hold of this weapon;
I quitclaim° it forever, keep it as his own,   *give it up*
And I shall stand him a stroke, steady on this floor,
295 So you grant me the guerdon° to give him another,   *reward*
              sans blame.
          In a twelvemonth and a day
          He shall have of me the same;
          Now be it seen straightway
300   Who dares take up the game."

If he astonished them at first, stiller were then
All that household in hall, the high and the low;
The stranger on his green steed stirred in the saddle,
And roisterously his red eyes he rolled all about,
305 Bent his bristling brows, that were bright green,
Wagged his beard as he watched who would arise.
When the court kept its counsel he coughed aloud,
And cleared his throat coolly, the clearer to speak:
"What, is this Arthur's house," said that horseman then,
310 "Whose fame is so fair in far realms and wide?
Where is now your arrogance and your awesome deeds,
Your valor and your victories and your vaunting° words?   *boastful*
Now are the revel and renown of the Round Table
Overwhelmed with a word of one man's speech,
315 For all cower and quake, and no cut felt!"
With this he laughs so loud that the lord grieved;
The blood for sheer shame shot to his face,
              and pride.
          With rage his face flushed red,
320   And so did all beside.
          Then the king as bold man bred
          Toward the stranger took a stride.

And said, "Sir, now we see you will say but folly,
Which whoso has sought, it suits that he find.
325 No guest here is aghast° of your great words.   *frightened*
Give to me your gisarme, in God's own name,
And the boon you have begged shall straight be granted."
He leaps to him lightly, lays hold of his weapon;
The green fellow on foot fiercely alights.
330 Now has Arthur his ax, and the haft grips,
And sternly stirs it about, on striking bent.
The stranger before him stood there erect,
Higher than any in the house by a head and more;

With stern look as he stood, he stroked his beard,
335 And with undaunted countenance drew down his coat,
No more moved nor dismayed for his mighty blows
Than any bold man on bench had brought him a drink
                                 of wine.
                  Gawain by Guenevere
340   Toward the king doth now incline:
                  "I beseech, before all here,
                  That this melee° may be mine."   *combat*

"Would you grant me the grace," said Gawain to the king,
"To be gone from this bench and stand by you there,
345 If I without discourtesy might quit this board,
And if my liege lady° misliked it not,   *wife of a feudal lord*
I would come to your counsel before your court noble.
For I find it not fit, as in faith it is known,
When such a boon is begged before all these knights,
350 Though you be tempted thereto, to take it on yourself
While so bold men about upon benches sit.
That no host under heaven is hardier of will,
Nor better brothers in arms where battle is joined;
I am the weakest, well I know, and of wit feeblest;
355 And the loss of my life would be least of any;
That I have you for uncle is my only praise;
My body, but for your blood, is barren of worth;
And for that this folly befits not a king,
And it is I that have asked it, it ought to be mine,
360 And if my claim be not comely let all this court judge,
                                 in sight."
                  The court assays the claim.
                  And in counsel all unite
                  To give Gawain the game
365   And release the king outright.

Then the king called the knight to come to his side,
And he rose up readily, and reached him with speed,
Bows low to his lord, lays hold of the weapon,
And he releases it lightly, and lifts up his hand,
370 And gives him God's blessing, and graciously prays
That his heart and his hand may be hardy both.
"Keep, cousin," said the king, "what you cut with this day,
And if you rule it aright, then readily, I know,
You shall stand the stroke it will strike after."
375 Gawain goes to the guest with gisarme in hand,
And boldly he bides there, abashed not a whit.

Then hails he Sir Gawain, the horseman in green:
"Recount we our contract, ere you come further.
First I ask and adjure° you, how you are called   *solemnly command*
380   That you tell me true, so that trust it I may."
"In good faith," said the good knight, "Gawain am I
Whose buffet befalls you, whate'er betide after,
And at this time twelvemonth take from you another
With what weapon you will, and with no man else
385   alive."
The other nods assent:
"Sir Gawain, as I may thrive,
I am wondrous well content
That you this dint shall drive."

390   "Sir Gawain," said the Green Knight, "By Gog, I rejoice[11]
That your fist shall fetch this favor I seek,
And you have readily rehearsed, and in right terms,
Each clause of my covenant with the king your lord,
Save that you shall assure me, sir, upon oath,
395   That you shall seek me yourself, wheresoever you think
My lodgings may lie, and look for such wages
As you have offered me here before all this host."
"What is the way there?" said Gawain. "Where do you live?
I never heard of your house, by Him that made me,
400   Nor I know you not, knight, your name nor your court.
But tell me truly thereof, and teach me your name,
And I shall fare forth to find you, so far as I may,
And this I say in good certain, and swear upon oath."
"That is enough in New Year, you need say no more,"
405   Said the knight in the green to Gawain the noble,
"If I tell you true, when I have taken your knock,
And if you handily have hit, you shall hear straightway
Of my house and my home and my own name;
Then follow in my footsteps by faithful accord.
410   And if I spend no speech, you shall speed the better:
You can feast with your friends, nor further trace
                  my tracks.
Now hold your grim tool steady
And show us how it hacks."
415   "Gladly, sir; all ready,"
Says Gawain; he strokes the ax.

The Green Knight upon ground girds him° with care;   *prepares himself*
Bows a bit with his head, and bares his flesh;

His long lovely locks he laid over his crown,
420   Let the naked nape for the need be shown.
Gawain grips to his ax and gathers it aloft—
The left foot on the floor before him he set—
Brought it down deftly upon the bare neck,
That the shock of the sharp blow shivered the bones
425   And cut the flesh cleanly and clove it in twain,
That the blade of bright steel bit into the ground.
The head fell to the floor as the ax hewed it off;
Many found it at their feet, as forth it rolled;
The blood gushed from the body, bright on the green,
430   Yet fell not the fellow, nor faltered a whit,
But stoutly he starts forth upon stiff shanks,
And as all stood staring he stretched forth his hand,
Laid hold of his head and heaved it aloft,
Then goes to the green steed, grasps the bridle,
435   Steps into the stirrup, bestrides his mount,
And his head by the hair in his hand holds,
And as steady he sits in the stately saddle
As he had met with no mishap, nor missing were
                         his head.
440   His bulk about he haled,°   *hauled*
           That fearsome body that bled;
           There were many in the court that quailed°   *cowered*
           Before all his say was said.

For the head in his hand he holds right up;
445   Toward the first on the dais directs he the face,
And it lifted up its lids, and looked with wide eyes,
And said as much with its mouth as now you may hear:
"Sir Gawain, forget not to go as agreed,
And cease not to seek till me, sir, you find,
450   As you promised in the presence of these proud knights.
To the Green Chapel come, I charge you, to take
Such a blow as you bestowed—you deserve, beyond doubt,
A knock on your neck next New Year's morn.
The Knight of the Green Chapel I am well known to many,
455   Wherefore you cannot fail to find me at last;
Therefore come, or be counted a recreant° knight."   *faithless*
With a roisterous rush he flings round the reins,
Hurtles out at the hall door, his head in his hand,
That the flint fire flew from the flashing hooves.
460   Which way he went, not one of them knew

Nor whence he was come in the wide world
                    so fair.
          The king and Gawain gay
          Make game of the Green Knight there,
465   Yet all who saw it say
          'Twas a wonder past compare.

Though high-born Arthur at heart had wonder,
He let no sign be seen, but said aloud
To the comely queen, with courteous speech,
470 "Dear dame, on this day dismay you no whit;
Such crafts are becoming at Christmastide,
Laughing at interludes,° light songs and mirth,   *short farcical plays*
Amid dancing of damsels with doughty° knights.   *stout-hearted*
Nevertheless of my meat now let me partake,
475 For I have met with a marvel, I may not deny."
He glanced at Sir Gawain, and gaily he said,
"Now, sir, hang up your ax, that has hewn enough,"[12]
And over the high dais it was hung on the wall
That men in amazement might on it look,
480 And tell in true terms the tale of the wonder.
Then they turned toward the table, these two together,
The good king and Gawain, and made great feast,
With all dainties double, dishes rare,
With all manner of meat and minstrelsy both,
485 Such happiness wholly had they that day
                    in hold.
          Now take care, Sir Gawain,
          That your courage wax not cold
          When you must turn again
490   To your enterprise foretold.

Part II

This adventure had Arthur of hand gifts first
When young was the year, for he yearned to hear tales;
Though they wanted for words when they went to sup,
Now are fierce deeds to follow, their fists stuffed full.
495 Gawain was glad to begin those games in hall,
But if the end be harsher, hold it no wonder,
For though men are merry in mind after much drink,
A year passes apace, and proves ever new:
First things and final conform but seldom.
500 And so this Yule to the young year yielded place,
And each season ensued at its set time;

After Christmas there came the cold cheer of Lent,
When with fish and plainer fare our flesh we reprove;
But then the world's weather with winter contends;
505 The keen cold lessens, the low clouds lift;
Fresh falls the rain in fostering showers
On the face of the fields; flowers appear.
The ground and the groves wear gowns of green;
Birds build their nests, and blithely sing
510 That solace of all sorrow with summer comes
                              ere long.
                    And blossoms day by day
                    Bloom rich and rife° in throng;   *numerous*
                    Then every grove so gay
515   Of the greenwood rings with song.

And then the season of summer with the soft winds,
When Zephyr sighs low over seeds and shoots;[13]
Glad is the green plant growing abroad,
When the dew at dawn drops from the leaves,
520 To get a gracious glance from the golden sun.
But harvest with harsher winds follows hard after,
Warns him to ripen well ere winter comes;
Drives forth the dust in the droughty season,
From the face of the fields to fly high in air.
525 Wroth winds in the welkin° wrestle with the sun,   *sky*
The leaves launch from the linden and light on the ground,
And the grass turns to gray, that once grew green.
Then all ripens and rots that rose up at first,
And so the year moves on in yesterdays many,
530 And winter once more, by the world's law,
                              draws nigh.
                    At Michaelmas° the moon   *September 29*
                    Hangs wintry pale in sky;
                    Sir Gawain girds him soon
535   For travails yet to try.

Till All Saints' Day° with Arthur he stays,   *November 1*
And he held a high feast to honor that knight
With great revels and rich, of the Round Table.
Then lovely ladies and lords debonair
540 With sorrow for Sir Gawain were sore at heart;
Yet they covered their care with countenance glad:
Many a mournful man made mirth for his sake.
So after supper soberly he speaks to his uncle
Of the hard hour at hand, and openly says,

545   "Now, liege lord of my life, my leave I take;
     The terms of this task too well you know—
     To count the cost over concerns me nothing.
     But I am bound forth betimes to bear a stroke
     From the grim man in green, as God may direct."
550   Then the first and foremost came forth in throng:
     Yvain and Eric and others of note,
     Sir Dodinal le Sauvage, the Duke of Clarence,
     Lionel and Lancelot and Lucan the good,
     Sir Bors and Sir Bedivere, big men both,
555   And many manly knights more, with Mador de la Porte,
     All this courtly company comes with the king
     To counsel their comrade, with care in their hearts;
     There was much secret sorrow suffered that day
     That one so good as Gawain must go in this fashion
560   To bear a bitter blow, and his bright sword
               lay by.
             He said, "Why should I tarry?"
             And smiled with tranquil eye;
             "In destinies sad or merry,
565   True men can but try."

     He dwelt there all that day, and dressed in the morning;
     Asked early for his arms, and all were brought.
     First a carpet of rare cost was cast on the floor
     Where much goodly gear gleamed golden bright;
570   He takes his place promptly and picks up the steel,
     Attired in a tight coat of Turkestan silk
     And a kingly cap-à-dos, closed at the throat,
     That was lavishly lined with a lustrous fur.
     Then they set the steel shoes on his sturdy feet
575   And clad his calves about with comely greaves,°   *leg armor*
     And plate well polished protected his knees,
     Affixed with fastenings of the finest gold.
     Fair cuisses enclosed, that were cunningly wrought,
     His thick-thewed° thighs, with thongs bound fast,   *well-muscled*
580   And massy chain mail of many a steel ring
     He bore on his body, above the best cloth,
     On his arms, at his elbows, armor well wrought
     Protected that prince, with plated gloves,
     And all the goodly gear to grace him well
585   that tide.
             His surcoat° blazoned bold;   *cloth tunic*
             Sharp spurs to prick with pride;

And a brave silk band to hold
The broadsword at his side.

590 When he had on his arms, his harness was rich,
The least latchet° or loop laden with gold;   *thong*
So armored as he was, he heard a mass,
Honored God humbly at the high altar.
Then he comes to the king and his comrades in arms,
595 Takes his leave at last of lords and ladies,
And they clasped and kissed him, commending him to Christ.
By then Gringolet was girt with a great saddle
That was gaily agleam with fine gilt fringe,
New furbished for the need with nail heads bright;
600 The bridle and the bars bedecked all with gold;
The breast plate, the saddlebow, the side panels both,
The caparison° and the crupper accorded in hue,   *decorated cloth cover*
And all ranged on the red the resplendent studs
That glittered and glowed like the glorious sun.
605 His helm now he holds up and hastily kisses,
Well closed with iron clinches, and cushioned within;
It was high on his head, with a hasp behind,
And a covering of cloth to encase the visor,
All bound and embroidered with the best gems
610 On broad bands of silk, and bordered with birds,
Parrots and popinjays preening their wings,
Lovebirds and love knots as lavishly wrought
As many women had worked seven winters thereon,
                    entire.
615   The diadem costlier yet
             That crowned that comely sire,
             With diamonds richly set,
             That flashed as if on fire.

Then they showed forth the shield, that shone all red,
620 With the pentangle portrayed in purest gold.[14]
About his broad neck by the baldric° he casts it,   *slantwise band*
That was meet° for the man, and matched him well.   *fitting*
And why the pentangle is proper to that peerless prince
I intend now to tell, though detain me it must.
625 It is a sign by Solomon sagely devised
To be a token of truth, by its title of old,
For it is a figure formed of five points,
And each line is linked and locked with the next
For ever and ever, and hence it is called
630 In all England, as I hear, the endless knot.[15]

And well may he wear it on his worthy arms,
For ever faithful fivefold in fivefold fashion
Was Gawain in good works, as gold unalloyed,°   *pure*
Devoid of all villainy, with virtues adorned
635   in sight.
    On shield and coat in view
    He bore that emblem bright,
    As to his word most true
    And in speech most courteous knight.

640 And first, he was faultless in his five senses,
    Nor found ever to fail in his five fingers,
    And all his fealty° was fixed upon the five wounds   *allegiance*
    That Christ got on the cross, as the Creed° tells;   *statement of belief*
    And wherever this man in melee took part,
645 His one thought was of this, past all things else,
    That all his force was founded on the five joys
    That the high Queen of Heaven had in her child.
    And therefore, as I find, he fittingly had
    On the inner part of his shield her image portrayed,
650 That when his look on it lighted, he never lost heart.
    The fifth of the five fives followed by this knight
    Were beneficence° boundless and brotherly love   *kindness*
    And pure mind and manners, that none might impeach,°   *discredit*
    And compassion most precious[16]—these peerless five
655 Were forged and made fast in him, foremost of men.
    Now all these five fives were confirmed in this knight,
    And each linked in other, that end there was none,
    And fixed to five points, whose force never failed,
    Nor assembled all on a side, nor asunder either,
660 Nor anywhere at an end, but whole and entire
    However the pattern proceeded or played out its course.
    And so on his shining shield shaped was the knot
    Royally in red gold against red gules,°   *red (heraldic)*
    That is the peerless pentangle, prized of old
665   in lore.
        Now armed is Gawain gay,
        And bears his lance before,
        And soberly said good day,
        He thought forevermore.

670 He struck his steed with the spurs and sped on his way
    So fast that the flint fire flashed from the stones.
    When they saw him set forth they were sore aggrieved,
    And all sighed softly, and said to each other,

Fearing for their fellow, "Ill fortune it is
675 That you, man, must be marred, that are most worthy!
His equal on this earth can hardly be found;
To have dealt more discreetly had done less harm,
And have dubbed° him a duke, with all due honor.   *appointed*
A great leader and lord he was like to become,
680 And better so to have been than battered to bits,
Beheaded by an elf man, for empty pride!
Who would credit that a king could be counseled so,
And caught in a cavil° in a Christmas game?"   *trivial argument*
Many were the warm tears they wept from their eyes
685 When goodly Sir Gawain was gone from the court
                    that day.
            No longer he abode,
            But speedily went his way
            Over many a wandering road,
690   As I heard my author say.

Now he rides in his array through the realm of Logres,[17]
Sir Gawain, God knows, though it gave him small joy!
All alone must he lodge through many a long night
Where the food that he fancied was far from his plate;
695 He had no mate but his mount, over mountain and plain,
Nor man to say his mind to but almighty God,
Till he had wandered well-nigh into North Wales.
All the islands of Anglesey he holds on his left,
And follows, as he fares, the fords by the coast,
700 Comes over at Holy Head, and enters next
The Wilderness of Wirral—few were within
That had great good will toward God or man.
And earnestly he asked of each mortal he met
If he had ever heard aught of a knight all green,
705 Or of a Green Chapel, on ground thereabouts,
And all said the same, and solemnly swore
They had seen no such knight all solely green
                    in hue.
            Over country wild and strange
710   The knight sets off anew;
            Often his course must change
            Ere the Chapel comes in view.

Many a cliff must he climb in country wild;
Far off from all his friends, forlorn must he ride;
715 At each strand or stream where the stalwart one passed
'Twere a marvel if he met not some monstrous foe,

And that so fierce and forbidding that fight he must.
So many were the wonders he wandered among
That to tell but the tenth part would tax my wits.
720 Now with serpents he wars, now with savage wolves,
Now with wild men of the woods, that watched from the rocks,
Both with bulls and with bears, and with boars besides,
And giants that came gibbering° from the jagged steeps.   *shouting crazily*
Had he not borne himself bravely, and been on God's side,
725 He had met with many mishaps and mortal harms.
And if the wars were unwelcome, the winter was worse,
When the cold clear rains rushed from the clouds
And froze before they could fall to the frosty earth.
Near slain by the sleet he sleeps in his irons
730 More nights than enough, among naked rocks,
Where clattering from the crest the cold stream ran
And hung in hard icicles high overhead.
Thus in peril and pain and predicaments dire
He rides across country till Christmas Eve,
735   our knight.
                And at that holy tide
                He prays with all his might
                That Mary may be his guide
                Till a dwelling comes in sight.

740 By a mountain next morning he makes his way
Into a forest fastness, fearsome and wild;
High hills on either hand, with hoar° woods below,   *gray with frost*
Oaks old and huge by the hundred together,
The hazel and the hawthorn were all intertwined
745 With rough raveled moss, that raggedly hung,
With many birds unblithe upon bare twigs
That peeped most piteously for pain of the cold.
The good knight on Gringolet glides thereunder
Through many a marsh and mire, a man all alone;
750 He feared for his default, should he fail to see
The service of that Sire that on that same night
Was born of a blessèd maid, to bring us His peace.
And therefore sighing he said, "I beseech of Thee, Lord,
And Mary, thou mildest mother so dear,
755 Some harborage where haply I might hear mass
And Thy matins tomorrow—meekly I ask it,
And thereto proffer and pray my Pater° and Ave°   *Our Father / Hail Mary*
                and Creed."
                He said his prayer with sighs,

760   Lamenting his misdeed;
         He crosses himself, and cries
         On Christ in his great need.

         No sooner had Sir Gawain signed° himself thrice   *crossed*
         Than he was ware, in the wood, of a wondrous dwelling,
765   Within a moat, on a mound, bright amid boughs
         Of many a tree great of girth that grew by the water—
         A castle as comely as a knight could own,
         On grounds fair and green, in a goodly park
         With a palisade of palings planted about
770   For two miles and more, round many a fair tree.
         The stout knight stared at that stronghold great
         As it shimmered and shone amid shining leaves,
         Then with helmet in hand he offers his thanks
         To Jesus and Saint Julian,° that are gentle both,   *travelers' protector*
775   That in courteous accord had inclined to his prayer;
         "Now fair harbor," said he, "I humbly beseech!"
         Then he pricks his proud steed with the plated spurs,
         And by chance he has chosen the chief path
         That brought the bold knight to the bridge's end
780   in haste.
                 The bridge hung high in air;
                 The gates were bolted fast;
                 The walls well framed to bear
                 The fury of the blast.

785   The man on his mount remained on the bank
         Of the deep double moat that defended the place.
         The wall went in the water wondrous deep,
         And a long way aloft it loomed overhead.
         It was built of stone blocks to the battlements' height,
790   With corbels° under cornices°   *supporting brackets /*
                 in comeliest style;   *projecting layers*
         Watchtowers trusty protected the gate,
         With many a lean loophole, to look from within:
         A better-made barbican° the knight beheld never.   *fortification*
         And behind it he beheld a great hall and fair:
795   Turrets rising in tiers, with tines at their tops,
         Spires set beside them, splendidly tall,
         With finials° well fashioned, as filigree fine.   *ornamental tops*
         Chalk-white chimneys over chambers high
         Gleamed in gay array upon gables and roofs;
800   The pinnacles in panoply, pointing in air,
         So vied there for his view that verily it seemed

A castle cut of paper for a king's feast.
The good knight on Gringolet thought it great luck
If he could but contrive to come there within
805 To keep the Christmas feast in that castle fair
                          and bright.
                 There answered to his call
                 A porter most polite;
                 From his station on the wall
810   He greets the errant knight.

"Good sir," said Gawain, "Would you go to inquire
If your lord would allow me to lodge here a space?"
"Peter!" said the porter. "For my part, I think
So noble a knight will not want for a welcome!"
815 Then he bustles off briskly, and comes back straight,
And many servants beside, to receive him the better.
They let down the drawbridge and duly went forth
And kneeled down on their knees on the naked earth
To welcome this warrior as best they were able.
820 They proffered him passage—the portals stood wide—
And he beckoned them to rise, and rode over the bridge.
Men steadied his saddle as he stepped to the ground,
And there stabled his steed many stalwart folk.
Now come the knights and the noble squires
825 To bring him with bliss into the bright hall.
When his high helm was off, there hastened a throng
Of attendants to take it, and see to its care;
They bore away his broad sword and blazoned shield;
Then graciously he greeted those gallants each one,
830 And many a noble drew near, to do the knight honor.
All in his armor into hall he was led,
Where fire on a fair hearth fiercely blazed.
And soon the lord himself descends from his chamber
To meet in mannerly fashion the man on his floor.
835 He said, "To this house you are heartily welcome:
What is here is wholly yours, to have in your power
                          and sway."°   *control*
                 Says Gawain with a smile
                 "May Christ your pains repay!"
840   They embrace in courteous style
                 As men well met that day.

Gawain gazed on the host that greeted him there,
And a lusty fellow he looked, the lord of that place:
A man of massive mold, and of middle age;

845 Broad, bright was his beard, of a beaver's hue,[18]
    Strong, steady his stance, upon stalwart shanks,
    His face fierce as fire, fair spoken withal,
    And well suited he seemed in Sir Gawain's sight
    To be a master of men in a mighty keep.°   *strong fort*
850 They pass into a parlor, where promptly the host
    Has a servant assigned him to see to his needs,
    And there came upon his call many courteous folk
    That brought him to a bower where bedding was noble,
    With heavy silk hangings hemmed all in gold,
855 Coverlets and counterpanes° curiously wrought,   *bedspreads*
    A canopy over the couch, clad all with fur,
    Curtains running on cords, caught to gold rings,
    Woven rugs on the walls of eastern work,
    And the floor, under foot, well furnished with the same.
860 With light talk and laughter they loosed from him then
    His war dress of weight and his worthy clothes.
    Robes richly wrought they brought him right soon,
    To change there in chamber and choose what he would.
    When he had found one he fancied, and flung it about,
865 Well fashioned for his frame, with flowing skirts,
    His face fair and fresh as the flowers of spring,
    All the good folk agreed, that gazed on him then,
    His limbs arrayed royally in radiant hues,
    That so comely a mortal never Christ made
870   as he.
                 Whatever his place of birth,
                 It seemed he well might be
                 Without a peer on earth
                 In martial rivalry.

875 A couch before the fire, where fresh coals burned,
    They spread for Sir Gawain splendidly now
    With quilts quaintly stitched, and cushions beside,
    And then a costly cloak they cast on his shoulders
    Of bright silk, embroidered on borders and hems,
880 With furs of the finest well furnished within,
    And bound about with ermine, both mantle and hood;
    And he sat at that fireside in sumptuous estate
    And warmed himself well, and soon he waxed merry.
    Then attendants set a table upon trestles broad,
885 And lustrous white linen they laid thereupon,
    A saltcellar of silver, spoons of the same.
    He washed himself well and went to his place,

Men set his fare before him in fashion most fit.
There were soups of all sorts, seasoned with skill,
890   Double-sized servings, and sundry fish,
Some baked, some breaded, some broiled on the coals,
Some simmered, some in stews, steaming with spices,
And with sauces to sup that suited his taste.
He confesses it a feast with free words and fair;
895   They requite° him as kindly with courteous jests,   *repay*
well sped.
"Tonight you fast and pray;
Tomorrow we'll see you fed."[19]
The knight grows wondrous gay
900   As the wine goes to his head.

Then at times and by turns, as at table he sat,
They questioned him quietly, with queries discreet,
And he courteously confessed that he comes from the court,
And owns him of the brotherhood of high-famed Arthur,
905   The right royal ruler of the Round Table,
And the guest by their fireside is Gawain himself,
Who has happened on their house at that holy feast.
When the name of the knight was made known to the lord,
Then loudly he laughed, so elated he was,
910   And the men in that household made haste with joy
To appear in his presence promptly that day,
That of courage ever constant, and customs pure,
Is pattern and paragon,° and praised without end: *model of perfection*
Of all knights on earth most honored is he.
915   Each said solemnly aside to his brother,
"Now displays of deportment shall dazzle our eyes
And the polished pearls of impeccable° speech;   *flawless*
The high art of eloquence is ours to pursue
Since the father of fine manners is found in our midst.
920   Great is God's grace, and goodly indeed,
That a guest such as Gawain He guides to us here
When men sit and sing of their Savior's birth
in view.
With command of manners pure
925   He shall each heart imbue;°   *fill*
Who shares his converse, sure,
Shall learn love's language true."

When the knight had done dining and duly arose,
The dark was drawing on; the day nigh ended.
930   Chaplains in chapels and churches about

Rang the bells aright, reminding all men
Of the holy evensong° of the high feast.   *evening service*
The lord attends alone; his fair lady sits
In a comely closet, secluded from sight.
935 Gawain in gay attire goes thither soon;
The lord catches his coat, and calls him by name,
And has him sit beside him, and says in good faith
No guest on God's earth would he gladlier greet.
For that Gawain thanked him; the two then embraced
940 And sat together soberly the service through.
Then the lady, that longed to look on the knight,
Came forth from her closet with her comely maids.
The fair hues of her flesh, her face and her hair
And her body and her bearing were beyond praise,
945 And excelled the queen herself, as Sir Gawain thought.
He goes forth to greet her with gracious intent;
Another lady led her by the left hand
That was older than she—an ancient, it seemed,
And held in high honor by all men about.
950 But unlike to look upon, those ladies were,[20]
For if the one was fresh, the other was faded:
Bedecked in bright red was the body of one;
Flesh hung in folds on the face of the other;
On one a high headdress, hung all with pearls;
955 Her bright throat and bosom fair to behold,
Fresh as the first snow fallen upon hills;
A wimple° the other one wore round her throat;   *cloth head covering*
Her swart° chin well swaddled, swathed all in white;   *dark*
Her forehead enfolded in flounces of silk
960 That framed a fair fillet,° of fashion ornate.   *headband*
And nothing bare beneath save the black brows,
The two eyes and the nose, the naked lips,
And they unsightly to see, and sorrily bleared.
A beldame,° by God, she may well be deemed,   *formidable lady*
965   of pride!
                She was short and thick of waist,
                Her buttocks round and wide;
                More toothsome, to his taste,
                Was the beauty by her side.

970 When Gawain had gazed on that gay lady,
With leave from her lord, he politely approached;
To the elder in homage he humbly bows;
The lovelier he salutes with a light embrace.

He claims a comely kiss, and courteously he speaks;
975   They welcome him warmly, and straightway he asks
To be received as their servant, if they so desire.
They take him between them; with talking they bring him
Beside a bright fire; bade then that spices
Be freely fetched forth, to refresh them the better,
980   And the good wine therewith, to warm their hearts.
The lord leaps about in light-hearted mood;
Contrives entertainments and timely sports;
Takes his hood from his head and hangs it on a spear,
And offers him openly the honor thereof
985   Who should promote the most mirth at that Christmas feast;
"And I shall try for it, trust me—contend with the best,
Ere I go without my headgear by grace of my friends!"
Thus with light talk and laughter the lord makes merry
To gladden the guest he had greeted in hall
990   that day.
                 At the last he called for light
                 The company to convey;
                 Gawain says goodnight
                 And retires to bed straightway.

995   On the morn when each man is mindful in heart
That God's son was sent down to suffer our death,
No household but is blithe for His blessed sake;
So was it there on that day, with many delights.
Both at larger meals and less they were lavishly served
1000   By doughty° lads on dais,° with delicate fare;   *capable / platform*
The old ancient lady, highest she sits;
The lord at her left hand leaned, as I hear;
Sir Gawain in the center, beside the gay lady,
Where the food was brought first to that festive board,
1005   And thence throughout the hall, as they held most fit,
To each man was offered in order of rank.
There was meat, there was mirth, there was much joy,
That to tell all the tale would tax my wits,
Though I pained me, perchance, to paint it with care;
1010   But yet I know that our knight and the noble lady
Were accorded so closely in company there,
With the seemly solace of their secret words,
With speeches well sped, spotless and pure,
That each prince's pastime their pleasures far
1015   outshone.
                 Sweet pipes beguile their cares,

And the trumpet of martial tone;
Each tends his affairs
And those two tend their own.

1020 That day and all the next, their disport was noble,
And the third day, I think, pleased them no less;
The joys of Saint John's Day were justly praised,[21]
And were the last of their like for those lords and ladies;
Then guests were to go in the gray morning,
1025 Wherefore they whiled the night away with wine and with mirth,
Moved to the measures of many a blithe carol;
At last, when it was late, took leave of each other,
Each one of those worthies, to wend his way.
Gawain bids goodbye to his goodly host
1030 Who brings him to his chamber, the chimney beside,
And detains him in talk, and tenders his thanks
And holds it an honor to him and his people
That he has harbored in his house at that holy time
And embellished his abode° with his inborn grace.   *adorned his dwelling*
1035 "As long as I may live, my luck is the better
That Gawain was my guest at God's own feast!"
"Noble sir," said the knight, "I cannot but think
All the honor is your own—may the high king repay you!
And your man to command I account myself here
1040 As I am bound and beholden, and shall be, come
                          what may."
                The lord with all his might
                Entreats his guest to stay;
                Brief answer makes the knight:
1045   Next morning he must away.

Then the lord of that land politely inquired
What dire affair had forced him, at that festive time,
So far from the king's court to fare forth alone
Ere the holidays wholly had ended in hall.
1050 "In good faith," said Gawain, "you have guessed the truth:
On a high errand and urgent I hastened away,
For I am summoned by myself to seek for a place—
I wish I knew whither, or where it might be!
Far rather would I find it before the New Year
1055 Than own the land of Logres, so help me our Lord!
Wherefore, sir, in friendship this favor I ask,
That you say in sober earnest, if something you know
Of the Green Chapel, on ground far or near,
Or the lone knight that lives there, of like hue of green.

1060 A certain day was set by assent of us both
To meet at that landmark, if I might last,
And from now to the New Year is nothing too long,
And I would greet the Green Knight there, would God but allow,
More gladly, by God's Son, than gain the world's wealth!
1065 And I must set forth to search, as soon as I may;
To be about the business I have but three days
And would as soon sink down dead as desist from my errand."
Then smiling said the lord, "Your search, sir, is done,
For we shall see you to that site by the set time.
1070 Let Gawain grieve no more over the Green Chapel;
You shall be in your own bed, in blissful ease,
All the forenoon, and fare forth the first of the year,
And make the goal by midmorn, to mind your affairs,
             no fear!
1075   Tarry till the fourth day
       And ride on the first of the year.
       We shall set you on your way;
       It is not two miles from here."

Then Gawain was glad, and gleefully he laughed:
1080 "Now I thank you for this, past all things else!
Now my goal is here at hand! With a glad heart I shall
Both tarry, and undertake any task you devise."
Then the host seized his arm and seated him there;
Let the ladies be brought, to delight them the better,
1085 And in fellowship fair by the fireside they sit;
So gay waxed the good host, so giddy his words,
All awaited in wonder what next he would say.
Then he stares on the stout knight, and sternly he speaks:
"You have bound yourself boldly my bidding to do—
1090 Will you stand by that boast, and obey me this once?"
"I shall do so indeed," said the doughty knight;
"While I lie in your lodging, your laws will I follow."
"As you have had," said the host, "many hardships abroad
And little sleep of late, you are lacking, I judge,
1095 Both in needful nourishment and nightly rest;
You shall lie abed late in your lofty chamber
Tomorrow until mass, and meet then to dine
When you will, with my wife, who will sit by your side
And talk with you at table, the better to cheer
1100   our guest.
       A-hunting I will go
       While you lie late and rest."

The knight, inclining low,
Assents to each behest.°   *command*

1105 "And Gawain," said the good host, "agree now to this:
Whatever I win in the woods I will give you at eve,
And all you have earned you must offer to me;
Swear now, sweet friend, to swap as I say,
Whether hands, in the end, go empty or no."
1110 "By God," said Sir Gawain, "I grant it forthwith!
If you find the game good, I shall gladly take part."
"Let the bright wine be brought, and our bargain is done,"
Said the lord of that land—the two laughed together.
Then they drank and they dallied and doffed all constraint,
1115 These lords and these ladies, as late as they chose,
And then with gaiety and gallantries and graceful adieux
They talked in low tones, and tarried at parting.
With compliments comely they kiss at the last;
There were brisk lads about with blazing torches
1120 To see them safe to bed, for soft repose
long due.
Their covenants,° yet awhile,   *agreements*
They repeat, and pledge anew;
That lord could well beguile
1125 Men's hearts, with mirth in view.

Part III

Long before daylight they left their beds;
Guests that wished to go gave word to their grooms,
And they set about briskly to bind on saddles,
Tend to their tackle, tie up trunks.
1130 The proud lords appear, appareled to ride.
Leap lightly astride, lay hold of their bridles,
Each one on his way to his worthy house.
The liege lord of the land was not the last
Arrayed there to ride, with retainers° many;   *attendants*
1135 He had a bite to eat when he had heard mass;
With horn to the hills he hastens betimes.°   *early*
By the dawn of that day over the dim earth,
Master and men were mounted and ready.
Then they harnessed in couples the keen-scented hounds,
1140 Cast wide the kennel door and called them forth,
Blew upon their bugles bold blasts three;[22]
The dogs began to bay with a deafening din,
And they quieted them quickly and called them to heel,

A hundred brave huntsmen, as I have heard tell,
1145   together.
    Men at stations meet;
    From the hounds they slip the tether;°   *leash*
    The echoing horns repeat,
    Clear in the merry weather.

1150 At the clamor of the quest, the quarry trembled;
Deer dashed through the dale, dazed with dread;
Hastened to the high ground, only to be
Turned back by the beaters, who boldly shouted.
They harmed not the harts, with their high heads,
1155 Let the bucks go by, with their broad antlers,
For it was counted a crime, in the close season,
If a man of that demesne° should molest the male deer.   *kingdom*
The hinds were headed up, with "Hey!" and "Ware!"° *Look out!*
The does with great din were driven to the valleys.
1160 Then you were ware,° as they went, of the whistling   *conscious*
    of arrows;
At each bend under boughs the bright shafts flew
That tore the tawny hide with their tapered heads.
Ah! they bray and they bleed, on banks they die,
And ever the pack pell mell comes panting behind;
1165 Hunters with shrill horns hot on their heels—
Like the cracking of cliffs their cries resounded.
What game got away from the gallant archers
Was promptly picked off at the posts below
When they were harried on the heights and
    herded to the streams:
1170 The watchers were so wary at the waiting-stations,
And the greyhounds so huge, that eagerly snatched,
And finished them off as fast as folk could see
        with sight.
    The lord, now here, now there,
1175   Spurs forth in sheer delight.
    And drives, with pleasures rare,
    The day to the dark night.

So the lord in the linden wood leads the hunt
And Gawain the good man in gay bed lies,
1180 Lingered while light shone late on the walls,
Under coverlet costly, curtained about.
And as he slips into slumber, slyly there comes
A little din at his door, and the latch lifted,
And he holds up his heavy head out of the clothes;

1185 A corner of the curtain he caught back a little
And kept watch warily, to see what befell.
Lo! it was the lady, loveliest to behold,
Who drew the door behind her deftly and still
And was bound for his bed—abashed was the knight,
1190 And laid his head low again in likeness of sleep;
And she stepped stealthily, and stole to his bed,
Cast aside the curtain and came within,
And set herself softly on the bedside there,
And lingered at her leisure, to look on his waking.
1195 The fair knight lay feigning for a long while,
Conning in his conscience what his case might
Mean or amount to—a marvel he thought it.
But yet he said to himself, "More seemly it were
To try her intent by talking a little."
1200 So he started and stretched, as if startled from sleep,
Lifts wide his eyelids in likeness of wonder,
And signs° himself swiftly, as safer to be,   *crosses*
               with art.
               Sweetly does she speak
1205   And kindling glances dart,
               Blent white and red on cheek
               And laughing lips apart.

"Good morning, Sir Gawain," said that gay lady,
"A slack sleeper you are, to let one slip in!
1210 Now you are taken in a trice—a truce we must make,
Or I shall bind you in your bed, of that be assured."
Thus laughing lightly that lady jested.
"Good morning, gay lady," said Gawain the blithe,
"Be it with me as you will; I am well content!
1215 For I surrender myself, and sue for your grace,
And that is best, I believe, and behooves me now."
Thus jested in answer that gentle knight.
"But if, lovely lady, you misliked it not,
And were pleased to permit your prisoner to rise,
1220 I should quit this couch and accoutre° me better,   *outfit*
And be clad in more comfort for converse here."
"Nay, not so, sweet sir," said the smiling lady;
"You shall not rise from your bed; I direct you better:
I shall hem and hold you on either hand,
1225 And keep company awhile with my captive knight.
For as certain as I sit here, Sir Gawain you are,
Whom all the world worships, whereso you ride;

Your honor, your courtesy are highest acclaimed
By lords and by ladies, by all living men;
1230 And lo! we are alone here, and left to ourselves;
My lord and his liegemen are long departed,
The household asleep, my handmaids too,
The door drawn, and held by a well-driven bolt,
And since I have in this house him whom all love,
1235 I shall while the time away with mirthful speech
at will.
My body is here at hand,
Your each wish to fulfill;
Your servant to command
1240 I am, and shall be still."²³

"In good faith," said Gawain, "my gain is the greater,
Though I am not he of whom you have heard;
To arrive at such reverence as you recount here
I am one all unworthy, and well do I know it.
1245 By heaven, I would hold me the happiest of men
If by word or by work I once might aspire
To the prize of your praise—'twere a pure joy!"
"In good faith, Sir Gawain," said that gay lady,
"The well-proven prowess that pleases all others,
1250 Did I scant or scout it, 'twere scarce becoming.
But there are ladies, believe me, that had liefer far
Have thee here in their hold, as I have today,
To pass an hour in pastime with pleasant words,
Assuage all their sorrows and solace their hearts,
1255 Than much of the goodly gems and gold they possess.
But lauded° be the Lord of the lofty skies,   *praised*
For here in my hands all hearts' desire
doth lie."
Great welcome got he there
1260 From the lady who sat him by;
With fitting speech and fair
The good knight makes reply.

"Madame," said the merry man, "Mary reward you!
For in good faith, I find your beneficence° noble.   *generosity*
1265 And the fame of fair deeds runs far and wide,
But the praise you report pertains not to me,
But comes of your courtesy and kindness of heart."
"By the high Queen of heaven" (said she) "I count it not so,
For were I worth all the women in this world alive,

1270 And all wealth and all worship were in my hands,
And I should hunt high and low, a husband to take,
For the nurture I have noted in you, knight, here,
The comeliness and courtesies and courtly mirth—
And so I had ever heard, and now hold it true—
1275 No other on this earth, should have me for wife."
"You are bound to a better man," the bold knight said,
"Yet I prize the praise you have proffered me here,
And soberly your servant, my sovereign I hold you,
And acknowledge me your knight, in the name of Christ."
1280 So they talked of this and that until 'twas nigh noon,
And ever the lady languishing in likeness of love.
With feat° words and fair he framed his defense,   *clever*
For were she never so winsome, the warrior had
The less will to woo, for the wound that his bane°   *doom*
1285   must be.
              He must bear the blinding blow,
              For such is fate's decree;
              The lady asks leave to go;
              He grants it full and free.

1290 Then she gaily said goodbye, and glanced at him, laughing,
And as she stood, she astonished him with a stern speech:
"Now may the Giver of all good words these glad hours repay!
But our guest is not Gawain—forgot is that thought."
"How so?" said the other, and asks in some haste,
1295 For he feared he had been at fault in the forms of his speech.
But she held up her hand, and made answer thus:
"So good a knight as Gawain is given out to be,
And the model of fair demeanor° and manners pure,   *behavior*
Had he lain so long at a lady's side,
1300 Would have claimed a kiss, by his courtesy,
Through some touch or trick of phrase at some tale's end."
Said Gawain, "Good lady, I grant it at once!
I shall kiss at your command, as becomes a knight,
And more, lest you mislike, so let be, I pray."
1305 With that she turns toward him, takes him in her arms,
Leans down her lovely head, and lo! he is kissed.
They commend each other to Christ with comely words,
He sees her forth safely, in silence they part,
And then he lies no later in his lofty bed,
1310 But calls to his chamberlain, chooses his clothes,
Goes in those garments gladly to mass,

Then takes his way to table, where attendants wait,
And made merry all day, till the moon rose
             in view.
1315   Was never knight beset
             'Twixt worthier ladies two:
             The crone° and the coquette,°   old lady / flirt
             Fair pastimes they pursue.

And the lord of the land rides late and long,
1320 Hunting the barren hinds over the broad heath.
He had slain such a sum, when the sun sank low,
Of does and other deer, as would dizzy one's wits.
Then they trooped in together in triumph at last,
And the count of the quarry quickly they take.
1325 The lords lent a hand²⁴ with their liegemen many,
Picked out the plumpest and put them together
And duly dressed the deer, as the deed requires.
Some were assigned the assay° of the fat: measurement
Two fingers' width fully they found on the leanest.
1330 Then they slit the slot open and searched out the paunch,
Trimmed it with trencher° knives and tied it up tight.   carving
They flayed the fair hide from the legs and trunk,
Then broke open the belly and laid bare the bowels,
Deftly detaching and drawing them forth.
1335 And next at the neck they neatly parted
The weasand° from the windpipe, and cast away the guts.   throat
At the shoulders with sharp blades they showed their skill,
Boning them from beneath, lest the sides be marred;
They breached the broad breast and broke it in twain,
1340 And again at the gullet they begin with their knives,
Cleave down the carcass clear to the breach;
Two tender morsels they take from the throat,
Then round the inner ribs they rid off a layer
And carve out the kidney fat, close to the spine,
1345 Hewing down to the haunch, that all hung together,
And held it up whole, and hacked it free,
And this they named the numbles,²⁵ that knew such terms
             of art.
             They divide the crotch in two,
1350   And straightway then they start
             To cut the backbone through
             And cleave the trunk apart.

With hard strokes they hewed off the head and the neck,
Then swiftly from the sides they severed the chine,°   backbone

1355 And the corbie's bone they cast on a branch.[26]
     Then they pierced the plump sides, impaled either one
     With the hock° of the hind foot, and hung it aloft,   *joint next to hoof*
     To each person his portion most proper and fit.
     On a hide of a hind the hounds they fed
1360 With the liver and the lights, the leathery paunches,
     And bread soaked in blood well blended therewith.
     With sound of shrill horns they signal their prize,
     Then merrily with their meat they make their way home,
     Blowing on their bugles many a brave blast.
1365 Ere dark had descended, that doughty° band   *brave*
     Was come within the walls where Gawain waits
                         at leisure.
               Bliss and hearth fire bright
               Await the master's pleasure;
1370   When the two men met that night,
               Joy surpassed all measure.

     Then the host in the hall his household assembles,
     With the dames of high degree and their damsels fair.
     In the presence of the people, a party he sends
1375 To convey him his venison in view of the knight.
     And in high good humor he hails him then,
     Counts over the kill, the cuts° on the tallies,°   *notches / measuring sticks*
     Holds high the hewn ribs, heavy with fat.
     "What think you, sir, of this? Have I thriven° well?   *prospered*
1380 Have I won with my woodcraft a worthy prize?"
     "In good earnest," said Gawain, "this game is the finest
     I have seen in seven years in the season of winter."
     "And I give it to you, Gawain," said the good host,
     "For according to our covenant, you claim it as your own."
1385 "That is so," said Sir Gawain, "and the same say I:
     What I worthily have won within these fair walls,
     Herewith I as willingly award it to you."
     He embraces his broad neck with both his arms,
     And confers on him a kiss, the comeliest that he could.
1390 "Have here my profit, it proved no better;
     Ungrudging do I grant it, were it greater far."
     "Such a gift," said the good host, "I gladly accept—
     Yet it might be all the better, would you but say
     Where you won this same award, by your wits alone."
1395 "That was no part of the pact; press me no further,
     For you have had what behooves; all other claims
                         forbear."

With jest and compliment
They conversed, and cast off care;
1400　To the table soon they went;
Fresh dainties wait them there.

And then by the chimney side they chat at their ease;
The best wine was brought them, and bounteously served;
And after in their jesting they jointly accord
1405　To do on the second day the deeds of the first:
That the two men should trade, betide as it may,
What each had taken in, at eve when they met.
They seal the pact solemnly in sight of the court;
Their cups were filled afresh to confirm the jest;
1410　Then at last they took their leave, for late was the hour,
Each to his own bed hastening away.
Before the barnyard cock had crowed but thrice
The lord had leapt from his rest, his liegemen as well.
Both of mass and their meal they made short work:
1415　By the dim light of dawn they were deep in the woods
　　　　　away.
With huntsmen and with horns
Over plains they pass that day;
They release, amid the thorns,
1420　Swift hounds that run and bay.

Soon some were on a scent by the side of a marsh;
When the hounds opened cry, the head of the hunt
Rallied them with rough words, raised a great noise.
The hounds that had heard it came hurrying straight
1425　And followed along with their fellows, forty together.
Then such a clamor and cry of coursing° hounds　　　　*racing*
Arose, that the rocks resounded again.
Hunters exhorted them with horn and with voice;
Then all in a body bore off together
1430　Between a mere° in the marsh and a menacing crag,　　*pool*
To a rise where the rock stood rugged and steep,
And boulders lay about, that blocked their approach.
Then the company in consort closed on their prey:
They surrounded the rise and the rocks both,
1435　For well they were aware that it waited within,
The beast that the bloodhounds boldly proclaimed.
Then they beat on the bushes and bade him appear,
And he made a murderous rush in the midst of them all;
The best of all boars broke from his cover,
1440　That had ranged long unrivaled, a renegade° old,　　*loner*

For of tough-brawned boars he was biggest far,
Most grim when he grunted—then grieved were many,
For three at the first thrust he threw to the earth,
And dashed away at once without more damage.
1445 With "Hi!" "Hi!" and "Hey!" "Hey!" the others followed,
Had horns at their lips, blew high and clear.
Merry was the music of men and of hounds
That were bound after this boar, his bloodthirsty heart
               to quell.°   *subdue*
1450   Often he stands at bay,
      Then scatters the pack pell mell;
      He hurts the hounds, and they
      Most dolefully yowl and yell.

Men then with mighty bows moved in to shoot,
1455 Aimed at him with their arrows and often hit,
But the points had no power to pierce through his hide,
And the barbs were brushed aside by his bristly brow;
Though the shank of the shaft shivered in pieces,
The head hopped away, wheresoever it struck.
1460 But when their stubborn strokes had stung him at last,
Then, foaming in his frenzy, fiercely he charges,
Hurtles at them headlong that hindered his flight,
And many feared for their lives, and fell back a little.
But the lord on a lively horse leads the chase;
1465 As a high-spirited huntsman his horn he blows;   .
He sounds the assembly and sweeps through the brush,
Pursuing this wild swine till the sunlight slanted.
All day with this deed they drive forth the time
While our lone knight so lovesome lies in his bed,
1470 Sir Gawain safe at home, in silken bower
                so gay;
      The lady, with guile in heart,
      Came early where he lay;
      She was at him with all her art
1475   To turn his mind her way.

She comes to the curtain and coyly peeps in;
Gawain thought it good to greet her at once,
And she richly repays him with her ready words,
Settles softly at his side, and suddenly she laughs,
1480 And with a gracious glance, she begins on him thus:
"Sir, if you be Gawain, it seems a great wonder—
A man so well meaning, and mannerly disposed,
And cannot act in company as courtesy bids,

And if one takes the trouble to teach him, 'tis all in vain.
1485 That lesson learned lately is lightly forgot,
Though I painted it as plain as my poor wit allowed."
"What lesson, dear lady?" he asked all alarmed;
"I have been much to blame, if your story be true."
"Yet my counsel was of kissing," came her answer then,
1490 "Where favor has been found, freely to claim
As accords with the conduct of courteous knights."
"My dear," said the doughty man, "dismiss that thought;
Such freedom, I fear, might offend you much;
It were rude to request if the right were denied."
1495 "But none can deny you," said the noble dame,
"You are stout enough to constrain with strength, if you choose,
Were any so ungracious as to grudge you aught."
"By heaven," said he, "you have answered well,
But threats never throve among those of my land,
1500 Nor any gift not freely given, good though it be.
I am yours to command, to kiss when you please;
You may lay on as you like, and leave off at will."
                    With this,
            The lady lightly bends
1505   And graciously gives him a kiss;
            The two converse as friends
            Of true love's trials and bliss.

"I should like, by your leave," said the lovely lady,
"If it did not annoy you, to know for what cause
1510 So brisk and so bold a young blood as you,
And acclaimed for all courtesies becoming a knight—
And name what knight you will, they are noblest esteemed
For loyal faith in love, in life as in story;
For to tell the tribulations° of these true hearts,   *troubles*
1515 Why, 'tis the very title and text of their deeds,
How bold knights for beauty have braved many a foe,
Suffered heavy sorrows out of secret love,
And then valorously° avenged them on villainous churls   *courageously*
And made happy ever after the hearts of their ladies.
1520 And you are the noblest knight known in your time;
No household under heaven but has heard of your fame,
And here by your side I have sat for two days
Yet never has a fair phrase fallen from your lips
Of the language of love, not one little word!
1525 And you, that with sweet vows sway women's hearts,
Should show your winsome ways, and woo a young thing,

And teach by some tokens the craft of true love.
How! are you artless, whom all men praise?
Or do you deem me so dull, or deaf to such words?
1530   Fie!° Fie!   *For shame!*
      In hope of pastimes new
      I have come where none can spy;
      Instruct me a little, do,
      While my husband is not nearby."

1535 "God love you, gracious lady!" said Gawain then;
      "It is a pleasure surpassing, and a peerless joy,
      That one so worthy as you would willingly come
      And take the time and trouble to talk with your knight
      And content you with his company—it comforts my heart.
1540 But to take on myself the task of telling of love,
      And touch upon its texts, and treat of its themes
      To one that, I know well, wields more power
      In that art, by a half, than a hundred such
      As I am where I live, or am like to become,
1545 It were folly, fair dame, in the first degree!
      In all that I am able, my aim is to please,
      As in honor behooves me,° and am evermore   *I am obliged to*
      Your servant heart and soul, so save me our Lord!"
      Thus she tested his temper and tried many a time,
1550 Whatever her true intent, to entice him to sin,
      But so fair was his defense that no fault appeared,
      Nor evil on either hand, but only bliss
                        they knew.
            They linger and laugh awhile;
1555   She kisses the knight so true,
            Takes leave in comeliest style
            And departs without more ado.

      Then he rose from his rest and made ready for mass,
      And then a meal was set and served, in sumptuous style;
1560 He dallied at home all day with the dear ladies,
      But the lord lingered late at his lusty sport;
      Pursued his sorry swine, that swerved as he fled,
      And bit asunder the backs of the best of his hounds
      When they brought him to bay, till the bowmen appeared
1565 And soon forced him forth, though he fought for dear life,
      So sharp were the shafts they shot at him there.
      But yet the boldest drew back from his battering head,
      Till at last he was so tired he could travel no more,
      But in as much haste as he might, he makes his retreat

1570 To a rise on rocky ground, by a rushing stream.
With the bank at his back he scrapes the bare earth,
The froth foams at his jaws, frightful to see.
He whets his white tusks—then weary were all
Those hunters so hardy that hovered about
1575 Of aiming from afar, but ever they mistrust
                    his mood.
          He had hurt so many by then
          That none had hardihood
          To be torn by his tusks again,
1580   That was brainsick, and out for blood.

Till the lord came at last on his lofty steed,
Beheld him there at bay before all his folk;
Lightly he leaps down, leaves his courser,
Bares his bright sword, and boldly advances;
1585 Straight into the stream he strides towards his foe.
The wild thing was wary of weapon and man;
His hackles rose high; so hotly he snorts
That many watched with alarm, lest the worst befall.
The boar makes for the man with a mighty bound
1590 So that he and his hunter came headlong together
Where the water ran wildest—the worse for the beast,
For the man, when they first met, marked him with care,
Sights well the slot, slips in the blade,
Shoves it home to the hilt, and the heart shattered,
1595 And he falls in his fury and floats down the water,
                    ill sped.
          Hounds hasten by the score
          To maul him, hide and head;
          Men drag him in to shore
1600   And dogs pronounce him dead.

With many a brave blast they boast of their prize,
All hallooed in high glee, that had their wind;
The hounds bayed for the beast, as the bold men bade
That were charged with chief rank in that chase of renown.
1605 Then one wise in woodcraft, and worthily skilled,
Began to dress the boar in becoming style:
He severs the savage head and sets it aloft,
Then rends the body roughly right down the spine;
Takes the bowels from the belly, broils them on coals,
1610 Blends them well with bread to bestow on the hounds.
Then he breaks out the brawn° in fair broad flitches,°   *meat / slabs*
And the innards to be eaten in order he takes.

The two sides, attached to each other all whole,
He suspended from a spar that was springy and tough;
1615 And so with this swine they set out for home;
The boar's head was borne before the same man
That had stabbed him in the stream with his strong arm,
                              right through.
          He thought it long indeed.
1620   Till he had the knight in view;
          At his call, he comes with speed
          To claim his payment due.

The lord laughed aloud, with many a light word,
When he greeted Sir Gawain—with good cheer he speaks.
1625 They fetch the fair dames and the folk of the house;
He brings forth the brawn, and begins the tale
Of the great length and girth, the grim rage as well,
Of the battle of the boar they beset in the wood.
The other man meetly commended his deeds
1630 And praised well the prize of his princely sport,
For the brawn of that boar, the bold knight said,
And the sides of that swine surpassed all others.
Then they handled the huge head; he owns it a wonder,
And eyes it with abhorrence, to heighten his praise.
1635 "Now, Gawain," said the good man, "this game becomes yours
By those fair terms we fixed, as you know full well."
"That is true," returned the knight, "and trust me, fair friend,
All my gains, as agreed, I shall give you forthwith."
He clasps him and kisses him in courteous style,
1640 Then serves him with the same fare a second time.
"Now we are even," said he, "at this evening feast,
And clear is every claim incurred here to date,
                              and debt."
          "By Saint Giles!" the host replies,
1645   "You're the best I ever met!
          If your profits are all this size,
          We'll see you wealthy yet!"

Then attendants set tables on trestles about,
And laid them with linen; light shone forth,
1650 Wakened along the walls in waxen torches.
The service was set and the supper brought;
Royal were the revels that rose then in hall
At that feast by the fire, with many fair sports:
Amid the meal and after, melody sweet,
1655 Carol dances comely and Christmas songs,

With all the mannerly mirth my tongue may describe.
And ever our gallant knight beside the gay lady;
So uncommonly kind and complaisant° was she,   *intent on pleasing*
With sweet stolen glances, that stirred his stout heart,
1660 That he was at his wits' end, and wondrous vexed;
But he could not in all conscience her courtship repay,
Yet took pains to please her, though the plan might
                    go wrong.
            When they to heart's delight
1665   Had reveled there in throng,
            To his chamber he calls the knight,
            And thither they go along.

And there they dallied and drank, and deemed it good sport
To enact their play anew on New Year's Eve,
1670 But Gawain asked again to go on the morrow,
For the time until his tryst was not two days.
The host hindered that, and urged him to stay,
And said, "On my honor, my oath here I take
That you shall get to the Green Chapel to begin your chores
1675 By dawn on New Year's Day, if you so desire.
Wherefore lie at your leisure in your lofty bed,
And I shall hunt hereabouts, and hold to our terms,
And we shall trade winnings when once more we meet,
For I have tested you twice, and true have I found you;
1680 Now think this tomorrow: the third pays for all;
Be we merry while we may, and mindful of joy,
For heaviness of heart can be had for the asking."
This is gravely agreed on and Gawain will stay.
They drink a last draught and with torches depart
1685   to rest.
            To bed Sir Gawain went;
            His sleep was of the best;
            The lord, on his craft intent,
            Was early up and dressed.

1690 After mass, with his men, a morsel he takes;
Clear and crisp the morning; he calls for his mount;
The folk that were to follow him afield that day
Were high astride their horses before the hall gates.
Wondrous fair were the fields, for the frost was light;
1695 The sun rises red amid radiant clouds,
Sails into the sky, and sends forth his beams.
They let loose the hounds by a leafy wood;
The rocks all around re-echo to their horns;

Soon some have set off in pursuit of the fox,
1700 Cast about with craft for a clearer scent;
A young dog yaps, and is yelled at in turn;
His fellows fall to sniffing, and follow his lead,
Running in a rabble on the right track,
And he scampers all before; they discover him soon,
1705 And when they see him with sight they pursue him the faster,
Railing at° him rudely with a wrathful din.   *scolding*
Often he reverses over rough terrain,
Or loops back to listen in the lee of a hedge;
At last, by a little ditch, he leaps over the brush,
1710 Comes into a clearing at a cautious pace,
Then he thought through his wiles to have thrown off the hounds
Till he was ware, as he went, of a waiting station
Where three athwart his path threatened him at once,
all gray.
1715   Quick as a flash he wheels
And darts off in dismay;
With hard luck at his heels
He is off to the wood away.

Then it was heaven on earth to hark to the hounds
1720 When they had come on their quarry, coursing together!
Such harsh cries and howls they hurled at his head
As all the cliffs with a crash had come down at once.
Here he was hailed, when huntsmen met him;
Yonder they yelled at him, yapping and snarling;
1725 There they cried "Thief!" and threatened his life,
And ever the harriers° at his heels, that he had no rest.   *pursuing hounds*
Often he was menaced when he made for the open,
And often rushed in again, for Reynard was wily;
And so he leads them a merry chase, the lord and his men,
1730 In this manner on the mountains, till midday or near,
While our hero lies at home in wholesome sleep
Within the comely curtains on the cold morning.
But the lady, as love would allow her no rest,
And pursuing ever the purpose that pricked her heart,
1735 Was awake with the dawn, and went to his chamber
In a fair flowing mantle that fell to the earth,
All edged and embellished with ermines fine;
No hood on her head, but heavy with gems
Were her fillet° and the fret° that confined her tresses;   *headband / net*
1740 Her face and her fair throat freely displayed;
Her bosom all but bare, and her back as well.

She comes in at the chamber door, and closes it with care,
Throws wide a window—then waits no longer,
But hails him thus airily with her artful words,
1745   with cheer:
      "Ah, man, how can you sleep?
      The morning is so clear!"
      Though dreams have drowned him deep,
      He cannot choose but hear.

1750 Deep in his dreams he darkly mutters
As a man may that mourns, with many grim thoughts
Of that day when destiny shall deal him his doom
When he greets his grim host at the Green Chapel
And must bow to his buffet, bating° all strife.   *giving up*
1755 But when he sees her at his side he summons his wits,
Breaks from the black dreams, and blithely answers.
That lovely lady comes laughing sweet,
Sinks down at his side, and salutes him with a kiss.
He accords her fair welcome in courtliest style;
1760 He sees her so glorious, so gaily attired,
So faultless her features, so fair and so bright,
His heart swelled swiftly with surging joys.
They melt into mirth with many a fond smile,
And there was bliss beyond telling between those two,
1765   at height.
      Good were their words of greeting;
      Each joyed in other's sight;
      Great peril attends that meeting
      Should Mary forget her knight.

1770 For that high-born beauty so hemmed him about,
Made so plain her meaning, the man must needs
Either take her tendered° love or distastefully refuse.   *offered*
His courtesy concerned him, lest crass he appear,
But more his soul's mischief, should he commit sin
1775 And belie his loyal oath to the lord of that house.
"God forbid!" said the bold knight, "That shall not befall!"
With a little fond laughter he lightly let pass
All the words of special weight that were sped his way;
"I find you much at fault," the fair one said,
1780 "Who can be cold toward a creature so close by your side,
Of all women in this world most wounded in heart,
Unless you have a sweetheart, one you hold dearer,
And allegiance to that lady so loyally knit
That you will never love another, as now I believe.

1785 And, sir, if it be so, then say it, I beg you;
     By all your heart holds dear, hide it no longer
                     with guile."
                 "Lady, by Saint John,"
                 He answers with a smile,
1790   "Lover have I none,
                 Nor will have, yet awhile."

     "Those words," said the woman, "are the worst of all,
     But I have had my answer, and hard do I find it!
     Kiss me now kindly; I can but go hence
1795 To lament my life long like a maid lovelorn."
     She inclines her head quickly and kisses the knight,
     Then straightens with a sigh, and says as she stands,
     "Now, dear, as I depart, do me this pleasure:
     Give me some little gift, your glove or the like,
1800 That I may think on you, man, and mourn the less."
     "Now by heaven," said he, "I wish I had here
     My most precious possession, to put it in your hands,
     For your deeds, beyond doubt, have often deserved
     A repayment far passing my power to bestow.
1805 But a love token, lady, were of little avail;
     It is not to your honor to have at this time
     A glove as a guerdon° from Gawain's hand,   *reward*
     And I am here on an errand in unknown realms
     And have no bearers with baggage with becoming gifts,
1810 Which distresses me, madame, for your dear sake.
     A man must keep within his compass:° account it neither grief   *limits*
                     nor slight."
                 "Nay, noblest knight alive,"
                 Said that beauty of body white,
1815   "Though you be loath to give,
                 Yet you shall take, by right."

     She reached out a rich ring, wrought all of gold,
     With a splendid stone displayed on the band
     That flashed before his eyes like a fiery sun;
1820 It was worth a king's wealth, you may well believe.
     But he waved it away with these ready words:
     "Before God, good lady, I forego all gifts;
     None have I to offer, nor any will I take."
     And she urged it on him eagerly, and ever he refused,
1825 And vowed in very earnest, prevail she would not.
     And she sad to find it so, and said to him then,
     "If my ring is refused for its rich cost—

You would not be my debtor for so dear a thing—
I shall give you my girdle; you gain less thereby."
1830 She released a knot lightly, and loosened a belt
That was caught about her kirtle,° the bright cloak beneath,   *dress*
Of a gay green silk, with gold overwrought,
And the borders all bound with embroidery fine,
And this she presses upon him, and pleads with a smile,
1835 Unworthy though it were, that it would not be scorned.
But the man still maintains that he means to accept
Neither gold nor any gift, till by God's grace
The fate that lay before him was fully achieved.
"And be not offended, fair lady, I beg,
1840 And give over your offer, for ever I must
                         decline.
             I am grateful for favor shown
             Past all deserts of mine,
             And ever shall be your own
1845   True servant, rain or shine."

"Now does my present displease you," she promptly inquired,
"Because it seems in your sight so simple a thing?
And belike, as it is little, it is less to praise,
But if the virtue that invests it were verily known,
1850 It would be held, I hope, in higher esteem.
For the man that possesses this piece of silk,
If he bore it on his body, belted about,
There is no hand under heaven that could hew him down,
For he could not be killed by any craft on earth."
1855 Then the man began to muse, and mainly he thought
It was a pearl for his plight, the peril to come
When he gains the Green Chapel to get his reward:
Could he escape unscathed,° the scheme were noble!   *unharmed*
Then he bore with her words and withstood them no more,
1860 And she repeated her petition and pleaded anew,
And he granted it, and gladly she gave him the belt,
And besought him for her sake to conceal it well,
Lest the noble lord should know—and the knight agrees
That not a soul save themselves shall see it thenceforth
1865   with sight.
             He thanked her with fervent heart,
             As often as ever he might;
             Three times, before they part,
             She has kissed the stalwart knight.

1870 Then the lady took her leave, and left him there,

For more mirth with that man she might not have.
When she was gone, Sir Gawain got from his bed,
Arose and arrayed him in his rich attire;
Tucked away the token the temptress had left,
1875 Laid it reliably where he looked for it after.
And then with good cheer to the chapel he goes,
Approached a priest in private, and prayed to be taught
To lead a better life and lift up his mind,
Lest he be among the lost when he must leave this world.
1880 And shamefaced at shrift° he showed his misdeeds   *confession*
From the largest to the least, and asked the Lord's mercy,[27]
And called on his confessor to cleanse his soul,
And he absolved him of his sins as safe and as clean
As if the dread Day of Judgment should dawn on the morrow.
1885 And then he made merry amid the fine ladies
With deft-footed dances and dalliance light,
As never until now, while the afternoon wore
                              away.
                    He delighted all around him,
1890   And all agreed, that day,
                    They never before had found him
                    So gracious and so gay.

Now peaceful be his pasture, and love play him fair!
The host is on horseback, hunting afield;
1895 He has finished off this fox that he followed so long:
As he leapt a low hedge to look for the villain
Where he heard all the hounds in hot pursuit,
Reynard comes racing out of a rough thicket,
And all the rabble in a rush, right at his heels.
1900 The man beholds the beast, and bides his time,
And bares his bright sword, and brings it down hard,
And he blenches from° the blade, and backward   *moves to avoid*
        he starts;
A hound hurries up and hinders that move,
And before the horse's feet they fell on him at once
1905 And ripped the rascal's throat with a wrathful din.
The lord soon alighted and lifted him free,
Swiftly snatched him up from the snapping jaws,
Holds him over his head, halloos with a will,
And the dogs bayed the dirge, that had done him to death.
1910 Hunters hastened thither with horns at their lips,
Sounding the assembly till they saw him at last.
When that comely company was come in together,

All that bore bugles blew them at once,
And the others all hallooed, that had no horns.
1915 It was the merriest medley° that ever a man heard,   *mixed chorus*
The racket that they raised for Sir Reynard's soul
                that died.
        Their hounds they praised and fed,
        Fondling their heads with pride,
1920   And they took Reynard the Red
        And stripped away his hide.

And then they headed homeward, for evening had come,
Blowing many a blast on their bugles bright.
The lord at long last alights at his house,
1925 Finds fire on the hearth where the fair knight waits,
Sir Gawain the good, that was glad in heart.
With the ladies, that loved him, he lingered at ease;
He wore a rich robe of blue that reached to the earth
And a surcoat° lined softly with sumptuous furs;   *loose outer coat*
1930 A hood of the same hue hung on his shoulders;
With bands of bright ermine embellished were both.
He comes to meet the man amid all the folk,
And greets him good humoredly, and gaily he says,
"I shall follow forthwith the form of our pledge
1935 That we framed to good effect amid fresh-filled cups."
He clasps him accordingly and kisses him thrice,
As amiably and as earnestly as ever he could.
"By heaven," said the host, "you have had some luck
Since you took up this trade, if the terms were good."
1940 "Never trouble about the terms," he returned at once,
"Since all that I owe here is openly paid."
"Marry!" said the other man, "mine is much less,
For I have hunted all day, and nought have I got
But this foul fox pelt, the fiend take the goods!
1945 Which but poorly repays those precious things
That you have cordially conferred, those kisses three
             so good."
        "Enough!" said Sir Gawain;
        "I thank you, by the rood!"°   *cross*
1950   And how the fox was slain
        He told him, as they stood.

With minstrelsy and mirth, with all manner of meats,
They made as much merriment as any men might
(Amid laughing of ladies and lighthearted girls,
1955 So gay grew Sir Gawain and the goodly host)

Unless they had been besotted,° or brainless fools.   *drunk*
The knight joined in jesting with that joyous folk,
Until at last it was late; before long they must part,
And be off to their beds, as behooved° them each one.   *was proper for*
1960   Then politely his leave of the lord of the house
Our noble knight takes, and renews his thanks:
"The courtesies countless accorded me here,
Your kindness at this Christmas, may heaven's King repay!
Henceforth, if you will have me, I hold you my liege,°   *feudal lord*
1965   And so, as I have said, I must set forth tomorrow,
If I may take some trusty man to teach, as you promised,
The way to the Green Chapel, that as God allows
I shall see my fate fulfilled on the first of the year."
"In good faith," said the good man, "with a good will
1970   Every promise on my part shall be fully performed."
He assigns him a servant to set him on the path,
To see him safe and sound over the snowy hills,
To follow the fastest way through forest green
                         and grove.
1975   Gawain thanks him again.
               So kind his favors prove,
               And of the ladies then
               He takes his leave, with love.

Courteously he kissed them, with care in his heart,
1980   And often wished them well, with warmest thanks,
Which they for their part were prompt to repay.
They commend him to Christ with disconsolate sighs;
And then in that hall with the household he parts—
Each man that he met, he remembered to thank
1985   For his deeds of devotion and diligent pains,
And the trouble he had taken to tend to his needs;
And each one as woeful, that watched him depart,
As he had lived with him loyally all his life long.
By lads bearing lights he was led to his chamber
1990   And blithely brought to his bed, to be at his rest.
How soundly he slept, I presume not to say,
For there were matters of moment his thoughts might well
                         pursue.
               Let him lie and wait;
1995   He has little more to do,
               Then listen, while I relate
               How they kept their rendezvous.

Part IV

Now the New Year draws near, and the night passes,
The day dispels the dark, by the Lord's decree;
2000 But wild weather awoke in the world without:
The clouds in the cold sky cast down their snow
With great gusts from the north, grievous to bear.
Sleet showered aslant upon shivering beasts;
The wind warbled wild as it whipped from aloft,
2005 And drove the drifts deep in the dales below.
Long and well he listens, that lies in his bed;
Though he lifts not his eyelids, little he sleeps;
Each crow of the cock he counts without fail.
Readily from his rest he rose before dawn,
2010 For a lamp had been left him, that lighted his chamber.
He called to his chamberlain,° who quickly   *personal attendant*
      appeared,
And bade him get him his gear, and gird° his good steed,   *equip*
And he sets about briskly to bring in his arms,
And makes ready his master in manner most fit.
2015 First he clad him in his clothes, to keep out the cold,
And then his other harness, made handsome anew,
His plate armor of proof,° polished with pains,   *impenetrable*
The rings of his rich mail rid of their rust,
And all was fresh as at first, and for this he gave thanks
2020   indeed.
        With pride he wears each piece,
        New furbished° for his need: *made bright*
        No gayer from here to Greece;
        He bids them bring his steed.

2025 In his richest raiment he robed himself then:
His crested coat armor,° close stitched with craft,   *cloth outer garment*
With stones of strange virtue on silk velvet set;
All bound with embroidery on borders and seams
And lined warmly and well with furs of the best.
2030 Yet he left not his love gift, the lady's girdle;
Gawain, for his own good, forgot not that:
When the bright sword was belted and bound on his haunches,
Then twice with that token he twined him about.
Sweetly did he swathe him in that swatch of silk,
2035 That girdle of green so goodly to see,
That against the gay red showed gorgeous bright.
Yet he wore not for its wealth that wondrous girdle,

Nor pride in its pendants, though polished they were,
Though glittering gold gleamed at the ends,
2040 But to keep himself safe when consent he must
To endure a deadly blow, and all defense
                    denied.
            And now the bold knight came
            Into the courtyard wide;
2045   That folk of worthy fame
            He thanks on every side.

Then was Gringolet girt, that was great and huge,
And had sojourned° safe and sound, and savored his fare;   *stayed there*
He pawed the earth in his pride, that princely steed.
2050 The good knight draws near him and notes well his look,
And says sagely to himself, and soberly swears,
"Here is a household in hall that upholds the right!
The man that maintains it, may happiness be his!
Likewise the dear lady, may love betide her!
2055 If thus they in charity cherish a guest
That are honored here on earth, may they have His reward
That reigns high in heaven—and also you all;
And were I to live in this land but a little while,
I should willingly reward you, and well, if I might."
2060 Then he steps into the stirrup and bestrides his mount;
His shield is shown forth; on his shoulder he casts it;
Strikes the side of his steed with his steel spurs,
And he starts across the stones, nor stands any longer
                    to prance.
2065   On horseback was the swain°   *fellow*
            That bore his spear and lance;
            "May Christ this house maintain
            And guard it from mischance!"

The bridge was brought down, and the broad gates
2070 Unbarred and carried back upon both sides;
He commended him to Christ, and crossed over the planks;
Praised the noble porter, who prayed on his knees
That God save Sir Gawain, and bade him good day,
And went on his way alone with the man
2075 That would lead him before long to that luckless place
To face the sad fate that must befall him there.
Under bare boughs they ride, where steep banks rise,
Over high cliffs they climb, where cold snow clings;
The heavens held aloof, but heavy thereunder
2080 Mist mantled the moors, moved on the slopes.

Each hill had a hat, a huge cape of cloud;
Brooks bubbled and broke as they ran between rocks,
Flashing in freshets° that waterfalls fed.   *streams*
Roundabout was the road that ran through the wood
2085 Till the sun at that season was soon to rise,
                    that day.
          They were on a hilltop high;
          The white snow round them lay;
          The man that rode nearby
2090   Now bade his master stay.

"For I have seen you here safe at the set time,
And now you are not far from that notable place
That you have sought for so long with such special pains.
But this I say for certain, since I know you, sir knight,
2095 And have your good at heart, and hold you dear—
Would you heed well my words, it were worth your while—
You are rushing into risks that you reck not° of: *are heedless*
There is a villain in yon valley, the veriest on earth,
For he is rugged and rude, and ready with his fists,
2100 And most immense in his mold of mortals alive,
And his body bigger than the best four
That are in Arthur's house, Hector or any.
He gets his grim way at the Green Chapel;
None passes by that place so proud in his arms
2105 That he does not dash him down with his deadly blows,
For he is heartless wholly, and heedless of right,
For be it chaplain or churl° that by the Chapel rides,   *person of low class*
Monk or mass-priest or any man else,
He would as soon strike him dead as stand on two feet.
2110 Wherefore I say, just as certain as you sit there astride,
You cannot but be killed, if his counsel holds,
For he would trounce° you in a trice,° had you   *thrash / an instant*
          twenty lives
                    for sale.
          He has lived long in this land
2115   And dealt out deadly bale;°   *harm*
          Against his heavy hand
          Your power cannot prevail.

"And so, good Sir Gawain, let the grim man be;
Go off by some other road, in God's own name!
2120 Leave by some other land, for the love of Christ,
And I shall get me home again, and give you my word
That I shall swear by God's self and the saints above,

By heaven and by my halidom° and other oaths more, *sacred relic*
To conceal this day's deed, nor say to a soul
2125 That ever you fled for fear from any that I knew."
"Many thanks!" said the other man—and
     demurring° he speaks— *objecting*
"Fair fortune befall you for your friendly words!
And conceal this day's deed I doubt not you would,
But though you never told the tale, if I turned back now,
2130 Forsook this place for fear, and fled, as you say,
I were a caitiff° coward; I could not be excused. *wretched*
But I must to the Chapel to chance my luck
And say to that same man such words as I please,
Befall what may befall through Fortune's will
2135   or whim.
     Though he be a quarrelsome knave
     With a cudgel° great and grim, *club*
     The Lord is strong to save:
     His servants trust in Him."

2140 "Marry," said the man, "since you tell me so much,
And I see you are set to seek your own harm,
If you crave a quick death, let me keep you no longer!
Put your helm on your head, your hand on your lance,
And ride the narrow road down yon rocky slope
2145 Till it brings you to the bottom of the broad valley.
Then look a little ahead, on your left hand,
And you will soon see before you that self-same Chapel,
And the man of great might that is master there.
Now goodbye in God's name, Gawain the noble!
2150 For all the world's wealth I would not stay here,
Or go with you in this wood one footstep further!"
He tarried no more to talk, but turned his bridle,
Hit his horse with his heels as hard as he might,
Leaves the knight alone, and off like the wind
2155   goes leaping.
     "By God," said Gawain then,
     "I shall not give way to weeping;
     God's will be done, amen!
     I commend me to His keeping."

2160 He puts his heels to his horse, and picks up the path;
Goes in beside a grove where the ground is steep,
Rides down the rough slope right to the valley;
And then he looked a little about him—the landscape was wild,
And not a soul to be seen, nor sign of a dwelling,

2165 But high banks on either hand hemmed it about,
With many a ragged rock and rough-hewn crag;
The skies seemed scored° by the scowling peaks.   *scraped*
Then he halted his horse, and held the rein fast,
And sought on every side for a sight of the Chapel,
2170 But no such place appeared, which puzzled him sore,
Yet he saw some way off what seemed like a mound,
A hillock high and broad, hard by the water,
Where the stream fell in foam down the face of the steep
And bubbled as if it boiled on its bed below.
2175 The knight urges his horse, and heads for the knoll;
Leaps lightly to earth; loops well the rein
Of his steed to a stout branch, and stations him there.
He strides straight to the mound, and strolls all about,
Much wondering what it was, but no whit the wiser;
2180 It had a hole at one end, and on either side,
And was covered with coarse grass in clumps all without,
And hollow all within, like some old cave,
Or a crevice of an old crag—he could not discern
               aright.
2185   "Can this be the Chapel Green?
        Alack!" said the man. "Here might
        The devil himself be seen
        Saying matins° at black midnight!"   *morning service*

"Now by heaven," said he, "it is bleak hereabouts;
2190 This prayer house is hideous, half covered with grass!
Well may the grim man mantled in green
Recite here his orisons,° in hell's own style!   *prayers*
Now I feel it is the Fiend, in my five wits,
That has tempted me to this tryst, to take my life;
2195 This is a Chapel of mischance, may the mischief take it!
As accursed a country church as I came upon ever!"
With his helm on his head, his lance in his hand,
He stalks toward the steep wall of that strange house.
Then he heard, on the hill, behind a hard rock,
2200 Beyond the brook, from the bank, a most barbarous din:
Lord! it clattered in the cliff fit to cleave it in two,
As if someone on a grindstone ground a great scythe!
Lord! it whirred like a mill wheel whirling around!
Lord! it echoed loud and long, lamentable to hear!
2205 Then "By heaven," said the bold knight, "That business up there
Is arranged for my arrival, or else I am much
              misled.
        Let God work! Ah me!

All hope of help has fled!
2210   Forfeit my life may be
But noise I do not dread."

Then he listened no longer, but loudly he called,
"Who has power in this place, high parley° to hold?   *conference*
For none greets Sir Gawain, or gives him good day;
2215   If any would a word with him, let him walk forth
And speak now or never, to speed his affairs."
"Abide," said one on the bank above over his head,
"And what I promised you once shall straightway be given."
Yet he stayed not his grindstone, nor stinted its noise,
2220   But worked awhile at his whetting before he would rest,
And then he comes around a crag, from a cave in the rocks,
Hurtling out of hiding with a hateful weapon,
A Danish ax devised for that day's deed,
With a broad blade and bright, bent in a curve,
2225   Filed to a fine edge—four feet it measured
By the length of the lace that was looped round the haft.
And in form as at first, the fellow all green,
His lordly face and his legs, his locks and his beard,
Save that firm upon two feet forward he strides,
2230   Sets a hand on the ax-head, the haft to the earth;
When he came to the cold stream, and cared not to wade,
He vaults over on his ax, and advances apace
On a broad bank of snow, overbearing and brisk
                    of mood.
2235   Little did the knight incline
When face to face they stood;
Said the other man, "Friend mine,
It seems your word holds good!"

"God love you, Sir Gawain!" said the Green Knight then,
2240   "And well met this morning, man, at my place!
And you have followed me faithfully and found me betimes,
And on the business between us we both are agreed:
Twelve months ago today you took what was yours,
And you at this New Year must yield me the same.
2245   And we have met in these mountains, remote from all eyes:
There is none here to halt us or hinder our sport;
Unhasp your high helm, and have here your wages;
Make no more demur than I did myself
When you hacked off my head with one hard blow."
2250   "No, by God," said Sir Gawain, "that granted me life,
I shall grudge not the guerdon,° grim though it prove;   *repayment*
Bestow but one stroke, and I shall stand still,

And you may lay on as you like till the last of my debt
is paid."

2255   He proffered, with good grace,
                His bare neck to the blade,
                And feigned a cheerful face:
                He scorned to seem afraid.

Then the grim man in green gathers his strength,
2260   Heaves high the heavy ax to hit him the blow.
With all the force in his frame he fetches it aloft,
With a grimace as grim as he would grind him to bits;
Had the blow he bestowed been as big as he threatened,
A good knight and gallant had gone to his grave.
2265   But Gawain at the great ax glanced up aside
As down it descended with death-dealing force,
And his shoulders shrank a little from the sharp iron.
Abruptly the brawny man breaks off the stroke,
And then reproved with proud words that prince among knights.
2270   "You are not Gawain the glorious," the green man said,
"That never fell back on field in the face of the foe,
And now you flee for fear, and have felt no harm:
Such news of that knight I never heard yet!
I moved not a muscle when you made to strike,
2275   Nor caviled at° the cut in King Arthur's house;   *raised objections to*
My head fell to my feet, yet steadfast I stood,
And you, all unharmed, are wholly dismayed—
Wherefore the better man I, by all odds,
must be."

2280   Said Gawain, "Strike once more;
                I shall neither flinch nor flee;
                But if my head falls to the floor
                There is no mending me!

"But go on, man, in God's name, and get to the point!
2285   Deliver me my destiny, and do it without delay,
For I shall stand to the stroke and stir not an inch
Till your ax has hit home—on my honor I swear it!"
"Have at you then!" said the other, and heaves it aloft,
And glares down as grimly as he had gone mad.
2290   He made a mighty feint, but marred not his hide;
Withdrew the ax adroitly before it did damage.
Gawain gave no ground, nor glanced up aside,
But stood still as a stone, or else a stout stump
That is held in hard earth by a hundred roots.
2295   Then merrily does he mock him, the man all in green:

"So now you have your nerve again, I needs must strike;
Uphold the high knighthood that Arthur bestowed,
And keep your collarbones clear, if this cut allows!"
Then was Gawain gripped with rage, and grimly he said,
2300 "Why, thrash away, tyrant, I tire of your threats;
You make such a scene, you must frighten yourself."
Said the green fellow, "In faith, so fiercely you speak
That I shall finish this affair, nor further grace
                allow."
2305   He stands prepared to strike
           And scowls with both lip and brow;
           No marvel if the man mislike
           Who can hope no rescue now.

He gathered up the grim ax and guided it well:
2310 Let the barb at the blade's end brush the bare throat;
He hammered down hard, yet harmed him no whit
Save a scratch on one side, that severed the skin;
The end of the hooked edge entered the flesh,
And a little blood lightly leapt to the earth.
2315 And when the man beheld his own blood bright on the snow,
He sprang a spear's length with feet spread wide,
Seized his high helmet, and set it on his head,
Shoved before his shoulders the shield at his back,
Bares his trusty blade, and boldly he speaks—
2320 Not since he was a babe born of his mother
Was he once in this world one half so blithe—
"Have done with your hacking—harry me no more!
I have borne, as behooved,° one blow in this place;   *was proper*
If you make another move I shall meet it midway
2325 And promptly, I promise you, pay back each blow
               with brand.°   *sword*
           One stroke acquits me here;
           So did our covenant stand
           In Arthur's court last year—
2330   Wherefore, sir, hold your hand!"

He lowers the long ax and leans on it there,
Sets his arms on the head, the haft on the earth,
And beholds the brave knight that bides there afoot,
How he faces him fearless, fierce in full arms,
2335 And plies him with proud words—it pleases him well.
Then once again gaily to Gawain he calls,
And in a loud voice and lusty, delivers these words:
"Bold fellow, on this field your anger forbear!

No man has made demands here in manner uncouth,
2340 Nor done, save as duly determined at court.
I owed you a hit and you have it; be happy therewith!
The rest of my rights here I freely resign.
Had I been a bit busier, a buffet, perhaps,
I could have dealt more directly, and done you some harm.
2345 First I flourished with a feint, in frolicsome mood,
And left your hide unhurt—and here I did well
By the fair terms we fixed on the first night;
And fully and faithfully you followed accord:
Gave over all your gains as a good man should.
2350 A second feint, sir, I assigned for the morning
You kissed my comely wife—each kiss you restored.
For both of these there behooved° but two   *were deserved*
      feigned blows
                 by right.
            True men pay all they owe;
2355   No danger then in sight.
           You failed at the third throw,
           So take my tap, sir knight.

"For that is my belt about you, that same braided girdle,
My wife it was that wore it; I know well the tale,
2360 And the count of your kisses and your conduct too,
And the wooing of my wife—it was all my scheme!
She made trial of a man most faultless by far
Of all that ever walked over the wide earth;
As pearls to white peas, more precious and prized,
2365 So is Gawain, in good faith, to other gay knights.
Yet you lacked, sir, a little in loyalty there,
But the cause was not cunning, nor courtship either,
But that you loved your own life; the less, then, to blame."
The other stout knight in a study stood a long while,
2370 So gripped with grim rage that his great heart shook.
All the blood of his body burned in his face
As he shrank back in shame from the man's sharp speech.
The first words that fell from the fair knight's lips:
"Cursed be a cowardly and covetous heart!
2375 In you is villainy and vice, and virtue laid low!"
Then he grasps the green girdle and lets go the knot,
Hands it over in haste, and hotly he says:
"Behold there my falsehood, ill hap betide it!
Your cut taught me cowardice, care for my life,
2380 And coveting came after, contrary both

To largesse and loyalty belonging to knights.
Now am I faulty and false, that fearful was ever
Of disloyalty and lies—bad luck to them both!—
             and greed.
2385   I confess, knight, in this place,
          My faults are grave indeed.
          Let me gain back your good grace,
          And hereafter I shall take heed."

Then the other laughed aloud, and lightly he said,
2390 "Such harm as I have had, I hold it quite healed.
You are so fully confessed, your failings made known,
And bear the plain penance of the point of my blade,
I hold you polished as a pearl, as pure and as bright
As you had lived free of fault since first you were born.
2395 And I give you, sir, this girdle that is gold hemmed
And green as my garments, that, Gawain, you may
Be mindful of this meeting when you mingle in throng
With nobles of renown—and known by this token
How it chanced at the Green Chapel, to chivalrous knights.
2400 And you shall in this New Year come yet again
And we shall finish out our feast in my fair hall,
             with cheer."
          He urged the knight to stay,
          And said, "With my wife so dear
2405   We shall see you friends this day,
          Whose enmity touched you near."

"Indeed," said the doughty knight, and doffed his high helm,
And held it in his hands as he offered his thanks,
"I have lingered long enough—may good luck be yours,
2410 And He reward you well that all worship bestows!
And commend me to that comely one, your courteous wife,
Both herself and that other, my honoured ladies,
That have trapped their true knight in their
          trammels° so quaint.   *nets*
But if a dullard should dote, deem it no wonder,
2415 And through the wiles of a woman be wooed into sorrow,
For so was Adam by one, when the world began,
And Solomon by many more, and Samson the mighty—
Delilah was his doom, and David thereafter
Was beguiled by Bathsheba, and bore much distress;
2420 Now these were vexed by their devices—'twere a very joy
Could one but learn to love, and believe them not.
For these were proud princes, most prosperous of old,

Past all lovers lucky, that languished under heaven,
        bemused.°   *bewildered*
2425   And one and all fell prey
        To women that they had used;
        If I be led astray,
        Methinks I may be excused.

"But your girdle, God love you! I gladly shall take
2430 And be pleased to possess, not for the pure gold,
Nor the bright belt itself, nor the beauteous pendants,
Nor for wealth, nor worldly state, nor workmanship fine,
But a sign of excess it shall seem oftentimes
When I ride in renown, and remember with shame
2435 The faults and the frailty of the flesh perverse,
How its tenderness entices the foul taint of sin;
And so when praise and high prowess have pleased my heart,
A look at this love-lace will lower my pride.
But one thing would I learn, if you were not loath,
2440 Since you are lord of yonder land where I have long sojourned
With honor in your house—may you have His reward
That upholds all the heavens, highest on throne!
How runs your right name?—and let the rest go."
"That shall I give you gladly," said the Green Knight then;
2445 "Bertilak de Hautdesert, this barony I hold,[28]
Through the might of Morgan le Fay, that lodges at my house,[29]
By subtleties of science and sorcerers' arts,
The mistress of Merlin, she has caught many a man,
For sweet love in secret she shared sometime
2450 With that wizard, that knows well each one of your knights
                and you.
        Morgan the Goddess, she,
        So styled by title true;
        None holds so high degree
2455   That her arts cannot subdue.

"She guided me in this guise to your glorious hall,
To assay,° if such it were, the surfeit° of pride   *test / excess*
That is rumored of the retinue of the Round Table.
She put this shape upon me to puzzle your wits,
2460 To afflict the fair queen, and frighten her to death
With awe of that elvish man that eerily spoke
With his head in his hand before the high table.[30]
She was with my wife at home, that old withered lady,
Your own aunt is she, Arthur's half sister,
2465 The duchess's daughter of Tintagel, that dear King Uther

Got Arthur on after, that honored is now.
And therefore, good friend, come feast with your aunt;
Make merry in my house; my men hold you dear,
And I wish you as well, sir, with all my heart,
2470 As any mortal man, for your matchless faith."
But the knight said him nay, that he might by no means.
They clasped then and kissed, and commended each other
To the Prince of Paradise, and parted with one
                              assent.
2475   Gawain sets out anew;
              Toward the court his course is bent;
              And the knight all green in hue,
              Wheresoever he wished, he went.

Wild ways in the world our worthy knight rides
2480 On Gringolet, that by grace had been granted his life.
He harbored often in houses, and often abroad,
And with many valiant adventures verily he met
That I shall not take time to tell in this story.
The hurt was whole that he had had in his neck,
2485 And the bright green belt on his body he bore,
Oblique, like a baldric,° bound at his side,   *band worn aslant*
Below his left shoulder, laced in a knot,
In betokening of the blame he had borne for his fault;
And so to court in due course he comes safe and sound.
2490 Bliss abounded in hall when the high born heard
That good Gawain was come; glad tidings they thought it.
The king kisses the knight, and the queen as well,
And many a comrade came to clasp him in arms,
And eagerly they asked, and awesomely he told,
2495 Confessed all his cares and discomfitures many,
How it chanced at the Chapel, what cheer made the knight,
The love of the lady, the green lace at last.
The nick on his neck he naked displayed
That he got in his disgrace at the Green Knight's hands,
2500   alone.
              With rage in heart he speaks,
              And grieves with many a groan;
              The blood burns in his cheeks
              For shame at what must be shown.

2505 "Behold, sir," said he, and handles the belt,
"This is the blazon° of the blemish that I bear on   *heraldic symbol*
        my neck;
This is the sign of sore loss that I have suffered there

For the cowardice and coveting that I came to there;
This is the badge of false faith that I was found in there,
2510 And I must bear it on my body till I breathe my last.
For one may keep a deed dark, but undo it no whit,
For where a fault is made fast, it is fixed evermore."
The king comforts the knight, and the court all together
Agree with gay laughter and gracious intent
2515 That the lords and the ladies belonging to the Table,
Each brother of that band, a baldric should have,
A belt borne oblique, of a bright green,
To be worn with one accord for that worthy's sake.
So that was taken as a token by the Table Round,
2520 And he honored that had it, evermore after,
As the best book of knighthood bids it be known.
In the old days of Arthur this happening befell;
The books of Brutus' deeds bear witness thereto
Since Brutus, the bold knight, embarked for this land
2525 After the siege ceased at Troy and the city fared
                              amiss.
          Many such, ere we were born,
          Have befallen here, ere this.
          May He that was crowned with thorn
2530   Bring all men to His bliss! Amen.

HONI SOIT QUI MAL PENCE[31]

Notes: *Sir Gawain and the Green Knight*

1. line 1: **Since the siege . . . ceased at Troy.** The poet begins his story, as he later ends it, by placing the reign of King Arthur in a broad historical perspective, which includes the fall of Troy. In accordance with medieval notions of history (though not all of his details can be found in the early chronicles), he visualizes Aeneas, son of the king of Troy, and his descendants as founding a series of western kingdoms to which each descendant gives his name.
2. lines 3–4: **The knight that had knotted . . . proven most true.** This deceitful knight is evidently Antenor, who in Virgil's *Aeneid* is a trusted counselor but who appears as a traitor in later versions of the Troy story.
3. line 13: **And far over the French Sea, Felix Brutus.** The westward movement ends with the crossing of the "French Sea," or English Channel, by Brutus, great-grandson of Aeneas, legendary founder of the kingdom of Britain. This Brutus, whom the poet calls *Felix*, or fortunate, is not to be confused with the Marcus Brutus of Roman history.
4. line 43: **Then came to the court for carol dancing.** In the original, the poet simply says that lords and ladies came to Arthur's court "to make carols"; there was

no need in late Middle English to add the word *dancing*. Caroling, in this context, means singing while dancing in a circle. Such carols were not necessarily religious, though at a Christmas feast some of them were probably what we think of as Christmas carols today.

5. line 66: **. . . hand gifts to make.** In the original, the poet says that the participants offered *hondeselle,* literally "hand" + "give," to each other. What seems to be meant is a game in which men concealed gifts in their outstretched hands, offering them to ladies who had to guess what the gift was or perhaps which hand held it (line 67). The forfeit for guessing wrong was a kiss.

6. lines 108–15: **Talking before the high table . . . many stalwart knights.** What we are asked to visualize here is not the "Table Round" at which no place was higher or lower than any other, though that table is referred to later by the Green Knight (li. 313). Rather, the poet describes the kind of seating arrangement that he might have seen in a baronial hall and that indeed is still seen in the dining halls at the universities of Oxford and Cambridge. The "high table," reserved for the most honored guests, stands on a dais opposite the entrance through which the Green Knight will ride. Those seated there face the rest of the company, who occupy tables ranged along either side of the hall (li. 115). The middle seat is the king's, though when the story opens it is vacant. A distinguished representative of the church, Bishop Baldwin, occupies the place of honor at the king's right. Next to the bishop sits Sir Yvain, who, as his partner at table, will share with him the twelve dishes served at the feast (line 128). At the king's left sits the queen; beside her, Sir Gawain, and beside him, his table partner, Sir Agravain.

7. line 182: **A beard big as a bush on his breast hangs.** This detail is one sign of a generation gap evidently envisioned by the poet between the Green Knight and the company at King Arthur's court. Abundance of beard and hair bespeak a man past his first youth, as do "bristling" eyebrows (line 305) such as the Green Knight is said to possess. Our attention is again drawn to the beard in line 306, when the knight wags it as he looks around, and in line 334, when he strokes it while awaiting a blow from the ax in the king's hands. His belittling reference to Arthur's knights as "beardless children" (line 280) further signifies this distance in age between them. See also line 2228.

8. line 186: **Of a king's cap-à-dos . . .** The word *capados* occurs in this form in Middle English only in *Sir Gawain,* here and in line 572. I have interpreted it, as the poet apparently did also, as *cap-à-dos*—that is, a garment covering its wearer "from head to back," on the model of *cap-à-pie,* "from head to foot," referring to armor.

9. lines 224–25: **. . . "Where is," he said, "The captain of this crowd? . . ."** The Green Knight's inability, or feigned inability, to tell which of the people before him is King Arthur has insulting implications; in heroic legend, a leader typically stands out in a crowd. In *Beowulf,* for example, the coast guard, greeting the band of Geats on their arrival in the land of the Danes, clearly refers to the hero when he says, "I have never seen a mightier warrior on earth than is one of you. That is no retainer made to seem good by his weapons" (trans. Donaldson).

10. lines 233–34: **For much did they marvel what it might mean / That a horseman and a horse should have such a hue.** The greenness of the Green Knight is susceptible of many interpretations, none of which need preclude the others. It is, most obviously, the color of vegetation and thus symbolizes the endless vegetative cycle of death and rebirth; the spectators are amazed that a horse

and his rider should "grow green as the grass" (line 235). But this image from the natural realm is immediately discarded in favor of one drawn from the realm of artifice, that of green enamel on gold. And in fact neither can compare, the poet thinks, with the "glorious" hue of the knight. Green also had associations in medieval thought with the infernal realm: a devil in Chaucer's *Friar's Tale*, for example, is dressed all in green. For the members of Arthur's court, the stranger's hue simply enhances his phantasmal and uncanny appearance (li. 239–40).

11. line 390: **"Sir Gawain," said the Green Knight, "by Gog, I rejoice.** In chapters 38–39 of the Old Testament Book of Ezekiel, the Lord says to the prophet "Son of man, set thy face against Gog" (38:2) and later tells him to "prophesy against Gog, and say: Thus saith the Lord God; Behold, I am against thee, O Gog. . . . Thou shalt fall upon the open field" (39:1, 6). Gog is also mentioned in Revelation as a power that appears when Satan is released from his thousand years of bondage and joins forces with him (20:7–9). The Green Knight's oath thus superficially resembles such innocuous expressions as "by golly" and "by gosh" but, at the same time, carries a fleeting suggestion of a demonic supernatural realm.

12. line 477: **"Now, sir, hang up your ax, that has hewn enough."** The "gay" remark with which the king counters the tension of the moment is a witty play on words; the phrase "to hang up one's ax" meant, in Middle English, to stop whatever one has been doing.

13. line 517: **When Zephyr sighs low . . .** Latin *Zephirus* (Greek *Zephyros*) was a name for the west wind in classical mythology. It was transmitted to the late Middle Ages in Latin works such as Guido delle Colonne's prose *History of the Destruction of Troy*, where the blowing of Zephyr forms part of a description of the coming of spring. Chaucer famously uses the detail in a similar description in the opening of the "General Prologue" to the *Canterbury Tales*. It appears also in *Destruction of Troy*, an adaptation of Guido's work belonging to the same alliterative tradition as the long lines of *Sir Gawain and the Green Knight*.

14. lines 619–20: **Then they showed forth the shield, that shone all red, / With the pentangle portrayed in purest gold.** The "pentangle" was a five-pointed star drawn in a continuous line and rejoining itself without a break. In the completed design, the line weaves in and out, going alternately over and under itself. The ancient concept of the five-pointed star merged in medieval thought with that of the six-pointed star of Solomon. Both emblems had magical and religious associations.

15. lines 629–30: **. . . and hence it is called / In all England, as I hear, the endless knot.** But in fact there is no recorded instance of such a phrase.

16. lines 652–54: **. . . beneficence boundless and brotherly love / And pure mind and manners, that none might impeach, / And compassion most precious.** In the poet's Middle English, the names of the five virtues are *franchise, fellowship, cleanness, courtesy,* and *pity.*

17. lines 691–701: **Now he rides in his array through the realm of Logres . . . The Wilderness of Wirral.** The poet evidently thought that Logres, King Arthur's kingdom, was in central or south Wales. Sir Gawain rides north and then turns eastward along the north coast of Wales, leaving Anglesey and its neighboring islands to his left. It was considered dangerous in the poet's time to pass through the forest of Wirral, which was a place of refuge for outlaws and other criminals.

18. line 845: **Broad, bright was his beard, of a beaver's hue.** See n. 7, p. 261 (li. 182).

19. lines 897–98: **Tonight you fast and pray; / Tomorrow we'll see you fed.** Those who serve Sir Gawain his meal are joking. On Christmas Eve, as on Fridays and during Lent, Christians were supposed to abstain from meat. The elaborate fish dishes, of course, make the meal anything but an occasion for self-denial.

20. line 950: **But unlike to look upon, those ladies were.** Underlying the double description is a message of religious import: mortal beauty is transitory. Such as the old lady now is, the desirable young lady will be.

21. line 1022: **The joys of Saint John's Day were justly praised.** The date of Saint John's Day is December 27, so there are four days left, not three, before New Year's morning, on which Sir Gawain is bound to set out to meet the Green Knight. But he lies late in bed at the lord's behest only three days. A line after 1022 may inadvertently have been omitted; in any case, a day seems to be missing.

22. line 1141: **Blew upon their bugles bold blasts three.** Three long notes, or *motes*, were sounded when the hunters unleashed the hounds. The words used by the poet are *thre bare mote*, an onomatopoeic sequence of three long syllables, which I have replicated in my version of the line.

23. lines 1239–40: **Your servant to command / I am, and shall be still.** *Servant* could have its innocuous modern meaning ("one who would be glad to be of service") in the poet's Late Middle English. But it also meant specifically "a professed lover." Sir Gawain takes advantage of this ambiguity in line 1278.

24. line 1325: **The lords lent a hand.** The skills proper to a nobleman in the poet's time included the dressing—disemboweling and dismembering—of deer killed in the hunt.

25. line 1347: **And this they named the numbles.** The modern expression "humble pie" comes from *umble*, a variant from of *numble*.

26. line 1355: **The corbie's bone they cast on a branch.** *Corbie* is a name for the raven (cf. French *corbeau*). Ravens, being carrion birds, would in all probability stay close at hand during the butchering that followed a hunt. It was customary to throw a small piece of gristle into the branches of a nearby tree for them.

27. lines 1880–81: **And shamefaced at shrift he showed his misdeeds / From the largest to the least, and asked the Lord's mercy.** Gawain evidently does not confess his intention of withholding from the lord the girdle he has been given by the lady, thus failing to live up to the terms of their agreement. Because the intention to commit a sin (in this case primarily the sin of failing to be true to one's word) is itself sinful, his confession would seem to be invalid. Perhaps, as has been suggested, he feels that it is not sinful to break the rules of a mere "game" (li. 1111) or "jest" (li. 1409). But he feels differently later, as is shown by his outburst in lines 2378–84. However Gawain's confession and absolution at Hautdesert are to be interpreted, it is fair to say that the absolution that strikes most readers of the poem as "real" is the secular one Sir Gawain receives later from the Green Knight (li. 2391–94).

28. line 2445: **"Bertilak de Hautdesert, this barony I hold."** The first name appears, though it is of minor importance, in Arthurian tradition. A Bertolais and a Bertelak figure in two stories, one French and one English, but neither one has the slightest resemblance to the Green Knight. The name *Hautdesert* is not found elsewhere; it seems to be composed of two French words that would mean "high

hermitage" and would thus imply the isolation of Lord Bertilak's castle from other human dwellings.

29. line 2446: **Through the might of Morgan le Fay, that lodges at my house.** Morgan le Fay, a famous "fairy" or enchantress, was, as we hear later (line 2464), the half sister of King Arthur. (Why she should be a member of Lord Bertilak's household is not so clear.) Merlin, her lover, was a magician who plays an important role in a number of the Arthurian stories. See also the following note.

30. lines 2456–62: **"She guided me in this guise to your glorious hall . . . / before the high table."** Few readers of the poem have been satisfied by this explanation of the opening episode. It is, however, in keeping with a tradition to the effect that Morgan le Fay was a bitter enemy of Queen Guenevere.

31. line 2531: **HONI SOIT QUI MAL PENCE,** Evil be to him who evil thinks, is the motto of the Order of the Garter. The words have been added to the manuscript, apparently by someone who thought there was, or wanted to suggest, a relationship between the adoption of the green girdle by Arthur's court and the founding of the order in 1350. But there is general agreement that there is little basis for interpreting one in terms of the other. (For one thing, the ceremonial Garter is not green but blue.) By allowing the motto to stand after the concluding "Amen," as it does in the manuscript, I do not mean to indicate that I consider it part of the poem.

The Authorship of *Saint Erkenwald*

It has long been the consensus among scholars that the four poems of the *Gawain* group are the work of a single author. Though the poems are compatible in subject matter, theme, and style, it is doubtful whether such a consensus would have established itself had it not been for the fact that they appear side by side, copied by a single hand, in a single manuscript. Though the language of *Saint Erkenwald* is thought to belong to the same dialect area as that of the *Gawain*-group poems, the single manuscript containing it was copied about seventy-five years later. (None of the poems is attributed to a named author.) Advocates of common authorship have therefore had to base their arguments on data identifiable in the language of all five poems and nowhere else.

Early in the twentieth century, such data seemed to have been found in the form of a distinctive vocabulary: words seemingly present only in *Pearl, Patience, Cleanness, Sir Gawain and the Green Knight,* and *Saint Erkenwald.* But as more and more Middle English texts came to be edited—and the successive volumes of the *Middle English Dictionary,* with its comprehensive lists of citations for each entry, were published—the words in this supposedly distinctive vocabulary were found in other texts and had to be disqualified as unique signs of authorship. Today, only a single word of the original group is left, but this word, a verb meaning "to offer" or "to utter," has not yet been found anywhere else. It appears a number of times in the five poems, is an important carrier of meaning, and constitutes a small but significant bit of evidence.

Today, anyone attempting to establish a presumption of authorial individuality (there can be no proof) in the five poems must deal with the fact that four of them are products of the so-called Alliterative Revival of the fourteenth century and share the traditional alliterative style with other poems by a variety of authors. All the poets of the revival used the same metrical form (the "long alliterative line"), the same words and phrases, the same grammatical structures, the same descriptive techniques, and even the same set topics, such as sieges (*Cleanness*) and sea storms (*Patience*). A potentially fruitful way of coping with this difficulty is to think of these aspects of style as constituting an inherited repertoire or storehouse of narrative devices. Each poet who had mastered the repertoire would have drawn on it according to his own bent, relying on some parts of it more than on others, and adapting the traditional features to reflect his way of imagining a given story. We will find the true individuality of the *Gawain* or *Erkenwald* poet vested not so much in his language itself as in the creative powers we see at work in it.

A feature of the inherited style that has proved rewarding in a study designed for this purpose is the recurrent presence of elaborated or descriptive references to characters. Instead of merely calling a character by name or using a pronoun, the alliterative poets add to the name some sort of descriptive material: an adjective, a modifying phrase, or a relative clause. This technique must have first been developed in the heroic poetry composed in preliterate societies (see the account in the General Introduction), including the Hellenic verse of the Homeric poems and the Germanic verse, marked by alliteration, of the Old English *Beowulf* and the earliest recorded poems of Continental Germanic provenience. The language of heroic poetry was formulaic, made up in large part of inherited, metrically shaped combinations of words; its purpose was to commemorate the exploits of ancestral chieftains and noble warriors. In Homer, members of the mythical pantheon of gods participate in the action together with mortals; in *Beowulf* and the early Germanic poems, the extant texts of which date from after the adoption of Christianity, heroic deeds take place in the earthly realm governed by the one true God. As one would expect, much of the descriptive material attached to proper names in this early poetry signified relevant virtues or powers. In the *Odyssey*, Zeus, the ruler of the gods, is called "Zeus who views the wide world," "the master of heaven and high thunder," and "the summoner of cloud," among other titles. Odysseus himself is called "the strategist," "the great-hearted hero," "the kingly man," and "the great tactician" (translated by Fitzgerald). In *Beowulf*, the Christian God is called "sovereign," "helm (i.e., ruler) of the heavens," "the father who rules times and seasons," and "the ruler over victories." Beowulf is called "Hygelac's thane, good among the Geats," "[he] who was the strongest of mankind in that day," "leader," and "son of Ecgtheow." (Translations are my own.)

All of these descriptive references are definitive—literally "definitional"—in that they signify the inherent identity of the being to whom they are applied. The virtues and powers attributed to him are always his, regardless of his situation or actions at any given point in the plot. They are thus independent of narrative time. Odysseus is always "the man of craft," whether or not he is acting craftily at a given moment; Beowulf, likewise, is always "good."

This stylistic feature descended into Late Middle English as an aspect of the shared style of the poems of the Alliterative Revival. In the "Alliterative *Morte Arthure*," King Arthur is called "the sovereign . . . who was deemed most doughty (stout hearted) of all dwellers on earth." In *Wars of Alexander*, Alexander the Great is called "the heir that rules all" and the "warrior to whom all the world bows." In *Sir Gawain*, Gawain is "he to whose person belong all refined manners," "he . . . who was ever stout hearted," and so on.

But in the poems of the *Gawain* group, descriptive references have, more often than not, a different kind of content whose recurrent presence distinguishes the *Gawain* poet's narratives from others. The attributes they confer on the person in question are time bound, applicable to him (or her) at a certain moment in the unfolding of the narrative, and subject to change. The story in Genesis 18, retold in *Cleanness*, of the visit paid to Abraham by God in the form of three men to whom he serves a meal, provides an apt example. In the Bible, Abraham is said to be seated, before his visitors arrive, "at the door of his tent." In *Cleanness*, he is seated "under a green oak,'" in "shadow under bright leaves" (602, 605). (The biblical source of the oak is apparently the statement that when Abraham sets food before his guests he stands by them "under the tree [Latin *arbor*];" the tree is mentioned only once.) When the poet says that Abraham immediately hastens to greet the strangers he sees coming toward him, he begins by calling him "the man who lay there under the leaves" (609). This is a time-located descriptive reference such as I have defined above; it identifies Abraham not in definitional terms (as, say, "the great Hebrew patriarch" or "the father of Isaac") but in temporary ones. I shall call such references "circumstantial." I have found them in every one of the poems of the *Gawain*-group and in *Saint Erkenwald*, but in none of the other poems of the alliterative revival.

Later in *Cleanness* the poet tells the story of the visit to Lot, in Sodom, by two angels (Genesis 19). In the Biblical account, "he rose up and went to meet them: and worshipped them prostrate to the ground." In *Cleanness*, the poet says that as Lot stared into the street from a door near the gates of his house, he saw two young men approaching him. They were beautiful in every respect because they were angels, "and *the quick-witted man who [sat] in the gate* understood that" (796), rose quickly, and ran to meet them." In *Patience*, Jonah goes below decks in the ship that is (supposedly) carrying him away from Nineveh, fearful of the storm that God has aroused to interrupt his voyage. All those aboard are summoned to participate in a lottery designed to identify the person whose presence has aroused the storm. Everyone is found except *"Jonah the Jew, who lay asleep in hiding"* (182). Later, when he is tossed overboard, a wandering whale becomes aware *"of the man who was going into the water"* (249). In *Sir Gawain*, Gawain, wandering in search of the Green Chapel on his horse Gringolet, finally sees Lord Bertilak's castle in the distance; as he stops to gaze on it, he is referred to as *"the man who tarried on his steed"* (785). Later, he is received by Bertilak as a guest. In the early darkness of the morning when he is to be escorted from the castle to the Green Chapel, a wild snowstorm rages, and *"the man who lay in his bed* listened well" (2006) to it. All these references are circumstantial, like the earlier reference to Abraham as the man who was lying in the shade of the oak leaves.

The references cited above, both definitional and circumstantial, contain relative clauses. Descriptive references to characters constructed in this way

---

° In the examples from the *Gawain* group that follow, I translate the original Middle English literally, whereas in my verse translations I have sometimes departed from the original syntax or wording to satisfy the formal requirements of the verse.

belonged to the repertoire of features inherited by the poets of the alliterative school; the *Gawain* poet made use of them frequently. A briefer, equally traditional, way of referring to a character was to combine a noun with a prepositional phrase expressing some aspect of professional identity; in the case of a knight or warrior, the wearing of a helmet or the possession of a sword or a warhorse. Two of these, linking words that alliterated in Middle English, were "hathel on hors" and "burne on blonk." (*Blonk* and *hathel/burne* belonged to the traditional groups of poetic words meaning, respectively, "horse" and "warrior.") The *Gawain* poet supplements the inherited combinations, which were of course definitional, with new ones having circumstantial force. In *Cleanness*, he refers to Noah on the ark as "the hathel under hach ('hatches')" (409), "the burne bynne bord ('within the ship')" (452), and, using a relative clause, "the chevetayn ('chieftain') . . . that the chyst yemed ('who governed the chest')" (464). When the flood abates, and those aboard the ark look out, the narrator says that "ledez loghen ('people laughed') in that lome ('vessel')" (495). In *Patience*, he calls Jonah, who wakens in his booth in the shade provided by the vine God has caused to grow over it, "the wyghe ('man') under wodbynde ('woodbine')" (446). In *Sir Gawain*, he uses the traditional combination "hathel on hors" in such a way as to give it circumstantial meaning: "His hathel ('attendant') on hors watz *thenne*" (2065)—that is, Sir Gawain's attendant had just mounted, prior to departing with him from Lord Bertilak's castle. Combinations devised "for the nonce," such as circumstantial references containing relative clauses, are peculiar to the *Gawain* poet's narratives—and to *Saint Erkenwald*.

What all the passages I have cited add up to is an important aspect of the poet's way of imagining his narratives: a habit of focusing, and thus leading his readers to focus, on the identity and actions of a central character in relative terms rather than absolute, as contingent on situation rather than determined by inherent traits. In *Sir Gawain and the Green Knight*, Gawain, apologizing to the wife of Lord Bertilak for having no suitable gift to give her, says "Iche tolke mon do as he is tan" (1811)—literally, "Each man must do as he is taken"; more freely, "Each man must act according to the circumstances in which he is caught."

I now return to the story of Abraham and his threefold divine visitor as the poet tells it, with a view to investigating his characteristic treatment of space. Abraham is introduced as lying "under a green oak" (602), but this is not, as in the Bible, the only reference to the tree. Rather, the poet keeps drawing our attention to it as we read on. A few lines later, Abraham is said to have "sought out the shade under bright leaves" (605). He pleads with the strangers, whom he has recognized as personifying God, not to depart until they have rested "under bough" (616) and asks them to "remain here on this root" (619) while he goes and gets them some refreshment. In the Bible, Abraham's tent is the only feature of the scene mentioned, except for a single reference to "the tree." Sara remains out of sight behind the tent door until after the meal is over, and later calls to Abraham and his guests but does not come out to speak to them as she does in *Cleanness*. In the Bible, the stewed veal and cakes are presumably prepared within the tent, though served out of doors. In *Cleanness*, Abraham goes into his "house" (623) to give instructions to Sara, and takes a calf from the "cowhouse" (629) to be stewed. He serves his guests in (British) picnic style, getting a "clean cloth" and throwing it on "the green [grass]" (634), presumably in the shade of the oak. These details define a limited space, bounded in one direction by the oak on the grass and in the opposite direction by the house. The action takes place within these limits as if within a stage set.

In *Patience*, spatial limits play a part in the poet's narrative of the swallowing of Jonah by the whale. In the great storm sent by God to prevent Jonah from voyaging to Joppa in defiance of his command, two different winds "wrestle" wildly (141). The sea rises in immense waves, then, as it falls, creates "abysses" so deep that terrified fish dare not rest near the bottom (143–44). When the whale is mentioned later, it is referred to, circumstantially, as a creature that had been "driven from the abyss" (248). (Needless to say, none of this is in the biblical account.)

Limitations of time and of space work together in the *Gawain* poet's narratives to portray a world in which the actions of living beings, whether human or animal, are intensely imagined as they are "defined" by circumstances at this or that moment in the action. Circumstantial conditions and constraints figure importantly in this poet's best-known work, starring Sir Gawain himself. In Part I of that poem, as in the story of Abraham, details otherwise inconspicuous lead us to imagine a kind of stage set, within which the Green Knight's challenge to the court and its acceptance by the hero take place. The rear wall of the set, so to speak, is formed by the high table or dais on which Sir Gawain sits beside the queen with other dignitaries. From the dais, the two side tables, on which the other knights and ladies are seated, extend like the sides of a capital U, leaving the "fourth wall" empty. The Green Knight enters this space and rides up to the dais, looks all around, insultingly asks which of the men present is the king, and challenges someone in the court to cut off his head with his ax, on condition that he accept a return stroke in a year's time. After King Arthur has accepted the challenge, Sir Gawain, referred to circumstantially as "Gawain, who sat by the queen" (339), intervenes, offering, in a speech of almost overly elaborate courtesy, to take it upon himself.

A year later, riding in search of the Green Chapel where he is to encounter the Green Knight, Sir Gawain becomes a guest at the castle of Lord Bertilak. He is assured by his host that the Green Chapel is less than two miles away and commanded to rest from his travels by staying in bed late for three successive days. On the first morning, hearing a sound at the door of his room and peering out from the curtains surrounding his bed, he discovers that Lord Bertilak's wife has come to visit him, lies back, and pretends to be still asleep. Here again, the action takes place within a perimeter in the form of the walls of the room and the latched door, which are mentioned in several descriptive details unnecessary for the narration. Within this enclosure is one smaller still: the curtained enclosure where Gawain is lying under a rich coverlet. The visiting lady unhesitatingly enters this space, sits down on the side of the bed, and waits for him to wake up. He finally opens his eyes, and a conversation ensues—one of three on the three successive mornings—in which she tries her best to seduce him. In this passage, physical constraints take on symbolic value because we perceive them as operating in tandem with constraints of a social and moral nature. As a Christian, Gawain knows that adultery is a sin; moreover, his temptress is the wife of the lord to whom he has sworn obedience. Aware of his reputation as a knight famed for his superlative courtesy, he must manage to refuse her advances without insulting her. Courtesy also obliges him to put on a cheerful front, even though he expects to be beheaded in three days.

Several details that appear in the poet's account of the visit of the Green Knight to King Arthur's court imply another kind of circumstance contributing to the spatial definition of the action, one that is mentioned again and again in later episodes. When the Green Knight first arrives, he is described in lavish detail, with emphasis on the greenness of his body, his garments, his ax, and his horse. So strange was his appearance, the narrator says, that "all who stood there" gazed at him intently (237). When his head was cut off, it fell to the floor and rolled around where "many kicked at it with their feet" (428). Immediately he strode over to it, "reached out uncannily where warriors stood" (432) and picked it up. These details play no part in the unfolding of the story. What they do is to remind us of the presence of spectators at a scene. The action in progress does not take place in isolation but is "framed" by people watching it. In two of the above details, these people are literally "bystanders," "supernumeraries," who have no function other than to stand watching. Later, during the first hunt, we are told that greyhounds seized the fleeing deer "as fast as warriors might look" (1172). In the second hunt, when the great boar was brought to bay, "all the bold warriors who stood near him were irked by him" (1574). But these bold warriors did not act; rather, they watched as Lord Bertilak rode up, dismounted, and attacked him.

Everything I have said about the poet's way of using the traditional style of alliterative poetry applies equally to *Saint Erkenwald*. To begin with, the latter poem contains circumstantial references to characters such as I have found distinctive in the poems of the *Gawain* group. They are used of the two main characters of the poem: Erkenwald, bishop of St. Paul's Cathedral in London; and a body, sumptuously dressed, that has been found in the foundations of the cathedral in a splendid tomb. Erkenwald is referred to definitionally as "he who had been consecrated bishop" (159), but also circumstantially, as the one who *"had said his prayers nearly all night to beseech his Lord to let him solve the mystery"* (119–21) presented by the entombed body. When he speaks to it that morning, he first addresses it as "corpse *that lies there*" (179). When the body is about to answer his question about the dwelling place of its soul, the poet refers to it as "he *that lay there*" (281). Earlier, when it is about to respond to Saint Erkenwald's exhortation to speak, it is referred to as "the bright body in the burynes ["tomb"]" (190). This phrase, like "hathel under hach" in *Patience*, uses two alliterating words in an original combination appropriate to the circumstances.

The dramatic action of *Saint Erkenwald* takes place within two bounded spaces. First, of course, there is the cathedral itself, in whose foundations the tomb is discovered. After the discovery, tomb and body are secured for safety in the space containing the excavated "floor" on which they were found. After conducting a mass, the bishop goes there, followed by a crowd made up of those who had attended the service. The statement that the "cloyster" was unlocked for him is followed by a detail whose wording is of particular interest for the purposes of this essay. The language of the original reads, "pyne wos wyt the grete prece that passyd hym after" (141)—literally, "[there was (*wos*)] difficulty (*pyne*) with the great crowd (*prece*) that passed [in] after him." We do or should take these words to mean that it was hard for everyone who had followed the bishop to find room in the enclosure. The word *pyne* is also used in *Sir Gawain and the Green Knight*, in the opening description of King Arthur's Christmas banquet. The narrator says that so many dishes were served that the servitors had "pine ("difficulty")" to fynde the place the people biforne" ("before the people [seated at table]") to set the silver dishes that held various stews (or soups) down on the cloth (122–25). In both details, the poet's awareness of spatial limitations brings about a kind of stereoscopic vividness. (In a similar description in the alliterative *Morte Arthure*, the list of dishes served is improbably long, and the banquet table seems to expand indefinitely as the details continue to accumulate.)

We see Bishop Erkenwald, like Sir Gawain during the lady's first entrance into his bedroom (and the curtains of his bed), as acting within limitations or constraints both physical and moral. The presence of the body on or off the scene, which we are reminded of partly by the poet's frequent use of the word and its synonyms (sixteen occurrences in 276 lines, beginning with line 76), insists on the urgency of a problem for whose solution the bishop, and he only, is responsible. The intensity of his feelings is revealed by the fact that he spends almost the entire night after his return to the cathedral praying that he may be allowed to solve "this marvel whose mystery amazes men so," and weeping as he prays (122–25). In the course of his anxious attempt to arrive at a solution, the answer to one question simply raises another. First, who is the man in the tomb? Second, given the man's identity as an impeccably righteous pagan, what has been the fate of his soul? Third, given the soul's pitiful and seemingly everlasting situation in limbo, can the dead man be saved? The unexpected answer to this last question comes fewer than thirty lines from the end of the poem. The entire conversation between Erkenwald and the body, and the inadvertently redemptive action to which it leads, takes place in the doubly limited space of the burial enclosure; once the salvation of the buried man's soul has taken place, space opens out into the poem's largest bounded scene, defined in its opening line: the city of London. All the church bells "in the city" miraculously chime as the bishop and his congregation pass out from the cathedral in procession, and "all the people follow" (351–52).

The important role of spectators throughout the poem is obvious. When the lid of the tomb is first lifted, before Saint Erkenwald has entered the action, we hear that "there was wonder aplenty among those who stood [there]" (73). Later, time elapsed as "each one asked the other" (95) who the dead body might be; "every man asked" (96) how it might be that its clothing had remained intact during its long stay in the tomb. The entire conversation between bishop and body, and its culmination in the inadvertent baptism, takes place in the presence of the crowd of spectators. We are reminded of them by several circumstantial references: during the body's first speech, not a word was spoken by "the people" nor was any sound made as "all stood and listened, as still as stone" (217–19), wondering and weeping. When the body describes its sad situation in the darkness of limbo, "all wepyd for woo *the words that herden* ("who heard the words")" (310).

The *Gawain* poet lived in a society in which the doctrines of the established Christian church pervaded all aspects of life. The burden of the "original sin" committed by Adam and Eve, inherited by every one of their descendants, had to be removed from the members of each new generation by baptism. The sins that human beings constantly committed had constantly to be absolved. Baptism and absolution were administered exclusively under the aegis of the institutional church. Truth and error, good and evil, salvation and damnation, were conceived of in absolute terms. The man who wrote the *Gawain* group and *Saint Erkenwald* lived in this intellectual milieu; moreover, the style in which he chose to narrate most of his stories took shape in a body of preliterate poetry originally designed for unquestioning praise and commemoration. Yet his writings portray the human predicament, the temporally evolving circumstances that limit intended action and thwart aspiration, from the human point of view. He tells the stories of his fallible heroes—the father in *Pearl* made obtuse by his earthly perspective, the prophet forced to prophesy falsely in *Patience*, the knight in *Sir Gawain* lapsing from the perfection of the pentangle, even the bishop in *Saint Erkenwald*, troubled by what seems to be God's consignment of an utterly righteous soul to eternal sorrow—in a poetic language that keeps the old patterns but modifies their import in accordance with his own deeply founded creative bias.

Details cited earlier—such as "he reached out *where warriors stood*," and "the man *who lay in his bed*," from *Sir Gawain*; "the *man* in the *boat*" and "the man *who had sought out the shade under bright leaves*," from *Cleanness*; "the man *under woodbine*," from *Patience*; and "corpse *that lies here*" and "all wept *who heard the words*" from *Saint Erkenwald*—are superfluous to the progress of the narratives where they appear and tend to pass beneath the reader's eye unnoticed. But they fulfill the criterion I stated at the outset as relevant to an investigation of authorship: they are found in the language of these five poems and nowhere else, and are thus valid signs of the unique working of one man's creative faculties. In helping to draw us imaginatively into three-dimensional scenes within which we witness predicaments that arouse our capacity to sympathize with mortal beings other than ourselves, they also bespeak his artistic power. No alliterative poet except the author of *Pearl, Patience, Cleanness, Sir Gawain and the Green Knight*—and *Saint Erkenwald*—had this distinctive power. In modern translations that do them justice, these poems can affect us and enrich our memories, despite the passage of six hundred years.

The Metrical Forms

Alliterative Verse

The Basic Form

The poems representing the Late Middle English alliterative school that have come down to the present day were composed in a verse form known as the "long alliterative line." This line has a basic structure that recurs throughout the poems and is a point of departure for a number of variants. The proportionate frequency of these variants generally, and the frequency with which particular ones are used, can differentiate the verse of one poet from that of another. The anonymous poet who wrote *Patience, Cleanness, Saint Erkenwald*, and *Sir Gawain and the Green Knight*, used variant forms freely and with great skill, while maintaining the continuous rhythmic momentum, or beat, of the basic form.

The rhythm of the basic form is easy to sense, as is the formal relationship between alliteration and stress. Each long line is divided into two half lines; the division between them, called the *caesura* (pronounced "see-SHU-rah"), corresponds to a grammatical division of at least minor importance. Each half line contains two syllables that clearly call for heavier stress than the others, so that four chief syllables, as I call them, occur in every line. Chief syllables are spaced in time as the downbeats of successive measures are spaced in a musical piece played with expressive flexibility rather than with strict correspondence to a metronomic beat; the listener hears them as occurring in a time continuum at regular, though not exactly equal, intervals. The line can thus be described as divided into four "measures" in the musical sense of that word.

Alliteration (repetition of the same consonant at the beginnings of stressed syllables) is not optional or ornamental in the line, as it is in most of the verse familiar to the modern reader. It is a formal requirement. In the pattern that appears most frequently, the two chief syllables in the first half line alliterate with each other and with the first chief syllable of the second half line, so that the line contains three alliterating chief syllables in all. The chief syllable at the end of the second half line normally does not alliterate. The following two lines of *Sir Gawain* exemplify the basic form (chief syllables are in capital letters):

HIGH were their HEARTS in HALLS and CHAMbers,
These LORDS and these LAdies, for LIFE was SWEET. (48–49)

The basic form can be expressed in metrical notation by marking chief syllables above the line with C, alliterating letters below the line with a, the first letter of the nonalliterating chief syllable at the end of the line with x, and the caesura in midline with /. In the following four examples, I have placed vertical lines before the chief syllables to indicate that, in musical terms, they constitute the "downbeats" of the four measures making up each line.

<pre>
        C   C   C   C
So he | passes to the | port, his | passage to | seek
    a   a   /   a   x
</pre>

(*Patience* 97)

<pre>
          C   C   C   C
Then the | lord of that | land found | little to | praise
      a   a   /   a   x
</pre>

<pre>
      C   C   C   C
In their | unfriendly | answers— | angrily he | speaks.
      a   a   / a   x
</pre>

(*Cleanness* 73–74)

In the third of these lines, as is permissible, different vowels alliterate wth each other; *h*, whether sounded or silent, may also alliterate with vowels.

<pre>
        C   C   C   C
Then he | turns to the | tomb, and | talks to the | dead
    a   a   /   a   x
</pre>

(*Erkenwald* 177)

As the above examples show, chief syllables may be separated by one, two, or three "intermediate" syllables. In *Patience* 97, there is one intermediate syllable between *port* and *passage*; there are two between the first syllable of *passage* and *seek*, and there are three between the first syllable of *passes* and *port*. It is natural to read measures containing two or three such syllables a little faster than those containing only one.

Occasionally, chief syllables are juxtaposed, usually in the second half line.

<pre>
        C   C   C   C
All the onlookers eyed him, and edged nearer
    a   a   /   a   x
</pre>

(*Gawain* 237)

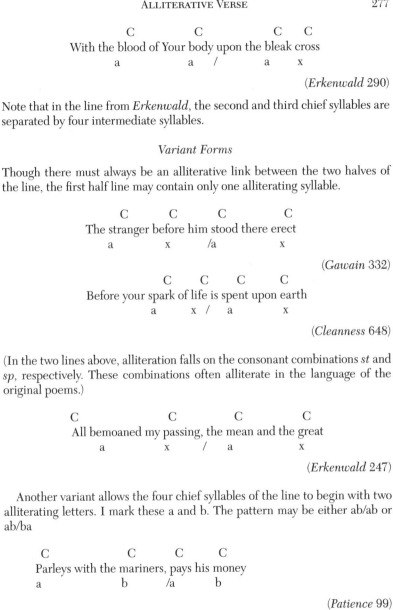

<pre>
        C   C   C   C
With the blood of Your body upon the bleak cross
        a   a   /   a   x
</pre>

(Erkenwald 290)

Note that in the line from Erkenwald, the second and third chief syllables are separated by four intermediate syllables.

Variant Forms

Though there must always be an alliterative link between the two halves of the line, the first half line may contain only one alliterating syllable.

<pre>
        C   C   C   C
The stranger before him stood there erect
        a   x   /a   x
</pre>

(Gawain 332)

<pre>
            C   C   C   C
Before your spark of life is spent upon earth
            a   x / a   x
</pre>

(Cleanness 648)

(In the two lines above, alliteration falls on the consonant combinations st and sp, respectively. These combinations often alliterate in the language of the original poems.)

<pre>
   C   C   C   C
All bemoaned my passing, the mean and the great
   a   x   /   a   x
</pre>

(Erkenwald 247)

Another variant allows the four chief syllables of the line to begin with two alliterating letters. I mark these a and b. The pattern may be either ab/ab or ab/ba

<pre>
 C   C   C   C
Parleys with the mariners, pays his money
 a   b   /a   b
</pre>

(Patience 99)

<pre>
     C   C   C   C
But in the third all were injured who ought to have thrived
     a   b   /   b   a
</pre>

(Cleanness 249)

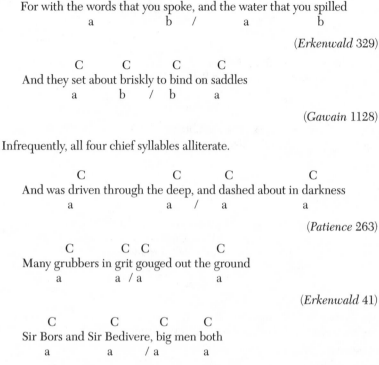

       C   C   C   C
For with the words that you spoke, and the water that you spilled
       a   b   /   a   b

(*Erkenwald* 329)

      C   C   C   C
And they set about briskly to bind on saddles
    a   b   /   b   a

(*Gawain* 1128)

Infrequently, all four chief syllables alliterate.

       C   C   C   C
And was driven through the deep, and dashed about in darkness
      a   a   /   a   a

(*Patience* 263)

     C   C C   C
Many grubbers in grit gouged out the ground
   a   a / a   a

(*Erkenwald* 41)

   C   C   C   C
Sir Bors and Sir Bedivere, big men both
 a   a   / a   a

(*Gawain* 554)

I take it that in all the lines I have cited so far, four chief syllables are clearly discernible—that is, it is easy, when reading them, to stress four of the syllables they contain more than the others. If one taps a finger while pronouncing each of these syllables, the taps create an ongoing rhythm, a quasi-musical beat.

An important group of variants in the verse of the *Gawain* poet is made up of lines in which chief stress and alliteration do not coincide. One of the two alliterating syllables in the first half line, or the single alliterating syllable required in the second, or both, may be an unstressed prefix or a word, such as a preposition, that receives comparatively light stress in the sentence.

Lines in which one or more alliterating syllables are prefixes:

       C   C   C   C
Why rush to revenge me, since some will repent?
     a   a   /   a x

(*Patience* 519)

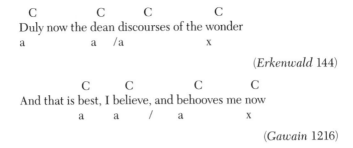

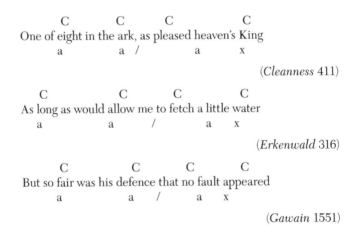

The Heavy Lines

A number of lines and groups of lines in the four poems exemplify variant forms of a different and more important sort. Their frequent and conspicuous presence in certain passages is a distinctive mark of the *Gawain* poet's artistry. In such lines, the count of stressed syllables exceeds in number the basic four. The first half line, for example, may contain three such syllables; so, less frequently, may the second. Scholars have differed regarding the correct scansion of such lines, the main question being whether they should be read with five chief syllables of equal rank, and thus divided into five quasi-musical measures, or four, as in the basic form. Consider, for example, the second lines of the following passages:

> "I worship the one God whose will all obey:
> The wide world with the welkin, the wind and the stars,
> And all that range in that realm, He wrought with His word"
>
> (*Patience* 206–8)

"I was no king or emperor, or a knight either,
But a leading light of the law that the land then used"

(*Erkenwald* 199–200)

He assigns a servant to set him on the path,
To see him safe and sound over the snowy hills.

(*Gawain* 1971–72)

If equal metrical rank were assigned to *wide, world,* and the first syllable of *welkin,* and similarly to the three alliterating syllables of the first half lines of *Erkenwald* 200 and *Gawain* 1972, these lines would have five measures, and would properly be read aloud with the three alliterating syllables in the first half line and the two chief syllables in the second half line of each falling at intervals felt as equivalent, to create a five-beat rhythm.

I contend, however, and have argued at length elsewhere,* that it is natural, when reading such lines aloud in the context of a four-beat rhythm, to subordinate the second alliterating syllables of the first half-lines to the first and third; in linguistic terms, to give primary stress to the first and third and secondary stress to the second. I call syllables bearing primary stress in such half lines "major chief" and those bearing secondary stress "minor chief." They exemplify what I call "compound" meter, containing syllables bearing two grades of stress (major and minor) alongside unstressed syllables. Scanned in this way, these heavier lines have four measures like the others, and the four-beat "swing" of the verse is uninterrupted.

If upper-case C indicates primary stress and lower-case c indicates secondary stress, and if vertical lines are placed before the downbeats of the measures, as in my first examples above, the three lines will be marked thus:

```
        C    c                  C          C            C
The | wide world with the | welkin, the | wind and the | stars
        a    a                  a     /    a            x
```

```
        C    c            C            C
But a | leading light of the | law that the | land then | used
        a    a                a /        a          x
```

```
        C      c        C                C      C
To | see him safe and | sound over the | snowy | hills
        a      a        a    /           a      x
```

An important argument for a four-measure reading of lines such as these can be made on the basis of the popular affinities of alliterative verse: its (mostly) down-to-earth style and plain diction, and the presence in it of combinations of

---

* See "The Alliterative Long Line: The Extended Form" in *Sir Gawain and the Green Knight: A Stylistic and Metrical Study.*

alliterating words that were also in use in the everyday language of the poet's day. In my translations, I have drawn, so far as possible, from the stock of alliterating phrases that is extant in the English of the present (see General Introduction, p. xviii). These popular affinities are present and important, side by side with the more literary aspects of the traditional style. These include the use, as an aid in composing lines expressing the intended meanings while also fulfilling the technical requirements of the verse, of the groups of poetic synonyms in Middle English, beginning with different consonants, expressing ideas that often figure in the narrative, such as *warrior, steed, to go* and *to speak* (see above, General Introduction, p. xx, and Introduction to *Sir Gawain and the Green Knight*, pp. 193–94.)

The metrical patterns of the compound measures of alliterative verse can easily be sensed because they are familiar to us from popular verse such as Mother Goose rhymes, jump-rope chants, and the like. Two such lines suggest themselves for purposes of comparison; I have marked them with the same notation I am using for alliterative verse.

C   c   C   C   c   C
Pease porridge hot, pease porridge cold,
a   a   x /a   a   x

C   c   C   c C   c C
Pease porridge in the pot, nine days old.
a   a   x   a /x   x   x

Despite the affinities I am suggesting, the meter of "Pease Porridge Hot" differs from that of the alliterative lines I have cited in that it is uniformly compound. In addition, the lines are read with slightly artificial patterns of emphasis (note particularly the stress on *in*), rather than as they would be spoken in the everyday language.

If *Patience* 207 read "The wide world with the welkin, the sun, wind, and stars"; if *Erkenwald* 200 read "I was a leading light of the law, who lived long in honor"; and if *Gawain* 1972 read "To see him safe and sound over the snow-covered hills," their meter would be uniformly compound, like that of "Pease porridge hot, pease porridge cold." Some scholars have in fact argued that the meter of the long alliterative line is of this sort. But most of the measures of these and other lines contain so few stressed syllables that to recite them with a uniform alternation between C and c would result in distortion:

C   c   C   c   C   c C
To see him safe and sound over the snow-ee hills

In *Patience* 207, *Erkenwald* 200, and *Gawain* 1972, compound meter relaxes into simple meter after the caesura break. The same pattern would be produced by rewriting the first line of the nursery rhyme as "Pease porridge hot, freshly prepared." The rewritten line would be perfectly acceptable as it stands in the alliterative verse of the *Gawain* poet, since the requirement that there be an alliterating syllable in the second half line is fulfilled by the prefix of *prepared*.

Varying Relationships between Alliteration and Stress in the Heavy Lines

In the examples I have discussed so far, compounding occurs in the first half line, and all three syllables bearing major and minor stress alliterate. In other lines, compounding occurs in the second half line, and one of the stress-bearing syllables fails to alliterate. The examples that follow illustrate some of the permutations and combinations of these patterns.

Compounding in one or both halves of the line, with alliteration on major chief syllables only:

$$
\begin{array}{ccccc}
C & c & C & C & c \\
\end{array}
$$
And when night draws near, to Noah she flies
$$
\begin{array}{cccccc}
a & x & a & / & a & x \\
\end{array}
$$

(*Cleanness* 484)

$$
\begin{array}{cccc}
C & C & c & C & C \\
\end{array}
$$
And Gawain the good knight in gay bed lies.
$$
\begin{array}{ccccc}
a & & a & x & / & a & x \\
\end{array}
$$

(*Gawain* 1179)

Compounding in the first half of the line, with alliteration lacking on one of the two major chief syllables:

$$
\begin{array}{ccccc}
C & c & C & C & C \\
\end{array}
$$
And there are many dumb beasts in barn and in field
$$
\begin{array}{ccccc}
x & x & a & / & a & x \\
\end{array}
$$

(*Patience* 517)

$$
\begin{array}{cccc}
C & c & C & C & C \\
\end{array}
$$
Now all these five fives were confirmed in this knight
$$
\begin{array}{ccccc}
x & a & a & / & a & x \\
\end{array}
$$

(*Gawain* 656)

Compounding in both halves of the line, with alliteration falling on minor chief rather than major chief syllables:

$$
\begin{array}{cccccc}
C & c & C & C & c & C \\
\end{array}
$$
To hew the hard stones with keen-edged tools
$$
\begin{array}{ccccccc}
a & & a & x & / & x & a & x \\
\end{array}
$$

(*Erkenwald* 40)

If the above line were read with artificially heightened stress on *with*, raising it from a weak to a minor chief syllable, it would be compound throughout. But such a reading would slow the line down and break the natural flow of the verse.

Compounding in lines with two alliterating letters:

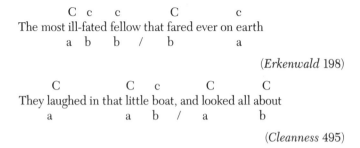

```
        C  c    c        C           c
The most ill-fated fellow that fared ever on earth
        a  b    b    /   b           a
```

(*Erkenwald* 198)

```
   C           C  c    C         C
They laughed in that little boat, and looked all about
   a           a  b /  a         b
```

(*Cleanness* 495)

The above and other patterns form a complicated array, but if one simply reads a given passage aloud without preliminary analysis, the relative degrees of stress called for by the syllables of successive phrases are easily felt, and a rhythmic continuum of four major chief syllables per line establishes itself.

Rhymed Verse

Gawain is composed partly in alliterative and partly in rhymed verse. The poem is made up of 101 "paragraphs" of long alliterating lines. These are of varying length: the first five paragraphs contain 14, 12, 18, 20, and 17 long lines, respectively. Each group of long lines is finished off by a two-syllable line called the "bob," consisting of an unstressed syllable followed by a stressed one (in classical metrical terminology, an iamb), and a stanza called the "wheel," consisting of four lines of verse containing three measures or beats. The five lines rhyme *ababa*.

  Pearl is composed entirely in rhymed verse. It is made up of 101 stanzas consisting of twelve lines, each containing four measures. The twelve lines rhyme *ababababbcbc*.

  The metrical patterns of the rhyming lines of *Gawain* and *Pearl* can appropriately be called "mixed," since they have affinities both with native alliterative verse and with the rhymed syllabic verse of Continental origin first used in English by Chaucer. The lines are simple in form. In what can be identified as a basic pattern having many variations, chief syllables alternate with single intermediate syllables:

```
   x  C  x    C  x   C
As lightning quick and light
```

```
x C      x C  x  C
```
He looked to all at hand;

```
x C        x  C  x   C
```
It seemed that no man might

```
x  C  x C     x   C
```
His deadly dints withstand.

(Gawain 199–202)

```
x   C x  C x    C x C
```
To that especial spot I hied

```
x   C x     C x    C x    C
```
And entered that same garden green

```
x C  x   C x C x    C
```
In August at a festive tide

```
x   C  x C  x   C   x    C
```
When corn is cut with scythe-edge keen.

(Pearl I.4.1–4)

As in the above examples, intermediate syllables are occasionally heavy (*man* in *Gawain* 201, *edge* in *Pearl* 40), but it is easy to identify three or four chief syllables as the downbeats of three or four measures in each line. There is thus no need, as there was in scanning the long alliterating lines, to invoke the concept of "minor chief" stress as an alternative to inserting an additional measure.

A feature of the mixed meter of the rhymed lines is the occasional presence of two intermediate syllables, rather than one, between chief syllables. (In classical metrical terminology, the prevailing iambic meter is occasionally varied by anapestic feet.) Entire wheels containing only single intermediate syllables are rare in *Gawain*, as are sequences of four such lines in *Pearl*.

```
x   C  xx    C   x  C
```
They linger and laugh awhile;

```
x C  x    x  C     x  C
```
She kisses the knight so true,

```
x    C   x  C  (x)x   C
```
Takes leave in comeliest style

```
x   x  C    x  x    C  x C
```
And departs without more ado.

(Gawain 1554–57)

```
x C   x  C     x   C x    C
```
My soul forsook that spot in space

```
x  C    x  C x x    C    x  C
```
And left my body on earth to bide.

```
x  Cx  C   x  C    x    C
```
My spirit sped, by God's good grace,

```
x x    C    x    C x    C x C
```
On a quest where marvels multiplied.

(*Pearl* II.1.1–4)

An intermediate syllable and a chief syllable may change places at the beginning of the line. Such lines are said to begin with a "reversed foot."

```
C    x    x    C  x    C  x
```
Hold now your grim tool steady

(*Gawain* 413)

The above line has what is called a "feminine ending," that is, the rhyming word is disyllabic and adds a fourth intermediate syllable.

```
Cx    x  C   x   C    x  C
```
"Duly the lord, at day's decline,

```
C   x   x  C x     C   x C
```
Said to the steward, 'Sir, proceed' "

(*Pearl* X.1.1–2)

The first intermediate syllable of a line may be omitted. Lines having this pattern are called "headless."

```
C   x  C    x    C
```
Bliss and hearth-fire bright

```
x  C    x  C  x    C  x
```
Await the master's pleasure;

```
x    x    C  x    C    x  C
```
When the two men met that night,

```
C  x  C    x    C  x
```
Joy surpassed all measure.

(*Gawain* 1368–71)

```
C   x   C  x    C    x  C
```
"Less of bliss none brings us here

```
x  C    x  C    x C  x    C
```
Who bear the pearl upon our breast."

(*Pearl* XV.2.1–2)

As the above examples show, chief syllables regularly alternate with inter-mediate syllables within the rhyming lines. In the rare cases where juxtaposition of chief syllables seems to occur, it can be avoided by the sounding of a final -e, as frequently happens in Chaucerian verse. That the sounding of -e is intentional is indicated by the fact that the first chief syllable of the seemingly juxtaposed pair is invariably a word whose ancestral form had -e. Such -es, like those that may have been sounded at the end of the long alliterating line, represent an archaic mode of pronunciation handed down in poetry from a time when syllabic -e was a feature of the spoken language. The following examples are quoted from the original.

> x   C x C   x   C
> Wyth rychë cote armure
>
> (*Gawain* 586)

> x   C x C x C
> He madë non abode
>
> (*Gawain* 687)

> x   x   C   x C   x   C x   C   x
> The more strengthe of ioye myn hertë straynez
>
> (*Pearl* III.1.8)

In *Pearl* III.1.8, the word *heart* (Old English *heorte*, Middle English *herte*) is spelled with a final *e*. In my next example (I.2.5), *e* is omitted. This difference is due to the inconsistent practice of the scribe, who copied out the poem at a time when spelling had not yet become fixed. The poet surely intended in the latter line, as in the earlier, to invoke an archaic pronunciation of the word with two syllables to avoid the illegitimate pattern x C x C x C C. The line should therefore be emended as follows:

> x   C   x   C   x C   x   C
> That dotz bot thrych my hert[ë] thrange
> (literally, "That does but oppress my heart sorely")
>
> (*Pearl* I.2.5)

More often, words such as *hert(e)* in the rhyming lines of *Gawain* and *Pearl* are pronounced, in modern fashion, as monosyllables. This indicates that the evolution of the language in the poet's Northwest Midland dialect had reached a later stage than it had in Chaucer's London dialect: in Chaucer's verse, such words are usually disyllabic. A radical difference between the *Gawain* poet and Chaucer in the treatment of -e in rhyme words provides further evidence to the same effect. Chaucer regularly rhymes words ending in -e with other words ending in -e, the implication being that we are to sound -e as a syllable in both members of a rhyming pair. The *Gawain* poet rhymes words that have, or originally had, -e with words in whose ancestral forms -e is lacking, the implication being that -e is to remain silent in words of the former sort. Thus Chaucer rhymes *face*, *place*, and *space*, from French *facë*, *placë*, and *espacë*, respectively. The *Gawain* poet also rhymes these words, but with them he combines *was* (Old English *wæs*) and *case* (Old French *cas*) in the sort of rhyme Chaucer does not use except when he is poking fun at "rym dogerel" in *Sir Thopas*, and rhymes *place*, spelled *plas*, with *gras* (779, 781).

In the mixed meter of the rhyming lines of *Gawain* and *Pearl*, formal metrical patterns correspond more closely to the natural stress patterns of the spoken language than they do in the iambic meters of classical English poetry. That is, syllables having chief rank are also, as a rule, strongly stressed, while those of intermediate rank are weakly stressed. In iambic meter, such alternation is less regularly maintained. The following lines of Emily Dickinson's, for example, contain three iambic feet:

> The Brain, within its Groove,
> Runs evenly—and true—

The second chief syllable of each is lighter than the first and third; one is part of a preposition, the other an adverbial suffix. A reading that stressed them as heavily as the others would sound unnatural. Yet all three chief syllables in each line are formally equal, having one and the same metrical rank. Translated into the three-beat mixed meter of the wheels in *Gawain*, Dickinson's lines might run

> The brain, in its well-worn groove,
> Keeps to a constant course.

The strong, even rhythms generated by such sequences as this tend to impose themselves (though not, in a good reading, to the point of distortion) on sequences in which alternation between heavy and light syllables is less marked.

The four-beat lines of *Pearl* create a similar effect on a slightly larger scale. Here, a well-known passage from Robert Frost's "Stopping by Woods on a Snowy Evening" suggests itself for comparison:

> My little horse must think it queer
> To stop without a farmhouse near
> Between the woods and frozen lake
> The darkest evening of the year.

Translated into the mixed meter of *Pearl*, it might run thus:

> My horse in harnesss must think it queer
> To stop with never a farmhouse near
> 'Twixt wintry woods and ice-locked lake
> On the darkest night of all the year.

Here, as with the Dickinson lines, light chief syllables (the second syllables of *without* and *between*, *of*) have been replaced by heavier ones.

The rewritten passages differ from the originals in another, equally important way. In them, a number of pairs of chief syllables are linked by alliteration; repetition of sound adds to their conspicuousness as lexically weighty, and hence emphatic, parts of speech. Though alliteration is not a formal component of the verse in the rhyming lines of *Gawain* and *Pearl* as it is in the long lines, alliterative combinations frequently occur in them. In *Pearl*, however, alliteration is not equally distributed; certain passages have it in abundance, whereas in other passages it is scarce. (I present a passage of each type in the "Specimen Scansions," below.) We find something like the heavily alliterating four-beat lines of *Pearl* in modern poetry in Gerard Manley Hopkins's "Inversnaid":

> This darksome burn, horseback brown,
> His rollrock highroad roaring down,
> In coop and in comb the fleece of his foam
> Flutes and low to the lake falls home.

But these lines are weightier still; a five-syllable sequence such as "rollrock highroad roar-" is not found in *Pearl*.

Compared with the four-line subdivisions of the *Pearl* stanza, the four-line stanzas of the wheel in *Gawain* are notably terse: they offer succinct summary and comment after the continuity of the narrative or descriptive paragraphs of alliterating lines, which come to a full stop with the bob. The three-beat line is the shortest line in which English poets have chosen to write entire poems, and the stanzas of the wheel are regularly divided into two halves, with a full stop at the end of the second line. In *Pearl*, the four-line subdivision is often a single syntactic unit (though there is usually a pause of at least comma strength at the end of each line, and a full stop at the end of every fourth line), and the three subdivisions of the stanza are themselves bound together by rhyme. Metrical units are marked off for the ear of the listener by repetition at regular intervals: the *b* rhyme recurs at lines 2, 4, 6, 8, defining and linking the first two subdivisions, and a pivotal repetition of the *b* rhyme in line 9 signals the beginning of the third, which rhymes *bcbc*. The second *c* rhyme in each section is also the repeated, and thematically important, link word; it is carried over from the fifth and last stanza to the first stanza of the next section, after which another takes its place.

The total effect, as the poem is heard or read in its entirety, is powerfully cumulative. The shift from link word to link word measures off in stages the rise in intensity of rhetoric and feeling, from the time of the introduction of the parable of the heavenly pearl in section XII until the dreamer rushes toward the stream at the beginning of section XX, rather like a series of shifts to the next higher musical key in successive choruses of a popular song. Toward the end, we experience vicariously the resolution of the human drama while recognizing, on the formal level, patterns of recurrence and return. Grasping the poem in the fullness of its mutually reinforcing meanings, we achieve a commensurate fullness of response.

Specimen Scansions

I have chosen two passages from *Gawain* and *Patience* and three from *Pearl*, presenting them first in the original, then in my translation. I quote the Middle English text of *Gawain* in the second edition, revised by Norman Davis, of the 1925 edition by J. R. R. Tolkien and E. V. Gordon (Clarendon Press, 1967), that of *Patience* as edited by J. J. Anderson (Manchester University Press, 1969), and that of *Pearl* as edited by E. V. Gordon (Clarendon Press, 1953). I have substituted *j* for *i, u* for *v*, and *v* for *u*, in accordance with modern spelling, and *th* for the Middle English letter *thorn*. For the Middle English letter *yogh*, I have substituted *y* at the beginnings of words and *gh* or *s/z* at the ends of words, depending on the sound represented.

From Sir Gawain and the Green Knight

Passage 1 and Passage 2 illustrate two different kinds of metrical effect. This difference in turn correlates with two differences that can be described statistically, in factual terms. The first passage, a description of Lord Bertilak's castle as Sir Gawain first sees it, contains, in the original poem, a sequence of five lines (785–89) in which a minor chief syllable is present in addition to the two major chief syllables of the first half line. In my translation, there is a sequence of four such first half lines (786–89). The second passage, taken from the conversation of the first bedroom scene (1208–17), contains, in the original, no such half lines. In my translation, there is one. In addition, the second passage contains, in the original, four sequences of three (or in one case, four) intermediate syllables between major chief syllables; there are five in my translation. The first passage contains only two such sequences (assuming that the *-ez* of *garytez* is not syllabic); there are two in my translation. The first passage is thus metrically heavier than the second; it contains a greater proportion of stressed to unstressed syllables and, as a result, is slower in pace.

"Clusters" of heavy lines appear in descriptive passages such as passage 1 and the description of the Green Knight when he first appears; sequences of lines that are comparatively light appear in passages of direct discourse, especially in conversations between Sir Gawain and the lady. The first effect seems to express the sustained impact of a remarkable sight on the beholder; the second, the fluency of casual repartee.

1. LINES 785–93

     C   c   C   C   C
The burne bode on bonk, that on blonk hoved,
     a   a   a   /   a   x

     C   c   C   C   C
Of the depe double dich that drof to the place;
     a   a   a   /   a   x

    C   c   C   C   C
The walle wod in the water wonderly depe,
    a   a   a   / a   a

    C   C c   C   C
And eft a ful huge heght hit haled up on lofte,
    a   a   a /   a   x

    C c   C C   C
Of harde hewen ston up to the tablez,
    a   a   x / a   x

    C   C   C C
Enbaned under the abataylment in the best lawe;
    a   a   /   a   x

      C   C C   C
And sythen garytez ful gaye gered bitwene,
      a   a / a   x

     C C   C   C
Wyth mony luflych loupe that louked ful clene:
      a   a /   a   x

  c C   C C   C
A better barbican that burne blusched upon never.
  a   a   a / a   x

    C   C   C   C
The man on his mount remained on the bank
    a   a / a   x

    C c   C   C   C
Of the deep double moat that defended the place.
    a a   x / a   x

    C c   C C   C
The wall went in the water wondrous deep,
    a a   a / a   x

    C c C C   C
And a long way aloft it loomed overhead.
    a   x   a / a   x

    C c C   C   C
It was built of stone blocks to the battlements' height,
    a   x   a /   a   x

<pre>
    C   C   C   C
With corbels under cornices in comeliest style;
      a   a   /   a   x

  C   c   C   C   C
Watch towers trusty protected the gate,
  x   a   a   /   a   x

      C   c   C   C   C
With many a lean loophole, to look from within:
        x   a   a   /   a   x

    C   c   C   C   c   C
A better-made barbican the knight beheld never.
    a   x   a   /   b   a   b
</pre>

2. LINES 1208–17

<pre>
      C   C   C C
"God moroun, Sir Gawayn," sayde that gay lady,
  a   a   /   a   x

        C   C   C   C
"Ye ar a sleper unslyghe, that mon may slyde hider;
        a   a   /   a   x

          C   C   C   C
Now ar ye tan astyt! Bot true uus may schape,
          a   a /   a   x

      C   C   C   c   C
I schal bynde you in your bedde, that be ye trayst!"
      a   a   /x   a   x

    C   C   C   C
Al laghande the lady lanced tho bourdez.
    a   a /a   x

        C   C   C   C
"Goud moroun, gay," quoth Gawayn the blythe,
  a   a   /   a   x

          C   C   C   c C
"Me schal worthe at your wille, and that me wel lykez,
            a   a   /   x   a   x

      C   C   C   C
For I yelde me yederly, and yeghe after grace,
      a   a   / a   x
</pre>

     C   C   C C
And that is the best, be my dome, for me byhovez nede!"
      a a   x /   a   x

     C   C   C c C
And thus he bourded ayayn with mony a blythe laghter.
        a   x /   x   a   x

     C   C   C C
"Good morning, Sir Gawain," said that gay lady,
 a   a   /   a x

   C c   C   C   C
"A slack sleeper you are, to let one slip in!
   a   a   x / x   a x

       C   C   C   C
Now you are taken in a trice—a truce we must make,
        a   a / a   x

     C   C   C   C
Or I shall bind you in your bed, of that be assured."
      a   a / x a   x

   C   C   C C
Thus laughing lightly that lady jested.
    a   a   /   a x

      C   C   C   C
"Good morning, good lady," said Gawain the blithe,
 a   a   /   a   x

    C   c   C   C
"Be it with me as you will; I am well content!
   a   a /   a   x

     C   C   C   C
For I surrender myself, and sue for your grace,
    a   a / a   x

      C C   C   C
And that is best, I believe, and behooves me now."
       a   a / a   x

    C   C   C   C
Thus jested in answer that gentle knight.
   a   x   /   a   x

From Patience

1. LINES 137–44

```
    C   c        C   c        C     C
An-on out of the north-east the noys bigynes,
    a    b        a   b   /    a     x

            C   c          C          C   C
When bothe brethes con blowe upon blo watteres;
            a    a          a    /     a   x

    C   c        C       C          C
Rogh rakkes ther ros with rudnyng an-under,
    a    a        a   /    a           x

        C   c        C     C       C
The see soghed ful sore, gret selly to here.
        a    a        a   /    a     x

        C                C     c      C     C
The wyndes on the wonne water so wrastel to-geder
        a                a     a   /   a      x

            C          C   C        C
That the wawes ful wode waltered so highe
            a          a   /a        x

            C               C          C   C
And efte busched to the abyme, that breed fysches
            a               a    /     a    x

        C        C     C          C
Durst nowhere for rogh arest at the bothem.
        x        a   /  a          x
```

```
        C   c        C   c      C     C
And now out of the northeast the noise begins
        a    b        a   b   /  a      x

            C          c        C          C   C
As they blow with both their breaths over bleak waters;
            a          a        a    /     a    x

        C   c   c   C        C          C
The cloud rack runs ragged, reddening beneath;
        x    a   a    a    /a           x

    C        c   C     C        C
The ocean howls hellishly, awful to hear;
    a        a   a     a    /a       a
```

   C   C c C C
The winds on the wan water so wildly contend
   a   a a / a   x

    C C   C   C
That the surges ascending are swept up so high
    a   a   / a   x

    C c   C   C c C
And then drawn back to the depths, that fear-dazed fish
    a x   a / x a   x

   C   C   C c C
Dare not rest, for that rage, at the roiled sea bottom.
    a   a /   a x x

2. LINES 413–24

  C   C   C C
I biseche the, syre, now thou self jugge,
  a   a /   a x

    C c   C   C   C
Watz not this ilk my worde that worthen is nouthe,
a b   x   a /   a   b

    C   C   C c C
That I kest in my cuntre, when thou thy carp sendez,
     a   a /   x   a x

      C   C   C   C
That I schulde tee to thys toun thi talent to preche?
      a   a / a   x

    C   C   C C
Wel knew I thi cortaysye, thy quoynt suffraunce,
    a   a   / a   x

   C   C   C C
Thy bounte of debonerte and thy bene grace,
   a   a   /   a x

   C c   C   C C
Thy longe abydyng wyth lur, thy late vengaunce,
   a   x   a / a x

     C   C   C   C
And ay thy mercy is mete, be mysse never so huge.
     a   a / a   x

 c C   C   C C
I wyst wel, when I hade worded quat-so-ever I cowthe
 a a (a)   a / a x   x

   C c   C c   C   c   C
To manace alle thise mody men that in this mote dowellez,
  a   b   a a / b   a   x

    C   C   C C
Wyth a prayer and a pyne thay myght her pese gete,
    a   a /   a x

   C   C   C   C
And ther-fore I wolde haf flowen fer in-to Tarce.
    a   a / a   x

NOTE: In line 418, *debonerte* is stressed on the second syllable, and the final *e* is syllabic, as also in *bounte*.

   C   C   C   C
I beseech You now, Sire, Yourself be the judge:
  a   a / a   x

 C   C   C   C
Were they not my words that forewarned of this change,
a   a /   a   x

   C   C   C   C
That I said when You summoned me to sail from Judea
   a   a   / a   x

  C   C   C   C
To travel to this town and teach them Your will?
(a) a   (a)   a / a   x

   C c   C   c   C   C
I knew well Your courteous ways, Your wise forbearance,
 x a   x   a / a   x

   C   C   C   C
Your abounding beneficence, the bounty of Your grace,
   a   a x   / a   x

  C   C   C C
Your leniency, Your longsuffering, Your delayed vengeance;
  a   a   /   a x

      C   C   C c   C
And ever mercy in full measure, though the misdeed be huge.
    a   a   /   a x   x

<pre>
         C   C   C   C
I knew well, when I had wielded such words as I could
      a   a   /   a   x
</pre>

<pre>
     C   C   c   C   C
To menace all these mighty men, the masters of this place,
  a   a   a /   a   x
</pre>

<pre>
            C   C   C   C
That for a prayer and a penance You would pardon them all,
         a   a   /   a   x
</pre>

<pre>
     C   C c C   C
And therefore I would have fled far off into Tarshish.
   x   (a)   a /a x   x
</pre>

From Pearl

To illustrate the metrical patterns of *Pearl*, I have chosen the opening stanza, a stanza from the pearl maiden's argument immediately following her narration of the parable of the vineyard, and a stanza from the dreamer's vision of the celestial Jerusalem.

The "rules" determining scansions are as described above. The inflectional endings *-ed* (as in *jugged* "judged") and *-ez* (as in *sydez* "sides") had continued to be pronounced as syllables in the language of the *Pearl* poet. He often used them to provide the necessary intermediate syllables within the line. They could also be contracted, as indicated by their presence in lines where their sounding would result in irregular sequences of three intermediate syllables. Where they are followed by a single intermediate syllable, I have left their metrical status indeterminate, though I am inclined to think that they should be contracted in most, if not all, such cases. I have left *-ez* silent in *hondelyngez* in example 2, on the linguistic grounds that in this word it falls after a syllable bearing less than primary stress; compare the pronunciation indicated by the meter for *planetez* in example 3.

1. LINES 1–12

<pre>
c x   c x   x   c   x   c
Perle, plesaunte to prynces paye,
</pre>

<pre>
  x   c   x   c x   c   x   c
To clanly clos in golde so clere,
</pre>

<pre>
c   x   c(x)x   x   c   x x   c
Oute of oryent, I hardyly saye,
</pre>

<pre>
   x   c(x) x   c x   x   c x   c
Ne proved I never her precios pere.
</pre>

<pre>
 x c   x c x x c   x c
So rounde, so reken in uche araye,
</pre>

<pre>
  x   c x   c   x   c x   c
So smal, so smothe her sydez were,
</pre>

<pre>
   x   x c x x c x   c   x   c
Quere-so-ever I jugged gemmez gaye,
</pre>

<pre>
 x c   x   c   x c x   c
I sette hyr sengeley in synglere.
</pre>

<pre>
 x c x c   x c x x c
Allas! I leste hyr in on erbere;
</pre>

<pre>
   x   c   x c   x   c x c
Thurgh gresse to grounde hit fro me yot.
</pre>

<pre>
  x   c   x c(x) x c   x   c
I dewyne, fordolked of luf-daungere
</pre>

<pre>
 x   x   c x c   x c x   c
Of that pryvy perle wythouten spot.
</pre>

NOTE: In line 1, *perle* was probably pronounced very much like modern English *peril*.

<pre>
 c   x x c   x c   x c
Pearl, that a prince is well content
</pre>

<pre>
 x c x c x x c   x c
To give a circle of gold to wear,
</pre>

<pre>
 c   x x c   x c x c
Boldly I say, all Orient
</pre>

<pre>
  x   c   x   c x c   x c
Brought forth none precious like to her;
</pre>

<pre>
 x c   x x c   x c x c
So comely in every ornament,
</pre>

<pre>
 x c x x c   x c   x   c
So slender her sides, so smooth they were,
</pre>

<pre>
 c x   x   c   x c   x   c
Ever my mind was bound and bent
</pre>

<pre>
  x c x x c   x c x c
To set her apart without a peer.
</pre>

<pre>
 x x c x x c   x c   x c
In a garden of herbs I lost my dear;
</pre>

     x   c x c   x c x   c
Through grass to ground away it shot;

    x   c   x   x c x c x   c
Now, lovesick, the heavy loss I bear

  x   x c x c   x c x   c
Of that secret pearl without a spot.

2. LINES 673–84

    x   c x c   x c   x c
"Ryght thus I knaw wel in this cas,

    c x x c   x c   x c
Two men to save is god by skylle:

    x c   x   c   x c x c
The ryghtwys man schal se hys face,

    x c   x   c x   x   c   x   c
The harmlez hathel schal com hym tylle.

    x c x x   c   c x x c
The Sauter hyt satz thus in a pace:

    c   x   x   c   x c   x   c
'Lorde, quo schal klymbe thy hygh[e] hylle,

  x (x) c   x   c   x c x c
Other rest wythinne thy holy place?' '

    x   c   x   c   x c x   c
Hymself to onsware he is not dylle:

    c   x   c   x c   x c
'Hondelyngez harme that dyt not ille,

    x c x   c   x   c   x   c
That is of hert bothe clene and lyght,

    c   x   x   c x   c x   c
Ther schal hys step[e] stable stylle':

    x c x x   c x   c   x c
The innosent is ay saf by ryght.

NOTE: *Hygh* (678) and *step* (683) have been emended to provide a necessary intermediate syllable; compare the general discussion of the metrical form, above. Note the rhyme *cas/face*, evidence that -e in *face* is silent as in modern English.

```
x   c   x    c  x  c   x   c
```
"I know right reason in this case

```
x    c   x  c   x    c x c
```
And thereto cite authority:

```
   x  c   x     c    x   c    x   c
```
The righteous man shall see His face

```
x     x c  x x    c     x    c   x c
```
And the innocent bear Him company.

```
 c x   x   c    x   c  x   c
```
So in a verse the psalter says,

```
   c     x   x   c    x    c x   c
```
'Lord, who shall climb Your hill on high

```
x   c    x  c   x    c x  c
```
Or rest within Your holy place?'

```
 x     c  xx   c   x   c    x   c
```
And readily then He makes reply:

```
   c     x   c   x c  x  c
```
'Hands that did no injury,

```
 c     x    x  c  x    c   x    c
```
Heart that was always pure and light:

```
   c    x   x   c    x  c    x    c
```
There shall his steps be stayed in joy';

```
  x c   x  c   x   c    x   c
```
The innocent is safe by right.

3. LINES 1069–80

```
  x   c    x    x c x  c    x    c
```
The mone may therof acroche no myghte;

```
 x   c x   x c   x   c x   x   c
```
To spotty ho is, of body to grym,

```
 x    c x   c x   c x   c
```
And also ther is never nyght.

```
    c    x     x   c     x   c    x    c
```
What schulde the mone ther compas clym?

```
x    x c x    c    x   c    x c
```
And to even wyth that worthly lyght

```
    x    c (x) x  c    x   c x     c
```
That schynez upon the brokez brym

```
    x  c  x    x   c  x  c     x   c
```
The planetez arn in to pouer a plyght

```
    x      x  c  x  c      x  c  x  c
```
And the sel[ve] sunne ful fer to dym.

```
    x  c     x   c x x      c  x     c
```
Aboute that water arn tres ful schym,

```
      x     c    x    x  c  x    c   x   c
```
That twelve frytez of lyf con bere ful sone;

```
    c    x     x   c   x   c(x)  x   c
```
Twelve sythez on yer thay beren ful frym,

```
    x     x c x   c x c    x   c
```
And renowlez nwe in uche a mone.

NOTE: *Self* (1076) has been emended to *selve*, a disyllablic "weak" form fol-
lowing the definite article. Compare Chaucer's line "Right in that selvë wisë,
soth to seyë" (*Troilus* 3.355).

```
      x   c   x  c   x   c     x  c
```
The moon has in that reign no right;

```
    x    c x   x c  x  c x x    c
```
Too spotty she is, of body austere;

```
    x    c    x   c    x     c   x  c
```
And they who dwell there know no night—

```
    x    c x c   x   c x      c
```
Of what avail her varying sphere?

```
    x    c   x c    x    c    x    c
```
And set beside that wondrous light

```
      x   c   x  c    x   c x    c
```
That shines upon the waters clear

```
    x  c  x   x     c    x   c   x  c
```
The planets would lose their luster quite

```
    x     x  c  x  c   x     c   x   c
```
And the sun itself would pale appear.

```
    x c     x  c x x    c     x   c
```
Beside the river are trees that bear

c   x   x c   x   c   x c
Twelve fruits of life their boughs upon;

c   x   x c   x   c x   c
Twelve times a year they burgeon there

x   x c   x   c   x c   x   c
And renew themselves with every moon.

Selected Bibliography

Aers, David. *Community, Virtue, and Individual Identity: English Writing, 1360–1430.* London: Routledge, 1988.

Anderson, J. J. *Language and Imagination in the Gawain-Poems.* Manchester: Manchester University Press, 2005.

———, ed. *Cleanness.* Manchester: Manchester University Press; New York: Barnes and Noble, 1977.

———, ed. *Patience.* Manchester: Manchester University Press; New York: Barnes and Noble, 1969.

Andrew, Malcolm, and Ronald Waldron, eds. *The Poems of the "Pearl" Manuscript.* York Medieval Texts, 2nd ser. Berkeley: University of California Press, 1979. Rpt.: Exeter: University of Exeter Press, 2002.

Bede's Ecclesiastical History of the English People. Edited by Bertram Colgrave and R. A. B. Mynors. Oxford: Oxford University Press, 1969.

Bennett, Michael J. *Community, Class, and Careerism: Cheshire and Lancashire Society in the Age of Sir Gawain and the Green Knight.* Cambridge: Cambridge University Press, 1983.

Benson, Larry D. *Art and Tradition in Sir Gawain and the Green Knight.* New Brunswick, N.J.: Rutgers University Press, 1965.

Bishop, Ian. *"Pearl" in Its Setting.* Oxford: Blackwell, 1968.

Blanch, Robert J., ed. *"Sir Gawain" and "Pearl": Critical Essays.* Bloomington: Indiana University Press, 1966.

Blanch, Robert J., and Julian N. Wasserman. *From "Pearl" to "Gawain": forme to fynisment.* Gainesville: University Press of Florida, 1993.

Blanch, Robert J., Miriam Youngerman Miller, and Julian N. Wasserman, eds. *Text and Matter: New Critical Perspectives on the Pearl-Poet.* Troy, N.Y.: Whitston, 1991.

Boitani, Piero. *English Medieval Narrative in the Thirteenth and Fourteenth Centuries.* Translated by Joan Krakover. Cambridge: Cambridge University Press, 1982.

Borroff, Marie. "Narrative Artistry in the *Gawain*-Group and 'St. Erkenwald': The Case for Common Authorship Reconsidered." *Studies in the Age of Chaucer* 28 (2006): 41–76.

———. *"Sir Gawain and the Green Knight": A Stylistic and Metrical Study.* Yale Studies in English, vol. 152. New Haven and London: Yale University Press, 1962.

————, *Traditions and Renewals: Chaucer, the Gawain-Poet, and Beyond.* New Haven and London: Yale University Press, 2003.

Brewer, D. S. "Courtesy and the *Gawain*-Poet." In *Patterns of Love and Courtesy: Essays in Memory of C. S. Lewis,* edited by John Lawlor. London: Edward Arnold, 1966.

Brewer, Derek S., ed. *Studies in Medieval English Romances: Some New Approaches.* Cambridge: D. S. Brewer, 1988.

Brewer, Derek S., and Jonathan Gibson, eds. *A Companion to the Gawain-Poet.* Cambridge: D. S. Brewer, 1997.

Brewer, Elizabeth, ed. *"Sir Gawain and the Green Knight": Sources and Analogues.* Woodbridge, Suffolk: D. S. Brewer, 1992.

Burrow, J. A. *A Reading of "Sir Gawain and the Green Knight."* London: Routledge and Kegan Paul, 1965.

————. *Ricardian Poetry: Chaucer, Gower, Langland, and the Gawain-Poet.* New Haven and London: Yale University Press, 1971.

Cawley, A. C., and J. J. Anderson, eds. *"Pearl," "Cleanness," "Patience," "Sir Gawain and the Green Knight."* London: Dent; New York: Dutton, 1972.

Condren, Edward J. *The Numerical Universe of the Gawain-Poet.* Gainesville: University Press of Florida, 2002.

Donaldson, E. Talbot, trans. *Beowulf: A Prose Translation: Contexts, Criticism.* Edited by Nicholas Howe. New York: W. W. Norton, 2001.

Everett, Dorothy. "The Alliterative Revival." In *Essays on English Literature,* edited by Patricia Kean. Oxford: Oxford University Press, 1955.

Fox, Denton, ed. *Twentieth-Century Interpretations of "Sir Gawain and the Green Knight."* Englewood Cliffs, N.J.: Prentice-Hall, 1968.

Ganim, John M. *Style and Consciousness in Middle English Narrative.* Princeton, N.J.: Princeton University Press, 1983.

Gollancz, Israel. *"Pearl," "Cleanness," "Patience," and "Sir Gawain and the Green Knight": Reproduced in Facsimile from the Unique MS. Cotton Nero A.x.* Early English Text Society, O. S. 162. London: Oxford University Press, 1923.

Gordon, E. V., ed. *Pearl.* Oxford: Clarendon, 1953.

Green, Richard Firth. *A Crisis of Truth: Literature and Law in Ricardian England.* Philadelphia: University of Pennsylvania Press, 1999.

Hanna, Ralph. "Alliterative Poetry." In *The Cambridge History of Medieval English Literature,* edited by David Wallace, 488–512. Cambridge: Cambridge University Press. 1999.

Hieatt, A. Kent. " 'Sir Gawain': Pentangle, 'Luf-Lace,' Numerical Structure." In *Silent Poetry: Essays in Numerological Analysis,* edited by Alastair Fowler, 116–40. New York: Barnes and Noble, 1970.

Homer. *The Odyssey.* Translated by Robert Fitzgerald. New York: Farrar, Straus and Giroux, 1998.

Johnston, R. C., and D. D. R. Owen, eds. *Two Old French Gauvain Romances.* Edinburgh: Scottish Academic Press, 1972.

Kean, P. M. *The Pearl: An Interpretation.* London: Routledge and Kegan Paul, 1967.

Keen, Maurice. *Chivalry.* New Haven and London: Yale University Press, 1984.

Keiser, Elizabeth B. *Courtly Desire and Medieval Homophobia: The Legitimation of Sexual Pleasure in "Cleanness" and Its Contexts.* New Haven and London: Yale University Press, 1997.

Kottler, Barnet, and Alan Mouns Markman. *A Concordance to Five Middle English Poems: Cleanness, St. Erkenwald, Sir Gawain and the Green Knight, Patience and Pearl.* Pittsburgh: University of Pittsburgh Press, 1966.

Levy, Bernard S., and Paul E. Szarmach, eds. *The Alliterative Tradition in the Fourteenth Century.* Kent, Ohio: Kent State University Press, 1981.

Mann, Jill. "Satisfaction and Payment in Middle English Literature." *Studies in the Age of Chaucer* 5 (1983): 17–48.

Loomis, Laura H. "*Gawain and the Green Knight.*" In *Arthurian Literature in the Middle Ages: A Collaborative History,* edited by Roger S. Loomis. Oxford: Oxford University Press, 1959.

Marvin, William Perry. *Hunting Law and Ritual in Medieval English Literature.* Cambridge: D. S. Brewer, 2006.

Menner, Robert J. *Purity.* Yale Studies in English 61. New Haven and London: Yale University Press, 1920.

Miller, Miriam Youngerman, and Jane Chance, eds. *Approaches to Teaching "Sir Gawain and the Green Knight."* New York: Modern Language Association of America, 1986.

Mitchell, Bruce, and Fred C. Robinson, eds. *Beowulf: An Edition with Relevant Shorter Texts.* Oxford and Malden, Mass.: Blackwell, 1998.

Morse, Charlotte C. "The Image of the Vessel in *Cleanness.*" *University of Toronto Quarterly* 40 (1970–71): 202–16.

———. *The Pattern of Judgment in the Queste and "Cleanness."* Columbia: Missouri University Press, 1978.

Muscatine, Charles. "The *Pearl*-Poet: Style as Defense." In *Poetry and Crisis in the Age of Chaucer,* 37–70. Notre Dame and London: Notre Dame University Press, 1972.

Nicholls, Jonathan. *The Matter of Courtesy: Medieval Courtesy Books and the Gawain-Poet.* Woodbridge, Suffolk: D. S. Brewer, 1985.

Oakden, J. P. *Alliterative Poetry in Middle English.* 2 vols. Manchester: Manchester University Press, 1920, 1935.

Peterson, Clifford, ed. *Saint Erkenwald.* Philadelphia: University of Pennsylvania Press, 1977.

Putter, Ad. *An Introduction to the Gawain-Poet.* London: Longman, 1996.

———. *"Sir Gawain and the Green Knight" and French Arthurian Romance.* Oxford: Clarendon, 1995.

Rhodes, Jim. *Poetry Does Theology: Chaucer, Grosseteste, and the 'Pearl'-Poet.* Notre Dame: Notre Dame University Press, 2001.

Robinson, Fred C. *"Beowulf" and the Appositive Style.* Knoxville: University of Tennessee Press, 1985.

Rooney, Anne. *Hunting in Middle English Literature.* Cambridge: Boydell Press, 1993.

Spearing, A. C. *Criticism and Medieval Poetry.* London: Edward Arnold, 1964.

————. "The Alliterative Tradition: *Pearl.*" In *Medieval Dream-Poetry,* 111–70. Cambridge: Cambridge University Press: 1976.

————. *The Gawain-Poet: A Critical Study.* Cambridge: Cambridge University Press, 1970.

Tolkien, J. R. R., and E. V. Gordon, eds. *Sir Gawain and the Green Knight.* 2nd ed., revised by Norman Davis. Oxford: Clarendon, 1967.

Turville-Petre, Thorlac. *The Alliterative Revival.* Cambridge and Totowa, N.J.: Boydell & Brewer, 1977.

Watts, Ann Chalmers. *The Lyre and the Harp: A Comparative Reconsideration of Oral Tradition in Homer and Old English Epic Poetry.* New Haven and London: Yale University Press, 1969.

————. "*Pearl,* Inexpressibility, and Poems of Human Loss." *PMLA* 99.1 (1984): 26–40.